THE EUROPEAN NEIGHBOURHOOD POLICY AND THE DEMOCRATIC VALUES OF THE EU

This book offers a legal analysis of the European Neighbourhood Policy (the ENP) as it applies to developing relations with the EU's neighbours. It explores the legal aspects of this policy, including ENP competence matters, institutional arrangements and substantive policy issues, using international relations theory as the starting point in defining the EU's role as a political actor. The book focuses on the adequacy of the ENP legal framework for transposing the EU's democratic values and upholding its political image. In this connection, the book also features an analysis of EU democratic values as they are intended to be understood by its neighbours. The relevant legal framework of this policy and its implementation in the states of the South Caucasus (Georgia, Armenia and Azerbaijan) is evaluated, revealing the effects of the ENP in their democratic processes and the shortfalls of the ENP conditionality.

Volume 41 in the series Modern Studies in European Law

Modern Studies in European Law
Recent titles in this series:

Professional Services in the EU Internal Market: Quality Regulation and Self-Regulation
Tinne Heremans

Environmental Integration in the EU's External Relations: Beyond Multilateral Dimensions
Gracia Marín Durán and Elisa Morgera

The Constitutional Dimension of European Criminal Law
Ester Herlin-Karnell

EU Counter-Terrorism Law: Pre-Emption and the Rule of Law
Cian Murphy

Children and the European Union: Rights, Welfare and Accountability
Helen Stalford

Federalism in the European Union
Edited by Elke Cloots, Geert De Baere and Stefan Sottiaux

Toward a Prosecutor for the European Union Volume 1: A Comparative Analysis
Edited by Katalin Ligeti

Empowerment and Disempowerment of the European Citizen
Edited by Michael Dougan, Niamh Nic Shuibhne and Eleanor Spaventa

Legal Reasoning and the European Court of Justice
Gunnar Beck

Lawyering Europe: European Law as a Transnational Social Field
Edited by Antoine Vauchez and Bruno de Witte

Services and the EU Citizen
Edited by Frank S Benyon

The Accession of the European Union to the European Convention on Human Rights
Paul Gragl

Normative Patterns and Legal Developments in the Social Dimension of the EU
Edited by Ann Numhauser-Henning and Mia Rönnmar

For the complete list of titles in this series, see
'Modern Studies in European Law' link at
www.hartpub.co.uk/books/series.asp

The European Neighbourhood Policy and the Democratic Values of the EU

A Legal Analysis

Nariné Ghazaryan

·HART·
PUBLISHING
OXFORD AND PORTLAND, OREGON
2014

Published in the United Kingdom by Hart Publishing Ltd
16C Worcester Place, Oxford, OX1 2JW
Telephone: +44 (0)1865 517530
Fax: +44 (0)1865 510710
E-mail: mail@hartpub.co.uk
Website: http://www.hartpub.co.uk

Published in North America (US and Canada) by
Hart Publishing
c/o International Specialized Book Services
920 NE 58th Avenue, Suite 300
Portland, OR 97213-3786
USA
Tel: +1 503 287 3093 or toll-free: (1) 800 944 6190
Fax: +1 503 280 8832
E-mail: orders@isbs.com
Website: http://www.isbs.com

Hart Publishing is an imprint of Bloomsbury Publishing plc.

British Library Cataloguing in Publication Data
Data Available

ISBN: 978-1-84946-278-5

Typeset by Hope Services, Abingdon
Printed and bound in Great Britain by
TJ International Ltd, Padstow

Acknowledgements

Many people have helped me while I was working on this book. Some influenced the research that had led to this publication, while others supported me personally. Some did both.

As the book is a substantially revised version of my PhD thesis, which I defended at the University of Nottingham in 2010, I would first of all like to thank my supervisor, Professor Jeffrey Kenner. I have been extremely fortunate to have his constant guidance during my time in Nottingham. His knowledge and insight into EU Law and legal research were invaluable, and as a highly skilled supervisor he was a constant source of encouragement. I looked forward to our regular meetings as a highlight of my studentship. Professor Kenner is also one of the kindest people I have met.

I would also like to express my gratitude to Professor Tamara Hervey for the support she showed when I was applying for a PhD project at the University of Nottingham.

I must thank my PhD examiners, Professors Christophe Hillion and Stefan Wolff. Their comments have helped me to improve my work and to reflect further on certain themes and central arguments of the thesis. The comments provided by the Hart Publishing independent reviewer were most helpful in developing the manuscript. The interviewees at the European Commission and various institutions in Georgia and Armenia have assisted this project by sharing their insight into respective policy issues.

Professor Robert Schütze has shared much needed practical advice and I thank him for this.

Throughout these years I was always in my family's thoughts, as they were in mine. I am grateful to my parents for the opportunities they allowed me to pursue despite the obstacles they faced in their lives. My life has been immeasurably enhanced by my friendships, which provide motivation, inspiration and support. I thank my friends for their presence during my time at Nottingham and beyond.

I have to say special thanks to Gerry Clare, whose support has meant so much to me. Thank you!

Contents

Abbreviations

ANCEI	Azerbaijan National Committee for European Integration
CCP	Common Commercial Policy
CEE	Central and Eastern European
CEPS	Centre for European Policy Studies
CFSP	Common Foreign and Security Policy
CSDP	Common Security and Defence Policy
COSAC	Conference of Parliamentary Committees for Union Affairs of Parliaments
DCFTA	Deep and Comprehensive Free Trade Area
DG	Directorate General
DG RELEX	Directorate General for External Relations
EEA	European Economic Area
EEAS	European External Action Service
EC	European Community
EFTA	European Free Trade Area
EIDHR	European Instrument for Democracy and Human Rights
ENP	European Neighbourhood Policy
ENPI	European Neighbourhood and Partnership Instrument
EaP	Eastern Partnership
EP	European Parliament
ESDP	European Security and Defence Policy
ESS	European Security Strategy
EU	European Union
FAC	Foreign Affairs Council
FTA	Free Trade Area
ICG	International Crisis Group
IGC	Intergovernmental Conference
NATO	North Atlantic Treaty Organization
NGO	Non-governmental organisation
OSCE	Organization for Security and Co-operation in Europe
PCA	Partnership and Cooperation Agreement
SEA	Single European Act
TACIS	Technical Aid to the Commonwealth of Independent States
TEU	Treaty on European Union
TFEU	Treaty on the Functioning of the European Union
UfM	Union for the Mediterranean
WTO	World Trade Organization

Table of Cases

Table of Treaties and Other Instruments

Other Primary Sopurces

1

*Introduction**

<p>
T</p>HE EUROPEAN NEIGHBOURHOOD Policy (ENP) was initiated in 2003 by the European Union (EU) in search of an international identity. The circumstances surrounding the launch of the policy were complex and multifaceted. The EU made a pledge to boost its economic might by becoming 'the most dynamic knowledge-based economy' by 2010 and launching a single currency on its path towards a monetary union.[1] Externally, the European continent and its vicinity were about to change irreversibly through the unification of Europe. On an unprecedented scale, the EU was to welcome ten new Member States in 2004, with Bulgaria and Romania expected to join in 2007. The Union was preparing to turn into an actor with a 'continental scale of operation'.[2]

Proclaiming itself a 'success story' in the Laeken Declaration, the EU sought a new role for itself not only on the continent but in the globalised world, acting within its own 'moral framework'.[3] Traditionally the preconditions for the EU international 'actorness' were set in its economic might and prosperity, attracting foreign partners and according the EU with a power of transformation. It is this very logic that laid the foundations of the ENP.

It is said that foreign policy decisions 'can be understood, predicted, and manipulated only in so far as the factors influencing the decisions can be identified and isolated'.[4] The EU foreign policy making has been perceived to be reactive to outside events, often attracting criticism.[5] While this in part explains the genesis of the ENP, it nevertheless falls short of acknowledging the internal rationale for policy formation.

The internal rationale is embodied in the 'environmental'[6] – in this case geographic – factors linked to the expansion of the EU. The anticipated 2004 round of enlargement would create a new physical proximity between the EU and the former

---

* The book represents the state of affairs as of 1 July 2013.
[1] Laeken European Council Conclusions, 14–15 December 2001, Laeken Declaration.
[2] W Kok, 'Enlarging the European Union: Achievements and Challenges', Report to the European Commission, EUI, 19 March 2003, 6.
[3] Laeken European Council, note 1 above, 19.
[4] A Wolfers, *Discord and Collaboration: Essays on International Politics* (Baltimore, The Johns Hopkins University Press, 1968) 37.
[5] KE Smith, *The Making of EU Foreign Policy: The Case of Eastern Europe* (Basingstoke, Palgrave, 1999) 4.
[6] Wolfers, note 4 above, 39–43.

Soviet Republics, which would become an inalienable element of its foreign policy.[7] The internal rationale thus primarily concerned the 'European' neighbours of the EU, namely Russia, Belarus, Ukraine and Moldova. Some of these states had European aspirations, which the Union was neither willing nor able to reciprocate at that stage. The failed ratification of the Draft Constitutional Treaty halted further constitutional development of the EU, which had yet to determine its *finalité politique*.[8] While the queue for membership already included a number of hopeful states, further 'deepening' was needed in terms of adapting the EU institutions and policy making, raising the issue of its 'absorption capacity'.[9] The Union was suffering from so-called 'enlargement fatigue'.[10]

Despite the suggestions for the enlargement to be crafted as a 'bridge building' to the former Soviet Union states,[11] it created a new dividing line with hard borders and differences across those borders.[12] The necessity of bridging this gap was

---

[7] C Patten and J Solana, Joint letter on Wider Europe, 7 August 2002; Council Conclusions, General Affairs, 15 April 2002; Copenhagen European Council Conclusions, 12 and 13 December 2002, 6; Commission Communication, Wider Europe – Neighbourhood: A New Framework for Relations with our Eastern and Southern Neighbours COM (2003) 104 final, 11 April 2003 (hereinafter Wider Europe Communication) 3, 4, 5, 9; E Johansson-Nogues, 'The EU and its Neighbourhood: an Overview' in K Weber, M Smith and M Baun (eds), *Governing Europe's Neighbourhood: Partners or Periphery* (Manchester, Manchester University Press, 2007) 21–35, 22; L Delcour, 'Does the European Neighbourhood Policy Make a Difference? Policy Patterns and Reception in Ukraine and Russia' (2007) 7 *European Political Economy Review* 118, 121.

[8] Treaty Establishing a Constitution for Europe [2004] OJ C310/47; R Dannreuther, 'Developing the Alternative to Enlargement: The European Neighbourhood Policy' (2006) 11 *European Foreign Affairs Review* 183, 186; G Meloni, 'Is the Same Toolkit Used during Enlargement Still Applicable to the Countries of the New Neighbourhood? A Problem of Mismatching between Objectives and Instruments' in M Cremona and G Meloni (eds), *The European Neighbourhood Policy: A New Framework for Modernisation?*, EUI Working Papers, LAW 2007/21, 97–111, 97; M Comelli, E Greco, N Tocci, 'From Boundary to Borderland: Transforming the Meaning of Borders through the European Neighbourhood Policy' (2007) 12 *European Foreign Affairs Review* 203, 214–15.

[9] Copenhagen European Council Conclusions, 21–22 June 1993, s 7; Commission Communication, 'Enlargement Strategy and Main Challenges 2006–2007' COM (2006) 649 final, 8 November 2006; C Hillion, 'Widen to Deepen? The Potential and Limits of Accession Treaties to Achieve EU Constitutional Reform' in S Blockmans and S Prechal (eds), *Reconciling the Deepening and Widening of the European Union* (The Hague, TMC Asser Press, 2007) 157–65, 158; S Blockmans and S Prechal, 'The European Integration Process: A Continuum of "Deepening" and "Widening"' in Blockmans and Prechal (eds), ibid, 1–12, 4; M Emerson et al, 'Just What is this "Absorption Capacity" of the European Union?' CESP Policy Brief No 113, 2006, 2–3.

[10] Comelli et al, note 8 above, 214–15; M Smith and K Webber, 'Political Dialogue and Security in the European Neighbourhood Policy: The Virtues and Limits of "New Partnership Perspective"' (2008) 13 *European Foreign Affairs Review* 73, 75; KE Smith, 'The Outsiders: The European Neighbourhood Policy' (2005) 81 *International Affairs* 757, 758; R Del Sarto and T Schumacher, 'From EMP to ENP: What's at Stake with the European Neighbourhood Policy towards the Southern Mediterranean?' (2005) 10 *European Foreign Affairs Review* 17, 25–26; B Ferrero-Waldner, 'The European Neighbourhood Policy: The EU's Newest Foreign Policy Instrument' (2006) 11 *European Foreign Affairs Review* 139, 139–40.

[11] A Hyde-Price, 'The New Pattern of International Relations in Europe' in V Curzon Price, A Landau and R Whitman (eds), *The Enlargement of the European Union: Issues and Strategies* (London, Routledge, 1999) 111–17, 116.

[12] A Mungiu-Pippidi, 'Facing the "Desert of Tartars": The Eastern Border of Europe' in J Zielonka (ed), *Europe Unbound: Enlarging and Reshaping the Boundaries of the European Union* (London, Routledge, 2002) 51–77, 55.

acknowledged by the Commission in 2001 with the concept of 'proximity'.[13] Some, though, argue that the idea of close relations with neighbours dates back in time to the 1997 enlargement momentum and the parallel conclusion of the Partnership and Cooperation Agreements (PCA) with the former Soviet Republics and the establishment of the Barcelona Process with the Southern partners in 1995.[14]

To bridge the gap the ENP was devised as a means to solve the 'inclusion-exclusion' dilemma of the EU.[15] Membership-like, it was to exclude accession while promising close political and economic cooperation with those neighbours ineligible for EU membership and those whose membership prospects the EU was not prepared to consider.[16]

Although the exclusionary rationale of the policy was directed at the Eastern neighbourhood, the Southern neighbourhood was also incorporated at the insistence of certain Member States.[17] It therefore transformed the concept of 'European' neighbourhood into a 'EUropean' one,[18] leading to an awkward geographic and political amalgamation. Unlike the Southern neighbours involved in the multilateral Barcelona Process, the Eastern neighbours were engaged in bilateral relations via the PCAs. Besides, the Southern dimension was based on a more beneficial bilateral framework through association agreements instead.[19] As a result, 16

[13] European Commission Strategy Paper, Towards the Enlarged Union COM (2002) 700 final, 9 October 2002, 6–7; Commission Strategy Paper, Making a Success of Enlargement COM (2001) 700 final, 17 November 2011, 7.

[14] In 1995 the EU launched a new policy towards the Mediterranean region, the Barcelona Process, aimed at creating a free trade area with the North African and Middle Eastern countries; Barcelona Declaration, Euro-Mediterranean Ministerial Council, 28–28 November 1995; Partnership and Cooperation Agreement between the European Communities and their Member States, of the one part, and Russia, of the other [1997] OJ L327; Partnership and Cooperation Agreement between the European Communities and their Member States, of the one part, and the Republic of Armenia, of the other [1999] OJ L239/3; Partnership and Cooperation Agreement between the European Communities and their Member States, of the one part, and the Republic of Azerbaijan, of the other [1999] OJ L246/3; Partnership and Cooperation Agreement between the European Communities and their Member States, of the one part, and the Republic of Georgia, of the other [1999] OJ L205/3; Partnership and Cooperation Agreement between the European Communities and their Member States, of the one part, and the Republic of Moldova, of the other [1998] OJ L181; Partnership and Cooperation Agreement between the European Communities and their Member States, of the one part, and Ukraine, of the other [1998] OJ L049; M Cremona, 'The European Neighbourhood Policy' in A Ott and E Vos (eds), *Fifty Years of European Integration: Foundations and Perspectives* (Hague, TMC Asser Press, 2009) 221–245, 221–222.

[15] Smith, note 10 above, 757–58; Cremona, note 14 above, 243.

[16] Wider Europe Communication, 5.

[17] Copenhagen European Council, note 7 above, 7; F Bicchi, *European Foreign Policy Making Towards the Mediterranean* (Basingstoke, Palgrave, 2007) 177; A Missiroli, 'The EU and its Changing Neighbourhood' in R Dannreuther (ed), *European Union Foreign and Security Policy: Towards a Neighbourhood Strategy* (London, Routledge, 2004) 12–26, 23.

[18] S Vasilyan, 'The "European" "Neighbourhood" "Policy" ' in J Wunderlich and DJ Bailey (eds), *The European Union and Global Governance: A Handbook* (London, Routledge, 2010) 177–86, 177.

[19] Euro–Mediterranean Agreement establishing an Association between the European Community and its Member States, of the one part, and the People's Democratic Republic of Algeria, of the other part [2005] OJ L265; Euro–Mediterranean Agreement establishing an Association between the European Communities and their Member States, of the one part, and the Arab Republic of Egypt, of the other part [2004] OJ L304; Euro–Mediterranean Agreement establishing an Association between

neighbours, including Ukraine, Moldova, Belarus and the South Caucasian Republics in the East, and Israel, the Occupied Palestinian Territories, Jordan, Syria, Lebanon, Libya, Tunisia, Morocco and Egypt have become the ENP addressees, with an opt-out from Russia.[20] A few years later, with the enterprise of certain pro-active Member States, a regional split occurred in the EU policies towards the neighbourhood, introducing the Eastern Partnership (hereinafter the EaP) in the East and a somewhat revamped Union for the Mediterranean (hereinafter the UfM) in the South.[21]

The external rationale for the development of the ENP is closely linked to the wider security challenges facing the EU from the beginning of the millennium.[22] Global security threats, such as international terrorism associated with the 9/11 attacks, and the EU's inability to react to external events due to Member States' divergences, apparent in the Iraq crisis, required the elaboration of a comprehensive security strategy for the Union.[23] The 2003 European Security Strategy (ESS) envisaged the EU's role in tackling global security threats but, most importantly, emphasised the significance of 'geography' in this task.[24]

The presence of frozen conflicts in the East, as well as the Arab–Israeli conflict continuously threatening the peace in the Middle East, in themselves justify the prioritisation of security issues in the neighbourhood.[25] Most recently, the Arab

the European Communities and their Member States, of the one part, and the Hashemite Kingdom of Jordan, of the other part [2002] OJ L129; Euro–Mediterranean Agreement establishing an Association between the European Communities and their Member States, of the one part, and the State of Israel, of the other part [2000] OJ L147; Euro–Mediterranean Agreement establishing an association between the European Communities and their Member States, of the one part, and the Kingdom of Morocco, of the other part [2000] OJ L070; Euro–Mediterranean Agreement establishing an Association between the European Communities and their Member States, of the one part, and the Republic of Tunisia, of the other part [1998] OJ L97.

[20]   Russia's reluctance to be an 'addressee' of the ENP with its conditionality resulted in its opt-out from the policy, and cooperation is instead pursued through a 'Strategic Partnership' framework; Council of the European Union, 'Joint Statement on EU Enlargement and EU–Russia Relations', Luxembourg, 27 April 2004; 'Commission Communication on Relations with Russia' COM (2004) 106, 9 February 2004; P Van Elsuwege, 'The Four Common Spaces: New Impetus to the EU–Russia Strategic Partnership?' in A Dashwood and M Maresceau (eds), *Law and Practice of EU External Relations: Salient Features of a Changing Landscape* (Cambridge, CUP, 2008) 334–59, 355.

[21]   For discussion of the Member States' position at this stage, see B Van Vooren, 'The European Union as an International Actor and Progressive Experimentation in Its Neighbourhood' in P Koutrakos (ed), *European Foreign Policy: Legal and Political Perspectives* (Cheltenham, Edward Elgar Publishing, 2011) 147–71, 152–53.

[22]   R Aliboni, 'The Geopolitical Implications of the European Neighbourhood Policy' (2005) 10 *European Foreign Affairs Review* 1, 1; M Cremona and C Hillion, 'L'Union Fait La Force? Potential and Limitations of the ENP as an Integrated EU Foreign and Security Policy' in N Copsey and A Mayhew (eds), *European Neighbourhood Policy: The Case of Europe*, Sussex European Institute, SEI Seminar Papers Series Number 1, 2006, 20–44, 23.

[23]   'A Secure Europe in a Better World', European Security Strategy Paper, Brussels, 12 December 2003 (hereinafter European Security Strategy Paper); A Missiroli and G Quille, 'European Security in Flux' in F Cameron (ed), *The Future of Europe: Integration and Enlargement* (London, Routledge, 2004) 114–34, 118–19; D Lynch, 'The European Neighbourhood Policy', Institute for Security Studies, Paper presented at the workshop 'European Neighbourhood Policy: Concepts and Instruments', Prague, June 2004, organised by the European Commission with DGAP, CEFRES and IIR, 2; Aliboni, note 22 above, 1.

[24]   European Security Strategy Paper 7.

[25]   Ibid 7–8.

Spring revolutions have illustrated the interlinked relationship between the stability of the EU and the events in its neighbourhood. The overthrowing of the ruling regimes in Tunisia, Libya and Egypt not only led to increased risks of illegal migration, arms proliferation, and even military intervention by EU Member States, but also placed question marks over the very nature of the EU's engagement in the South. Thus, the security rationale of the ENP is ever present, and the neighbourhood cannot be ignored.

These internal and external determinants were to have an irrevocable impact on the legal nature of the ENP and the role of the EU democratic values within the latter.

1.1 AIMS AND APPROACHES

As a political instrument, the ENP is a fusion of wide-ranging objectives, policies and instruments. Its ambition and vast content immediately attracted much attention.

One of the distinctive approaches in the studies on the ENP has been the regional contextualisation of the policy.[26] A prominent line of research has been the study of the ENP mechanisms, instruments and objectives with reference to the enlargement experience.[27] Others have explored the security dimension of the policy.[28] Legal scholars analysed inter alia the role of the ENP in EU external relations law, its legal instruments and mechanisms.[29]

The discussion that follows is set to contribute to the debate on the legal aspects of the ENP. The analysis offered aims in particular at linking the legal aspects of the ENP with the discourse on democracy promotion by the EU. The latter has become a prominent line of research in EU external relations. Although initially the human rights discourse dominated the literature, a much wider approach based on the ethical aspects and value dimension of EU foreign policy has emerged

[26] See for instance Del Sarto and Schumacher, note 10 above, 17; E Baracani, 'From the EMP to the ENP: A New European Pressure for Democratisation?' (2005) 1 *Journal of Contemporary European Research* 54; V Stritecky, 'The South Caucasus: A Challenge for the ENP' in P Kratochvil (ed), *The European Union and Its Neighbourhood: Policies, Problems and Priorities* (Prague, Institute of International Relations, 2006) 59–76; K Longhurst and S Nies, 'Recasting Relations with the Neighbours – Prospects for the Eastern Partnership' Institut Français des Relations Internationales, February 2009.

[27] For instance J Kelley, 'New Wine in Old Wineskins: Policy Learning and Adaptation in the New European Neighbourhood Policy' (2006) 44 *Journal of Common Market Studies* 29; A Magen, 'The Shadow of Enlargement: Can the European Neighbourhood Policy Achieve Compliance?', Center on Democracy, Development and the Rule of Law, Stanford Institute for International Studies, Working Papers, No 68, August 2006; Meloni, note 8 above, 97–111; R Balfour and A Rotta, 'Beyond Enlargement. The European Neighbourhood Policy and its Tools' (2005) 40 *International Spectator* 7.

[28] D Lynch, 'The Security Dimension of the European Neighbourhood Policy' (2005) 40 *The International Spectator* 33; Smith and Webber, note 10 above, 73.

[29] Cremona and Hillion, note 22 above, 20–44; M Cremona, 'The European Neighbourhood Policy: More than a Partnership?' in M Cremona (ed), *Developments in EU External Relations Law* (Oxford, OUP, 2008) 244–99; B Van Vooren, 'A Case-study of "Soft Law" in EU External Relations: the European Neighbourhood Policy' (2009) 34 *European Law Review* 696; B Van Vooren, *EU External Relations Law and the European Neighbourhood Policy: A Paradigm for Coherence* (London, Routledge, 2011).

in recent years.[30] The ENP occupies a special place in this discourse due to the apparent prominence of democracy promotion on its agenda. The transformationist rationale associated with the export of EU values was injected into the ENP from the start on the high wave of the EU's 'political and moral weight' to promote democracy abroad.[31]

However, this raises another 'capability–expectations gap':[32] can the ENP uphold democracy, as an EU value, in its neighbourhood? Besides, what is to be understood as 'democracy' that is being promoted on the ENP territory? Although the Commission justifies the EU's standing to promote democracy on the basis of its Member States being democracies,[33] it cannot possibly promote their model of democracy, as no single or common model can be discerned. It is rather an 'EU' concept of democratic values that lays the foundations for democracy promotion within the ENP. This concept can be revealed with reference to the constitutional development of the EU, allowing the distillation of those features of its governance that can credibly be called 'values'.

It is in this light that the study also necessitates the analysis of the enlargement practices. First, the accession of Central and Eastern European (CEE) states is perceived to be one of the most successful foreign policy actions of the EU in achieving political and economic transformation in third states, despite general scepticism regarding *ab extra* democracy imposition. Moreover, the ENP has been devised predominantly on the basis of the pre-accession instruments and methodology, including the conditionality principle. It is therefore considered that the enlargement and the ENP policies 'can be treated within the same brackets' as regards democracy promotion.[34] The comparison between the legal aspects of the ENP and the enlargement policy therefore contributes to the identification of the prominence of democracy promotion within the ENP.

The proclamation of the objective to promote democracy abroad in the revised Treaties, as well as the prominence of the discourse on 'values' in the ENP documents compel an investigation into the EU's 'normative' identity. As a foreign policy instrument, the ENP and its elements are at a crossroads between the disciplines

---

[30] M Cremona, 'Human Rights and Democracy Clauses in the EC's Trade Agreements' in N Emiliou and D O'Keeffe (eds), *The European Union and World Trade Law: After the GATT Uruguay Round* (Chichester, Wiley, 1996) 62–77; E Fierro, *The EU's Approach to Human Rights Conditionality in Practice* (The Hague, Martinus Nijhoff, 2003); U Khaliq, *Ethical Dimensions of the Foreign Policy of the European Union: A Legal Appraisal* (Cambridge, CUP, 2008); R Balfour, *Human Rights and Democracy in EU Foreign Policy: The Cases of Ukraine and Egypt* (London, Routledge, 2012); N Tocci, 'Can the EU Promote Democracy and Human Rights Through the ENP? The Case for Refocusing on the Rule of Law' in Cremona and Meloni (eds), note 8 above, 23–35; PJ Cardwell, 'Mapping Out Democracy Promotion in the EU's External Relations' (2011) 16 *European Foreign Affairs Review* 21.

[31] Commission Communication, 'The European Union's Role in Promoting Human Rights and Democratisation in Third Countries' COM (2001) 252 final, 8 May 2001, 3–4; Copenhagen European Council Conclusions, 12–13 December 2002, 4.

[32] C Hill, 'The Capability–Expectations Gap, or Conceptualizing Europe's International Role' (1993) 31 *Journal of Common Market Studies* 305, 321–322.

[33] Commission Communication, 'The European Union's Role in Promoting Human Rights and Democratisation in Third Countries' COM (2001) 252 final, 8 May 2001, 3.

[34] Cardwell, note 30 above, 32.

of international relations and external relations law of the EU. To understand the ENP and in particular the role of the democratic values therein, one needs to creep into the realm of international relations theory. Mere reliance on legal studies carries the risk of omitting the comprehensive picture of the ENP: the identification of the EU's nature as a political actor provides the background against which to analyse the role of the democratic values in the ENP legal framework.

In a departure from rationalist approaches, both realist and liberal, with their focus on exogenous factors such as interests and self-interest detached from social structures,[35] constructivists suggest that social structures influence actions. According to Wendt, identities formed by agents in their socialisation predetermine the subsequent action.[36] As opposed to rationalist perspective, it is the 'logic of appropriateness' which is the driving force behind the action predetermined by established identity.[37] Identity, ideas, norms and values are the concepts most frequently used within this approach. Constructivist accounts of the EU foreign policy have been explored by various scholars,[38] based on a presumption of shared identity and understanding stemming from certain values as a basis for a collective action aimed at transformation.[39] These include the 'civilian power' of Duchêne with the characterisation of the then European Community (EC) as 'a force for the international diffusion of civilian and democratic standards' which achieves foreign policy objectives via economic means.[40] Where the first element of this conceptualisation acquired centrality in analysing the EU foreign policy subsequently,[41] others brought the focus back to the second, normative element of Duchêne's definition, where the 'civilian nature' of the power is not determined by the use of force per se, but rather by the way in which the force is used, ie for the promotion of civilian values.[42]

---

[35] GJ March and GR Olsen, *Rediscovering Institutions: The Organisational Basis of Politics* (New York, Free Press, 1989) 160; B Rosamond, 'New Theories of European Integration' in M Cini (ed), *European Union Politics*, 2nd edn (Oxford, OUP, 2007) 130; U Sedelmeier, *Constructing the Path to Eastern Enlargement* (Manchester, Manchester University Press, 2005) 18.

[36] A Wendt, *Social Theory of International Politics* (Cambridge, CUP, 1999) 41, 371.

[37] Sedelmeier, note 35 above, 18.

[38] T Christiansen, KE Jorgensen and A Weiner, 'The Social Construction of Europe' (1999) 6 *Journal of European Public Policy* 528; KE Jorgensen (ed), *Reflective Approaches to European Governance* (London, Macmillan, 1997); B Tonra, 'Constructing the Common Foreign and Security Policy: The Utility of a Cognitive Approach' (2003) 41 *Journal of Common Market Studies* 731; JT Checkel, 'Why Comply? Social Learning and European Identity Change' (2001) 55 *International Organisation* 553.

[39] Tonra, note 38 above, 741, 747.

[40] F Duchêne, 'The EC and the Uncertainties of Interdependence' in M Kohnstamm and W Hager (eds), *A Nation Writ Large? Foreign Policy Problems before the European Community* (London, Macmillan, 1973) 1–21, 19–20.

[41] C Hill, 'European Foreign Policy: Power Bloc, Civilian Model – or Flop?' in R Rummel (ed), *The Evolution of an International Actor: Western Europe's New Assertiveness* (Boulder, Westview Press, 1990) 31–55, 41–48; KE Smith, 'The End of Civilian Power EU: A Welcome Demise or Cause for Concern?' (2000) 35 *The International Spectator* 11, 13; J Howorth, 'European Defence and the Changing Politics of the European Union: Hanging Together or Hanging Separately' (2001) 39 *Journal of Common Market Studies* 765, 767, 769.

[42] S Stavridis, '"Militarising" the EU: the Concept of Civilian Power Revisited' (2001) *The International Spectator* 43, 44, 48; H Sjursen, 'The EU as a "Normative" Power: How Can This Be?' (2006) 13 *Journal of European Public Policy* 235, 238; S Biscop, 'The European Security Strategy and the Neighbourhood Policy:

The most recent identity-based understanding of the EU has been the 'norma-tive power' of Manners. Accordingly, the unique normative basis of the EU is 'diffused' in its international relations, predisposing the latter to act 'normatively'.[43] This normative basis comprises norms defining the EU's identity, including democracy and human rights. The norms not only influence the foreign policy, but they become the very constituents of it. The promotion of democracy and human rights are considered to be 'identity objectives' for the EU, manifesting its value-driven power as opposed to other actors on the international scene.[44] It has been noted that the EU's 'self-representation' – even on a rhetorical level – can be 'performative', which, given necessary structural context, can contribute to the formulation of identity of relevant actors.[45] Furthermore, it is also considered to be a factor enhancing the EU's identity and its values internally in reference to its 'democratic deficit' debate.[46]

However, the identification of the EU in constructivist terms does not ulti-mately dismiss the rationalist accounts of its foreign policy action. According to Diez, no facile distinction can be discerned between norms and strategic interests: there is no normative existence without accompanying interests.[47] Hence, the general debate between rationalists and constructivists in international relations theory has been reflected in EU studies.[48] In particular, the current level of EU integration has been identified as one of the factors affecting its international identity, which continues to represent a fusion of both supranationalism and intergovernmentalism.[49] The inability of the EU to act as a unitary actor in foreign relations is influenced by the complexity of its internal decision-making and spo-radic and ad hoc manner of reacting to international events.[50] Most importantly, the presence of multiple policymakers increases scepticism as to the possibility of

A New Starting Point for a Euro–Mediterranean Security Partnership?' in F Attina and R Rossi (eds), *European Neighbourhood Policy: Political, Economic and Social Issues*, The Jean Monnet Centre 'Euro-Med', Department of Political Studies, 2004, 25–36, 29.

[43] I Manners, 'Normative Power Europe: A Contradiction in Terms' (2002) 40 *Journal of Common Market Studies* 235, 236, 244, 252.

[44] S Keukeleire and J MacNaughtan, *The Foreign Policy of the European Union* (Basingstoke, Palgrave, 2008) 223; R Youngs, 'Normative Dynamics and Strategic Interests in the EU's External Identity' (2004) 42 *Journal of Common Market Studies* 415, 416; GR Olsen, 'Promotion of Democracy as a Foreign Policy Instrument of "Europe": Limits to International Idealism' (2000) 7 *Democratisation* 142, 143.

[45] S Lucarelli, 'Values, Identity and Ideational Shocks in the Transatlantic Rift' (2006) 9 *Journal of International Relations and Development* 304, 319–20.

[46] Youngs, note 44 above, 415, 419.

[47] T Diez, 'Constructing the Self and Changing Others: Reconsidering Normative Power Europe' (2005) 33 *Journal of International Studies* 613, 625.

[48] M Aspinal and G Schneider (eds), *The Rules of Integration: Institutionalist Approaches to the Study of Europe* (Manchester, Manchester University Press, 2001); JT Checkel and A Moravcsik, 'A Constructivist Research Programme in EU Studies?' (2001) 2 *European Union Politics* 219.

[49] R Whitman, *From Civilian Power to Superpower? The International Identity of the European Union* (Basingstoke, Palgrave, 1998) 28, 205; A Bendiek, 'European Realism in the EU's Common Foreign and Security Poilicy' in PJ Cardwell (ed), *EU External Relations Law and Policy in the Post-Lisbon Era* (The Hague, TMC Asser Press, 2012) 35–57, 48, 51.

[50] R Dannreuther (ed), *European Union Foreign and Security Policy: Towards a Neighbourhood Strategy* (London, Routledge, 2004) 207.

formulating a single presumption of the EU's identity and upholding it with equal intensity.[51]

Thus, the legal analysis of the ENP will be grounded on the definition of the EU in the following terms: it is an actor whose identity requires it to act 'normatively' in its external action, which nevertheless is not devoid of rationalist motivations.

1.2 STRUCTURE

The book is structured as follows. Chapter 2 considers the role of democracy promotion within the external relations agenda of the EU, and within the ENP framework in particular. It analyses the objectives of the foreign policy of the EU as established in the Treaties. The ENP-specific objectives are discussed to reveal the focus or lack of it on the promotion of democratic values in the neighbourhood.

Chapter 3 analyses substantive legal issues arising in relation to the ENP. It first refers to the institutional arrangements of policy initiation and formation and the subsequent impact of the Lisbon Treaty on those arrangements. Matters related to legal competence in EU external relations law as applied to the ENP contribute to the discussion in the next part of the chapter. Further, the instruments and methods of the policy are considered with a view to determining their appropriateness for promoting the democratic values of the EU. The EaP, as a regional dimension of the ENP affecting the Eastern neighbours, is analysed to identify the impact it has had on the legal aspects of the policy and the democracy promotion within it. The discussion of the EaP as opposed to the Union for the Mediterranean is dictated by the choice of the case study identified below.

To trace the role of EU democratic values within the implementation of the ENP, Chapter 4 identifies those values with reference to EU constitutional evolution as legalised in the provisions of the Lisbon Treaty. The practice of the 2004 and 2007 accession rounds is reflected upon as a precedent of promoting democratic values, on which the ENP heavily draws.

Chapters 5 and 6 are dedicated to the ENP implementation process in Georgia, Armenia and Azerbaijan and comprise the case study chosen. Constituting the so-called region of the South Caucasus the three countries were latecomers to the ENP. The first phase of EU relations with the three states via the establishment of almost identical PCAs was part of a more general approach towards the former Soviet Union states, itself a regional category for the EU.[52] This so-called '1990s style' approach[53] was marked by a lack of a coordinated policy, and a reluctance to become involved in the South Caucasian conflicts.[54]

---

[51] Sedelmeier, note 35 above, 36.

[52] D Lynch, 'The EU: Towards a Strategy' in 'The South Caucasus: A Challenge for the EU', Chaillot Papers No 65, EU Institute for Security Studies, Paris, 2003, 9–21, 179.

[53] N Popescu, 'Europe's Unrecognised Neighbours: The EU in Abkhazia and South Ossetia', CEPS Working Document No 260, 2007, 4.

[54] N Ghazaryan, 'The ENP and the South Caucasus: Meeting Expectations?' in R Whitman and S Wolff (eds), *The European Neighbourhood Policy in Perspective* (Basingstoke, Palgrave, 2010) 223–46,

A shift in the relationship between the EU and the three states occurred at the beginning of the new millennium with a view to contributing towards conflict prevention and post-conflict rehabilitation.[55] This eagerness was translated into a number of ad hoc Common Foreign and Security Policy (CFSP) initiatives in Georgia, as well as the appointment of a Special Representative for the South Caucasus in 2003.[56] The initial omission of the South Caucasian states from the list of the ENP addressees, therefore, came as a counter-trend. Due to the importance accorded to the region in the ESS,[57] the 'Rose Revolution' in Georgia,[58] and the inter-institutional stance taken by the European Parliament (EP), the Commission and the High Representative for CFSP, the three states were included within the list of the ENP addressees in 2004.[59]

The interests of the EU in the region, where Azerbaijan is a significant exporter of oil and gas, while Georgia and Armenia can secure an alternative transit route,[60] are closely linked to the pressure of diversifying its energy supplies. The Baku-Tbilisi-Ceyhan and the Baku-Tbilisi-Erzurum pipelines for oil and gas secured Georgian–Azerbaijani cooperation, but left Armenia isolated due to its problematic relations with Azerbaijan and Turkey.[61] This suggests that security understood in broad terms occupies a prominent role in the politics of the EU in the

---

224; B Coppieters, 'An EU Special Representative to a New Periphery' in 'The South Caucasus: A Challenge for the EU', note 52 above, 159–70, 169; U Halbach, 'The European Union in the South Caucasus: Story of A Hesitant Approximation' in *South Caucasus: 20 Years of Independence* (Friedrich Ebert Stiftung, 2011) 300–15, 301–02.

[55] Council Conclusions, General Affairs, 26–27 February 2001.

[56] Joint Action 2000/456/CFSP regarding a contribution of the European Union towards reinforcing the capacity of the Georgian authorities to support and protect the OSCE observer mission on the border of the Republic of Georgia with the Chechen Republic of the Russian Federation [2000] OJ L183/3, as amended [2001] OJ L2002/2; Joint Action 2002/373/CFSP regarding a contribution of the European Union towards reinforcing the capacity of the Georgian authorities to support and protect the OSCE observer mission on the border of Georgia with the Ingush and Chechen Republics of the Russian Federation [2002] OJ L134/1; Joint Action 2001/759/CFSP regarding a contribution from the European Union to the conflict settlement process in South Ossetia [2001] OJ L286/4; Joint Action 2003/473/CFSP regarding a contribution of the EU to the conflict settlement in Georgia/South Ossetia [2003] OJ L157/72; Joint Action 2003/496/CFSP concerning the appointment of an EU Special Representative for the South Caucasus [2003] OJ L169/74; Council Decision 2004/924/CFSP [2004] OJ L389/41.

[57] European Security Strategy Paper, 8.

[58] N Tocci, 'Does the ENP Respond to the EU's Post-Enlargement Challenges?' (2005) 40 *International Spectator* 21, 23; 'Georgia: Sliding Towards Authoritarianism?' ICG, Europe Report No 189, 19 December 2007, 1.

[59] Council Conclusions, General Affairs and External Relations, 14 June 2004, para 12.

[60] Commission Communication, Development of Energy Policy for the Enlarged European Union, its Neighbours and Partner Countries COM (2003) 262 final, 13 March 2003.

[61] Turkey closed its border with Armenia in response to Armenian advances in the Nagorno–Karabakh war in 2003. Differences also exist regarding the legal qualification of the mass massacres of Armenians in Ottoman Turkey at the beginning of the 20th century. The Baku-Tbilisi-Ceyhan pipeline launched in May 2005 transports oil from the Caspian Sea to the Mediterranean port of Ceyhan. The Baku-Tbilisi-Erzurum natural gas pipeline was launched in 2006 and transports gas from the Azeri Shah-Deniz gas field. A Labedzska, 'The Southern Caucasus' in S Blockmans and A Lazowski (eds), *The European Union and Its Neighbours: A Legal Appraisal of the EU's Policies of Stabilisation, Partnership and Integration* (The Hague, TMC Asser Press, 2006) 575–612, 582.

region. Moreover, the presence of unresolved conflicts in Nagorno-Karabakh,[62] South Ossetia and Abkhazia[63] also support the presumption that rationalist considerations cannot be dismissed, particularly in a region prone to influences form other international actors.[64]

The choice of the case study is conditioned also by the continuous political transition in the three states. Although according to their national constitutions they have embraced liberal democracy as a political model, supported by membership of international organisations,[65] none has succeeded in realising a full transition to a liberal democratic regime, while Azerbaijan is also characterised by authoritarian features.[66]

Within this context, Chapters 5 and 6 are aimed at revealing the consistency of the EU's self-representation as a normative actor. The two chapters trace the operative elements of the policy implementation, that is the Action Plans setting the main parameters of cooperation, the monitoring and assistance provided. Chapter 5 focuses on the Action Plans established with each of the countries in comparative perspective, while Chapter 6 discusses the role of democratic values with a focus on monitoring of progress and financial assistance provided.

Finally, Chapter 7 summarises the main findings of the book.

[62] The conflict erupted over the status of the largely Armenian-populated autonomous oblast in Azerbaijan at the end of 1980s. Full-scale military activities intensified after the break-up of the Soviet Union. A ceasefire was signed in May 1994 with the efforts of the OSCE. Negotiations over the conflict settlement are pursued within the OSCE Minsk Group.

[63] The dispute commenced over South Ossetia's attempts to upgrade its status to 'autonomous republic' in 1989. Armed violence broke out in 1991, until the signing of the 'Agreement on the Principle of the Settlement of the Georgian–Ossetian conflict between Georgia and Russia' in 1992, establishing a Joint Control Commission and deploying joint peacekeepers combining Russians, Georgians and Ossetians. Nationalist tendencies in Georgia stirred the ethnic tension in the Abkhaz Autonomous Republic at the end of the 1980s leading to the declaration of its independence in July 1992. A military intervention by the Georgian forces followed, which was nevertheless halted by Abkhazia in 1993. The latter proclaimed its independence in 1999.

[64] On the role of the US, Russia and Turkey, see *South Caucasus: 20 Years of Independence*, note 54 above, 241–98.

[65] The Constitution of Georgia, 24 August 1995, Arts 1, 5, 7; The Constitution of the Republic of Azerbaijan, 12 November 1995, Arts 7, 26; The Constitution of the Republic of Armenia, 5 July 1995, Arts 1, 4, 5, 7; All three states joined the UN and the OSCE in 1992. Armenia and Azerbaijan became members of the Council of Europe in January 2001, Georgia was admitted earlier in April 1999.

[66] In the freedom of press rankings Georgia is ranked 111th, Armenia is 149th, and Azerbaijan is 172nd; *A Freedom of the Press 2012*, Freedom House: available at www.freedomhouse.org. Transparency International in its corruption perception index ranked Azerbaijan as 142nd, Armenia 129th and Georgia as 64th among 182 states: available at www.transparency.org. See also 'Armenia: Picking up the Pieces' ICG, Europe Briefing No 48, 8 April 2008; 'Armenia: An Opportunity for Statesmanship' IGC, Europe Report No 217, 25 June 2012; 'Honouring of obligations and commitments by Armenia' Report, Doc 10027, 27 January 2004, Parliamentary Assembly of the Council of Europe; 'Azerbaijan's 2005 Elections: Lost Opportunity' ICG, Europe Briefing No 40, 21 November 2005; 'Azerbaijan: Vulnerable Stability' ICG, Europe Report No 207, 3 September 2010; 'The Functioning of Democratic Institutions in Azerbaijan', Report of Monitoring Committee, Doc 11627, 6 June 2008, Parliamentary Assembly of the Council of Europe; Resolution 1359 (2004) on Political Prisoners in Azerbaijan of the Parliamentary Assembly of the Council of Europe; 'Honouring of obligations and commitments by Georgia' Report, Doc 10383, 21 December 2004, Parliamentary Assembly of the Council of Europe; 'Honouring of obligations and commitments by Georgia', Resolution 1603 (2008), Parliamentary Assembly of Council of Europe 24 January 2008; 'Georgia: Securing a Stable Future' ICG, Europe Briefing No 58, 13 December 2010; 'Georgia: Sliding Towards Authoritarianism?' ICG, Europe Report No 189, 19 December 2007.

2

Democracy Promotion, EU External Relations Law and ENP Objectives

2.1 INTRODUCTION

THE ENP HAS presented an opportunity to challenge the perception of the EU as a weak foreign policy actor and to act 'beyond the dichotomy of accession/non-accession'.[1] The policy can be suggested to have become a regional manifestation of the Union's growing sense of 'actorness'. This actor was required to determine its interests in its vicinity and identify the necessary instruments for their pursuit.

A vast – geographically speaking and diverse – politically speaking – territory was subsumed by an overarching rationale of securing the borders of the EU.[2] In each of the regions, namely Eastern Europe, the South Caucasus and the Mediterranean, the EU had interests of its own. In the South Caucasus, despite a common regional approach, relations between the EU and each state concerned acquired their own distinct patterns, with varying objectives and interests pursued.[3]

The pursuit of any foreign policy agenda by the EU is based on the legal framework of EU external relations, and in particular the objectives defined in the Treaties. The Lisbon Treaty introduced for the first time a uniform list of objectives for all areas of EU external relations, equally binding on the Member States and EU institutions. To accommodate all areas of EU external action the objectives are defined widely and also include democracy promotion. The latter has acquired a multifaceted and multilayered expression: it is reflected in separate objectives, but is also a 'principle' guiding foreign policy, as well as a 'value' which is to be promoted.

---

[1] M Emerson, 'The Wider Europe as the European Union's Friendly Monroe Doctrine' CEPS Policy Brief No 27, 2002, 2; D Lynch, 'The Security Dimension of the European Neighbourhood Policy' (2005) 40 *International Spectator* 33, 33–34.

[2] M Cremona, 'The European Neighbourhood Policy: More than a Partnership?' in M Cremona (ed), *Developments in EU External Relations Law* (Oxford, OUP, 2008) 244–99, 251.

[3] N Ghazaryan, 'The ENP and the South Caucasus: Meeting Expectations?' in R Whitman and S Wolff (eds), *The European Neighbourhood Policy in Perspective* (Basingstoke, Palgrave, 2010) 223–46, 226–30; P Van Elsuwege, 'Variable Geometry in the European Neighbourhood Policy: The Principle of Differentiation and its Consequences' in E Lannon (ed), *The European Neighbourhood Policy's Challenges* (Brussels, PIE Peter Lang, 2012) 59–84, 69–70.

Under this general umbrella, the new Article 8 of the Treaty on European Union (TEU) specifies the objectives to be pursued in the neighbourhood.[4]

The objectives of the ENP have been formulated and reformulated, often changing from document to document. Despite the ambiguity surrounding the policy at the initial stage of its conceptualisation, it transpires that security is the central matter of concern. It is therefore necessary to clarify to what extent the Union's normative identity has been translated into the objectives of the ENP.

Against this background, the chapter first seeks to identify the role of democracy promotion within EU external relations objectives. The pursuit of democratic values as a foreign policy objective in the Treaties will be considered both prior to and following the ratification of the Lisbon Treaty. The documents initiating and shaping the ENP are analysed next to reveal the specific set of objectives pursued within the policy. The identification of the role of democracy promotion within the ENP objectives constitutes a part of this discussion. Finally, the chapter is summarised with brief conclusions on the role of democratic values within the ENP policy objectives.

2.2 DEMOCRACY PROMOTION AND EU EXTERNAL RELATIONS OBJECTIVES

In political science, foreign policy objectives pursued by nations have been classified to include possession goals and milieu goals.[5] In pursuing its possession goals a nation follows its interests and pursues those issues to which 'it attaches value'. The milieu goals are concerned with transforming the environment outside the borders of the nation pursuing them. With its identified political agenda, this classification can equally apply to the foreign policy objectives of the EU, although not a nation state.[6] In the ENP context Tocci identifies the milieu goals to include the promotion of democracy and human rights, as well as the rule of law, international law, conflict resolution and good neighbourly relations.[7] In contrast, the possession goals, or alternatively strategic objectives, include advancing narrower EU interests in commercial relations, migration, border management and energy security.[8] The latter group, arguably including also conflict resolution, can be summarised in the broader concept of security.

Democracy promotion, as a milieu goal, is currently provided for in the founding Treaties of the EU: it is a constituent element of the latter's normative image. The first allusion to democracy promotion was in the Preamble to the Single

---

[4] Treaty on European Union [2012] OJ C326 (hereinafter TEU).

[5] A Wolfers, *Discord and Collaboration: Essays on International Politics* (Baltimore, The Johns Hopkins University Press, 1968) 73–74.

[6] See for instance N Tocci, 'Can the EU Promote Democracy and Human Rights Through the ENP? The Case for Refocusing on the Rule of Law' in M Cremona and G Meloni (eds), *The European Neighbourhood Policy: A New Framework for Modernisation?*, EUI Working Papers, LAW 2007/21, 23–35.

[7] Ibid 29.

[8] Ibid 29–30.

European Act (SEA) referring to the role of the Member States in upholding democracy based on international law.[9] Democracy promotion is currently inevitably associated with the Union's own external relations framework, within which the ENP is bound to operate.

2.2.1 Democracy Promotion Prior to the Lisbon Treaty

At the time of the ENP initiation the EU foreign policy objectives were scattered across the EU Treaty and the EC Treaty, reflecting the pillar division of the EU constitutional framework.[10] Articles 133, 177 and 181a EC respectively established the Community's objectives on Common Commercial Policy (CCP), development cooperation and economic, financial and technical cooperation with third countries, while Article 11 EU established the objectives for the CFSP action. Although Article 29 EU on police and judicial cooperation did not directly refer to the foreign policy objectives, it has been argued that the objectives set for the third pillar therein would have been legitimate also for the external aspects of that policy.[11] In practice this meant that the various areas of EU external relations pursued an agenda of their own in the absence of a common denominator in terms of policy objectives.

Article 11 EU provided for the development and consolidation of democracy and the rule of law, and respect for human rights and fundamental freedoms among the list of CFSP objectives. It referred also to the safeguarding of 'common values', although no clarification was provided as to what those values might mean.[12] Because no 'values' as such were identified in the Treaties at the time, the 'principles' to which the Member States adhered were to be relied upon.[13] These were defined in the Preamble to the Maastricht Treaty to include inter alia democracy.[14] A few years later, the Amsterdam Treaty elevated the status of the Preamble principles to 'founding' in Article 6 EU to include democracy, liberty, respect for human rights and fundamental freedoms, and the rule of law.[15] The understanding of 'common values' as 'principles' raised the issue of the correlation between the objective to 'develop and consolidate democracy' in Article 11(5) EU and 'to safeguard the common values' in Article 11(1) TEU. It can be suggested that this

---

[9] [1987] OJ L169.

[10] Consolidated Version of the Treaty Establishing the European Community and the Treaty on European Union [2006] OJ C321.

[11] F Hoffmeister, 'The Contribution of European Union Practice to International Law' in Cremona (ed), note 2 above, 37–127, 45.

[12] M Koskenniemi, 'International Law Aspects of the Common Foreign and Security Policy' in M Koskenniemi (ed), *International Law Aspects of the European Union* (Leiden, Martinus Nijhoff Publishers, 1998) 27–44, 27–28.

[13] R Wessel, *The European Union's Foreign and Security Policy: A Legal Institutional Perspective* (The Hague, Kluwer Law International, 1999) 60.

[14] The preamble to the EU Treaty confirmed the attachment of the Member States 'to the principles of liberty, democracy and respect for human rights and fundamental freedoms and of the rule of law'.

[15] Treaty of Amsterdam [1997] OJ C340.

indicates the level of integration in the EU, where the 'common values' were linked to the central role the Member States played within the CFSP. On the other hand, the inclusion of the objective on developing and consolidating democracy could have been linked to the 'generalisation' of democracy promotion as a foreign policy objective.

The objective of democracy promotion was also formulated in both Articles 177 and 181a EC as 'a general objective' without further qualification. Democracy promotion, as an external objective, appeared to have crossed the pillars, and therefore had been considered to be 'a general objective of EU foreign policy'.[16] The cross-Treaty references to democracy are said to have contributed to the constructivist understanding of the EU.[17]

Despite the 'generalisation' of democracy promotion, the latter played a more prominent role within the context of the development policies, where the lack of democracy was viewed as an obstacle to the policy itself.[18] On the other hand, it can be suggested that Article 11 EU mainstreamed democracy promotion, since political dialogue and 'essential' clauses have become common practice in the conclusion of international agreements.[19] It therefore ensured that democracy-related issues made an appearance in bilateral cooperation between the EU and third states.

2.2.2 The Lisbon Treaty: A New Role for Democratic Values within EU Foreign Policy?

An initial consideration of the provisions of the Lisbon Treaty support the presumption of the Union's general mandate to promote democracy abroad.[20] This mandate is expressed in various, at times confusing, ways.

Article 3 TEU defines the general aims of the Union, which include promotion of peace and EU values. Paragraph 5 specifies this aim in external relations, where:

> the Union shall uphold and promote its values and interests and contribute to the protection of its citizens. It shall contribute to [. . .] the protection of human rights, in particular the rights of the child, as well as to the strict observance and the development of international law, including respect for the principles of the United Nations Charter.

In contrast with previous Treaties, the Lisbon Treaty identifies the 'values' of the EU which resemble the former 'founding' principles. Article 2 TEU defines the

---

[16] G de Baere, *Principles of EU External Relations Law* (Oxford, OUP, 2008) 108; P Koutrakos, *EU International Relations Law* (Oxford, Hart Publishing, 2006) 484.

[17] PJ Cardwell, *EU External Relations and Systems of Governance: The CFSP, Euro–Mediterranean Partnership and Migration* (London, Routledge, 2009) 9.

[18] U Khaliq, *Ethical Dimensions of the Foreign Policy of the European Union: A Legal Appraisal* (Cambridge, CUP, 2008) 74.

[19] For instance PCAs with former Soviet Union states, see note 14, chapter one.

[20] PJ Cardwell, 'Mapping Out Democracy Promotion in the EU's External Relations' (2011) 16 *European Foreign Affairs Review* 21, 24.

founding values with reference to human dignity, freedom, democracy, equality, the rule of law and respect for human rights, including the rights of persons belonging to minorities. These are, therefore, the foundations of the normative identity of the EU, whereby its legitimacy for outsiders in promoting democracy lies in the fact that these values have their roots in Europe.[21]

A few observations should be made regarding Articles 2 and 3 TEU. First, there is an overlap between the provisions referring to both values and objectives.[22] Besides, Article 3(5) TEU appears to emphasise values and interests in equal measure without any prioritisation. In addition, the aims in Article 3(5) are formulated so widely that they are sufficient 'to elude any direct measure of many actions against declared objectives'.[23]

Similar fusion is present in Article 21 TEU representing the latest stage in the process of 'legalisation' or 'constitutionalisation' of EU foreign policy.[24] For the first time, a single set of objectives is directly prescribed for all areas of EU external action. Together with the formal abolition of pillar structure, Article 21 TEU is considered to be a significant improvement to the Union's 'unitary legal system'.[25] Article 21(1) requires the EU international action to 'be guided by the principles which have inspired its own creation'. However, the principles cited in the same paragraph include the values of Article 2 TEU, which in their turn replaced the 'founding' principles as noted above. It is therefore apparent that the concepts of 'principle' and 'value' are used interchangeably.[26]

Second, the list of specific objectives in Article 21(2) TEU adds extra layers to the obligation to promote democracy in relations with the wider world. The Union is said to (a) safeguard its values and fundamental interests, and (b) consolidate and support democracy. The question to ask is whether such formulations suggest that democracy could also be understood outside the framework of EU values. On the one hand, Article 21(2)(b) in addition to consolidating and supporting democracy also mentions the rule of law and human rights which similarly constitute the values of the EU as defined in Article 2 TEU. On the other

---

[21] C Carta, 'Close Enough? The EU's Global Role Described by Non-European Diplomats in Brussels' in S Lucarelli and L Fiaramonti (eds), *External Perceptions of the European Union as a Global Actor* (London, Routledge, 2009) 207–17, 213.

[22] LS Rossi, 'Does the Lisbon Treaty Provide a Clearer Separation of Competences between EU and Member States?' in A Biondi, P Eeckout and S Ripley (eds), *EU Law After Lisbon* (Oxford, OUP, 2012) 85–106, 91.

[23] S Duke, 'Consistency, Coherence and European Union External Action: The Path to Lisbon and Beyond' in P Koutrakos (ed), *European Foreign Policy: Legal and Political Perspectives* (Cheltenham, Edward Elgar Publishing, 2011) 15–54, 20.

[24] B de Witte, 'Too Much Constitutional Law in the European Union's Foreign Relations' in M Cremona and B de Witte (eds), *EU Foreign Relations Law: Constitutional Fundamentals* (Oxford, Hart Publishing, 2008) 3–15, 5.

[25] R Wessel, 'The Multilevel Constitution of European Foreign Relations in Transnational Constitutionalism: International and European Perspectives' in N Tsagourias (ed), *Transnational Constitutionalism: International and European Perspectives* (Cambridge, CUP, 2010) 160–206, 202; DM Curtin and IF Dekker, 'The European Union From Maastricht to Lisbon: Institutional and Legal Unity of the Shadows' in P Craig and G de Búrca (eds), *Evolution of EU Law* (Oxford, OUP, 2011) 155–85, 171.

[26] Rossi, note 22 above, 91.

hand, one might argue that the combination of these objectives in Article 21(2)(a) and (b) alludes to a stronger obligation attached to democracy which is not only 'safeguarded' but also 'consolidated and supported', suggesting a more proactive attitude. However, Article 21(2)(a) TEU in line with Article 3(5) TEU puts on an equal footing the 'values, fundamental interests, security, independence and integrity' of the EU.

Thus, according to Article 21 TEU in its external relations the Union's action shall be 'guided' by democracy as a principle, the Union shall 'safeguard' democracy as a value, and it shall 'consolidate and support' democracy as an objective.

Article 205 of the Treaty on the Functioning of the European Union (TFEU) in its turn confirms this fusion of the concepts of values, principles and objectives:

> The Union's action on the international scene, pursuant to this Part, shall be guided by the principles, pursue the objectives and be conducted in accordance with the general provisions laid down in Chapter 1 of Title V of the Treaty on European Union.

It therefore appears that democracy features in EU external relations as a value, a principle and as an objective. These concepts are not interchangeable, nonetheless, as they denote distinct ideas. While principles are characterised as legal norms used to denominate limitations on the Union's actions, values have been noted to have 'intrinsic worth' of their own as an 'ethical conviction'.[27] According to Von Bogdandy the use of 'value' instead of a 'principle' demonstrates a present lack of determination as regards the founding EU principles,[28] which had a precedent in the EU Treaty as noted above. Moreover, in terms of legal enforcement, principles are more meaningful: as basic legal norms they must be complied with, even if it is at the expense of the values.[29]

Principles should also be distinguished from objectives: the latter are indicative in terms of the end goal of the action.[30] Therefore, the external actions of the EU are limited by the principle of democracy by which it has to be 'guided', at the same time attempting to achieve consolidation of democracy as an end goal of its international efforts.

The confusion between values, principles and objectives, however, is not the only issue arising from Article 21 TEU. It has been noted that the list of the objectives is not balanced, and the CFSP (with former Article 11 objectives) occupies the central place.[31] The objectives are formulated widely to reflect the EU interests in international security, economic development, multilateral cooperation and

---

[27] A Von Bogdandy, 'Founding Principles' in A Von Bogdandy and J Bast (eds), *Principles of European Constitutional Law*, 2nd edn (Oxford, Hart Publishing, 2010) 11–54, 22; M Cremona, 'Values in EU Foreign Policy' in M Evans and T Tridimas (eds), *Beyond Established Legal Orders: Policy Interconnections between the EU and the Rest of the World* (Oxford, Hart Publishing, 2011) 275–315, 281.

[28] Von Bogdandy, note 27 above, 22.

[29] EO Eriksen and JE Fossum, 'A Done Deal? The EU's Legitimacy Conundrum Revisited' in EO Eriksen, C Joerges and F Rodl (eds), *Law, Democracy and Solidarity in Post-National Union: The Unsettled Political Order of Europe* (London, Routledge, 2008) 230–25, 239.

[30] Von Bogdandy, note 27 above, 23.

[31] A Dashwood, M Dougan et al, *Wyatt and Dashwood's European Union Law*, 6th edn (Oxford, Hart Publishing, 2011) 904–05.

other areas. The wide list of objectives creates the necessary legal framework for pursuing both possession and milieu goals identified above. In other words within this framework the EU can pursue both its identity objectives, as well as rationalist interests. Precisely for this reason Article 21 TEU is not sufficient on its own to secure unitary external action, and a balance needs to be struck between various objectives and interests.

This can be problematic for a number of reasons. First of all, when a relevant legal basis is to be determined, it is important to distinguish between the CFSP and other external actions based on a TFEU legal basis due to the distinctions still existing in the decision-making processes.[32] Such drafting of Treaty provisions can potentially lead to securitisation of other policy areas, especially taking into account the text of Article 24 TEU defining the scope of the CFSP to include 'all areas' of external action. As established in *Titanium Dioxide* and applied in the subsequent case law, the aim of the measure is one of the 'objective factors' defining the legal basis for decision making.[33] The objectives of the CFSP played an important role in delimiting the CFSP competence from other areas of EU foreign policy.[34] On the other hand, the common list of objectives is less of a concern for the CFSP due to the exclusion of the latter from the list of shared competences in Article 4 TFEU, as well as Article 352 TFEU limiting the application of the flexibility clause.[35]

It is the opposite, namely the securitisation of other areas of external action, that should be of concern.[36] The preservation of the mostly intergovernmental nature of the CFSP, devoid of scrutiny from the Court of Justice and the Parliament, has been viewed to amount to retention of a separate 'pillar'.[37] Some even argue that due to its legal substance it rather should be a subject of political analysis.[38] Thus, the CFSP continues to provide the domain for pursuing political interests by the Member States.

Some relief in terms of the threat of 'securitisation' must be sought in the *ECOWAS* judgment on the application of what is currently Article 40 TEU guaranteeing the intactness of the procedures and the scope of competences in other

---

[32]   Art 24(1) TEU.

[33]   Case C-300/89 *Titanium Dioxide* [1991] ECR I-0286, para 10; Case C-36/98 *Spain v Council* [2001] ECR I-779, paras 58–59; Case C-281/01 *The Energy Star Agreement* [2002] I-12049, paras 33–34.

[34]   de Baere, note 16 above; D MacGoldrick, *International Relations Law of the European Union* (London, Longman, 1997) 142.

[35]   Rossi, note 22 above, 92.

[36]   In relation to development policy see P Koutrakos, 'The Nexus Between the European Union's Common Security and Defence Policy and Development' in A Arnull, C Barnard et al (eds), *A Constitutional Order of States? Essays in EU Law in Honour of Alan Dashwood* (Oxford, Hart Publishing, 2011) 589–608, 590.

[37]   Art 24 TEU restricts the competence of the Court in this area to delimitation of competence under Art 40 TEU, while the role of the Parliament is restricted under Art 36 TEU; DM Curtin and IF Dekker, 'The European Union From Maastricht to Lisbon: Institutional and Legal Unity of the Shadows' in P Craig and G de Burca (eds), note 25 above, 155–85, 172.

[38]   P Eeckout, *External Relations of the European Union: Legal and Constitutional Functions* (Oxford, OUP, 2011) 420; Cardwell, note 17 above, 27.

areas.[39] The function of Article 40 TEU, however, acquired a dual character, as it operates also to protect the CFSP from encroachment by other policies. It is therefore suggested that despite the 'commonisation' of objectives, the different decision-making procedures will still necessitate the identification of policy-specific objectives.

While certain objectives in Article 21 TEU are more easily attributable to a specific policy area, others are viewed to be 'cross-sectoral' in essence.[40] As mentioned earlier, democracy promotion even previously was perceived to be a general obligation. Safeguarding the Union's values and fundamental interests, as well as consolidating and supporting democracy are of a cross-sectoral nature, and therefore applicable to both CFSP and non-CFSP action. This proposition is supported by the language of Articles 3(5) and 21(1) TEU, whereby the references to 'upholding and promoting' democracy as a value or being 'guided' by democracy as a 'principle' suggest general application, as both refer to the 'relations with the wider world' or 'action on the international scene'. Therefore, one can conclude that promoting democracy as a Union value applies to the entire spectrum of EU external action. Furthermore, the expansion of the scope of Article 49 TEU suggests that democracy promotion is at the core of the EU identity. The candidate states are required not only to adhere to the values of the EU themselves, but they should also 'commit' to promoting those values abroad.

The incorporation of democracy promotion within the legal framework of EU foreign policy objectives affirms the EU's identity and its normative image in the founding Treaties. Nevertheless, the Treaties do not require that the identity of the EU be upheld at the expense of other policy objectives. The status of democracy promotion as a cross-sector objective of a general application does not necessarily entail its prioritisation vis-à-vis other objectives. Instead of a hierarchical pursuit of policy objectives, Article 21 TEU deploys 'complementarity' between various external policy areas as the main rationale behind the common list of objectives.[41] Although this suggests that the objectives have to complement each other, there is, however, no requirement that the objectives should be linked to each other.[42] In addition, the language of Article 3(5) TEU, as well as Article 21(2)(a), equally requires safeguarding of values and interests. Thus, democracy promotion measures should be balanced against other policy objectives.[43] As a milieu

---

[39] The Court established that the Union cannot adopt a measure through a CFSP legal basis if its provisions also fall under Community competences; Case C-91/05 *Commission v Council* [2008] ECR I-03651, paras 76–77.

[40] P Eeckhout, 'The EU's Common Foreign and Security Policy after Lisbon: From Pillar Talk to Constitutionalism in EU Law After Lisbon' in Biondi, Eeckout, and Ripley (eds), note 22 above, 266–91, 268.

[41] M Cremona, 'Coherence in European Union Foreign Relations Law' in Koutrakos (ed), note 23 above, 55–92, 77.

[42] J Wouters, D Coppens and B de Meester, 'The European Union's External Relations after the Lisbon Treaty' in S Griller and J Ziller (eds), *The Lisbon Treaty: EU Constitutionalism without a Constitutional Treaty* (New York, Springer, 2008) 143–203, 149.

[43] Cardwell, note 20 above, 29; M Cremona, 'The Draft Constitutional Treaty: External Relations and External Action (2003) 40 *Common Market Law Review* 1347, 1349.

goal, there is a risk that it could be overtaken by 'vital' possession goals,[44] where practice demonstrates that democracy promotion is ranked low in terms of priority.[45]

Furthermore, there is no absolute level required in promoting or consolidating democracy as an objective. In *Portugal v Council* concerning development policy the Court established that the Commission ought to 'take account' of the objective of respect of human rights when adopting a measure related to the development area.[46] While the judgment confirms that democracy needs to feature in EU foreign policy, it might entail that, for instance, the inclusion of an essential elements clause in a trade agreement will satisfy the requirement of 'taking account' of the particular objective. It would not suggest, however, that cooperation cannot continue with a country failing to respect human rights or democracy after incorporating such a clause.

It can therefore be concluded that the Treaty creates a scope for achieving traditional interest-orientated objectives alongside or instead of democracy promotion. The latter, whether in the form of upholding a value, principle or pursuing an objective, depends on the consistency and coherence of the Union's actions, as there is a 'direct correlation' between consistency and coherence and the promotion of democracy.[47]

2.2.3 Consistent Democracy Promotion?

The issue of coherence and consistency in exercising external action has attracted significant attention in EU external relations discourse. The SEA, the Maastricht Treaty and the Amsterdam Treaty each contributed in their own way to the development of the notion of consistency within EU foreign policy.[48] The quest for consistency inter alia motivated the revision of the Treaty provisions on external relations at the Intergovernmental Conference (IGC) on the Draft Constitutional Treaty,[49] leading some to argue that the EU was devising a 'grand strategy' for its foreign policy.[50]

---

[44] Wolfers, note 5 above, 75.

[45] See also note 119 below; R Youngs, *The EU's Role in the World Politics: A Retreat from Liberal Intergovernmentalism* (London, Routledge, 2011) 57–58.

[46] Case C-268/94 [1996] ECR I-6177, para 23.

[47] P Koutrakos, 'Primary Law and Policy in EU External Relations: Moving Away from the Big Picture' (2008) *European Law Review* 666, 675.

[48] Art 30 of the SEA imposed a duty on the Presidency and the Commission to ensure consistency between EC policies and the European Political Cooperation; Art C EU put an emphasis on the single institutional framework serving both the CFSP and the EC policies as a means of ensuring consistency; Art C(6) of the Amsterdam Treaty [1997] OJ C340.

[49] Report of Working Group VII, The European Convention, Brussels, 16 December 2002, CONV 459/02.

[50] M Smith, 'The Accidental Strategist? Military Power, Grand Strategy and the EU's Changing Global Role' 2008, European Institute, Edinburgh, Mitchell Working Paper Series 2008, 5.

Article 21(3) imposes an obligation on the Union 'to ensure consistency between the different areas of its external action and between these and its other policies'. It also specifies the institutions responsible for this task, including the Commission and the Council, assisted by the High Representative for Foreign Affairs and Security Policy (High Representative). Article 7 TFEU refers to a consistency obligation of a general application, that is between policies and activities, with a view to achieving all of the EU objectives. Such formulation of a duty to ensure consistency has been viewed to have become 'part of the equation in any action carried out by the Union'.[51]

Although the Treaty provisions refer to 'consistency', there is a major consensus that it is 'coherence' which is at stake. The understanding of 'consistency' as 'coherence' first of all stems from the versions of the Treaty in other languages where the equivalent of 'coherence' is used in place of consistency.[52] Nevertheless these concepts are not synonymous.[53] Consistency has been noted to refer merely to the elimination of contradictions, whereas coherence is to be understood in much wider terms: it requires 'positive' links between various elements, where one contributes to another.[54] Thus, consistency is understood as a 'minimalist requirement',[55] or a prerequisite for coherence.[56] Hillion notes that in its functional understanding, even consistency can be understood as going beyond simple absence of contradictions, where it can also presuppose 'synergy and added value'.[57] Such conceptualisation of consistency would suggest that a foreign policy action should not contradict other foreign policy actions taken by the EU, while possibly even contributing to the achievement of objectives other than its own policy-specific aims. In addition to conflict avoidance and synergy, Van Vooren also highlights the element of effective task allocation within the concept of consistency.[58] It can be argued that the latter relates to the role of various actors in securing consistency.

---

[51] U Khaliq, 'The External Action of the European Union under the Treaty of Lisbon' in M Trybus and L Rubini (eds), *The Treaty of Lisbon and the Future of European Law and Policy* (Cheltenham, Edward Elgar Publishing, 2012) 239–61, 247.

[52] C Hillion, 'Tous pour un, un pour tous! Coherence in the External Relations of the European Union' in Cremona (ed), note 2 above,10–36, 12–13; Khaliq, note 51 above, 247; Duke, note 23 above, 18.

[53] Certain support can be found in case law, where the Court did not elaborate on the substance of these two notions, but referred to 'coherence and consistency', suggesting that they are distinct notions; Case C-266/03 *Commission v Luxembourg* [2005] ECR I-4805, para 60; Case C-433/03 *Commission v Germany* [2005] ECR I-6985, para 66.

[54] Hillion, note 52 above, 14.

[55] C Gebhard, 'Coherence' in C Hill and M Smith (eds), *International Relations and the European Union*, 2nd edn (Oxford, OUP, 2011) 101–27, 106.

[56] P Koutrakos, *Trade, Foreign Policy and Defence* (Oxford, Hart Publishing, 2001) 39–40.

[57] E Denza, *The Intergovernmental Pillars of the European Union* (Oxford, OUP, 2002) 89, 290; Hillion, note 52 above, 17; S Blockmans and M Laatsit, 'The European External Action Service: Enhancing Coherence in EU External Action?' in PJ Cardwell (ed), *EU External Relations Law and Policy in the Post-Lisbon Era* (The Hague, TMC Asser Press, 2012) 135–59, 138.

[58] B Van Vooren, *EU External Relations Law and the European Neighbourhood Policy: A Paradigm for Coherence* (London, Routledge, 2011) 69.

Vertical and horizontal consistency are the most often-cited types of consistency.[59] Vertical consistency refers to the actions of the EU institutions and its Member States, supported by the duty of loyal cooperation in Article 4 TEU.[60] It is this particular aspect of consistency, and the lack of unity between the Member States, that weakens the role of the EU abroad,[61] as the intergovernmental nature of the CFSP decision making allows for pursuing national interests. The institutional innovations introduced by the Lisbon Treaty, including the double-hatted position of the High Representative, are expected to contribute to vertical consistency, which will be discussed below.[62] Nuttal also identifies institutional coherence based on different procedural rules and institutional arrangements in CFSP and other areas of external action.[63] The lack of consistency has been pointed out as a cause of concern even within the confines of the same institution.[64]

The notion of consistency within Article 21(3) TEU appears to refer to horizontal consistency: various areas of external relations should not contradict each other. The same logic can be viewed to have been included in Article 7 TFEU requiring consistency between all EU policies, whether external or internal. Moreover, coherence/consistency repeatedly appears in various Treaty provisions regarding specific institutions and policy areas.[65] The inclusion of the principle of consistency within Article 21 TEU suggests that a stronger case is made for achieving EU foreign policy objectives across all areas of external action. It is, therefore, considered that the combination of Articles 3(5) TEU, 21(3) TEU and 7 TFEU create a general legal obligation to act consistently,[66] including when promoting the values of the EU. However, Nuttal argues the spelling out of the principle of consistency can hardly change much in practice, as the Treaties do not establish a new mechanism for ensuring consistency.[67]

Within horizontal consistency more specific types of 'inter-policy' and 'inter-pillar' consistency have been identified.[68] Within the ENP that would translate into

---

[59] S Nuttal, 'Coherence and Consistency' in Hill and Smith, note 55 above, 91–112, 92; Hillion, note 52 above, 17.

[60] See in the context of mixed agreements Opinion 1/94 [1994] ECR I-5267, para 108; Opinion 2/00 [2001] ECR I-09713, para 18; C Hillion, 'Mixity and Coherence in EU External Relations: The Significance of the "Duty of Cooperation"' in C Hillion and P Koutrakos (eds), *Mixed Agreements Revisited: The EU and its Member States in the World* (Oxford, Hart Publishing, 2010) 87–114, 114.

[61] L Fiaramonti and S Lucarelli, 'Self-Representation and External Perceptions – Can the EU Bridge the Gap?' in S Lucarelli and L Fiaramonti (eds), *External Perceptions of the European Union as a Global Actor* (London, Routledge, 2009) 218–25; Carta, note 21 above, 211.

[62] See Chapter 3, section 3.2.2.

[63] Nuttal, note 59 above, 92.

[64] Khaliq, note 51 above, 247.

[65] Arts 13(1) TEU, 16(6) TEU, 18(4), 26(2) TEU, 208(1) TFEU, 212(1) TFEU, 214(1) TFEU.

[66] Van Vooren, note 58 above, 51, 60; In relation to development policy see MP Broberg, 'Don't Mess with the Missionary Man! On the Principle of Coherence, the Missionary Principle and the European Union's Development Policy' in PJ Cardwell (ed), *EU External Relations Law and Policy in the Post-Lisbon Era* (The Hague, TMC Asser Press, 2012) 181–196, 193; S Duke, 'The European External Action Service: Antidote Against Incoherence?' (2012) 17 *European Foreign Affairs Review* 45, 49.

[67] Nuttal, note 59 above, 109.

[68] Cremona, note 41 above, 70.

intra-policy consistency. The ENP is an 'umbrella' policy,[69] with elements combined from all areas of EU foreign policy action, each pursuing sector-specific policy objectives. The consistency in the pursuit of foreign policy objectives in various areas within the same policy is the ultimate test for the efficiency of the ENP. The discussion that follows is focused on a functional understanding of consistency in the promotion of democratic values in the EU neighbourhood. It is therefore apt to consider whether the promotion of democratic values features consistently within the ENP agenda, namely the policy objectives, the legal framework, including its institutional and instrumental aspects, its methodology and implementation. Besides, the comparative analysis undertaken attempts to identify whether there is consistency between the implementation of policy as regards similar treatment of third states, also identified as a possible understanding of consistency.[70]

The significance of coherence/consistency has been acknowledged in the EU both in relation to democracy promotion and the ENP. In 2001 the Commission stressed the importance of coherence for democracy promotion, in particular coherence between the EC policies at the time, between the EC policies and the CFSP, as well as between the EU and the Member States,[71] ie vertically and horizontally. In setting the EU Agenda for action on democracy support in EU external relations the Council highlighted the need for coherence between various links in the chain of policy formation, implementation, its evaluation and monitoring.[72] Within the ENP, the Council acknowledged the necessity for coherence of the policy with reference to its content, instruments and final objectives.[73] A combination of these factors leads to the conclusion that there is a presumption that democracy should be consistently promoted within the ENP.

2.3 ENP OBJECTIVES: DEMOCRACY PROMOTION WITHIN A SECURITY FRAMEWORK?

The changing language of the policy documents of the ENP and their grand rhetoric has created ambiguity as to the general aims of the policy and the appropriateness of the instruments chosen to achieve them. Is the ENP about preventing the emergence of new dividing lines in the European neighbourhood or is this a secondary objective? Or is it about creating 'good' neighbours who share the values of the EU, as well as its laws and regulations in economic and social areas which would promote prosperity and security in the neighbourhood?

[69] A Lazowski, 'With but Without You . . . The Europeanisation of Legal Orders of the Neighbouring Countries' in A Ott and E Vos (eds), *Fifty Years of European Integration: Foundations and Perspectives* (The Hague, TMC Asser Press, 2009) 247–70, 266.

[70] KE Smith, *European Union Foreign Policy in a Changing World* (Cambridge, Polity Press, 2003) 65.

[71] Commission Communication, 'The European Union's Role in Promoting Human Rights and Democratisation in Third Countries' COM (2001) 252 final, 8 May 2001, 5.

[72] Council Conclusions on Democracy Support in the EU's External Relations, External Relations, 17 November 2009, 5.

[73] Council Conclusions, General Affairs and External Relations, 14 June 2004, 10.

Some view the 'border-related' objectives of the ENP to be central, including the development and exchange within border regions, and fostering a 'ring of well-governed countries' which can enjoy close relations with the Union.[74] Alternatively, considering the EU as a 'gravity centre' for stabilisation, the latter becomes the central objective of the policy.[75] Thus, the shift towards a trans-formationist agenda has been emphasised as a specific feature within the ENP in addition to more traditional concerns in international relations.[76] Although all these observations are supported by the founding ENP documents, they neverthe-less can be considered to be sub-goals or means of achieving the goals of the policy, which are primarily concerned with the security of the EU.

2.3.1 The Security Agenda of the ENP

The European security rationale acquired an expressed outwards orientation fol-lowing the transition from the EC to the EU and the introduction of the CFSP and (European Security and Defence Policy (ESDP), creating a new international role for the EU outside its traditional economic spectrum.[77] A renewed emphasis on security surfaced at the beginning of the new millennium in response to global security threats and in anticipation of the most extensive enlargement, transform-ing the borders of the EU and bringing it closer to new neighbours, as mentioned in Chapter 1. Even the earlier engagement by the EU in its neighbourhood is per-ceived to have been aimed at security concerns.[78]

When the idea of the neighbourhood policy appeared for the first time in the joint Solana/Patten letter of 7 August 2002, special attention was devoted to the issue of security:

> there are a number of overriding objectives for our neighbourhood policy: stability, prosperity, shared values and the rule of law along our borders are all fundamental for our own security. Failure in any of these areas will lead to increased risks of negative spillover on the Union.[79]

---

[74] M Comelli, E Greco and N Tocci, 'From Boundary to Borderland: Transforming the Meaning of Borders through the European Neighbourhood Policy' (2007) 12 *European Foreign Affairs Review* 203, 203, 208.

[75] G Meloni, 'Is the Same Toolkit Used during Enlargement Still Applicable to the Countries of the New Neighbourhood? A Problem of Mismatching between Objectives and Instruments' in M Cremona and G Meloni (eds), *The European Neighbourhood Policy: A New Framework for Modernisation?*, EUI Working Papers, LAW 2007/21, 97–111, 99.

[76] R Dannreuther, 'Developing the Alternative to Enlargement: The European Neighbourhood Policy' (2006) 11 *European Foreign Affairs Review* 183, 184, 194–96.

[77] A Marchetti, 'The European Neighbourhood Policy: Foreign Policy at the EU's Periphery', Discussion Paper C158, Centre for European Integration Studies 2006, 5.

[78] Pace makes this observation in relation to the Barcelona Process: M Pace, 'Paradoxes and Contradictions in EU Democracy Promotion in the Mediterranean: The Limits of EU Normative Power' (2009) 16 *Democratisation* 39–58, 45.

[79] Joint letter by EU Commissioner Chris Patten and the EU High Representative for the Common Foreign and Security Policy on Wider Europe, 7 August 2002.

Thus, the first steps towards the policy formation highlighted the interdependence between the security of the Union and the developments in the neighbourhood, which required the action to start from abroad.[80]

In its Conclusions, the European Council in December 2002 appeared to confirm the intention of avoiding divisions and to promote stability and prosperity beyond the expanded Union.[81] The issue of the borders, however, is to be understood in a wider context. As noted by the then External Relations Commissioner Ferrero-Waldner, it is not the definition of borders that matters, but rather their upholding, which is relevant for 'citizens' urgent concerns – security, migration and economic growth'.[82] The focus is then on the changes occurring in the Union due to its new geographical location,[83] and therefore the policy is not primarily about the prosperity of the neighbours and their economic progress, but rather the security and stability of the Union itself.

The logic of protecting the Union from any 'negative spillover' in the neighbourhood is apparent in the language of the Wider Europe Communication, which acknowledged that within the current and future decades the Union's task to ensure its own security and stability would not be distinguishable from that of its neighbours.[84] In rhetoric, the Council in June 2003 appeared to have taken the security focus away from the policy objectives. The goals highlighted were '[t]o work with the partners to reduce poverty and create an area of shared prosperity and values', and '[t]o anchor the EU's offer of concrete benefits and preferential relations within a differentiated framework which responds to progress made by the partner countries' in the areas of political and economic reform, justice and home affairs.[85] Nevertheless, a closer look at the areas of cooperation emphasised by the Council demonstrates that the central role is accorded to preventing and combating security threats, while the incentives for integration are downgraded with the language of enhanced cooperation and preferential treatment.[86] It has been suggested that by asserting its presence in the policy the Council introduced 'a securitarian outlook' to the ENP and reorientated the Commission's agenda.[87]

This becomes apparent in the ENP Strategy Paper, where the Commission explicitly shifted its emphasis to stressing the notions of security and stability. Two objectives are a focal point of the policy: strengthening stability, security and

---

[80] Lynch, note 1 above, 34–35.

[81] Wider Europe Communication 3–4.

[82] B Ferrero-Waldner, 'The European Neighbourhood Policy: The EU's Newest Foreign Policy Instrument' (2006) 11 *European Foreign Affairs Review* 139, 140.

[83] R Del Sarto and T Schumacher, 'From EMP to ENP: What's at Stake with the European Neighbourhood Policy towards the Southern Mediterranean? (2005) 10 *European Foreign Affairs Review* 17, 25–26.

[84] Wider Europe Communication 3.

[85] Council Conclusions, Wider Europe – New Neighbourhood, General Affairs and External Relations, 16 June 2003.

[86] Council Conclusions, ibid. A detailed comparison is undertaken in R Balfour and A Rotta, 'Beyond Enlargement. The European Neighbourhood Policy and its Tools' (2005) 40 *International Spectator* 7, 12–14; Cremona, note 2 above, 292.

[87] R Zaiotti, 'Of Friends and Fences: Europe's Neighbourhood Policy and the "Gated Community Syndrome"' (2007) 29 *European Integration* 143, 157.

well-being for EU Member States and neighbouring countries, and preventing the emergence of new dividing lines between the enlarged EU and its neighbours.[88]

The prominence of security issues within the ENP is also evident in the links existing between the policy and the ESS, as noted in Chapter 1. The formulation of the ENP coincided with the launch of the ESS in 2003, which aimed at enhancing the Union's role as a world player capable of responding to global security threats.[89] The ENP Strategy Paper in its introduction provided that the ENP would 'also support efforts to realise the objectives of the [ESS]'.[90] The ESS Paper in its turn gave important meaning to the idea of 'building security in the neighbourhood' by declaring that the EU needed 'to extend the benefits of economic and political cooperation to [the] neighbours in the East while tackling political problems there'.[91] The ENP Strategy Paper adopts a similar pattern by incorporating a task of making a contribution to stability and good governance in the immediate neighbourhood and promoting 'a ring of well governed countries to the East of the [EU] and on the borders of the Mediterranean with whom [the EU] can enjoy close and cooperative relations'.[92] In addition to the cross-references in both documents, the terminology used for both the ENP and the ESS Paper are noticeably similar. These observations are therefore inclined to support the view that the ENP embodies the 'regional implementation of the ESS'.[93]

In the same light the ENP has been viewed as the 'logical extension of CFSP concerns',[94] where the CFSP would be 'a contradiction in terms' if it lacked a coherent strategy at its centre towards EU neighbours.[95] Such a perception suggests an ancillary or a secondary role for any other policy objectives within the ENP.

Within this context, the security aspects should be considered to be fundamental to the policy, where achievement of security plays the role of a central objective, while the objectives of stability and prosperity are designed to lead to that aim through political and economic development.[96] Security on the EU borders

---

[88] Commission Communication, European Neighbourhood Policy Strategy Paper, COM (2004) 373 final, 12 May 2004 (hereinafter ENP Strategy Paper) 3; Council Conclusions, General Affairs and External Relations, 14 June 2004.

[89] A Secure Europe in a Better World, European Security Strategy Paper, Brussels, 12 December 2003 (hereinafter the European Security Strategy Paper).

[90] ENP Strategy Paper, 2, 6.

[91] European Security Strategy Paper, 8.

[92] ENP Strategy Paper, 6.

[93] C Hillion, 'The EU's Neighbourhood Policy towards Eastern Europe' in A Dashwood and M Maresceau (eds), *Law and Practice of EU External Relations* (Cambridge, CUP, 2008) 309–33, 314.

[94] M Smith and K Webber, 'Political Dialogue and Security in the European Neighbourhood Policy: The Virtues and Limits of "New Partnership Perspective"' (2008) 13 *European Foreign Affairs Review* 73, 81.

[95] W Wallace, 'Looking after the Neighbourhood: Responsibilities for the EU-25', Policy Paper No 4, Notre Europe 2003, 27.

[96] M Cremona and C Hillion, 'L'Union fait la force? Potential and Limitations of the ENP as an Integrated EU Foreign and Security Policy' in N Copsey and A Mayhew (eds), *European Neighbourhood Policy: The Case of Europe*, Sussex European Institute, SEI Seminar Papers Series Number 1, 2006, 20–44, 22–23; M Cremona, 'The European Neighbourhood Policy' in Ott and Vos (eds), note 69 above, 221–45, 225.

will be increased if stability is spread among the neighbouring states and their prosperity is guaranteed through social and economic development.[97] It should be noted that the concept of security is no longer understood in narrow terms, and it encompasses non-traditional threats, including environmental, energy, cyber security and other threats.[98] Such conceptualisation of the notion of security is not unique to the Union, which resembles other international actors in this respect.[99] Therefore, also the all-encompassing content of the ENP in terms of the cooperation offered in most areas of the EU competence is linked to its comprehensive security agenda.

The neighbourhood plays a twofold role within the Union's security agenda. First, the neighbourhood is a threat of its own representing a 'malevolent neighbour problem'.[100] Conflicts, political instability and poverty are all factors in this one-dimensional understanding of security and their significance has been acknowledged by the EU institutions.[101] For instance, the conflicts in the South Caucasus, Transnistria and in the Middle East present direct security threats at the EU periphery and have the potential to lead to migration, arms flow, trafficking, or suspension in energy flows. Second, transforming its neighbours into politically and economically stable states leads to the establishment of a 'buffer zone' or 'functioning semi-periphery' between the EU and the troubled areas further to the east and south.[102] Therefore the neighbourhood is also instrumental in achieving objectives stretching beyond the neighbourhood. Thus, one can hardly reject the rationalist presumption that stabilising the neighbours serves the aim of the EU's security and facilitates the achievement of its political agenda. The ENP is explicitly framed in terms of EU interests.[103]

Nevertheless, despite the traditional rationalist core of the ENP objectives, it has been suggested that the ENP is 'the example par excellence of civilian power', where the security element is 'devoid of military component',[104] therefore allowing for constructivist characterisation of the EU within the ENP. Certainly, the instruments of the policy are clearly civilian, focused on 'persuasion and negotiation'

---

[97] M Cremona, 'The European Neighbourhood Policy as a Framework for Modernisation' in F Maiani, R Petrov and E Mouliarova (eds), *European Integration without EU Membership: Models, Experiences, Perspectives*, EUI Working Papers, MWP 2009/10, 5–15, 7.

[98] Such a wide understanding of security is present in the 2008 evaluation of the ESS; Report on the Implementation of the European Security Strategy, 'Providing Security in a Changing World', European Council, 11 and 12 December 2008, 5–6.

[99] Koutrakos, note 36 above, 592; Wessel, note 13 above, 62.

[100] R Seidelmann, 'The EU's Neighbourhood Policies' in M Telo (ed), *The EU and Global Governance* (London, Routledge, 2009) 261–82, 276; G Meloni, 'Who's My Neighbour?' (2007) 7 *European Political Economy Review* 24, 33.

[101] Council Conclusions, Strengthening the European Neighbourhood Policy, General Affairs and External Relations, 18–19 June 2007, 2.

[102] Zaiotti, note 87 above, 149; Marchetti, note 77 above, 16–17.

[103] Wider Europe Communication, 3, 9; ENP Strategy Paper, 10.

[104] V Khasson, S Vasilyan and H Vos, ' "Everybody Needs Good Neighbours": The EU and its Neighbourhood' in J Orbie (ed), *Europe's Global Role: External Policies of the EU* (Aldershot, Ashgate, 2008) 217–37, 220, 223.

and are based on the EU's economic power.[105] In addition, the ENP instruments incorporate the EU's normative identity within the policy objectives, albeit in an indirect manner.

2.3.2 Democracy Promotion and ENP Objectives

That ENP is not an instrument primarily created to promote democracy is beyond doubt. In its overview of the EU's efforts to promote democracy and human rights in the world, the Commission does not single out the ENP as an avenue for democracy promotion, and instead notes that the policy is 'based' on democracy.[106] Bearing in mind the prominence of security issues within the ENP objectives and the framing of the policy with reference to EU interests, scepticism arises as to what the notion of 'being based' on democracy means. It is therefore suggested that democratic values play an indirect or intermediary role within the policy.

While there is an opinion that together with stability democracy appears as one of the overarching goals of the entire policy,[107] the analysis of the policy documents reveal no precise role for democracy per se within the objectives of the policy. Rather, democracy promotion is present within the objectives of the policy as an element of stability, which is perceived to be closely linked to political reform and democratisation.[108] According to the ESS Paper, '[t]he best protection for our security is a world of well-governed democratic states'.[109] Democracy promotion, therefore, is a means to an end, that is to achieve stability and security: promotion of democracy is vital 'if the deeper roots of insecurity are to be resolved effectively'.[110] Such relationship between democracy promotion and the main objectives of the ENP support the proposition that milieu goals at times serve as a means to achieve a possession goal.[111]

On the other hand, there is a fear that stability might be interpreted narrowly as 'an instrument to achieve an overarching security goal', risking the exclusion of democracy promotion altogether, since strictly speaking it is not necessary for the purposes of EU security.[112] This seeming contradiction derives from long-term or

---

[105] KE Smith, 'The End of Civilian Power EU: A Welcome Demise or Cause for Concern?' (2000) 35 *The International Spectator* 11, 13.

[106] Furthering Human Rights and Democracy Across the Globe, European Commission, 2007, 4.

[107] F Schimmelfennig, 'European Neighbourhood Policy: Political Conditionality and its Impact on Democracy in Non-Candidate Neighbouring Countries', Paper prepared for the EUSA Ninth Biennial International Conference, Austin, 31 March–2 April 2005.

[108] Cremona, note 96 above, 227; R Balfour, *Human Rights and Democracy in EU Foreign Policy: The Cases of Ukraine and Egypt* (London, Routledge, 2012) 19; S Stewart, 'EU Democracy Promotion in the Eastern Neighbourhood: One Template, Multiple Approaches' (2011) 16 *European Foreign Affairs Review* 607, 610.

[109] European Security Strategy Paper, 10.

[110] Dannreuther, note 76 above, 201; Pace, note 78 above, 42.

[111] Wolfers, note 5 above, 74.

[112] G Meloni, 'Is the Same Toolkit Used during Enlargement Still Applicable to the Countries of the New Neighbourhood? A Problem of Mismatching between Objectives and Instruments' in Cremona and Meloni (eds), note 75 above, 97–111, 102.

short-term perspectives on stability and security. If stability and security is the end goal, in a short-term perspective democracy can be compromised for preserving the status quo. However, in the long term efficient security cannot be achieved without stable democracies functioning in the neighbouring states. The lack of prioritisation of the objectives within Article 21 TEU would suggest an inherent flexibility in balancing long-term and short-term considerations, including vis-à-vis democracy promotion. Thus, although a general objective, democracy promotion has been included within the ENP objectives through the back door.

Democracy promotion also appears within the ENP in another indirect way, which is the concept of 'shared values' on which the cooperation between the parties is based. Borrowing Manners' terminology, the EU, through the rhetoric of shared values, 'diffuses' its normative basis, including democracy as a norm, in its relations with neighbours.[113] It is this 'value dimension' which is often referred to as a significant development introduced by the ENP in comparison with previous EU policies.[114] Due to this element of the ENP certain commentators conclude that the policy incorporates the objective of exporting the EU's values to its immediate periphery.[115] Nevertheless, it is suggested that this element is related more to the content of the policy, rather than its objectives.

The concept of 'shared values' does not represent the end goal of the EU's involvement in the neighbourhood, in a way an objective would denote. Rather, it is the preferred basis for cooperation to achieve other objectives. In this understanding, the promotion of democracy has been present on the ENP agenda since the launch of the project. In December 2002 the European Council declared that the enlargement 'presents an important opportunity to take forward relations with neighbouring countries based on shared political and economic values'.[116] The notion of 'shared values' was subsequently incorporated in central policy documents. The function of the notion of 'shared values' is associated with the methodology of the ENP, namely its conditionality element, which is discussed below.[117]

Consequently, one can conclude that democracy promotion found its indirect place not only within the ENP objectives, but also its methodology. Such indirect representation of democracy within policy objectives subordinates it to the primary goals of achieving security and stability. Since there is no prioritisation of foreign policy objectives within Article 21 TEU, it technically does not create any legal complications. Besides, it could be argued that even such incorporation of democracy within the policy suggests that the objective of democracy promotion has been taken into account.

---

[113] I Manners, 'Normative Power Europe: A Contradiction in Terms' (2002) 40 *Journal of Common Market Studies* 235, 236, 244.

[114] G Bosse, 'Values in the EU's Neighbourhood Policy: Political Rhetoric or Reflection of a Coherent Policy?' (2007) 7 *European Political Economy Review* 38, 39.

[115] Del Sarto and Schumacher, note 83 above, 23; Tocci, note 6 above, 27.

[116] Copenhagen European Council Conclusions, 12–13 December 2002, para 22.

[117] See Chapter 3, section 3.4.3.2.

In practice the EU has been noted to have a record of undermining the normative objectives versus the strategic ones when it comes to exercising a balance between the two.[118] Even though most of the time the EU incorporates the normative rhetoric in its relations with the wider world, it ultimately acts in a realist, imperialist or status quo-orientated way,[119] at times displaying differentiated attitudes towards undemocratic regimes.[120]

The inconsistency on behalf of the EU in its approach to democracy promotion has been noted particularly outside the enlargement framework.[121] This can be linked to the distinct objectives of the enlargement and other EU policies. The EU identity objectives are not as compelling as in the enlargement case, especially taking into account the rationalist considerations behind the ENP. In the Eastern neighbourhood an example of rationalist considerations overtaking democracy promotion before the ENP included the conclusion of the PCA with Azerbaijan despite the criticism of its political profile.[122]

The ENP unfortunately did not escape this trend. Shortly after the establishment of the ENP, actions driven by rationalist considerations were noted towards Azerbaijan, Morocco, Tunisia, Egypt, Jordan and Lebanon,[123] suggesting that the EU is nothing but a 'normal' political actor within the ENP.[124]

There is, therefore, an apparent complication between the rationalist and constructivist conceptualisation of the EU's foreign policy in its proximity, or – to put it in simple terms – the EU's interests in its neighbourhood and its legal obligation to uphold its identity internationally. Despite ostensibly being committed to EU values, the objectives of the ENP are set to be more important than the normative stance of the EU, which will most certainly preserve the rhetoric, but not necessarily be faithful to it.

---

[118] M Emerson et al, 'The Reluctant Debutante: The European Union as Promoter of Democracy in its Neighbourhood', CEPS Working Document No 223, 2005, 3; S Keukeleire and J MacNaughtan, *The Foreign Policy of the European Union* (Basingstoke, Palgrave, 2008) 334; R Youngs, 'Normative Dynamics and Strategic Interests in the EU's External Identity' (2004) 42 *Journal of Common Market Studies* 415, 431; S Lucarelli, 'Values, Identity and Ideational Shocks in the Transatlantic Rift' (2006) 9 *Journal of International Relations and Development* 304, 320; KE Smith, 'The Use of Political Conditionality in the EU's Relations with Third Countries: How Effective?' (1998) 3 *European Foreign Affairs Review* 253, 254, 272, 273; N Tocci, 'The European Union as a Normative Foreign Policy Actor', CEPS Working Document No 281, 2008; E Johansson-Nogues, 'The (Non-)Normative Power EU and the European Neighbourhood Policy: An Exceptional Policy for an Exceptional Actor?' (2007) 7 *European Political Economy Review* 181, 185–86.

[119] Tocci, note 118 above.

[120] Smith, note 70 above, 142.

[121] Schimmelfennig, note 107 above; K Raik, 'Promoting Democracy through Civil Society: How to Step up the EU's Policy towards the Eastern Neighbourhood', CEPS Working Document No 237, 2006, 18.

[122] J Kelley, 'New Wine in Old Wineskins: Policy Learning and Adaptation in the New European Neighbourhood Policy' (2006) 44 *Journal of Common Market Studies* 29, 48.

[123] M Emerson, G Noutcheva and N Popescu, 'European Neighbourhood Policy Two Years On: Time Indeed for an "ENP Plus"', CEPS Policy Brief No 126, 2007, 15; P Seeberg, 'The EU as a Realist Actor in Normative Clothes: EU Democracy Promotion in Lebanon and the European Neighbourhood Policy' (2009) 16 *Democratisation* 81, 94; Tocci, note 118 above, 19–22, 25–28.

[124] Johansson-Nogues, note 118 above, 187.

The difference between the ENP milieu and possession goals is based not only on their roots in norms and interests, but also the distinct means of engagement required to pursue the two groups of objectives. 'Conditional engagement' is required to promote the milieu goals, while the strategic objectives are achieved by means of cooperation with de facto actors, irrelevant of their authoritarian or democratic record.[125] In this scenario the democratisation agenda can even become a complication for the pursuit of such rationalist interests as energy cooperation or the fight against terrorism, which require collaboration with strong, even if authoritarian, regimes 'à la Aliev'.[126] Therefore, the ENP suffers not only from its 'goal conflict',[127] but also from a syndrome of 'norm versus interest'.[128]

In the case of the South Caucasian states, it is precisely security-orientated concerns that prompted a shift of attitude from the EU at the beginning of the millennium. In addition to conflict prevention and post-conflict rehabilitation, the importance of this region is also linked to EU energy security as noted in Chapter 1. The EU's continuous support for the evolving Organization of the Black Sea Economic Cooperation also highlights the importance of energy cooperation for the latter.[129] Thus, the interests of the EU in the region presuppose rationalist involvement, where the EU needs to cooperate with the existing regimes to reach its energy targets and ensure stability of energy supply.

In its most recent conclusions on the South Caucasus, the Council refers to the Union's 'core interests' therein, which are related to security and stability, democratic reforms, energy and economic investments, which suggests that promotion of democracy is also perceived as an interest rather than an identity-related objective.[130]

The neighbourhood-specific provision in Article 8 TEU will hardly alter the policy objectives pursued. It preserves the security rationale of the policy in a number of ways. First of all, the language of the article on establishing 'an area of prosperity and good neighbourliness [. . .] characterised by close and peaceful relations based on cooperation' closely resembles the ENP documents' language on 'friendly neighbourhood' or 'good neighbourliness'.[131] 'Good neighbourliness'

---

[125] Tocci, note 6 above, 30.

[126] Aliev is the long-ruling President of Azerbaijan who inherited power from his father in 2003; N MacFarlane, 'The Caucasus and Central Asia: Towards a Non-Strategy' in R Dannreuther (ed), *European Foreign and Security Policy: Towards a Neighbourhood Strategy* (London, Routledge, 2004) 118–34, 131.

[127] S Maier and F Schimmelfennig, 'Shared Values: Democracy and Human Rights' in K Weber, M Smith and M Baun (eds), *Governing Europe's Neighbourhood: Partners or Periphery* (Manchester, Manchester University Press, 2007) 39–57, 43.

[128] Seidelmann, note 100 above, 275.

[129] Founded in 1992, it involves Albania, Armenia, Azerbaijan, Bulgaria, Romania, Greece, Moldova, Georgia, Ukraine, Russia and Turkey, see www.bsec.gov.tr; D Lynch, 'Why Georgia Matters', Chaillot Paper No 86, February 2006, Institute for Security Studies, 84.

[130] Council Conclusions on the South Caucasus, Foreign Affairs, 27 February 2012.

[131] For instance, the ENP country reports for individual states note that '[t]he overarching objective of the European Neighbourhood Policy . . . is to promote the development of an area of prosperity and good neighbourliness between the European Union and the partner countries covered by the ENP'; see also Wider Europe Communication, 4; P Van Elsuwege and R Petrov, 'Article 8 TEU: Towards a New

on the other hand is an additional accession criterion, also referred to as the Essen condition.[132] According to the latter the applicant countries must cooperate with each other with an accent on peaceful resolution of any possible conflicts, and its adoption was primarily aimed at Turkey.[133] It is suggested that the inclusion of 'peaceful relations based on cooperation' could indicate the importance of security on the agenda of the EU. The idea of 'cooperation' in its turn is to be linked with the joint ownership principle incorporated in the ENP methodology.[134] Besides, 'peaceful relations based on cooperation' can also allude to the perception of the Union as a 'civilian' or 'soft' power. The 'area of prosperity', on the other hand, refers to the Commission's rhetoric contained in the ENP documents, which consider the economic well-being of the neighbouring states to be vital for ultimately guaranteeing security.

Furthermore, embodying the CFSP concerns on a regional level suggests that the neighbourhood policies under Article 8 TEU must pursue the CFSP objectives, including preserving peace, preventing conflicts and strengthening international security. Article 21(3) TEU applies the common list of objectives to the EU external action covered by Title V of the TEU and by Part Five of the TFEU, and technically leaves Article 8 TEU outside its scope. However, the ENP as an initially cross-pillar, and currently a cross-Treaty, policy comprising elements from various areas of EU foreign action, necessarily has to pursue the common objectives set out in Article 21 TEU. The latter, as noted earlier, provides no hierarchy between the normative and strategic objectives of foreign policy, suggesting therefore that Article 8 TEU preserves the status quo.

As to the reference to the 'Union's values' in Article 8 TEU, it hardly alters the objectives of the policy. Rather, it can be suggested that it clarified the conditionality element of the ENP by specifying that the values are those of the EU, which will be discussed in the next chapter.

2.4 CONCLUSION

The legal framework of EU external relations has evolved in its reflection of the Union's values and their promotion in relations with the wider world. Despite the coalescence of values, principles and objectives in the EU Treaties, a general duty to promote democracy abroad can be identified throughout. With varying intensity evident in the language used, the EU 'shall uphold and promote' and

---

Generation of Agreements with the Neighbouring Countries of the European Union?' (2011) 36 *European Law Review* 688, 695.

[132]   Essen European Council Conclusions, 9–10 December 1994.

[133]   K Inglis, 'EU Enlargement: Membership Conditions Applied to Future and Potential Member States' in S Blockmans and A Łazowski (eds), *The European Union and its Neighbours: a Legal Appraisal of the EU's Policies of Stabilisation, Partnership and Integration* (The Hague, TMC Asser Press, 2006) 61–92, 74; KE Smith, 'The Evolution and Application of EU Membership Conditionality' in M Cremona, *The Enlargement of the European Union* (Oxford, OUP, 2003) 105–39, 114–15.

[134]   See Chapter 3, section 3.4.3.3.

'safeguard' its values, 'be guided by' its founding principles, and 'consolidate and support democracy' in its foreign relations, thereby constituting a mosaic of its normative identity. Although it is a general duty applicable to all areas of EU external action, the common list of external action objectives does not prioritise democracy promotion over other objectives. Article 21(2) TEU is drafted rather extensively to accommodate all areas of EU external relations, therefore providing scope for pursuing possession and milieu goals simultaneously. A balancing exercise is therefore required to ensure that the efforts to achieve certain objectives through a particular policy instrument do not contradict others, and most importantly do not undermine democracy promotion. The principle of consistency plays a significant role in the success of this venture. Lack of contradictions or even added value between the ENP objectives, legal framework, including its institutional and instrumental aspects, methodology and implementation, is required to consistently promote democracy in relations with neighbouring states.

Democracy promotion cannot be considered to be a primary aim of the ENP. It is rather the strategic objectives of the EU, namely security and stability, widely understood, which dominate the agenda of the cooperation. The promotion of democracy is part of the package of attaining stability in the neighbourhood, which can therefore be compromised when strategic objectives so require. Democracy as an EU value also appears within the ENP framework through the notion of 'shared values' as the basis for cooperation between the parties. Although this preserves the Union's normative image in rhetoric, it nevertheless highlights the intermediary role of democracy promotion within the ENP, confirming that the latter is not directed chiefly at democracy promotion. On the contrary, democracy's role is instrumental, and possibly expendable.

The political ambitions of the ENP as embodied in its objectives can be advanced as far as the legal framework of EU external action facilitates it. Given the complications inherent in the political nature of the ENP, the consistency of the legal elements of the policy is vital for its success in general, and for democracy promotion in particular.

3

Legal Aspects of ENP

Institutions, Competence and Instruments

3.1 INTRODUCTION

THE UNION'S CAPACITY to act is determined by the competence conferred upon it – a principle which applies equally to its internal and external actions.[1] The pursuit of multidimensional security requires a comprehensive cooperation agenda to tackle possible sources of instability and insecurity. The ENP was designed therefore as a comprehensive policy instrument combining elements from the so-called three pillars of the EU constitutional order.[2] The multi-pillar structure of its legal order was established in the Treaty of Maastricht and subsequently developed by the Amsterdam Treaty.[3] It comprised three pillars, namely the three founding Communities,[4] the CFSP and Cooperation in the Fields of Justice and Home Affairs, which was divided later on to create a revised third pillar.[5]

In substantive terms the ENP cooperation extends to the internal market, border management and migration, preventing and combating common security threats, conflict prevention and crisis management, cultural cooperation, enhanced relations in transport, energy, telecommunications, support for foreign and domestic investment and other areas of EU competence.[6] This comprehensive arrangement was an indication of the willingness to engage with the neighbourhood à la membership, but without the promise of membership itself.

It is precisely this cross-pillar feature of the ENP which represented the longstanding weakness of the EU foreign policy action, that is the differentiated nature

[1] Art 5 TEU; *Opinion 2/94 Accession of the Community to the European Convention for the Protection of Human Rights and Fundamental Freedoms* [1996] ECR I-1759, para 24.

[2] Commission Communication, 'European Neighbourhood Policy Strategy Paper' COM (2004) 373 final, 12 May 2004 (hereinafter ENP Strategy Paper) 6.

[3] Art 1 EU provided that the Union shall be founded on the European Communities, supplemented by the policies and forms of cooperation established by the Treaty [2006] OJ C321 E/1.

[4] The European Community, the European Coal and Steel Community, and the European Atomic Energy Community.

[5] The Amsterdam Treaty separated asylum, immigration by nationals of non-Member States, and judicial cooperation in civil matters from the third pillar and formed a new Title IV in the EC Treaty, while the third pillar was renamed Police and Judicial Cooperation in Criminal Matters; E Denza, *The Intergovernmental Pillars of the European Union* (Oxford, OUP, 2002) 2.

[6] Commission Communication, Wider Europe-Neighbourhood: A New Framework for Relations with our Eastern and Southern Neighbours COM (2003) 104 final, 11 April 2003 (hereinafter Wider Europe Communication) 10–14.

of its decision-making procedures.[7] The CFSP has been a forum for a predominantly intergovernmental cooperation between the Member States without judicial scrutiny or parliamentary involvement as mentioned earlier.[8] The ENP had therefore inherited the dichotomy of the legal framework of the EU external relations, which was to influence the choices of its legal instruments.

Besides the legal complexities affecting the policy, the ENP had to be elaborated in a hurry to coincide with the 2004 enlargement round.[9] The drafting of the 'Wider Europe' concept explains the automatic reliance on the perceived success of already existing tools, namely the enlargement policy. The transfer of the various components of the enlargement policy, including its institutional set-up, mechanisms and instruments, has been viewed as a 'mechanical borrowing'.[10] However, the divergent objectives of the enlargement experience and the ENP necessarily entailed substantive distinctions between the two policies. Moreover, the reliance on the enlargement policy, which the ENP was destined to replace, raised a question mark over the ultimate success of the latter in the absence of a membership perspective.

The Lisbon Treaty marks the latest stage in the legalisation of the EU external relations as noted previously. Although on the face of it, it has made the pillar structure redundant, it has nevertheless preserved the distinctness of the CFSP, suggesting continuing competence inquiries. It has also introduced certain innovations capable of influencing the legal aspects of the ENP. The codification of the objectives of the external action was discussed in the previous chapter. The recent developments as regards the permanent Presidency of the European Council, the bridging position of the High Representative and the role of the European External Action Service (EEAS) instil certain new dynamics into the established institutional arrangements of the ENP. Most importantly, a new neighbourhood-specific provision has been included in the Treaties for the first time. Although repeating the ENP rhetoric at large, Article 8 TEU needs to be analysed with reference to its added value as a potential legal basis for action in the neighbourhood, as well as its importance for reflecting the EU democratic values.

The legal aspects of the ENP have arguably been affected by the regional split in the policy with the emergence of the EaP and the UfM, as noted in Chapter 1. The inclusion of the South Caucasian states within the EaP raises the issue of the extent to which the nature of the cooperation has been affected.

---

[7] C Hill and M Smith (eds), *International Relations and the European Union* (Oxford, OUP, 2005) 401.

[8] See Chapter 2, note 37.

[9] The General Affairs European Council of 15 April 2002 welcomed the intention of the Commission and the High Representative for the CFSP to prepare contributions for development of the relations with the neighbours. The Commission's Wider Europe Initiative was presented in March 2003.

[10] J Kelley, 'New Wine in Old Wineskins: Policy Learning and Adaptation in the New European Neighbourhood Policy' (2006) 44 *Journal of Common Market Studies* 29, 32.

In this light the chapter first addresses the role of the EU institutions and Member States in policy formation and its subsequent development. The pre- and post-Lisbon arrangements are reflected in this section. Next, legal competence issues arising from the ENP, as well as the impact of Article 8 TEU on the commitments the EU undertakes in its neighbourhood, are addressed. The instruments and methodology of the ENP are discussed further to draw a picture of the legal framework for democracy promotion. Finally, the legal framework and methodology of the EaP is discussed to reveal its effect on the original ENP. The chapter will be summarised with conclusions on the ENP and its legal nature, and the suitability of its legal framework for democracy promotion outside the borders of the EU.

3.2 PRE- AND POST-LISBON INSTITUTIONAL ASPECTS

The multiplicity of actors in the area of EU external relations and the interplay between them is an essential part of foreign policy making in the EU. While the Commission has been the main mastermind behind the policy, the rotating Presidency, the position of the Member States in the Council and the European Council played a significant role in the conceptualisation and the future development of the ENP.

In an attempt to tackle the lack of coherence in EU international action, the Treaty of Lisbon introduced new institutional arrangements. Nevertheless, their positive effect on policy coherence cannot be perceived as a given, since they can complicate rather than simplify foreign action. Each stage is addressed in turn below.

3.2.1 EU Institutions and Member States: Pre-Lisbon Arrangements

The overall pattern of the inter-institutional dynamics at the stage of ENP formation appeared to be explicable with reference to liberal intergovernmentalism.[11] Thus, following the appearance of the initiative at an intergovernmental meeting, the task of policy elaboration had been assigned to the Commission, which executed this function, and then the Council, as an agent of the Member States, made a decision.[12] The Member States could be seen to act as principals, whereas the Commission and the then Council's High Representative for the Common Foreign and Security Policy were the agents.[13]

---

[11] A Moravcsik, 'Preferences and Power in the European Community: A Liberal Intergovernmentalist Approach' (1993) 31 *Journal of Common Market Studies* 473, 480.

[12] Council Conclusions, General Affairs, 15 April 2002, 10; Copenhagen European Council Conclusions, 12–13 December 2002, 7; Council Conclusions, General Affairs and External Relations, 18 March 2003, 6.

[13] M Emerson et al, 'The Reluctant Debutante: The European Union as Promoter of Democracy in its Neighbourhood' CEPS Working Document No 223, 2005, 32.

The 2002 Copenhagen summit acknowledged the opportunity provided by the enlargement 'to take forward relations with neighbouring countries based on shared political and economic values', paving the way for subsequent policy development.[14] The task of policy development was therefore assigned to the Commission, which in the following months presented its Wider Europe Communication to the Council and the Parliament to set the ground for future involvement in the neighbourhood. After receiving a green light from the European Council, the Commission, alongside the Council, embarked on a mission of bridging the existential gap with its neighbours.[15]

Nevertheless, the position of the Commission transgressed the role of an agent within liberal intergovernmentalist understanding, as it had assumed the role of a significant policy actor with its impact on the scope and content of the policy. The Commission's prominent role was predetermined by the 'real' power it exercised in foreign policy prior to the ENP,[16] including within the enlargement policy. The latter was described by 'a high level of integration' involving a special arrangement between the institutions and the Member States led by the Commission.[17] Thus, the ENP presented an opportunity for the Commission to extend and mainstream its key role in EU external affairs. The way to secure its salient position was therefore the institutional 'mission creep' via the adaptation of the enlargement practices to the neighbourhood initiative.[18]

There were therefore no surprises when the Directorate General (DG) Enlargement of the Commission was entrusted with the task of elaborating the ENP. A Wider Europe Task Force was established under the guidance of the Enlargement Commissioner with a view to drawing the political concepts and methodologies of the ENP. Even following the transfer of the ENP to the DG External Relations (with Commissioner Ferrero-Waldner undertaking the responsibility for External Relations and Neighbourhood Policy at the end of 2004),[19] the DG Enlargement was reluctant to retreat in its struggle with DG RELEX in influencing the policy formation.[20]

---

[14] Copenhagen European Council, note 12 above, 6.

[15] Thessaloniki European Council Conclusions, 19–20 June 2003, 13.

[16] Citation in Kelley, note 10 above, 31.

[17] M Cremona and C Hillion, 'L'Union fait la force? Potential and Limitations of the ENP as an Integrated EU Foreign and Security Policy' in N Copsey and A Mayhew (eds), *European Neighbourhood Policy: The Case of Europe*, Sussex European Institute, SEI Seminar Papers Series, 1 Number 2006, 20–44, 28.

[18] A Magen, 'The Shadow of Enlargement: Can the European Neighbourhood Policy Achieve Compliance?' Center on Democracy, Development and the Rule of Law, Stanford Institute for International Studies, Working Papers, No 68, August 2006, 396; Emerson et al, note 13 above, 5.

[19] M Comelli, E Greco and N Tocci, 'From Boundary to Borderland: Transforming the Meaning of Borders through the European Neighbourhood Policy' (2007) 12 *European Foreign Affairs Review* 203, 213; E Tulmets, 'Adapting the Experience of Enlargement to the Neighbourhood Policy: the ENP as a Substitute to Enlargement?' in P Kratochvil (ed), *The European Union and Its Neighbourhood: Policies, Problems and Priorities* (Prague, Institute of International Relations, 2006) 29–57, 30.

[20] R Zaiotti, 'Of Friends and Fences: Europe's Neighbourhood Policy and the "Gated Community Syndrome"' (2007) 29 *European Integration* 143, 156; Comelli et al, note 19 above, 213; Tulmets, note 19 above, 30.

At the outset the Commission prepared Country Reports assessing the political and economic situation of relevant states. The reports were submitted to the Council, which decided whether to proceed to the elaboration and signing of the Action Plans.[21] Following the enlargement practices, the Commission acquired a similar role of monitoring the progress of the neighbours in implementing their respective Action Plans.[22] Thus, the leading role assumed by the Commission in the policy elaboration and monitoring has been evaluated with positive connotations: it would pursue the Union's interests impartially therefore, bypassing the effect of Member States' diverging interests.[23]

The role acquired by the Commission almost by default was not eagerly accepted by the Member States, which went into the shadows or to some extent lost interest following the initiation of the policy.[24] The Member States, despite their seeming apathy, could not easily have been dismissed, as they possessed important avenues for steering the policy agenda in the direction and at a time they favoured.

First of all, the Council was the ultimate decision-making body within the ENP.[25] It had demonstrated willingness to limit the role of the Commission and to ensure its presence in the process of policy formation in a number of ways. For instance, after the approval from the Council, the ENP Strategy Paper provided for the participation of the High Representative for the CFSP on the issues of political cooperation and CFSP matters during the Action Plans' preparation.[26] Accordingly, while drafting national reports, the Commission worked in close cooperation with the Council's High Representative. Specifically for the Action Plans with South Caucasian states, the Council instructed the Commission to act jointly – 'in close cooperation' – with the Presidency and the High Representative and, where appropriate, with the Special Representative for the South Caucasus on the issues concerning political cooperation and the CFSP.[27]

Close cooperation with the High Representative was also required for drafting progress reports on the issues related to political dialogue and cooperation, as well as CFSP matters.[28] This cooperation between the Commission and the High Representative for the CFSP was considered to be out of the ordinary in comparison with the institutional practice of the enlargement policy demonstrating the first steps towards the 'double-hatting' system proposed by the Constitutional

---

[21] Available at www.ec.europa.eu/world/enp/howitworks_en.htm.

[22] ENP Strategy Paper 10.

[23] A Ott and R Wessel, 'The EU's External Relations Regime: Multilevel Complexity in an Expanding Union' in S Blockmans and A Lazowski (eds), *The European Union and its Neighbours: A Legal Appraisal of the EU's Policies of Stabilisation, Partnership and Integration* (The Hague, TMC Asser Press, 2006) 19–59, 51.

[24] F Bicchi, *European Foreign Policy Making towards the Mediterranean* (Basingstoke, Palgrave, 2007) 177; Zaiotti, note 20 above, 156.

[25] R Balfour and A Missiroli, 'Reassessing the European Neighbourhood Policy', European Policy Centre, Issue Paper No 54, June 2007, 21.

[26] ENP Strategy Paper 4.

[27] Council Conclusions, 25 April 2005, 11.

[28] Council Conclusions, General Affairs and External Relations, 16–17 December 2004.

Treaty and later incorporated in the Lisbon Treaty.[29] The collaboration was to ensure a common position between the Commission and the Council, in particular a coordinated action on behalf of the External Relations Commissioner and the High Representative for CFSP.

Second, the Council significantly influenced the pragmatic and rationalist turn the policy took after the Commission's Wider Europe Communication as noted in Chapter 2. The promise of 'everything but institutions' and 'a stake in the EU's internal market' in the initial speeches and Wider Europe Communication was substantially abandoned following the ENP Strategy Paper.[30] Not only did the Council 'shuffle priorities' by shifting the focus to the security challenges of the neighbourhood, but it also limited the incentives, where the freedom of movement of persons was noted to be 'the first victim' of its intervention'.[31] However, it is also worth observing that the blame for policy 'securitisation' does not lie solely with the Council due to the influence of DG Justice, Liberty and Security within the Commission, resulting in a more prominent profile for such issues as asylum, illegal immigration and trafficking within the policy.[32]

The Commission–Council interactions therefore contributed to the view that the institutional rivalry had affected the direction taken by ENP.[33] The institutional arrangements as they were no doubt allowed the Member States to play their part in forming the content of the ENP. The latter could not have avoided the effects of intergovernmental aspects of the EU's foreign policy. However, the trend of reassertion by the Member States of their role was not confined to the ENP, and had been present already within the enlargement experience.[34] It was noted that the Commission created policy proposals with a view to what the Council would ultimately approve.[35] The same pattern is visible with the ENP Strategy Paper, which reflected the Council's previous position, and was subsequently approved without obstacles.

In addition to the Council's participation, the European Council, heads of governments or states served as an alternative arena for Member States to influence the elaboration and subsequent development of the policy. It was the European Council, in accordance with the former Article 13 EU, that defined the 'general guidelines of the common foreign and security policy'. In practice, however, this

---

[29] See section 3.2.2 below; Cremona and Hillion, note 17 above, 33.

[30] R Prodi, 'A Wider Europe – A Proximity Policy as the Key to Stability', Speech to the Sixth ECSA-World Conference, 5–6 December 2002, Speech/02/619; Wider Europe Communication, 4.

[31] R Balfour and A Rotta, 'Beyond Enlargement. The European Neighbourhood Policy and its Tools' (2005) 40 *International Spectator* 7, 9, 12–13.

[32] Zaiotti, note 20 above 156–57.

[33] D Kochenov, 'The ENP Conditionality: Pre-Accession Mistakes Repeated' in L Delcour and E Tulmets (eds), *Pioneer Europe? Testing EU Foreign Policy in the Neighbourhood* (Baden-Baden, Nomos, 2008) 105–20, 115.

[34] C Hillion, 'Enlarging the Constitutional Order of States' in A Arnull, C Barnard et al (eds), *A Constitutional Order of States? Essays in EU Law in Honour of Alan Dashwood* (Oxford, Hart Publishing, 2011) 485–99, 490–91.

[35] MA Vachudova, *Europe Undivided: Democracy, Leverage, and Integration after Communism* (Oxford, OUP, 2005) 119.

role extended beyond CFSP matters. As noted above, it was the European Council's conclusions that paved the way for policy formation. After the 2002 Copenhagen European Council, its role seemed to be marginal, leaving the tasks of policy formation to the Commission and the Council.

Nonetheless, where a serious political decision was to be initiated or made, the European Council was the platform for such decision making, and the rotating Presidency was the driving force behind it.[36] As noted previously, the new initiative was stretched to the Southern neighbours under the influence of certain Member States, fearful of the diminishing importance of their historic partners.[37] Others did not take a particular interest in the ENP, favouring previously existing frameworks.[38] Later on, the Member States orchestrated the regional split of the policy. The historical links of southern European Member States with the Mediterranean region influenced the decision of the French Presidency to launch the UfM within the ENP in 2008.[39] On the other hand, Sweden and Poland advocated a distinct approach to the Eastern neighbourhood, which materialised in the EaP initiative shortly afterwards.[40] The role of the Presidency was key also for supporting relevant regional cooperation initiatives, such as the Black Sea Synergy and the Northern Dimension.[41] Beside the role of the Presidency, the European Council provided the forum where the Member States played out their dissenting positions on international events. In contrast to the enlargement, where it was considered that the Member States' ultimate decision to enlarge was to a great extent motivated by identity considerations,[42] the 27, and now 28 Member States are more likely to be guided by rationalist considerations in relation to the Eastern neighbours. This is particularly so when the Member States have to react to events in the Union's neighbourhood.

[36] Lang, for instance, explores the role of the German and Czech presidency in 2007 and 2009 respectively: KO Lang, 'The Role of the German and the Czech Presidencies in the Definition of an Eastern Dimension for the ENP' in L Delcour and E Tulmets (eds), *Pioneer Europe: Testing EU Foreign Policy in the Neighbourhood* (Baden-Baden, Nomos, 2008) 77–101.

[37] Copenhagen Presidency Conclusions, European Council, 12–13 December 2002; Bicchi, note 24 above, 177; A Missiroli, 'The EU and its Changing Neighbourhood' in R Dannreuther (ed), *European Union Foreign and Security Policy: Towards a Neighbourhood Strategy* (London, Routledge, 2004) 12–26, 23.

[38] See for instance the position of Spain in M Natorski, 'National Concerns in the EU Neighbourhood: Spanish and Polish Policies on the Southern and Eastern Dimensions' in L Delcour and E Tulmets (eds), *Pioneer Europe: Testing EU Foreign Policy in the Neighbourhood* (Baden-Baden, Nomos, 2008) 57–75, 59–62.

[39] Brussels European Council Conclusions, 13–14 March 2008, 19; Commission Communication on the Barcelona Process: Union for the Mediterranean COM (2008) 319 final, 20 May 2008; Joint Declaration of the Paris Summit for the Mediterranean, Paris, 13 July 2008,11887/08 (Presse 213) 15 July 2008.

[40] Council Conclusions, General Affairs and External Relations, 26–27 May 2008, 24; Brussels European Council Conclusions, 19–20 June 2008, 19.

[41] E Lannon and P Van Elsuwege, 'The Eastern Partnership: Prospects of a New Regional Dimension within the ENP' in E Lannon (ed), *The European Neighbourhood Policy's Challenges* (Brussels, College of Europe Studies, PIE Peter Lang, 2012) 285–322, 287.

[42] KE Smith, *The Making of EU Foreign Policy: The Case of Eastern Europe* (Basingstoke, Palgrave, 2004) 180–81; U Sedelmeier, *Constructing the Path to Eastern Enlargement* (Manchester, Manchester University Press, 2005) 9.

The lack of unity among the Member States became particularly evident following the 2008 Russian–Georgian war, when the mediation by the Council President Nicolas Sarkozy led to a six-point ceasefire document on 12 August.[43] Although the mediation was a testimony to the role the EU could play in its neighbourhood, the Member States could not agree on a response to Russia with Baltic and Eastern European states calling for a tougher reaction, and most of the old Member States opting for a more careful approach.[44] Ultimately, a consensus was reached on the suspension of negotiations on a new agreement with Russia until the withdrawal of its troops from the Georgian territory.[45]

Besides the prominence of the Commission and the Council within the ENP institutional landscape, the role of the Parliament prior to the Lisbon Treaty should also be acknowledged. Although the EP is considered to be weaker in comparison with its national counterparts in the area of foreign affairs,[46] its role varies depending on the particular area of foreign affairs. The statement is most true in respect of CFSP, where the EP has been marginalised due to the intergovernmental nature of the decision-making procedures. The minuscule role of consultation by the Presidency on 'the main aspects and the basic choices' of the policy in former Article 21 EU did not ensure any influence for the Parliament, and is said to not have been efficiently implemented.[47]

Outside the CFSP domain, however, the Parliament gradually acquired a noticeable presence in EU foreign policy in a number of ways. First, it gained considerable weight through its partial powers over the budget,[48] which were accompanied by a certain supervisory role.[49] Second, in terms of its legislative involvement, former Article 300 EC ensured a consultative role for the Parliament as a general rule for the conclusion of international agreements with certain exceptions, including CCP-related agreements.[50] As a derogation from the general

---

[43] Russia's suspicious attitude to the political orientation of its neighbours became evident in the case of Georgia. The worsening of Russian–Georgian relations after the 'Rose Revolution', the proclamation of independence by Kosovo in February 2008, as well as a promise of NATO membership to Ukraine and Georgia, led to an increased Russian presence in Abkhazia and South Ossetia. The tension between the two states culminated in the Georgian military intervention in South Ossetia on 7 August 2008, followed by the Russian and Abkhaz military involvement.

[44] 'EU Shies Away from Strong Action against Russia', *EU Observer*, 1 September 2008; 'EU Diplomats Keen to Avoid Russia Controversy', *EU Observer*, 13 August 2008; 'EU Suspends Talks on Russia Pact', *BBC News*, 1 September 2008; 'EU Secures Deal on Russia Withdrawal', *EU Observer*, 9 September 2008; KE Smith, 'Enlargement, the Neighbourhood, and European Order' in C Hill and M Smith (eds), *International Relations and the European Union*, 2nd edn (Oxford, OUP, 2011) 299–323, 319.

[45] Brussels Extraordinary European Council, 1 September 2008, 1.

[46] D Thym, 'Parliamentary Involvement in European International Relations' in M Cremona and B de Witte (eds), *EU Foreign Relations Law: Constitutional Fundamentals* (Oxford, Hart Publishing, 2008) 201–32, 201.

[47] R Wessel, *The European Union's Foreign and Security Policy: A Legal Institutional Perspective* (The Hague, Kluwer Law International, 1999) 95; G de Baere, *Principles of EU External Relations Law* (Oxford, OUP, 2008) 161.

[48] Former Art 272 EC, Art 28 EU; Emerson et al, note 13 above, 34.

[49] Raube, K, 'Parliamentary Legitimacy in EU External Relations: How So?' Paper Presented at UACES 42 Annual Conference, 'Old Borders, New Frontiers' 3–5 September 2012, Passau.

[50] Art 300(3) EC.

rule the Parliament had to consent to only four types of agreements, including association agreements, over which the EP was noted to have acquired significant practical authority.[51]

Key in the increasing role of the Parliament has been its own activism in enhancing its profile in external relations.[52] The Parliament is keen to make its position known and call for action if considered necessary. In the case of the ENP, the Parliament has continuously supported the initiative, inviting attention to various policy issues, regions or countries.[53] It often demonstrated the vision other institutions lacked. For instance, the appointment of the Special Representative for the South Caucasus had been advocated by the Parliament.[54] Also significant was the Parliament's role in lobbying for the inclusion of Georgia, Armenia and Azerbaijan within the ENP with a view to supporting reforms and ensuring greater EU involvement in conflict zones.[55]

The Parliament's role is particularly important in placing the issues of democracy and human rights on the external agenda of the EU, especially when concluding international agreements.[56] An early example of the Parliament upholding these values in the neighbourhood included the conclusion of the PCAs with the South Caucasian states. The Parliament threatened to block the agreements if the Council did not include a separate title on democratic clauses.[57] Already at this stage, its willingness to play a more active role led to its assumption of a diplomatic role in promoting democracy abroad, acknowledged by the Commission.[58]

A similar stance on democracy and human rights-related issues was taken by the Parliament within the ENP. In its 2006 Resolution the Parliament emphasised the necessity of establishing an effective monitoring mechanism and demonstrated its readiness to restrict or suspend aid to, and even to cancel agreements

---

[51]   Art 300(6) EC; Thym, note 46 above 201; R Passos, 'Mixed Agreements from the Perspective of the European Parliament' in C Hillion and P Koutrakos (eds), *Mixed Agreements Revisited: The EU and its Member States in the World* (Oxford, Hart Publishing, 2010) 269–94, 273–374.

[52]   Parliament's aspirations come across strongly in its own Rules of Procedure – Rule 90; D MacGoldrick, *International Relations Law of the European Union* (London, Longman, 1997) 113–14; de Baere, note 47 above, 166; Passos, note 51 above, 277.

[53]   See, for instance, European Parliament Resolution on the European Neighbourhood Policy (2004/2166(INI) 19 January 2006; European Parliament Resolution on Strengthening the European Neighbourhood Policy (2007/2088(INI)) 15 November 2007; European Parliament Report on the Review of the European Neighbourhood and Partnership Instrument (2008/2236(INI)) 19 February 2009.

[54]   European Parliament Resolution on EU Relations with South Caucasus P5_TA(2002)0085, 28 February 2002, para 7.

[55]   European Parliament Resolution on the Communication from the Commission to the Council and the European Parliament on The European Union's Relations with the South Caucasus under the Partnership and Cooperation Agreements P5_TA (2002) 0085, 28 November 2002.

[56]   C Lord, 'Accountable and Legitimate? The EU's International Role' in C Hill and M Smith (eds), *International Relations and the European Union* (Oxford, OUP, 2005) 113–33, 121; G Edwards, 'The Pattern of the EU's Global Activity' in Hill and Smith (eds), note 44 above, 65.

[57]   European Parliament Report, The European Parliament and the Defence of Human Rights, Sanctions, 2006.

[58]   Commission Communication, 'The European Union's Role in Promoting Human Rights and Democratisation in Third Countries' COM (2001) 252 final, 8 May 2001, 6.

with, countries violating European and international standards of democracy.[59] In its 2008 Resolution on South Caucasus the Parliament stressed that the ENP revisions and assistance should be aimed at promoting institution building, respect for human rights, the rule of law and democratisation.[60] Under the Regulation on the European Neighbourhood and Partnership Instrument (ENPI), the main instrument for financing the ENP to this date, the Council is entitled to suspend aid to a misbehaving state following a recommendation by the Commission.[61] Nevertheless, a certain role is provided for the Parliament: a dialogue should be maintained between the Commission and the Parliament and an annual report on the implementation of the assistance allocation should be presented to the Parliament and the Council.[62]

Such institutional interactions support the standpoint that the role of the EU institutions within the ENP overstepped the ordinary constitutional set-up envisaged by the Treaties.[63] The Commission's activity is more than as a mere guardian of the Treaty vis-à-vis the Member States, and the Parliament is eager to transcend the limitations imposed on its role. Thus, the visions of these different institutions and Member States for the vicinity of the Union had to be reconciled within the same policy.[64]

3.2.2 Post-Lisbon Role of EU Institutions

One of the developments introduced in the Lisbon Treaty to enhance the Union's capacity to act in a global world might be argued to be the introduction of legal personality of the EU in Article 47 TEU.[65] Combined with the pillar structure of the EU constitutional order and the intergovernmental nature of the CFSP, the lack of legal personality contributed to the perception of the EU's weak role externally.[66] However, the absence of legal personality was not a major obstacle for the

---

[59] European Parliament Resolution on the European Neighbourhood Policy (2004/2166(INI)) 19 January 2006.

[60] European Parliament Resolution on a more Effective EU Policy for the South Caucasus: from Promises to Actions (2007/2076(INI)) 17 January 2008, para 6.

[61] See Chapter 6, section 6.3; Regulation No 1638/2006 of the European Parliament and of the Council laying down general provisions establishing a European Neighbourhood and Partnership Instrument (ENPI Regulation) [2006] OJ L310/1.

[62] Arts 25 and 26, ENPI Regulation.

[63] C Hillion, 'The EU's Neighbourhood Policy towards Eastern Europe' in A Dashwood and M Maresceau (eds), *Law and Practice of EU External Relations* (Cambridge, CUP, 2008) 309–33, 317; Cremona and Hillion, note 17 above, 28.

[64] On the role of the pre-Lisbon arrangements see also N Ghazaryan, 'Pre- and Post-Lisbon Institutional Trends in the EU's Neighbourhood' in PJ Cardwell (ed), *EU External Relations Law and Policy in the Post-Lisbon Era* (The Hague, TMC Asser Press, 2012) 199–216.

[65] Previously the EU lacked legal personality as such, and only the EC had legal personality under former Art 281 EC.

[66] M Cremona, 'External Relations and External Competence of the European Union' in P Craig and G de Búrca (eds), *Evolution of EU Law*, 2nd edn (Oxford, OUP, 2011) 261.

successful conduct of foreign policy. As a 'federal technique',[67] mixity in concluding international agreements allowed for combined action between the EC and all or some Member States.[68] In addition former Article 24 EU allowed the Union to enter into international agreements for CFSP matters. The introduction of a single legal personality therefore merely signified the establishment of a single framework for concluding international agreements, although with certain distinctions still preserved for the CFSP.[69]

It was rather the intergovernmental nature of the CFSP/ESDP that represented a major crack in the EU's external action, one that has been perpetuated in the Lisbon Treaty. In its specific provisions on the CFSP the modified TEU requires unanimity for adopting decisions related to CFSP/CSDP in both the European Council and the Council suggesting that 'mixity' in the representation of the EU will be a constant feature of its foreign policy, including the ENP.[70] As discussed in the previous chapter, the single list of foreign policy objectives formally establishes a common denominator for any EU foreign policy action, but it does not on its own guarantee coherent international action or a unified vision of the Union's role in its neighbourhood. A number of institutional arrangements introduced in the Lisbon Treaty are to play their part in achieving unity and synergy in EU external relations.

It should be noted that the European Council has been officially listed as one of the EU institutions: it defines the general political directions and choices of the Union not only in the CFSP, but also in other areas of EU external action.[71] The new Treaty provisions essentially codify the significance the European Council previously acquired in the decision making of the EU.[72] It is said that strengthening the role of the European Council potentially raises the profile of the Member States.[73] The former, therefore, continues to serve as a platform for the Member States to promote their own agenda concerning the ENP. Related to this development is the drawback of hijacking of the Commission's power of initiative, where a tendency has been observed to set detailed agendas, therefore limiting the Commission's scope for manoeuvre.[74]

The new permanent position of the President of the European Council has been introduced to contribute to the continuity of established policies under

---

[67] R Schütze, *From Dual to Cooperative Federalism: The Changing Structure of European Law* (Oxford, OUP, 2009) 308.

[68] M Maresceau, 'A Typology of Mixed Bilateral Agreements' in Hillion and Koutrakos (eds), note 51 above, 15; Smith, note 42 above, 7.

[69] JC Piris, *The Lisbon Treaty: A Legal and Political Analysis* (Cambridge, CUP, 2010) 88.

[70] Art 24 TEU.

[71] Arts 13, 15, 22(1), 26 TEU.

[72] U Puetter, 'The Latest Attempt at Institutional Engineering: The Treaty of Lisbon and Deliberative Intergovernmentalism in EU Foreign and Security Policy Coordination' in Cardwell (ed), note 64 above, 17–34, 27–28.

[73] J Wouters, D Coppens and B de Meester, 'The European Union's External Relations after the Lisbon Treaty' in S Griller and J Ziller (eds), *The Lisbon Treaty: EU Constitutionalism without a Constitutional Treaty* (Dordrecht, Springer, 2008) 143–203, 149–50.

[74] T Christiansen, 'The European Union after the Lisbon Treaty: An Elusive "Institutional Balance"?' in A Biondi and P Eeckhout (eds), *European Union Law After Lisbon* (Oxford, OUP, 2012) 228–47, 237.

Article 15 TEU. This office therefore intends to diminish the importance of the rotating Presidency, which was rather influential in steering and directing the foreign policy agenda. Nevertheless, the presence of the permanent President of the European Council did not completely sideline the significance of the rotating Presidency of the Council, which continues to influence the conduct of policy. For instance, Poland during its Presidency in 2011 prioritised the EaP and the democratisation agenda in the ENP, while the Cypriot Presidency in the second half of 2012 emphasised the Southern dimension of the ENP as opposed to the Eastern.[75]

Another major development was the creation of the position of High Representative for Foreign Affairs and Security Policy acting as the Vice-President of the Commission, while being directly responsible to the European Council.[76] The merger of the former positions of the High Representative for CFSP and the Commissioner for External Relations into a single office, simultaneously occupying the Vice-Presidency of the Commission, represents the so-called 'double-hatting', and is primarily aimed at increasing the consistency of EU foreign policy.[77] Even the appointment procedure for the High Representative is set to demonstrate the linking function of this new office.[78] The Representative is appointed by the European Council with the agreement of the President of the Commission. The position of the High Representative is viewed also as 'triple-hatting' with reference to her power of chairing the Foreign Affairs Council (FAC).[79]

It has been noted that the complexity and multiplicity of the tasks assigned to the High Representative required the candidate for this position 'to have political weight, managerial capability, experience of at least one side – one hat, as it were – and external credibility'.[80] This captures the challenges facing the High Representative linked to her mandate, representational functions and the bridging role between the Commission and the Council, particularly relevant for the ENP.

3.2.2.1 Mandate

As an added value to the previous position of the High Representative for CFSP, the duties of the new High Representative have been significantly expanded.

---

[75] Similarly the Lithuanian presidency commencing on 1 July 2013 declared its intentions to develop EU cooperation with the Eastern neighbours; 'Lithuania Gives Ukraine Extra Time to Meet EU Demands', *Euractiv*, 14 May 2013; Programme of the Polish Presidency of the Council of the European Union, 1 July 2011–31 December 2001, available at www.pl2011.eu; Priorities of the Cyprus Presidency of the Council of the European Union, 1 July–31 December 2012, available at www.cy2012.eu.

[76] Art 18 TEU.

[77] Final Report of Working Group VII on External Action, CONV 459/02, Brussels, 16 December 2002, 6–7.

[78] C Kaddous, 'Role and Position of the High Representative of the Union for Foreign Affairs and Security Policy under the Lisbon Treaty' in Griller and Ziller (eds), note 73 above, 206–21, 208.

[79] Piris, note 69 above, 245; P Morillas, 'Institutionalisation or Intergovernmental Decision-Taking in Foreign Policy: The Implementation of the Lisbon Treaty' in Cardwell (ed), note 64 above, 119–34, 123.

[80] *Foreign Policy Aspects of the Lisbon Treaty*, Third Report of Session 2007–08, House of Commons, Foreign Affairs Committee, UK, 16 January 2008, Point 175, 62.

Under Article 15 TEU the High Representative shall take part in the work of the European Council although without a power to vote. As noted above the High Representative chairs the FAC and is responsible for the conduct of external relations as the Vice-President of the European Commission.[81] In particular, she is responsible for putting the CFSP into effect.[82] The High Representative on her own or with the Commission's support may submit initiatives to the Council for consideration.[83] She also convenes an extraordinary Council when circumstances so require, and plays a leading part in the appointment of Special Representatives.[84] The combination of all these tasks is overwhelming and has been branded a 'mission impossible'.[85]

Besides the 'impossibility' of the mission, it is also not possible to determine the clear mandate of the High Representative based solely on the language of Article 18 TEU, which is perceived to create a certain margin of flexibility for securing political consensus.[86] According to Article 18(4) the High Representative 'shall be responsible within the Commission for responsibilities incumbent on it in external relations and for coordinating other aspects of the Union's external action'. This is remarkably general and vague for the purposes of drawing any conclusions as to the role of the High Representative vis-à-vis the Commission or within the latter. A central role in this respect belongs to the EU institutions together with the Member States, and importantly to the President of the Commission, whose 'right-hand man' the High Representative is meant to become. When Commission President Barroso announced the line-up of the 2009 Commission, the enlargement and the ENP, the humanitarian aid and development policies were notably excluded from the mandate of the High Representative.[87] The most obvious explanation for this exclusion was the Commission's intent to retain certain competencies within the institution.[88] Taking into account the Commission's eagerness to increase its presence in foreign affairs by its active role in the ENP domain, transferring the latter to the High Representative would have signified a loss of influence across the neighbourhood. In this scenario, the exclusion of the High Representative from these areas potentially creates a scope for rivalry between individual Commissioners and the High Representative,[89] especially taking into

---

[81] Art 18 TEU.

[82] Arts 24(1), 26(3), 27(1) TEU.

[83] Art 13(1) TEU.

[84] Art 33 TEU.

[85] S Blockmans and ML Laatsit, 'The European External Action Service: Enhancing Coherence in EU External Action?' in Cardwell (ed), note 64 above, 135–59, 140.

[86] P Koutrakos, 'Primary Law and Policy in EU External Relations: Moving Away from the Big Picture' (2008) 14 *European Law Review* 666, 671–72; JC Piris, 'Where Will the Lisbon Treaty Lead Us' in Arnull, Barnard et al (eds), note 34 above, 59–74, 59.

[87] 'President Barroso Unveils His New Team', Press Release, IP/09/1837, 27 November 2009.

[88] C Hillion and M Lefebvre, 'The European External Action Service: Towards a Common Diplomacy', European Issue No 184, Swedish Institute for European Policy Studies, 25 October 2010, 3; S Stoss, 'The Review of the European Neighbourhood Policy: Increasing the Coherence and Coordination of EU External Action?' *TEPSA Brief* (2011) 2.

[89] AC Marangoni, 'One Hat Too Many for the High Representative – Vice President? The Coherence of EU's External Policies after Lisbon' EU Foreign Affairs Review, *Global Europe*, July 2012, 11.

account the role of the High Representative in 'coordinating other aspects of the Union's external action' under Article 18(4) TEU. On the other hand, it has been noted that the High Representative does not have concrete powers to impose any position on the DGs retaining foreign competence, rendering her role to be a purely 'diplomatic undertaking'.[90]

Besides, transferring all the units dealing with foreign policy to the High Representative at once would have been an impossible task to perform.[91] Most importantly, it can be argued that the retention of the ENP within the Commission signifies that the latter, similar to the enlargement, is more than a traditional foreign policy. It is an area where the Commission is not yet prepared to give up its leading role. However, there are no limitations to be found in the Treaties to suggest that such a development is not possible in the future.[92]

3.2.2.2 Representational Functions

Even after the Lisbon amendments, there is no single face that is associated with the EU in the world, and currently there is more and not less representation of the EU. There is no clear consensus as to who truly represents the EU, as demonstrated by the debates as to who should receive the Nobel Peace Prize on behalf of the Union in 2012.[93]

Both the permanent Presidency and the High Representative are responsible for the representation of the EU internationally in CFSP matters.[94] Upon a closer reading of Article 15(6) TEU, Duke suggests that the High Representative's representation would be limited to the ministerial level.[95] At the EaP summits, held at the level of heads of states or governments, the President of the European Council and the High Representative however jointly represented the EU. In terms of asserting the representational functions, criticism was directed at Baroness Ashton, the first High Representative under the Lisbon Treaty, for her failure to assert herself on the international stage.[96]

In the neighbourhood the confusion as to who represents the EU in which matters continues to reign, as both the President of the European Council and the High Representative continue representing the EU in addition to the President of

---

[90] U Khaliq, 'The External Action of the European Union under the Treaty of Lisbon' in M Trybus and L Rubini (eds), *The Treaty of Lisbon and the Future of European Law and Policy* (Cheltenham, Edward Elgar Publishing, 2012) 239–61, 250–51.

[91] L Van Hoof, 'Why the EU is Failing in its Neighbourhood: The Case of Armenia' (2012) 17 *European Foreign Affairs Review* 285, 300.

[92] See, for instance, 'Ashton Drops Big Ideas on EU Foreign Service', *EU Observer*, 13 June 2013.

[93] 'Three Presidents to Collect Nobel Prize', *Euractiv*, 18 October 2012.

[94] Arts 15(6), 27(2) TEU.

[95] S Duke, 'Consistency, Coherence and European Union External Action: The Path to Lisbon and Beyond' in P Koutrakos (ed), *European Foreign Policy: Legal and Political Perspectives* (Cheltenham, Edward Elgar Publishing, 2011) 15–54, 31.

[96] The handling of the aftermath of the Haiti earthquake was the first instance raising such criticism due to the low profile the High Representative had assumed: 'Ashton under Fire for Not Going to Haiti', *EU Observer*, 19 January 2010.

the Commission and the Commissioner for Enlargement and the ENP 2010–2014, Štefan Füle. Therefore, the unclear nature as well as the significant overlap in the mandate of the positions of the President of the European Council and the High Representative should be considered as a drawback in presenting a unified front to the outside world.

A practice has developed in relation to political *démarches* addressed to the neighbouring states, where the Commissioner for the Enlargement and ENP and the High Representative jointly issue statements regarding political developments in the neighbourhood.[97] While creating a united front, it is nevertheless problematic as it assumes a slower reaction on behalf of the EU due to the necessity of reaching a common understanding between the two actors, which inevitably influences the tone of the reaction. For instance, in August 2012 upon his extradition, Ramil Safarov, a murderer of an Armenian officer convicted to life imprisonment in Hungary, was released in Azerbaijan raising serious concerns regarding the rule of law in the country and causing a diplomatic breakdown between Armenia and Hungary. It took a few days for the High Representative and the ENP Commissioner to issue a cautiously worded statement expressing 'concern' and calling both the Armenian and the Azerbaijani sides to 'exercise restraint'.[98] As a result the EU comes across as not being capable of taking a stance on matters involving its Member States and capable of triggering instability in its neighbourhood.

3.2.2.3 Commission–Council Synergy?

The 'double-hatting' of the High Representative's position has been viewed as a significant achievement in the constitutional development of the EU. The function of this institution, however, depends on the personality of the High Representative and her institutional loyalties.

On the one hand, it might be considered that the position adds strength to the powers of the Commission in relation to the CFSP matters, as the de facto Vice-President of the Commission acquires a leading role in this field. However, if the loyalties of the High Representative lie with the Council, then the position leads to the diminishing of the already 'secondary' role of the Commission,[99] since the latter no longer has an individual right of initiative, which was perceived to be its 'most powerful tool' in the CFSP area.[100] Moreover, it has been noted that being

---

[97] See for instance, Joint Statement by High Representative Catherine Ashton and Commissioner Štefan Füle on the Parliamentary Elections in Ukraine, MEMO/480/12, 29 October 2012; Joint Statement by High Representative Catherine Ashton and Commissioner Štefan Füle on EU–Georgia relations and Upcoming Elections, MEMO/12/640, 3 September 2012; Joint statement by High Representative Catherine Ashton and Commissioner Štefan Füle on the formation of new government of the Republic of Moldova, MEMO/11/20, 14 January 2011.

[98] Statement by the Spokespersons of EU High Representative Catherine Ashton and Commissioner Štefan Füle on the release of Ramil Safarov, Brussels, 3 September 2012, A 389/12.

[99] P Koutrakos, *EU International Relations Law* (Oxford, Hart Publishing, 2006) 392.

[100] Under Art 22 EU the Commission had a right of initiative in CFSP matters; N Neuwahl, 'Foreign and Security Policy and the Implementation of the Requirement of "Consistency" under the Treaty on European Union' in D O'Keeffe and PM Twomey (eds), *Legal Issues of the Maastricht Treaty* (Chichester, Chancery Law Publishing, 1994) 227–46, 241–42.

appointed by the European Council, as well as entertaining privileged links with the latter and the FAC, carries a risk of strengthening the European Council and weakening of the Commission's role and its 'communitarian' method.[101] Hence, the 'double-hatting' can result in one hat being worn on top of the other: the making of the decisions in the FAC has been suggested to support placing the Council hat on top of the Commission one.[102] The High Representative seemed to have had an insignificant role as the Vice-President of the Commission. Her record of attendance at the Commission meetings, let alone chairing them, points to this conclusion.[103]

Besides, the High Representative does not necessarily guarantee the continuity of the previous approaches in the neighbourhood. One of the first steps the High Representative intended to undertake after her appointment was scrapping the mandates of the Special Representative for the South Caucasus and Moldova, a move that was not a welcome development.[104] It went against the previous position of actively contributing to conflict resolution and peace building in the region. The move was later rectified by appointing a new Special Representative in September 2011 for the South Caucasus and the crisis in Georgia.[105]

An example of less than smooth cooperation was the delay in presenting the Joint Communication on 'A New Response to a Changing Neighbourhood' due to the differences between the Commissioner for ENP and the High Representative.[106] Therefore, a unified position between the Commission and the High Representative is not a given constant, and the differences in their visions can turn against the very idea the new office was to embody. In contrast, the High Representative for CFSP, Javier Solana, had more success in building bridges with the Commission,[107] as well as carving out a role for himself in comparison with the 'minimalist' approach of Baroness Ashton.[108] Thus, the office per se does not make much difference: it is the personality that is crucial.

As to the High Representative's role in creating a united front among the Member States and her ability to mobilise them, it has been noted that the Member States have more success in mobilising the High Representative rather than the opposite.[109] Others consider that the position of High Representative was

[101] P Craig, *The Lisbon Treaty: Law, Politics, and Treaty Reform* (Oxford, OUP, 2010) 427.

[102] M Dougan, 'The Treaty of Lisbon 2007: Winning Minds, Not Hearts' (2008) 45 *Common Market Law Review* 617– 703, 637.

[103] 'Baroness Ashton Absent from Two Thirds of European Commission Meetings', *The Telegraph*, 20 September 2012.

[104] 'EU Plans To Scrap South Caucasus, Moldova Envoys', *Radio Free Europe*, 31 May 2010; U Halbach, 'The European Union in the South Caucasus: Story of a Hesitant Approximation' in *South Caucasus: 20 Years of Independence* (Friedrich Ebert Stiftung, 2011) 300–15, 314.

[105] Philippe Lefort was appointed by Council Decision 2011/518/CFSP [2011] OJ L221/5, and his mandate was extended until 30 June 2013 by Council Decision 2012/326/CFSP [2012] OJ L165/53.

[106] COM (2011) 303, 25 May 2011; Van Hoof, note 91 above, 300.

[107] S Vanhoonacker, 'The Institutional Framework' in Hill and Smith (eds), note 56 above, 67–90, 82.

[108] Christiansen, note 74 above, 239.

[109] S Vanhoonacker, 'Inter-Institutional Dynamics in Common Foreign and Security Policy Post-Lisbon: Who are the Winners?', Paper presented at UACES 42 Annual Conference, 'Old Borders, New Frontiers', 3–5 September 2012, Passau.

doomed to failure in creating a single voice for the EU due to the Member States' prerogative of action in international relations.[110]

Much depends on the smooth operation of the EEAS, established to assist the High Representative in exercising her mandate. Similar to Article 18 TEU, Article 27 TEU has a general nature and allows for flexibility in defining the role of the service. Thus, depending on the role the latter assumes, the EEAS has the potential to serve either the Commission or the Council. If the High Representative's role as a Vice-President of the Commission is fulfilled, then it has been noted that the EEAS can operate as a 'service' to the Commission.[111]

However, the Council decision establishing the EEAS makes it clear that the EEAS is a 'functionally autonomous' body, which was judged to be a loss for the Parliament as it had advocated for a more significant role for the Commission.[112] As an independent body, it is required to assist the High Representative in her three tasks of conducting the CFSP and acting in her capacity as Vice-President of the Commission and as President of the FAC.[113] The initial appointment by the High Representative of a large number of Commission officials to the EEAS has been viewed as an example of adopting a pro-Commission stance.[114] Nevertheless, the most recent appointments represent a departure from that approach.[115] It has also been noted that the EEAS can split into various streams represented by those transferred from DG RELEX of the Commission, and those whose loyalties lie with the Council.[116]

The Council decision prescribes a general consultative practice between the EEAS and the Commission on all matters of foreign policy,[117] therefore ensuring a significant role in policy shaping. One of the prominent roles envisaged for the EEAS is related to certain areas of the Commission's expertise, in particular the management of the EU external cooperation programmes. Most importantly, with regard to the ENPI, the EEAS decision requires all the documents relating to changes in basic regulations and programming to be prepared both in the EEAS and the Commission under the direct supervision of the responsible Commissioner. This requires not only a united vision of the neighbourhood, but also highly coordinated action on behalf of relevant units in the EEAS and the Commission. Besides,

---

[110]   Khaliq, note 90 above, 253; Wouters et al, note 73 above, 153.

[111]   G Avery, 'The EU's External Action Service: New Actor on the Scene', European Policy Centre, 28 January 2011, 2.

[112]   B Van Vooren, 'A Legal-Institutional Perspective of the European External Action Service' (2011) 48 *Common Market Law Review* 475, 482.

[113]   Arts 1, 2; Council Decision 2010/427/EU Establishing the Organisation and Functioning of the European External Action Service [2010] OJ L201/30.

[114]   Morillas, note 79 above, 129.

[115]   Among 10 appointments (six definite and four suggested), five candidates are representatives of the Member States, three candidate have a Commission background, one candidate is from the Council and the appointment of the last candidate is the result of a reshuffle within the EEAS; 'High Representative/Vice President Catherine Ashton makes a number of new appointments in the European External Action Service', Press Release, IP/12/1195, 9 November 2012.

[116]   Hillion and Lefebvre, note 88 above, 7.

[117]   Art 3, note 113 above.

although the EEAS is to assist both the Council and the Commission, its very success depends on successful cooperation between the Council and Commission.[118]

For instance, the Medium Term Programme for a renewed European Neighbourhood Policy for the period 2011–2014, derived from the Office of the High Representative, was ultimately presented as a joint working document.[119] The latter identifies the actions to be undertaken within this period and assigns the responsibility to relevant institutions, and most significantly allocates a role to the EEAS, often jointly with relevant Commission DGs, in the majority of the areas of cooperation. The EEAS's leadership became prominent, for instance in establishing the European Endowment for Democracy – a financial support mechanism potentially competing with those deployed by the Commission.[120]

On the other hand, if a smooth cooperation is ensured between the Commission and the Council via the role of the High Representative and the EEAS, then it strengthens the executive branch vis-à-vis the Parliament, which so far has been supportive of the Commission in this institutional interplay.

The Parliament continued displaying its activism in the post-Lisbon era. Despite its limited consultative role over the EEAS decision, it took a strong position on the issues of the Commission's involvement in the new service, as well as the institutional accountability of the EEAS.[121] The Lisbon Treaty also expanded the role of the Parliament in the conclusion of international agreements, where the consent procedure has become a general rule.[122] The Parliament has to be informed at all stages of the negotiation procedure, and because its consent will ultimately be required, it is considered that the latter's opinions would have to be taken into account even at the negotiation phase.[123] In line with its proactive attitude, the Parliament has already demonstrated a willingness to turn the consent procedure into a force to be reckoned with in the case of the SWIFT agreement.[124] Particularly important for the neighbourhood is the Parliament's consent to the conclusion of association agreements, which will provide another outlet for its influence in neighbourhood matters, as association agreements are expected to be concluded in the East.[125]

---

[118] Blockmans and Laatsit, note 85 above, 157.

[119] Joint Staff Working Paper, A Medium Term Programme for a Renewed European Neighbourhood Policy 2011–2014 COM (2011) 303, 25 May 2011.

[120] See Chapter 6, section 6.3.3.

[121] Hillion and Lefebvre, note 88 above, 4; Khaliq, note 90 above, 256; Morillas, note 79, above 129.

[122] Art 218(6) TEU.

[123] P Eeckhout, *EU External Relations Law*, 2nd edn (Oxford, OUP, 2011) 199; R Corbett, 'The Evolving Roles of the European Parliament and of National Parliaments' in Biondi and Eeckhout (eds), note 74 above, 248–61, 249–50.

[124] The Parliament threatened to withdraw its consent if its opinions were not taken into account in negotiating the SWIFT agreement with the US on the exchange of financial information related to terrorists; 'SWIFT: European Parliament votes down agreement with the US', European Parliament, Plenary Session, 11 February 2010.

[125] 'European Parliament Remains Divided over Signing of Association Agreement with Ukraine', *KyivPost*, 13 December 2012; European Parliament Resolution containing the European Parliament's Recommendations to the Council, Commission and the European External Action Service on the Negotiation of the EU–Armenia Association Agreement (2011/2315(INI)) 18 April 2012; European Parliament Report containing the European Parliament's Recommendations to the Council, Commission and the European External Action Service on the Negotiation of the EU–Georgia

Nevertheless, no amendments have been made regarding the Parliament's involvement in CFSP matters, as it would have been an encroachment on the intergovernmental nature of this policy, raising democratic and legitimacy concerns.[126] The Lisbon Treaty merely transfers the consultation duty to the High Representative instead of the Presidency under Article 36 TEU. Following her appointment to the office the High Representative pledged to cooperate closely with the Parliament. However, the collaboration commenced from a low note following Baroness Ashton's first appearance in the Parliament, where her competence came to be doubted.[127] On the other hand, the regularity of appearances of the High Representative in front of the EP and its Foreign Affairs Committee indicate a certain extent of accountability.[128]

Although the Parliament has been given credit for gaining a significant diplomatic role over the years,[129] at times national interests play their part even within the latter. Its role as a diplomatic actor has to a certain extent been damaged in the South Caucasus with its 2010 Resolution No 2216. In particular, the EP requested the Armenian government to withdraw forces from occupied territories around the Nagorno-Karabakh enclave, a condition which is not in accordance with the Madrid 'Basic Principles' setting the possible framework for the conflict resolution supported by the EU.[130] This stance has not been particularly welcomed by the diplomats in the EEAS and the Member States, and had a chilling effect on EU–Armenia relations, where Armenia perceived the Resolution to be pro-Azerbaijani.[131]

To summarise the legal-institutional aspects of the ENP, they represent a complex interplay between various actors, at times with divergent interests. The Lisbon Treaty, with the creation of the office of the High Representative and the EEAS,

Association Agreement (2011/2133(INI)) 27 October 2011; Report containing the European Parliament's recommendations to the Council, the Commission and the European External Action Service on the negotiations of the EU–Azerbaijan Association Agreement, (2011/2316(INI)) 18 April 2012.

[126] Instead of the Presidency, the High Representative must currently consult the Parliament on the basic choices of foreign policy, Art 36 TEU; H Sjursen, 'The EU's Common Foreign and Security Policy: The Quest for Democracy' (2011) 18 *Journal of European Public Policy* 1069, 1073; F Mancini, *Democracy and Constitutionalism in the European Union: Collected Essays* (Oxford, Hart Publishing, 2000) 65.

[127] 'Parliament Grills Ashton for "Specific" Answers', *Euractiv*, 3 December 2009.

[128] Speech/10/82, 10 March 2010; Catherine Ashton High Representative/Vice President, Speech to the European Parliament's Foreign Affairs Committee, European Parliament Brussels, Speech/10/120, 23 March 2010; Catherine Ashton EU High Representative for Foreign Affairs and Security Policy and Vice President of the European Commission, Speech to the European Parliament on the creation of the European External Action Service, European Parliament Strasbourg, Speech/10/310, 7 July 2010; Speech/10/315, 16 June 2010; Speech Catherine Ashton High Representative of the Union for Foreign Affairs and Security Policy/Vice-President of the European Commission Statement at the European Parliament debate on the Middle East Peace Process European Parliament Strasbourg, Speech/09/584, 15 December 2009; speech on Myanmar, Speech/12/273, 17 April 2012; speech on North Africa and the Arab World, Speech/11/054, 6 July 2011; speech on the Report on Human Rights in the World and the EU's policy in the matter, Speech/12/178, 17 April 2012.

[129] Thym, note 46 above, 225; Raube, note 49 above.

[130] European Parliament Resolution on the Need for an EU strategy for the South Caucasus (2009/2216(INI)) 20 May 2010, para 8.

[131] Van Hoof, note 91 above, 291.

contributes to the already existing complexity. The role of the High Representative and the EEAS in bridging the existing gaps cannot be taken for granted: it instead depends on personalities and– cooperation between the Council and the Commission.

3.3 EU EXTERNAL COMPETENCE AND ENP

As a policy combining various areas of EU external action the ENP raises issues of competence and the appropriate legal basis for any binding legal measure.

The scope of the policy is very broad as mentioned in the introduction to this chapter. It was the intention of the Commission to make the ENP a 'comprehensive policy' cutting across the rationale of EU foreign relations. Craig identifies four rationales for EU external relations, including the external dimension of the internal market, implied competence of the EU, the EU's role as an important international player in development cooperation and humanitarian aid and aid to third countries, and finally the security rationale embodied in the CFSP and ESDP.[132] If this rationale is translated into the legal framework of EU external action, then the ENP appears to cross over different types of EU competences and its entire legal order.

3.3.1 Across the Spectrum of EU External Competence

Identifying a correct legal basis is essential for the validity of any EU external measure,[133] as it is linked to the principle of conferral of powers defining and limiting the Union competences.[134] As noted earlier, the latter is as important for EU external competence, as it is for internal competence.

The Rome Treaty contained few express provisions on external action, and their number was gradually expanded through Treaty amendments in the process of 'legalisation' or 'constitutionalisation' of EU foreign policy.[135] The express external provisions include those particularly dedicated to external actions, such as CCP, development policy etc, and those provisions including external aspects for internal policies, eg monetary union or environment.

---

[132] Craig, note 101 above, 423–24.
[133] *Opinion 2/00* [2001] ECR I-09713, para 5.
[134] Art 5(1) and (2) TEU.
[135] Original provisions were (as codified before the Lisbon Treaty) Arts 131–133 EC on CCP and Art 300 EC on concluding international agreements, Art 310 EC on association agreements, Arts 302–304 EC on relations with the UN, Council of Europe and the OECD. Later on Art 170 EC on cooperation in research and technological development and Art 174(4) EC on environmental cooperation added in the SEA. The EU Treaty added Art 111 EC on monetary policy and Arts 177–181 on development cooperation. The Amsterdam Treaty added Art 133(5) on trade agreements in services and the commercial aspects of intellectual property. The Nice Treaty added Art 181a EC on economic, financial and technical cooperation.

The external competence of the EU, however, stretches beyond the express powers in the Treaties due to the doctrine of 'implied powers'. In its seminal *ERTA* judgment the Court of Justice ruled that external competence might arise from other non-express Treaty provisions and measures adopted within those provisions.[136] This was subsequently refined and somewhat expanded in *Kramer* and *Opinion 1/76*. External competence was implied on the basis of mere existence of an internal competence, where the internal objective would be best achieved via an external measure, embodying the idea of 'effectiveness'.[137] These cases also provided a ground for the notion of 'parallelism' describing the implied external powers: external power exists in parallel with the internal decision-making capacity.[138] The latter has been criticised for its failure to capture the essence of implied powers. Instead the 'principle of complementarity' has been advocated: the external competence is required to achieve an objective with an express internal power.[139]

While the cases noted above primarily concerned the issue of existence of external competence as such, later the nature of the competence acquired prominence. The main issue of contestation therefore was whether a competence is exclusive or shared between the then Community and the Member States. As a general rule the competence is assumed to be shared, unless there are clear indications as to its exclusive nature.[140] However, there are certain qualifications to this general rule.

In addition to indications in the Treaties,[141] shared competence is said to arise when (a) internal competence has not been yet exercised, (b) an international agreement covers issues falling under the competence of both the EU and the Member States,[142] (c) the EU's external role is confined to minimum domestic requirements, and finally (d) where competences exist at the same time, rather than one at the expense of another.[143] Within the latter instance when competences exist simultaneously, two types of competence have been identified, including 'coexistent' and 'concurrent' or 'truly shared'.[144] The Court of Justice went on to

---

[136] Case 22/70 *Commission v Council* [1971] ECR 263, para 16.

[137] Joined Cases 3, 4 and 6/76 *Cornelis Kramer and Others* [1976] ECR 1279, paras 20, 30–33; *Opinion 1/76 on the Draft Agreement Establishing a Laying-up Fund for Inland Waterway Vessels* [1977] ECR 741, paras 3–4; A Dashwood, 'Implied External Competence of the EC' in M Koskenniemi (ed), *International Law Aspects of the European Union* (Leiden, Martinus Nijhoff, 1998) 113–23, 119–20, 122.

[138] T Tridimas and P Eeckhout, 'The External Competence of the Community and the Case-Law of the Court of Justice: Principle versus Pragmatism' (1994) 14 *Yearbook of European Law* 143, 151; A Dashwood, 'The Attribution of External Relations Competence' in A Dashwood and C Hillion (eds), *General Law of EC External Relations* (London, Sweet and Maxwell, 2000) 115–38, 128.

[139] According to Dashwood, if parallelism was taken literally, then a different conclusion would have been reached in *Opinion 1/94*; Dashwood, note 138 above, 130.

[140] D O'Keeffe, 'Exclusive, Concurrent and Shared Competence' in Dashwood and Hillion (eds), note 138 above, 179–99, 193.

[141] For instance Art 208 TFEU (former Art 177 EC) makes it clear that the actions of the EU and the Member States complement each other.

[142] *Opinion 1/78 on International Agreement on Natural Rubber* [1979] ECR 02871, para 60.

[143] I MacLeod, ID Hendry and S Hyett, *The External Relations of the European Communities* (Oxford, Clarendon Press, 1996) 63–64.

[144] A Rosas, 'The European Union and Mixed Agreements' in Dashwood and Hillion (eds), note 138 above, 200–20, 205.

establish the doctrine of pre-emption, said 'normally' to apply to shared competences.[145] Accordingly, if the Union has adopted any measures to exercise its powers internally or externally, the Member States can no longer act.[146] These parameters are therefore relevant for identifying not the existence, but rather the exclusive or shared nature, of the competence.[147]

Exclusive competence, on the other hand, is characterised by an arrangement whereby the Member States no longer have a power to act, that is when the competence has been 'completely' transferred to the Union at the expense of the Member States.[148] Prior to the Lisbon Treaty exclusive competence was defined with reference to the grounds giving rise to exclusivity. These would include the cases where there are express provisions in the Treaties to that effect, where the scope of internal measures of institutions have presumed so,[149] where internal measures contain external provisions,[150] and where the effective exercising of internal power could be achieved only in combination with external powers.[151]

Thus, the external competence of the EU before the Lisbon Treaty could best be described as a complex web of express and implied ways of exercising external action, which at times was shared with the Member States. The vast nature of the cooperation offered through the ENP inevitably involved areas where the competence was exclusive, such as CCP, or shared, such as development cooperation, as well as areas where the EU could not act without its Member States, such as the CFSP.

Matters were also complicated by the divided constitutional framework of the EU. From the outset the ENP was designed to be a 'comprehensive' policy, suggesting that its elaborate content would cross the EU's multi-pillar legal order. For instance, the Action Plans with the South Caucasian states envisage cooperation on foreign and security policy, economic development, poverty reduction, cooperation on trade-related issues, development of the energy sector, cooperation in the field of justice, freedom and security, conflict resolution, the fight against terrorism and other matters.[152] This cross-pillar dimension has been considered to be an important aspect of the ENPs security rationale: various specific objectives eventually contribute to the overall security objective.[153] It is the complexity of security issues challenging the EU in the neighbourhood which requires diffusion

---

[145] M Cremona, 'The Draft Constitutional Treaty: External Relations and External Action (2003) 40 *Common Market Law Review* 1347, 1364.

[146] Case 22/70 *Commission v Council* [1971] ECR 263, para 17.

[147] Cremona, note 66 above, 221.

[148] O'Keeffe, note 140 above, 181.

[149] For instance when maximum harmonisation is achieved; *Opinion 1/94 Competence of the Community to Conclude International Agreements Concerning Services and the Protection of Intellectual Property* [1994] ECR I-5267, para 96.

[150] *Opinion 1/94*, para 95.

[151] *Opinion 1/76*, paras 4 and 7; O'Keeffe, note 140 above, 181.

[152] EU–Armenia Action Plan, EU–Georgia Action Plan, EU–Azerbaijan Action Plan. Available at www.ec.europa.eu/world/enp.

[153] Cremona and Hillion, note 17 above, 24.

of various elements from different pillars.[154] Therefore, not only the aims of the policy, but also its very content, have been assembled around the security concerns of the EU.[155]

Thus, the ENP prior to the Lisbon Treaty could be qualified as a joint venture between the Member States, the Community for the issues under the first pillar, and the broader European Union for the second and third pillars.[156] While this aspect of the ENP was considered to be 'a clear innovation' of the new policy,[157] it nevertheless raised the old issues of legal basis and competence. The relevance of competence matters came to the fore particularly when the ENP documents raised the possibility of concluding new bilateral agreements with the neighbours to reflect the intense level of cooperation on offer.[158]

Prior to the Lisbon Treaty there were suggestions that the new 'neighbourhood' agreements would likely be concluded as association agreements based on Article 310 EC jointly by the Community and the Member States.[159] That mixity will be a way ahead for the new agreements was not doubted. Mixity has been noted to have prevailed over the last two decades for a number of reasons.[160] It represents the 'political compromise' agreed by the Member States to abandon delimitation of competence.[161] Most importantly, mixity allows for accommodating the interests of Member States who prefer the latter as it ensures a right of veto,[162] as well as their presence and visibility on the international stage.[163]

The largely anticipated type of new agreement would have been a standard mixed agreement with the EC and Member State participation. More innovative options would have been based on former Article 24 EU for the CFSP and Articles 308 and 310 EC.[164] Nevertheless, the first new agreement to be negotiated in the neighbourhood, the so-called 'new enhanced agreement' with Ukraine soon

[154] D Lynch, 'The Security Dimension of the European Neighbourhood Policy' (2005) 40 *International Spectator* 33, 35.

[155] Zaiotti, note 20 above, 148.

[156] Cremona and Hillion, note 17 above, 20.

[157] M Comelli, 'The Challenges of the European Neighbourhood Policy' (2004) 3 *The International Spectator* 97, 105–06.

[158] Wider Europe Communication, 17; ENP Strategy Paper, 3; Commission Communication, Strengthening the European Neighbourhood Policy COM(2006) 726 final, 4 December 2006 (hereinafter Communication on Strengthening the ENP) 4–5.

[159] C Hillion, 'A New Framework for the Relations between the Union and its East-European Neighbours' in M Cremona and G Meloni (eds), *The European Neighbourhood Policy: A New Framework for Modernisation?*, EUI Working Papers, LAW 2007/21, 147–54, 149, 151; M Cremona, 'The European Neighbourhood Policy: More than a Partnership?' in M Cremona (ed), *Developments in EU External Relations Law* (Oxford, OUP, 2008) 244–99, 290.

[160] C Timmermans, 'Opening Remarks – Evolution of Mixity since the Leiden 1982 Conference' in Hillion and Koutrakos (eds), note 51 above, 1–8, 2.

[161] Wouters et al, note 73 above, 180–81.

[162] Rosas, note 144 above, 201–02.

[163] R Schütze, 'Federalism and Foreign Affairs: Mixity as a (Inter)-national Phenomenon' in Hillion and Koutrakos (eds), note 51 above, 57–86, 81.

[164] M Cremona, 'The European Neighbourhood Policy as a Framework for Modernisation' in F Maiani, R Petrov and E Mouliarova (eds), *European Integration without EU Membership: Models, Experiences, Perspectives*, EUI Working Papers, MWP 2009/10, 5–15, 12.

turned into an association agreement.[165] The choice of association agreements is also an indication in favour of mixity, as they are the oldest type of the mixed agreements.[166] The conclusion of the new agreements as association agreements seemed to be inevitable.

Concluding a new agreement through other legal bases, such as the then Article 300 EC, Article 308 EC or Article 181a EC would not have marked a step forward in relations with the Eastern partners for a number of reasons.[167] Signing an agreement falling short of 'special, privileged links' as interpreted by the Court in *Demirel* in relation to the association agreement with Turkey[168] would not have proved a major development or a step change in the relationship which the ENP intended to embody. Besides, it was no longer necessary to make a political distinction, as in the case of Europe Agreements with the CEE states and the PCAs with the post-Soviet states.[169] Moreover, association agreements were already in place with some Southern neighbours as noted in Chapter 1, and offering less beneficial cooperation to the Eastern neighbours would not have been seen as advantageous, even more so when taking into account that the policy was originally initiated to advance relations with the Eastern partners.

The mixed nature of such agreements would have introduced a major brake on the progress of the policy, as their negotiation, signature and ratification would have required a few years.[170] In addition to the complexities of the mixity brought about by competence issues, concluding a binding Treaty with the neighbouring countries was not yet desirable for another reason. The first few years of formulating and establishing the ENP were characterised by indecisiveness as to the level of integration the EU was willing to commit to.[171] This in practice meant a lack of clarity as to the nature of the cooperation offered and the possibility of accessing the internal market, which in addition to political considerations constitute the factors influencing the choice of the type of international agreement.[172]

Furthermore, any new agreement would have become part of the EC/EU legal order and would have implied legal obligations for the institutions and the

---

[165] 'EU–Ukraine Start Negotiations on New Enhanced Agreement', IP/07/275, 2 March 2007.

[166] The first examples of association agreements were those concluded with Greece and Turkey in 1961 and 1963 respectively: the Member States participated alongside the EC; Maresceau, note 68 above, 16.

[167] Cremona, note 159 above, 290.

[168] Case 12/86 *Demirel v City of Schwabisch Gmund* [1987] ECR 3719, para 9; P Van Elsuwege and R Petrov, 'Article 8 TEU: Towards a New Generation of Agreements with the Neighbouring Countries of the European Union?' (2011) 36 *European Law Review* 688, 693; Cremona, note 145 above, 1365; Hillion, note 159 above, 149–50.

[169] C Hillion, 'Mapping-Out the New Contractual Relations between the European Union and its Neighbours: Learning from the EU–Ukraine "Enhanced Agreement"' (2007) 12 *European Foreign Affairs Review* 169, 175–76.

[170] It has been estimated that nearly three years usually pass between the signature and conclusion of a mixed agreement: F Hoffmeister, 'Curse or Blessing? Mixed Agreements in the Recent Practice of the European Union and its Member States' in Hillion and Koutrakos (eds), note 51 above, 249–68, 256.

[171] See section 3.4.3.3 below.

[172] MacGoldrick, note 52 above, 182.

Member States.[173] To avoid such consequences and to acquire certain flexibility in identifying the direction the policy was to take, other instruments, soft law in nature, were preferred in the short term to the new agreements.[174] The practice of opting out for soft law to avoid concluding cumbersome mixed agreements is not unique to the ENP and has been noted to have developed in the 1990s.[175] Nevertheless, it has been taken to a new level within the ENP as discussed further.

As noted earlier, despite the formal abolition of the pillar structure there is no single legal framework for conducting all external action on behalf of the EU. The Lisbon Treaty codified the EU competences by providing a list of shared and exclusive competences in Articles 3 and 4 TFEU. However, the competence list has not eliminated the complexities in defining the EU external competence, especially when some of these provisions create confusion as to established boundaries of the EU competence. For instance, Article 3(2) TFEU on the exclusive competence to conclude international agreements has been criticised for extending the competence beyond its previously understood boundaries.[176] Similarly, Article 216(1) TFEU codifying the implied competence doctrine, is wider in scope than the previously accepted limits of such competence,[177] and is said to have failed to translate the intricacies of the case law, namely on the distinction between exclusive and shared competences.[178]

In terms of the Treaty structure, the TFEU contains the majority of the legal basis for external action within Part Five on the Union's external action. The express provisions include the association of the overseas countries and territories, the CCP, development cooperation and humanitarian aid, restrictive measures, and EU relations with international organisations.[179] In addition to the express provisions directly dealing with external action, other provisions provide for the conclusion of international agreements or international cooperation.[180] However, the CFSP still stands separately in Chapter 2 of the TEU Title V, which includes general provisions on external action and specific provisions on the CFSP.

Importantly, the CFSP has not been classified as a shared competence under Article 4 TFEU. This has been considered to be a deliberate attempt at highlighting the distinctive nature of the CFSP.[181] If classified as a shared competence, on

---

[173] Case 181/73 *Haegeman v Belgium* [1974] ECR 449, para 5; Case 104/81 *Hauptzollamt Mainz v Kupferberg* [1982] ECR 3641, para 22.

[174] For instance, the Action Plans with South Caucasian states provide for the possibility to review the content and renew the documents; B Van Vooren, 'The Hybrid Legal Nature of the European Neighbourhood Policy' in Maiani, Petrov and Mouliarova (eds), note 164 above, 17–27, 22–23.

[175] A Rosas, 'Mixed Union – Mixed Agreements' in Koskenniemi (ed), note 137 above, 125–48,143.

[176] Dougan, note 102 above, 656.

[177] Cremona, note 66 above, 225.

[178] Eeckhout, note 123 above, 113.

[179] Arts 198, 206–207, 208–214, 215, 220 TFEU.

[180] Art 79(3) on readmission agreements, Art 186 on research and technological development cooperation, Art 191(4) on environmental cooperation and agreements, Art 217 on association agreements, Art 219 on monetary cooperation.

[181] M Cremona, 'The Two (or Three) Treaty Solution: The New Treaty Structure of the EU' in Biondi, Eeckhout and Ripley (eds), note 74 above, 40–61, 54.

the basis of the doctrine of pre-emption it could have led to the 'corruption' of the CFSP, that is to say the exclusion of the Member States after the Union has acted.[182] Article 40 TEU therefore makes it clear that the CFSP is 'opposed' to the competences in Articles 3–6 TFEU.[183] The delimitation of the CFSP and other foreign policy areas can be even more problematic than before, since the former applies to 'all areas of foreign policy', and there is no longer a separate list of objectives to make reference to, which potentially contributes to 'blurring the boundaries' between competences.[184] Therein lies the 'paradox' of the interaction between CFSP and other areas of EU external action: it has a starkly different character, yet it intends to cover 'all areas' of external action.[185] Others view the reference to 'all questions relating to the Union's security, including the progressive framing of a common defence policy' as a qualifying statement suggesting the distinctness of the CFSP.[186]

Thus, the distinct nature of the CFSP is confirmed due to the preservation of its 'specific rules and procedures' and the unanimity requirement.[187] It can be contested therefore that mixity will be a constant feature of EU foreign policy, and therefore also the ENP with its inherent security component.

Whether the new Article 8 TEU as a neighbourhood-specific provision brings added value to the legal aspects of the ENP is considered next.

3.3.2 Article 8 TEU and its Added Value

Although Article 8 TEU does not refer to the ENP, it has clearly been drafted with the latter in mind. The initial ideas around the new neighbourhood policy found their way into EU documents at the same time as the IGC was deliberating on the constitutional future of the EU, inter alia reflecting on the EU role in its neighbourhood.[188] Many aspects of the article appear to codify the already existing ENP practices in rather familiar language, giving grounds for it to be considered as a 'constitutionalisation' of the ENP.[189]

Precisely because of such 'constitutionalisation' it can be argued that the new provision transgressed the current ENP framework to create a legal obligation for

---

[182] Craig, note 101 above, 182; P Eeckhout, 'The EU's Common Foreign and Security Policy after Lisbon: From Pillar Talk to Constitutionalism in EU Law After Lisbon' in Biondi, Eeckout, Ripley (eds), note 74 above, 266–91, 268; M Cremona, 'The Union's External Action: Constitutional Perspectives' in G Amato, H Bribosia and B de Witte (eds), *Genesis and Destiny of the European Constitution* (Brussels, Bruylant, 2007) 1173–218, 1194–97.

[183] A Dashwood et al, *Wyatt and Dashwood's European Union Law*, 6th edn (Oxford, Hart Publishing, 2011) 932.

[184] A Dashwood, 'Mixity in the Era of the Treaty of Lisbon' in Hillion and Koutrakos, note 51 above, 351–66, 363; C Herrmann, 'Much Ado About Pluto? The "Unity of the Legal Order of the European Union" Revisited' in Cremona and de Witte (eds), note 46 above, 19–51, 47.

[185] Eeckhout, note 123 above, 172.

[186] Dashwood et al, note 183 above, 905.

[187] Art 24(1) TEU.

[188] Van Elsuwege and Petrov, note 168 above, 690.

[189] de Baere, note 47 above, 16.

the Union to develop relations with its neighbours. Prior to the Lisbon Treaty there were no specific constitutional obligations or requirements to develop a close cooperation with neighbours. Although the ENP proclaimed the intention of the EU to develop a special relationship, it nevertheless did not create traditional legal obligations for the EU. Article 8 TEU therefore qualifies the ENP in legal terms and establishes certain conditions for the cooperation to be pursued with Union's neighbours. Nevertheless, this suggestion does not mean that the new provision has changed the rationale or the motivation behind the ENP. On the contrary, the ENP rationale discussed in Chapter 1 appears to remain intact within the new provision.

Article 8 TEU cannot be restricted to the ENP in terms of its geographic scope, as the provision does not even mention the policy. It can therefore be used to pursue relations with Russia for instance, although whether this would be desirable for the latter is doubted in the view of the reference to the values of the EU as the basis for cooperation, assuming certain level of conditionality. Furthermore, the targeting of the 'neighbouring countries' in the provision does not necessarily mean that these states have to share a border with the Union.[190] The ENP itself includes states which share no border with the Union, Armenia and Azerbaijan being examples.

The main question concerning the added value of Article 8 TEU is tied to its potential of providing an additional legal basis, as well as new instruments. It is in this respect that the article can be criticised the most. First of all, the provision has been noted to be full of 'indefinite legal terms'.[191] This is most certainly true when considering the first paragraph:

> The Union shall develop a special relationship with neighbouring countries, aiming to establish an area of prosperity and good neighbourliness, founded on the values of the Union and characterised by close and peaceful relations based on cooperation.

Although the notions of 'special relationship', 'area of prosperity and good neighbourliness', 'close and peaceful relations based on cooperation' etc are not precise legal categories, some explanation for their legal content can be found in the previous practices of the EU. For instance, 'special relationship' can be associated with 'privileged links' identified in *Demirel* with regard to association agreements.[192] The other references in Article 8(1) TEU were discussed in Chapter 2 in relation to the objectives of the policy.

That Article 8 incorporates the political nature of the neighbourhood policies is apparent particularly in its textual location within the amended Treaties.

As noted previously, Part Five of the TFEU on external action includes all areas of the EU external action, apart from the CFSP which is located in the TEU. This

---

[190]   Van Elsuwege and Petrov, note 168 above, 692.
[191]   D Hanf, 'The European Neighbourhood Policy in the Light of the New "Neighbourhood Clause" (Article 8 TEU)' in E Lannon (ed), *The European Neighbourhood Policy's Challenges* (Brussels, College of Europe Studies, PIE Peter Lang, 2012) 109–23, 110.
[192]   Van Elsuwege and Petrov, note 168 above, 692.

has created a basis for some to argue that the TEU does not provide a legal basis other than for the CFSP.[193] Such an understanding would therefore exclude the potential role of Article 8 TEU as a legal basis if by 'legislation making' we also assume conclusion of international agreements. However, the latter expressly imposes a legal commitment on the EU towards its neighbourhood, and therefore cannot be dismissed altogether.[194] Besides, Van Elsuwege and Petrov observe that support for the proposition that the TEU contains a legal basis for concluding international agreements can be found in Article 216(1) TFEU.[195]

The exclusion of Article 8 TEU from both Part Five TFEU and Title V TEU on External Action of the EU and CFSP is peculiar nevertheless. In contrast to any other external policy, it is incorporated among the Common Provisions in Title I of the TEU. A number of considerations can explain this placement of the provision. The easiest explanation might be that the special place accorded to the neighbourhood provision suggests a certain prominence attributed by the EU to its neighbourhood, ie relations with neighbours can no longer be overlooked. This is nevertheless rather simplistic and other motives can be found for the isolation of Article 8 TEU. First, providing an article expressly referring to the neighbours of the EU in the first part of the TEU is said to be aimed at accentuating the distinct nature of this policy compared to the accession process.[196] Unlike the Draft Constitutional Treaty, where the corresponding Article I-57 was closely followed by the article on membership, the Lisbon Treaty clearly avoided similar textual proximation.[197] Perhaps, taking into account that the ENP did not satisfy the willing states in their eagerness to join the EU, the Lisbon Treaty was adamant in highlighting the very distinct nature of the cooperation on offer. Since the membership perspective was excluded for the Southern neighbours following the Moroccan application,[198] and because at the stage of the adoption of the Lisbon Treaty states like Ukraine and Georgia continued expressing their European aspirations, it can be argued that Article 8 TEU, in the spirit of the ENP, was directed at the exclusion of the Eastern partners.

Others argue that the provision does not necessarily have to be viewed as excluding accession and it can be viewed as a 'pre-pre-accession' stage in a certain context.[199] If the willing 'European' neighbouring country transforms itself politically and economically under the ENP there is nothing in the Treaty to prevent an accession application under Article 49 TEU. However, the very existence of a separate neighbourhood clause offering similar, yet distinct cooperation is

---

[193] Dougan, note 102 above, 637.

[194] Chalmers and others consider that the TEU establishes two external policies, that is the neighbourhood policy and the CFSP; D Chalmers, G Davies and G Monti, *European Union Law: Text and Materials*, 2nd edn (Cambridge, CUP, 2010) 640.

[195] Van Elsuwege and Petrov, note 168 above, 696.

[196] M Cremona, note 145 above, 1365.

[197] Treaty Establishing a Constitution for Europe [2004] OJ C310/47.

[198] The application was rejected on the ground that Morocco is not a 'European' state: Council Decision of 1 October 1987, cited in Europe Archives, Z 207.

[199] D Bechev and K Nicolaidis 'From Policy to Polity: Can the EU's Special Relations with its "Neighbourhood" Be Decentred?' (2010) 48 *Journal of Common Market Studies* 475, 494.

included in the Treaty to create scope for political manoeuvre depending on the context. After all, even the association agreements with the CEE states were not initially concluded for accession purposes, and had rather undergone a 'political reorientation' after the Copenhagen summit in 1993.[200] It can thus be argued that Article 8 TEU secures a legal margin for avoiding the application of Article 49 TEU.

Besides, the exclusion of the neighbourhood policies from Part Five TFEU indicates that the latter is not merely *another type* of EU external action. It is more a policy or a framework rather than a type of external *legal* action. Thus, reflecting the ENP's former cross-pillar nature, Article 8 TEU incorporates all those areas where the EU has an external competence as noted before, and as such can be considered to be a cross-Treaty provision rendering the ENP a cross-Treaty policy. By incorporating both TFEU external action and CFSP and being included within the TEU Title 1 on common provisions, it is a linking provision between the two Treaties.[201] So, if Article 8 essentially combines aspects of already established areas of EU external action, what does it offer in terms of its legal effect?

As noted earlier it is a 'special relationship' based on the EU values that is offered to the neighbouring states. However, the article is said to be vague on the instruments to be used for establishing such 'special relationship'.[202] According to Article 8(2) TEU:

> The Union may conclude specific agreements with the countries concerned. These agreements may contain reciprocal rights and obligations as well as the possibility of undertaking activities jointly . . .

The question to ask is whether this provision provides for a new type of agreement to be concluded with the neighbours. Despite the general nature of Article 8(2) TEU, certain observations can be made in the context of Article 8(1) TEU. If the reference to 'special relationship' is to denominate association agreements, such interpretation would suggest that Article 8 TEU is simply an instance of Article 217 TFEU, and therefore has no added value as such since association agreements can be concluded on the basis of the latter instead. Nevertheless, due to the fact that association agreements have been most recently linked to the accession process, that would strip Article 8 TEU of its rationale of excluding membership. The reluctance of the EU and certain Member States to conclude the association agreement with Ukraine on the basis of article 217 TFEU reinstates the distinction of the neighbourhood policies.[203] On the other hand, association agreements can be concluded *also* in replacement of enlargement.[204] The

---

[200] M Maresceau and E Montaguti, 'The Relations between the European Union and Central and Eastern Europe: A Legal Appraisal' (1995) 32 *Common Market Law Review* 1327, 1342.

[201] M Cremona, The Two (or Three) Treaty Solution, note 181 above, 46.

[202] R Dragneva and K Wolczuk, 'EU Law Export to the Eastern Neighbourhood' in PJ Cardwell (ed) *EU External Relations Law and Policy in Post-Lisbon Era* (Hague, TMC Asser Press, 2012) 217–240, 233.

[203] Lannon and Van Elsuwege, note 41 above, 292.

[204] E Fierro, *The EU's Approach to Human Rights Conditionality in Practice* (The Hague, Martinus Nijhoff, 2003) 27.

association agreements concluded with the Southern neighbours can be seen as such an example. Concluding similar-type agreements on the basis of Article 8 TEU will serve as a confirmation of distinctions as to the political aims of the cooperation.

Besides, the concept of 'special relationship', although associated with the terminology of *Demirel*, can give rise to an alternative interpretation. Article 8 TEU does not provide any 'blueprint' for the special relationship.[205] It requires a 'special', but not 'specific' relationship. The 'special' nature of the relations can be understood in wide terms to include different levels of proximity the cooperation might offer, be it a deep and comprehensive free trade area (DCFTA) or more enhanced cooperation in one particular area only. The imprecision of the language of Article 8 TEU can be considered to incorporate a long-standing feature of the ENP, namely its flexibility: the vaguer the provision, the more flexible is the EU in its choice of actions in the neighbourhood. Moreover, the vague language of this clause is considered to create scope for the optimal application of the principle of differentiation, discussed below.[206]

In comparison with Article 217 TFEU, the neighbourhood provision is notable for its more reserved language. While the former is clear on any association agreement containing reciprocal rights and obligations, Article 8 TEU merely notes that the agreement 'may contain reciprocal rights and obligations'. The reference to 'reciprocal rights and obligations' does not necessarily mean equal rights: even within association agreements responsibilities can be different.[207] If the new agreement were to reflect any conditionality, then it will be followed by a presumption of distinct legal obligations for the parties.

Thus, one can conclude that Article 8 TEU does not specifically oblige the EU to conclude association agreements with the neighbouring states. Instead it leaves a margin for flexibility in deciding what level of cooperation to offer. Instead of association agreements the EU might wish to opt for a low-key agreement. If so, it can rely instead on Article 212 on economic, financial and technical cooperation with third countries. That might be, for instance, a partnership and cooperation agreement, which, according to *Simutenkov*, also entails 'close' political and economic relations,[208] rendering Article 212 TFEU a potential legal basis for any new partnership agreement in the neighbourhood.[209] Eventually, the preference for either Articles 217 or 212 TFEU or 8 TEU will be one of a political and not legal nature.[210]

---

[205] Hanf, note 191 above, 110.

[206] P Van Elsuwege, 'Variable Geometry in the European Neighbourhood Policy: The Principle of Differentiation and its Consequences' in Lannon (ed), note 191 above, 59–84, 72.

[207] Macleod, Hendry and Hyett, note 143 above, 369.

[208] Case C-265/03 *Igor Simutenkov v Ministerio de Educación y Cultura and Real Federación Española de Fútbol* [2005] ECR I-02579, paras 27–28.

[209] R Petrov, 'Association Agreement versus Partnership and Co-operation Agreement. What is the Difference?' Eastern Partnership Community, 27 January 2011. Available at www.easternpartnership.org.

[210] M Cremona, 'Coherence in European Union Foreign Relations Law' in Koutrakos (ed), note 95 above, 55–92, 85.

It will rather become a signal as to the particular neighbour's status in relations with the EU,[211] as well as the 'international posture' of the Union.[212]

Therefore, at risk of tautology, one might suggest that the choice of legal basis would not be about the legal basis itself, ie the competence itself, but rather about the political message which such choice would herald. In addition to the importance of the political message, procedural considerations will also play a part in choosing Article 212 TFEU as a legal basis which requires a qualified majority vote as opposed to the unanimity requirement under Article 217 TFEU.[213]

Within this context one is inclined to note that Article 8 TEU is not *stricto sensu* necessary for concluding an agreement with a neighbouring state, as other Treaty provisions would be used in its absence. Even Article 216 TFEU could have been used for concluding new agreements as a new fallback provision embodying implied competence. In view of Article 37 TEU Wessel notes that Article 216 TFEU can be used to conclude agreements extending beyond the competences of the TFEU, therefore incorporating CFSP elements.[214]

Nevertheless, Article 8 TEU contains a legal obligation for the EU, therefore indicating the potential for serving as a separate legal basis. If it is to be used as such on its own merit, the following developments can be envisaged. In continuation of the standing practice on the political dialogue clauses, together with a stronger commitment envisaged in Article 21 TEU and the emphasis on the EU values in Article 8 TEU, a provision on political dialogue will necessarily be included in any new agreement concluded under the neighbourhood clause, therefore requiring mixity for the agreement. If the new neighbourhood agreements also contain other aspects of CFSP, then technically there is nothing to suggest that Articles 8 and 37 TEU cannot be used in combination. Nevertheless, the TEU itself would not be sufficient for concluding such an agreement, as the procedural rules are contained in the TFEU for all EU agreements.[215] For the first time the Lisbon Treaty provides for a uniform procedure for negotiating and concluding international agreements in Article 218 TFEU with certain variations concerning the CFSP.[216]

---

[211] Cremona, note 181 above, 46.

[212] P Koutrakos, 'Legal Basis and Delimitation of Competence in EU External Relations' in Cremona and de Witte (eds), note 46 above, 171–98, 173.

[213] R Petrov, 'The New EU Ukraine Enhanced Agreement versus the EU–Ukraine Partnership and Cooperation Agreement: Transitional Path or Final Destination?' in Maiani, Petrov, Mouliarova (eds), note 164 above, 39–45, 41.

[214] R Wessel, 'Cross-pillar Mixity: Combining Competences in the Conclusion of EU International Agreements' in Hillion and Koutrakos, note 51 above, 30–54, 51.

[215] Art 8 TEU bears a general character with no reference to procedural rules unlike its counterpart in the initial version of the Draft Constitutional Treaty, which made reference to the procedure for concluding agreements in Art III-227 (currently Art 218 TFEU). However, this initial reference was excluded from the final text of the Draft Constitutional Treaty, and likewise did not find a place in the Lisbon Treaty.

[216] Art 218(3) allows the Council to nominate a negotiator when the agreement exclusively or predominantly concerns the CFSP. Art 218(6) excludes the Parliament's assent or consultation when it comes to the CFSP, while Art 218(8) ensures unanimity for CFSP-related agreements.

Thus, Article 8 TEU ultimately guarantees certain flexibility as to the TFEU legal bases, allowing for provision shopping, which affects the level of cooperation a given agreement provides for. It should be also noted that Article 8 TEU provides for the conclusion of agreements setting a comprehensive framework for relations between the parties.[217] The sectoral agreements are concluded instead on the basis of sector-specific provisions. For instance, the EU–Israel Agreement on Conformity Assessment and Acceptance of Industrial Products relies on Article 207 TFEU for CCP and Article 218 TFEU for procedural rules. Similarly, visa facilitation agreements concluded with a number of neighbouring states rely on Articles 77 and 218 TFEU as their legal bases.[218]

Lastly, the significance of Article 8 TEU should be considered specifically in relation to the values of the EU. The reference to the EU values as the foundation of the relations with the neighbours suggests that any new agreement will have to make a provision on adherence to democracy and other values identified in Article 2 TEU, and therefore should be assessed positively. On the other hand the incorporation of 'values' as essential provisions in the EU agreements has been an established practice since the early 1990s.[219] For instance, the PCAs with South Caucasian states provide for a separate title on 'Cooperation on matters relating to democracy and human rights', representing the 'strong version' of the so-called 'standard clause' included in EU trade agreements.[220] The essential element clause fulfils a number of functions, including the linking of political reforms with the assistance provided,[221] as well as establishing a political dialogue necessitating mixity in light of *Opinion 1/94*.[222] Hence, Article 8 TEU does not make a new contribution in this context.

[217] Van Elsuwege and Petrov, note 168 above, 696.

[218] EU–Armenia Visa Facilitation Agreement, signed on 17 December 2012; 'Commission Proposal for a Council Decision concerning the conclusion of the Agreement between the European Community and the Republic of Armenia on the facilitation of the issuance of visas' COM (2012) 707 final, 27 November 2012, s I; EU–Georgia Visa Facilitation Agreement [2011] OJ L52/34; 'Commission Proposal for a Council Decision on the conclusion of the Agreement between the European Union and Ukraine amending the Agreement between the European Community and Ukraine on the facilitation of the issuance of visas' COM (2012) 266 final, 5 July 2012, s I.

[219] M Cremona, 'Values in EU Foreign Policy' in M Evans and T Tridimas, *Beyond Established Legal Orders: Policy Interconnections between the EU and the Rest of the World* (Oxford, Hart Publishing, 2011) 275– 315, 304. COM(95) 216 final, 23 May 1995.

[220] The strong version is related to the classification of this provision as essential, the serious breach of which can lead to the termination of the agreement. Common Art 2 of the PCAs with the South Caucasian countries states that respect for democracy promotion, inter alia, as defined in international law is an essential element of the agreements and the partnership established by the latter. Art 2 contains references to international documents, including the UN Charter, the Helsinki Final Act and the Charter of Paris for a New Europe; B Berdiyev, 'The EU and Former Soviet Central Asia: An Analysis of the Partnership and Cooperation Agreements' (2003) 22 *Yearbook of European Law* 463, 469; S Peers, 'From Cold War to Lukewarm Embrace: the European Union's Agreements with the CIS states' (1995) 44 *International and Comparative Law Quarterly* 829, 831; M Cremona, 'Human Rights and Democracy Clauses in the EC's Trade Agreements' in N Emiliou and D O'Keeffe (eds), *The European Union and World Trade Law: After the GATT Uruguay Round* (Chichester, Wiley, 1996) 62–77, 66–69.

[221] PJ Cardwell, 'Mapping Out Democracy Promotion in the EU's External Relations' (2011) 16 *European Foreign Affairs Review* 21, 34.

[222] As long as there is a provision on political dialogues, the Court is unwilling to attack mixity. 'The European Union's Role in Promoting Human Rights and Democratisation in Third Countries', Communication from the Commission to the Council and the European Parliament, COM (2001) 252

Besides, the reference to the Union's values in Article 8 TEU can be viewed as a specific instance of the general duty to promote the EU values in external relations, discussed in Chapter 2. Thus, it has been noted that in the view of Article 21 TEU any association agreement in the Eastern neighbourhood would incorporate an obligation to adhere to values in Article 2 TEU.[223] In this context it can be suggested that even in the absence of the reference to EU values in Article 8 TEU, democracy promotion would have been part of the cooperation required by the common list of objectives.

On the other hand, the language of Article 8 TEU and the common provisions on democracy promotion can be argued to pertain to more than merely political dialogue. According to the former the relationship between the EU and its neighbours is 'founded on the values' of the Union instead of those values being 'promoted'. Article 8 TEU therefore reflects the value dimension of the ENP, which is not an objective per se, but rather a precondition for cooperation linked to the conditional aspect of its methodology. In this context Article 8 TEU clarifies the conditionality element of the ENP by making a reference to the 'values of the Union' instead of previously used 'shared values'.[224] The combination of Article 8 and 2 TEU therefore clarifies the normative basis of the policy.

The incorporation of the conditionality element into Article 8 TEU is suggestive of a number of scenarios. First, the relationship is established only when there is adherence to EU values. The first scenario goes against the practice of the ENP, as relations were established with the majority of the neighbours, including those with authoritarian regimes or authoritarian political tendencies. Second, it can mean that the cooperation between the parties cannot progress unless a certain level of adherence is secured. The proponents of the second approach suggest that enhanced relations with the neighbours cannot progress unless they adhere to the EU values, and therefore Article 8 TEU imposes a strict conditionality on the ENP.[225] Related to this is the third interpretation, which can be argued to be an instance of the previous one, that is whether the direct reference to the EU values in the article suggests that the adherence to the Union's values will be a prerequisite for concluding a new agreement. As mentioned earlier, association agreements have been in force with certain Southern neighbours despite a lack of commitment to democracy and human rights. On the other hand, the halting of the initiation of the Ukrainian association agreement can be interpreted as a result of non-adherence to the Union's values as required by Article 8 TEU. The process has been suspended due to the political developments in the country, including the selective application of justice and the criminal prosecution of the former

---

final, 8 May 2001, 9; Rosas, note 144 above, 218; Eeckhout, note 123 above, 127; S Peers, 'EC Frameworks of International Relations: Co-operation, Partnership and Association' in Dashwood and Hillion (eds), note 138 above, 160–76, 164–65.

[223] Petrov, note 209 above.
[224] Van Elsuwege and Petrov, note 168 above, 693–94. On 'shared values' see section 3.4.3.2 below.
[225] Hanf, note 191 above, 116–17.

Prime Minister Yulia Timoshenko.[226] Nevertheless such interpretation is somewhat hasty as the progression of relations with the South Caucasian states demonstrates.[227]

Ultimately the conclusion of a new agreement, even if it does not alter the pattern of democracy promotion, will nevertheless contribute to the strengthening of the ENP legal framework.

3.4 INSTRUMENTS AND METHODOLOGY

The ENP legal framework is remarkable in a number of aspects. First, the formation of the policy and of its main concepts has largely taken place via soft law instruments. Almost 10 years later, the main framework documents are still soft law in nature. Second, many ENP instruments are the progeny of the accession practice, deployed here with a different purpose. Lastly, few binding instruments were involved in the formulation of the policy. Some of them, including the previously existing PCAs in the East, did not entirely sit well with either the ambitions of the policy or the aspirations of some of the neighbours. Moreover, the choices of the main instruments had to be reconciled with the ENP methodology, reflective of the objectives of the policy. These features of the ENP legal instruments will be considered in turn, followed by a discussion on the ENP methodology.

3.4.1 Soft Law: Rendering Cooperation Possible

Among the instruments through which the EU institutions exercise their competence, Article 288 TFEU includes recommendations and opinions alongside the regulations, directives and decisions.[228] In contrast with regulations, directives and decisions, the former have no binding force. The practice of non-binding instruments is not restricted to recommendations and opinions only, and the ENP provides a striking example of the tendency to rely on instruments not directly mentioned in the Treaties.[229] Currently, the instrumental framework of the ENP comprises a wide range of tools with no traditional legal obligations, which can be brought under the general concept of soft law, suggesting no binding force per se, but capable of producing certain practical or even legal effects.[230]

The majority of the instruments through which the main ENP concepts were elaborated can be argued to have been aimed at securing the neighbours' willingness to cooperate towards achieving the objectives of the policy, while simultaneously benefiting from it. Thus, the short-term practical effect was the engagement

---

[226] Conclusions, Foreign Affairs Council on Ukraine, 10 December 2012; 'EU–Ukraine Association Pact: Avoiding Ratification', *EU Observer*, 2 May 2012.

[227] See Chapter 6, section 6.4.

[228] Former Art 249 EC.

[229] Hillion, note 63 above, 309.

[230] See the definition in L Senden, *Soft Law in European Community Law* (Oxford, Hart Publishing, 2005) 112.

of the neighbours, with a view to possible legal effects in the medium and long term. The main ideas of the ENP were circulated through the conclusions of the Council and the European Council, Commission communications and other policy documents, including papers and non-papers, joint letters, statements, EP resolutions and recommendations. None of these documents have binding legal force, and neither do they require any legal bases to authorise the EU institutions to act.[231] The Action Plans with neighbouring states, as the main policy document, are not legally binding on either the Union or the relevant countries.

The various soft law instruments perform various tasks within the ENP. Based on Senden's categorisation, Van Vooren identifies preparatory and informative, interpretative and decisional, and steering instruments within this range.[232] It should be noted that one instrument can perform more than one function at times. Most of the Commission's initial communications were preparatory in nature as they intended to give shape to the policy. At the same time, they could be considered to be steering instruments as they allowed the Commission to take the policy in its favoured direction. The Council conclusions were also steering in nature, as they were indicative for the Commission as to the latter's preferences. For instance, the reduction of the free movement of persons ambition to merely visa liberalisation and better mobility is a result of the Council's 'steering' intervention. To the functions identified by Van Vooren, a supervisory function should also be added, as the Commission exercises monitoring via soft law instruments. In all these tasks soft law comprehensively enabled the elaboration of the initial concept of the policy, sufficient to engage the neighbours in a joint venture of securing EU interests. In this sense they were documents that were more political than legal in nature.

The choice of soft law instruments is not merely a continuation of a trend, it is rather a solution to problematic legal issues, as well as a means to a political end. First of all, to adopt any of the measures mentioned above the EU institutions did not require the appropriate legal basis to be established. By drafting the ENP based on soft law, the Union institutions succeeded in avoiding 'long competence discussions and "pillar politics" from stalling and undermining policy development and coherence'.[233] As noted earlier, any proposals for a new agreement would have stalled the relationship before it began and would have become an integral part of the EU legal order, which was not yet desirable inter alia for practical considerations.

These considerations were linked to the fact that though the concept of the ENP appeared rather swiftly, the same cannot be said about its content. Here, the non-binding instruments offer another advantage, as they allowed a progressive conceptualisation of the policy without tying the hands of the EU institutions, supporting the general presumption that soft law allows for responsiveness to

---

[231] Cremona, note 159 above, 264.
[232] B Van Vooren, *External Relations Law of the EU and the European Neighbourhood Policy: A Paradigm for Coherence* (London, Routledge, 2011) 181; Senden, note 230 above, 118–19.
[233] Cremona and Hillion, note 17 above, 30–31.

political considerations.[234] Flexibility together with 'incrementalism' has been identified as one of the advantages of the soft law. While flexibility or adaptability of the soft law allows the agenda to be shaped and adapted when the circumstances change, incrementalism refers to the potential of these measures to change into something 'harder' in legal terms.[235]

The flexibility of the soft law instruments is linked to the absence of legal terms and the general nature of their content. The expression of the flexibility becomes most apparent as regards the Action Plans, which are the central instruments in defining the scope of the cooperation between the EU and each of the neighbours. Although they offered unhindered adoption and incorporation of both the CFSP and other external competences with the involvement of different EU institutions,[236] they nevertheless come across as little more than a political 'wish list'. As pointed out by the Commission, these documents are 'political' in nature,[237] which inter alia suggests that few expectations were attached to their legal effects.

On the other hand, the Commission intended to draft the Action Plans to be more than declaratory in nature: '[i]ndividual priorities identified in the Action Plan aim to be both ambitious and realistic, and formulated in a manner as precise and specific as possible so as to allow concrete follow-up and monitoring of the commitments taken by both sides'.[238] Nevertheless, in practice the content of the Action Plans is much criticised in terms of 'precision' and 'specificity'.[239] Despite their 'quasi-informal character',[240] the Action Plans did not prove easy to adapt or amend. Although they provided for the possibility of regular reviews or updates, none of the Action Plans in the South Caucasus has been revised. For instance, Georgia's willingness to highlight the priority of conflict resolution in its Action Plan after the 2008 war with Russia was rejected by the Commission based on a pretext that the Action Plans were long-term documents and they were not intended to address immediate concerns.[241]

Although the soft law allowed legal complications for the ENP to be avoided, it simultaneously resulted in minimising legal effects, as there are no legal obligations for which the parties can be held accountable. It is for this reason that soft

---

[234] J Klabbers, *The Concept of Treaty in International Law* (The Hague, Kluwer Law International, 1996) 163.

[235] DM Trubek, P Cottrell, and M Nance ' "Soft Law", "Hard Law", and European Integration' in G De Burca and J Scott (eds), *Law and New Governance in the EU and the US* (Oxford, Hart Publishing, 2006) 65–94, 74; B Van Vooren, 'The European Union as an International Actor and Progressive Experimentation in its Neighbourhood' in Koutrakos (ed), note 95 above, 147–71, 161.

[236] Van Vooren, note 235 above, 161.

[237] Wider Europe Communication, 16.

[238] 'Commission Communication on the Proposals for Action Plans under the European Neighbourhood Policy' COM (2004) 795 final, 9 December 2004, 3.

[239] See Chapter 5 below.

[240] M Cremona, 'The European Neighbourhood Policy' in A Ott and E Vos (eds), *Fifty Years of European Integration: Foundations and Perspectives* (The Hague, TMC Asser Press, 2009) 221–45, 232.

[241] M Merlingen and R Ostrauskaite, 'EU Peacebuilding in Georgia: Limits and Achievements' in S Blockmans, J Wouters and T Ruys (eds), *The European Union and Peace Building: Policy and Legal Aspects* (The Hague, TMC Asser Press, 2010) 269–93, 282.

law has been viewed to be a contradiction in itself.[242] A related criticism raised in domestic context is that soft law, although raising expectations, does not always have the ability to deliver in practice.[243] The Action Plans themselves cannot materialise into a set of political and economic reforms on a grand scale. First of all, their implementation depends on the adoption of binding legal instruments.[244] Second, their existence for the longer term fails to signify the level of commitment and change the ENP promised to introduce into the cooperation between the EU and its partners. Therefore, the Action Plans should be viewed as primarily *scene-setting* instruments, which are to be followed by legally binding measures expressing the commitments of the ENP.

The ENP legal framework, however, did not progress by making a leap from soft law towards hard law. Instead new instruments have been developed which are viewed as 'second-generation' ENP instruments, among which Van Vooren includes the memoranda of understanding on energy cooperation, association agenda, and mobility partnerships.[245] Each of these instruments is telling in terms of the ENP's political nature.

The first Association Agenda was established with Ukraine in 2009 to replace the EU–Ukraine Action Plan and to prepare the ground for the new association agreement.[246] It is considered that the Association Agenda has arguably 'hardened' the soft law framework of the Action Plans, and reorientated the core of cooperation from the PCA implementation towards the new agreement.[247] It can also be suggested that the Association Agenda was introduced as an alternative to revising the Action Plan, which would not have signified any novelty or advancement in the relationship. Arguably, the establishment of the Association Agenda was to mark an improvement in the relations with Ukraine, which by 2009 was the front runner in the region. During the course of 2013 an association agenda is to be established with Moldova, demonstrating significant efforts to deliver on the cooperation agenda,[248] as well as with Georgia and Armenia, whose progress has also been evaluated mostly as positive.[249] No such possibility is envisaged for Azerbaijan or Belarus.[250]

Mobility partnerships were introduced by the Commission in a global instrument in 2008, and applied later also to the ENP countries.[251] It is argued that new soft law instruments are introduced to encourage the neighbours and ensure their continuous engagement. By replacing the prospect of free movement of persons

---

[242] Klabbers, note 234 above, 157–61.

[243] Trubek et al, note 235 above, 66.

[244] Van Elsuwege, note 206 above, 70.

[245] Van Vooren, note 232 above, 203–10.

[246] EU–Ukraine Association Agenda, 2.

[247] Van Vooren, note 235 above, 169.

[248] Joint Communication, 'European Neighbourhood Policy: Working towards a Stronger Partnership', JOIN (2013) 4 final, Brussels, 20 March 2013, 4–5.

[249] Ibid.

[250] No Action Plan has been adopted for Belarus to this date.

[251] 'Commission Communication on Strengthening the Global Approach to Migration and the European Pact on Immigration and Asylum' COM (2008) 611 final, 8 November 2008.

with mobility issues, the mobility partnerships focus on migration, readmission and visa policy, in order to ensure secure border control. In the East they were established with Moldova in 2008, followed by Georgia in 2009 and Armenia in 2011.[252] Their soft law nature also leaves their success in the hands of the governments of not only the partner countries, but also the participating EU Member States. The difficulty in monitoring them has also been highlighted as an outstanding problem.[253]

As to the memorandum of understanding on energy cooperation, it cannot strictly be viewed as a 'second generation' instrument, since the memorandum of understanding was signed with Azerbaijan in 2006, the same year as the respective Action Plan. Although the latter establishes no legal obligations for the parties, it nevertheless sets the ground for 'future possible discussion between the parties concerning a legal agreement'.[254] The significance of this instrument can be linked to the EU's energy interests: this was a specific document indicating the core of the cooperation between the parties in addition to the more comprehensive Action Plan. It can be argued therefore that the security rationale also required a diversification of the soft law toolbox of the ENP. That such trends might turn into a composite part of the ENP in the East is supported by the rumoured possibility of offering an alternative framework of cooperation to Azerbaijan. Initiated by the latter, a so-called 'Strategic Modernisation Partnership' would in substance acknowledge Azerbaijan's special role within the EaP.[255] If the proposal is to materialise it might be accommodated within the current ENP framework and therefore further diversify its instruments. Alternatively, if the new framework is to abandon the principle of conditionality (which seems to be the preference of the Azerbaijani government), then it might suggest the ultimate non-application of the ENP and its conditionality to the country concerned. However, it can be argued that any such new framework will have to be reconciled with Article 8 TEU.

3.4.2 Hard Law Instruments: Adaptation and 'Softening'

The main hard law instruments within the ENP are the Eastern PCAs and the Association Agreements with the Southern neighbours inherited from the

---

[252] Press Release, 'The European Union and the Republic of Moldova Enter into a Mobility Partnership', IP/08/893, Brussels, 5 June 2008; Press Release, 'The European Union and Georgia Enter into a Mobility Partnership', IP/09/1853, Brussels, 30 November 2009; Press Release, 'Better Mobility between the EU and Armenia', IP/11/1257, 27 November 2011.

[253] RH Sagrera, 'Moldova: Pioneering Justice and Home Affairs Cooperation with the EU in the Eastern Partnership?' Moldova's Foreign Policy Statewatch, Issue 30, July 2011, 3.

[254] Memorandum of Understanding on a Strategic Partnership between the European Union and the Republic of Azerbaijan in the Field of Energy, 12.

[255] I would like to thank Professor P van Elsuwege for bringing these developments to my attention. 'Azerbaijan Chief Paints Rosy Picture on EU Visit', *EU Observer*, 21 June 2013; 'Aliev Seeks EU Strategic Partner Status', *European Voice*, 19 June 2013.

previously existing bilateral relations, with the ENPI envisaged to continue their financing.[256]

The continuation of the PCAs in the ENP was apparent from the fact that the development and implementation of the Action Plans would start from analysis of the achievements and failures of the PCAs. The ENP Strategy Paper further stressed that the Action Plans will be aimed at the implementation of the provisions of the PCAs.[257] For instance, the Action Plans with the three South Caucasian countries make reference to the PCA in certain priority areas.[258] In fact, when including the countries of the South Caucasus in the ENP, the Commission inter alia stressed the need for partner countries to make further progress in implementing their respective PCAs.[259] Linking the new and old instruments in this fashion has been considered to provide the Action Plans with an interpretative function as regards the PCAs.[260]

Besides, the parties were to benefit from the institutional structures of the PCA which were already in place for the purposes of political dialogue and monitoring.[261] Certain new features of the ENP such as the new system of monitoring and new incentives were noted to potentially 'instil dynamism in the relationship' and cause 'political reorientation'.[262] Indeed, the ENP documents attempted to revive the contractual obligations between the parties by stressing that full implementation of the provisions of already existing agreements was a necessary precondition for any new development.[263]

However, the enhanced focus on the PCAs within the Action Plans per se did not inject new dynamics into the entire spectrum of relations between the parties. The ENP as a primarily security-driven policy was to be based on the PCA framework concerned predominantly with trade and economic development, and was symbolic of the EU's distant attitude in the first phase of its relations with the South Caucasus.

First, the trade-orientated core of the PCAs is relevant for the issues of economic integration without having a major impact on other areas of cooperation including political reform. Although, the ENP benefited from the PCA structures in terms of the continuation of political dialogue, which distinguished the PCAs from a standard trade agreement,[264] the essential clauses with their negative conditionality did not correspond to the positive conditionality the ENP meant to introduce.

---

[256] Wider Europe Communication, 15; European Council Conclusions on Wider Europe – New Neighbourhood, 19–20 June 2003; Art 2, ENPI Regulation.

[257] ENP Strategy Paper, 15; B Ferrero-Waldner, 'Europe's Neighbours – Towards Closer Integration', speech given at the Brussels Economic Forum, 22 April 2005.

[258] Priority Area 5 of EU–Armenia Action Plan; EU–Georgia Action Plan, General Actions 4.3, 4.5; EU–Azerbaijan Action Plan, Priority Area 7.

[259] ENP Strategy Paper, 11.

[260] Van Vooren, note 232 above, 182.

[261] ENP Strategy Paper, 7.

[262] Hillion, note 63 above, 319, 321.

[263] Wider Europe Communication, 17.

[264] Peers, note 20 above, 829; Koutrakos, note 99 above, 364.

Second, domestic elites were not necessarily keen on the PCA implementation. For instance, in Georgia the post-Rose Revolution authorities were not willing to implement the PCA, as it had been concluded by the previous government. In Armenia, the efforts to implement the PCAs through a national programme encompassing major legislative and institutional reforms have been mainly left on paper, currently serving as a point of reference for ad hoc reforms within the Action Plan. In Azerbaijan the first efforts to implement the PCA materialised on paper only in 2010.[265] The inability of the PCA Cooperation Councils to adopt legally binding decisions also contributed to the stagnation of the PCA implementation alongside the reinforced ENP commitments.

Another important hard law instrument is the ENPI Regulation on financial assistance which was introduced to replace the previous instruments financing the neighbourhood.[266] Although the details of the financial assistance with reference to democracy promotion are addressed in Chapter 6, the correlation between the Regulation as a hard law instrument and the soft law framework of the ENP should be pointed out. The Regulation itself mainly relies on soft law instruments. First of all, the Action Plans serve as a point of reference for establishing assistance priorities.[267] Also the Commission Communications and Council Conclusions are included within the ENPI 'policy framework', serving as a point of reference and therefore making the framework as wide as possible.[268] The actual allocation is also undertaken on the basis of soft law instruments, ultimately resulting in the 'softening' of the assistance provision.

The predominant role of the soft law within the ENP instruments and the unclear position of the hard law instruments should be viewed within the context of policy methodology.

3.4.3 ENP Methodology

The ENP has been noted to contain 'diluted versions of enlargement methodologies'.[269] The 'diluted' presence of conditionality is most certainly apparent. The ENP methodology is further weakened, with the conflicting nature of the principles of conditionality, joint ownership and differentiation reflecting the interest-based core of the ENP.

---

[265] See Chapter 5, section 5.3.

[266] The previous instruments were established under Council Regulation No 1279/96 concerning the provision of assistance to economic reform and recovery in the New Independent States and Mongolia [1996] OJ L165; Council Regulation No 99/2000 concerning the provision of assistance to the partner states in Eastern Europe and Central Asia [2000] OJ L12; Council Regulation No 1488/96 on financial and technical measures to accompany (MEDA) the reform of economic and social structures in the framework of the Euro-Mediterranean partnership as amended by Council Regulation No 780/98 [1998] OJ L113/3, and Council Regulation No 2698/2000 [2000] OJ L311/1.

[267] Art 3, ENPI Regulation.

[268] Art 3, ENPI Regulation.

[269] Magen, note 18 above, 386.

3.4.3.1 Accession Progeny and the Principle of Conditionality

The enlargement policy is recognised as one of the most successful instruments of EU foreign policy.[270] The success of this policy should be seen in its perceived ability to increase political stability and prosperity and to boost radical economic reforms based on adoption of a new transparent and stable legislative and regulatory framework in the candidate countries by a sole promise of membership of the Union. A number of rounds of accession have increased the number of the EU Member States to 28.[271] Most notably, the 2004 accession round prompted the formulation of the ENP: the latter was launched 12 days after the enlargement of 1 May 2004.[272]

Although nearly all official ENP-related documents are silent on the obvious similarities of the ENP and the enlargement process,[273] from the early stages of the circulation of the Wider Europe idea, it was clear that the Union would heavily rely on its experience with the enlargement process.[274] Besides its perceived success, there is another side to the rationale of relying on the enlargement experience. It derives from the presumption that in times of crisis the EU has a tendency of drawing on its previous policies 'even if it is clearly no longer appropriate'.[275] The urgency of reacting to new challenges compelled the EU institutions to rely on the existing resources and maximise previous experiences,[276] which is not surprising due to the transfer of human resources discussed earlier.

The similarities with the pre-accession strategy are particularly striking as regards the instruments, such as the legal and policy documents, and mechanisms of the ENP. The ENP's soft law framework includes the Country Reports resembling the Opinions and Progress Reports with the CEE countries during the pre-accession process. The Country Reports accompanying the ENP Strategy Paper

[270] Wider Europe Communication, 5; M Cremona, 'The European Neighbourhood Policy: Legal and Institutional Issues', Center on Democracy, Development and the Rule of Law, Stanford Institute for International Studies, Working Paper No 25, 2 November 2004, 6–7; M Cremona, 'Enlargement: A Successful Instrument of EU Foreign Policy?' in T Tridimas and P Nebbia (eds), *European Union Law for the Twenty-First Century* (Oxford, Hart Publishing, 2004) 317–414, 397; Hillion, note 63 above, 311; W Kok, 'Enlarging the European Union: Achievements and Challenges', Report to the European Commission, EUI, 19 March 2003; Comelli et al, note 19 above, 210; M Smith, 'Enlargement and European Order' in C Hill and M Smith (eds), note 56 above, 270–91, 271.

[271] Croatian accession is the latest stage of the EU expansion. The country joined the Union on 1 July 2013.

[272] A Harasimowicz, 'European Neighbourhood Policy, 2004–2006: the Growing Need for Strategy' in Cremona and Meloni (eds), note 159 above, 81–94, 81.

[273] P Kratochvil, 'The European Neighbourhood Policy: A Clash of Incompatible Interpretations' in P Kratochvil (ed), *The European Union and Its Neighbourhood: Policies, Problems and Priorities* (Prague, Institute of International Relations, 2006) 13–28, 15.

[274] Prodi, note 30 above; C Hillion, 'The Copenhagen Criteria and their Progeny' in C Hillion (ed), *EU Enlargement: A Legal Approach* (Oxford, Hart Publishing, 2004) 1–22, 14; Kelley, note 10 above, 35.

[275] Magen, note 18 above, 401.

[276] L Delcour, 'Does the European Neighbourhood Policy Make a Difference? Policy Patterns and Reception in Ukraine and Russia' (2007) 7 *European Political Economy Review* 118, 122; Ott and Wessel, note 23 above, 48–49; Hillion, note 63 above, 310; G Meloni, 'Is the Same Toolkit Used during Enlargement Still Applicable to the Countries of the New Neighbourhood? A Problem of Mismatching between Objectives and Instruments' in Cremona and Meloni (eds), note 159 above, 97–111, 105.

presented the state of relations between the EU and each partner at the time, constructing the priorities for cooperation along the lines of the Copenhagen criteria.[277]

Based on the Country Reports, the Action Plans were elaborated in 2006 and established the main priorities for cooperation for a period of five years for the South Caucasian countries. In contrast to Accession Partnerships adopted by Council decisions based on former Article 308 EC Council Regulation,[278] the Action Plans have been endorsed by the Cooperation Councils established by the PCAs.[279] Adapted from the enlargement is also the mechanism of monitoring undertaken by the Commission on an annual basis since 2008.[280] Based on the results of the revision, the EU decides on the adaptation and renewal of the Action Plans, whereas in the case of the enlargement process the Union updates the priorities contained in the Accession Partnerships almost every year.[281]

The adaptation of the mentioned documents and mechanisms from the accession practice implies the attractiveness of its conditionality mechanism. Conditionality is described as the linking by an international organisation or a state of perceived benefits to another state to the fulfilment of economic and/or political conditions.[282] Elements of positive and negative conditionality were incorporated in the EU strategy of human rights and democracy promotion early on in 1991.[283] However, conditionality in EU foreign policy is most commonly identified with the positive conditions a candidate country must satisfy to become a member of the Union under Article 49 TEU. It is therefore the mechanism which allows the EU to use its 'power of attraction' to change and adapt its milieu.[284] Cremona links these conditions generally to foreign policy objectives, including good neighbourliness, settlement of border disputes, economic reforms and the strengthening of democracy.[285]

Conditionality is also classified as *ex ante* and *ex post*. The former refers to the fulfilment of certain conditions before establishing the relations, while the latter assumes the emergence of certain conditions after the relations have been established.[286] In the context of EU foreign relations, *ex-post* conditionality refers to the

[277] Magen, note 18 above, 407–08.

[278] C Hillion, 'Enlargement of the European Union: A Legal Analysis' in A Arnull and D Wincott (eds), *Accountability and Legitimacy in the European Union* (Oxford, OUP, 2002) 401–18, 416–17.

[279] See Chapter 6, section 6.2.1.

[280] See Chapter 6, section 6.2.2.

[281] E Baracani, 'The EU and Democracy Promotion: A Strategy of Democratisation in the Framework of Neighbourhood Policy?' in F Attina and R Rossi (eds), *European Neighbourhood Policy: Political, Economic and Social Issues*, The Jean Monnet Centre 'Euro-Med', Department of Political Studies: 2004, 37–57, 55.

[282] KE Smith, 'Engagement and Conditionality: Incompatible or Mutually Reinforcing?' in R Youngs (ed), *Global Europe: New Terms of Engagement* (UK, The Foreign Policy Centre, 2005) 28.

[283] Resolution of the Council and of its Member States on Human Rights, Democracy and Development, Bull EC No 11/1991, s 3.

[284] KE Smith, 'The Evolution and Application of EU Membership Conditionality' in M Cremona (ed), *The Enlargement of the European Union* (Oxford, OUP, 2003) 23–29, 136.

[285] Cremona, 'Enlargement', note 270 above, 400.

[286] Fierro, note 204 above, 98.

possibility of withdrawing support in case of serious breaches of defined obligations.[287] The ENP should be considered to include both elements of *ex-post* and *ex-ante* conditionality. Although it can be noted that for establishing relations within the ENP the neighbours did not have to satisfy any conditions, on its surface *ex-ante* conditionality is present in the policy as the further development of relations will depend on fulfilling certain criteria referring to the ENP positive conditionality.

3.4.3.2 Positive Conditionality à la Copenhagen?

The last two rounds of enlargement are considered to be unprecedented due to the definition of the accession criteria and the predictability of their application.[288] In addition, the Commission undertook a rigorous role of monitoring the progress of the candidate countries. The accession criteria were defined at the 1993 Copenhagen European Council opening the prospect of enlargement for the CEE states. They include:

1. stability of institutions guaranteeing democracy, the rule of law, human rights, and respect for human rights and respect for and protection of minorities;
2. a functioning market economy with the capacity to cope with competitive pressures and market forces within the EU;
3. ability to adopt the *acquis* and accept the aims of economic and political union.[289]

Following the European Council in Copenhagen certain other requirements were added, including the 'good neighbourliness' mentioned above.[290] In December 1995 the Madrid European Council added the requirement for the candidate state to adjust its administrative structures to ensure not only the adoption but also the implementation of the *acquis*.[291] The aim of this criterion is to assess the 'ability to take on the obligations of membership, including adhering to the aim of political, economic and monetary union'.[292]

An additional, unusual condition for membership, also referred to as the fourth Copenhagen criterion, is addressed not to the candidates but to the Union itself.[293] It refers to the Union's ability to absorb new Member States without stretching its institutional and other capacities,[294] which led to seeking an alternative to the enlargement.

---

[287] N Tocci, 'Comparing the EU's Role in Neighbourhood Conflicts' in Cremona (ed), note 159 above, 216–43, 221.

[288] Hillion, 'Enlargement', note 278 above, 405–07; Hillion, note 274 above, 3–4; A Inotai, 'The CEECs: From the Association Agreements to Full Membership?' in J Redmond and G Rosenthal (eds), *The Expanding European Union: Past, Present, Future* (London, Linne Rienner Publishers, 1997) 157–76, 159.

[289] Copenhagen European Council Conclusions, 21–22 June 1993, 12.

[290] See notes 133, chapter two.

[291] Tulmets, note 19 above, 31.

[292] European Council Conclusions, 15–16 December 1995.

[293] K Inglis, 'EU Enlargement: Membership Conditions Applied to Future and Potential Member States' in Blockmans and Łazowski, (eds), note 23 above, 61–92, 65–67.

[294] Copenhagen European Council, note 289 above, 13.

The Copenhagen criteria demonstrate the civilian power of the EU: the latter influences the transformation of the candidate countries through adding a 'coercive', though still civilian, element to its power.[295] Adopting enlargement-like conditionality was supposed to accord the ENP with a similar 'transformationist rationale'.[296] However, borrowing the conditionality principle from enlargement has not been a straightforward exercise.

First of all, the accession criteria have been replaced with the concept of 'shared values'.[297] Thus, the prospect of closer economic integration with the EU depends on the progress in demonstrating shared values.[298] It is said that the Commission officials included respect for human rights, including minority rights, the rule of law, good governance, the promotion of good neighbourly relations, and the principles of a market economy and sustainable development within the concept of 'shared values' based on accession criteria.[299] However, the progress of the ENP partners does not depend solely on the adherence to shared values, but also on the 'will and capacity to implement agreed priorities'.[300] It is therefore not clear whether the values should be adhered to as a precondition or alongside the priorities agreed.

Moreover, the reliance on the idea of 'sharedness' of the values undermines the nature of conditionality. First, it creates an impression that the adherence to the values is not questioned.[301] Second, the language of 'shared values' is problematic as it does not clarify whose values are at stake and potentially suggests that the EU *does* share certain values with its neighbours or shares them to a certain extent. Already at the stage of ENP formation it was obvious that few, if any, of the neighbouring states shared the values of the Union in practice. Therefore, the assumption that the EU 'shares' the values of Belarus, for instance, or any other authoritarian neighbour for that matter, first of all discredits the EU's normative image. Clearly this was not the intention behind the language of 'sharedness', and it is the EU values that are be promoted, which transpired from various ENP sources.[302] These values must have referred to the principles contained in the former Article 6 EU, as no 'values' were defined as such in the Treaties at the time.

In terms of conditionality, the concept of 'shared values' bears another risk linked to its abstract nature. Although following Article 8 TEU, it is clear that it is the *EU's* values that are to be shared by the neighbours, the language of 'values' is still rather vague. As noted by Leino and Petrov, the abstraction in the notion of 'common values' implies their very general nature and allows flexibility in terms

---

[295] Smith, note 270 above, 271; E Ridder, A Schrijvers and H Vos, 'Civilian Power Europe and Eastern Enlargement: The More the Merrier' in J Orbie (ed), *Europe's Global Role: External Policies of the EU* (Aldershot, Ashgate, 2008) 240–57, 244.

[296] Comelli et al, note 19 above, 210.

[297] Tulmets, note 19 above, 30.

[298] Wider Europe Communication, 4; ENP Strategy Paper, 8.

[299] Tulmets, note 19 above, 32.

[300] ENP Strategy Paper, 8.

[301] N Tocci, 'Can the EU Promote Democracy and Human Rights Through the ENP? The Case for Refocusing on the Rule of Law' in Cremona and Meloni (eds), note 159 above, 23–35, 28.

[302] ENP Strategy Paper, 12.

of their monitoring.[303] Thus, despite finding a footing in the EU legal framework, the concept of 'values' nevertheless provides scope for political choices in terms of which values to include or prioritise or what level of adherence to require. The 'sharedness' also creates an impression that the values have been defined and promoted jointly, thus linking the conditionality principle to joint ownership.[304]

Despite the vagueness of the language of 'shared values', some considered that the ENP conditionality was different as it moved away from political conditionality to more precise 'benchmarking'.[305] This view is perhaps based on the premise that the cooperation is based on the priorities defined in the Action Plans. Nevertheless the latter fall short of providing clear benchmarking, discussed further in Chapter 5 below.

Besides positive conditionality, the ENP also incorporates negative conditionality, referring to the possible adverse impact that can occur in relations between the parties once the preconditions are breached. The negative impact can take the form of suspension of aid, imposition of sanctions or even suspension of relations between the parties.[306] First of all, by incorporating the PCA, the policy inherits an element of negative conditionality implied in the 'essential element' clauses of these agreements. The ENPI Regulation also incorporates negative conditionality allowing for suspension of aid representing *ex-post* conditionality.[307] While Chapter 6 addresses the issue of assistance provision, suffice it to say here that negative conditionality is not a mechanism favoured by the EU.

3.4.3.3 Conditionality to What End?

One of the main peculiarities of borrowing the conditionality principle from enlargement is linked to the question of incentives, or 'disincentives' borrowing the language of Blockmans and Prechal.[308] The Wider Europe Communication made it clear that the development of a new cooperation through the ENP would not include the membership perspective.[309] At the outset there was a predominant scepticism among the commentators as to the ability of conditionality to boost reforms in the neighbourhood similar to the accession process without the membership promise at stake.[310]

---

[303] P Leino and R Petrov, 'Between "Common Values" and Competing Universals – The Promotion of the EU's Common Values through the European Neighbourhood Policy' (2009) 15 *European Law Journal* 654, 665–66.

[304] M Cremona, 'Values in the EU Constitution: the External Dimension', Center on Democracy, Development and the Rule of Law, Stanford Institute for International Studies, Working Papers, No 26, 2 November 2004, 10; Cremona, note 219 above, 303.

[305] R Rossi, 'The European Neighbourhood Policy' in Attina and Rossi (eds), note 281 above, 8–14, 11.

[306] Fierro, note 204 above, 100–01.

[307] Cremona, note 159 above, 284.

[308] S Blockmans and S Prechal, 'The European Integration Process: A Continuum of "Deepening" and "Widening"' in S Blockmans and S Prechal (eds), *Reconciling the Deepening and Widening of the European Union* (The Hague, TMC Asser Press, 2007) 1–12, 3.

[309] Wider Europe Communication, 5.

[310] C Hill and M Smith (eds), *International Relations and the European Union* (Oxford, OUP, 2005) 287–88; Cremona and Hillion, note 17 above, 39; Missiroli, note 37 above, 19.

At the time, the President of the Commission Romano Prodi asked 'Why should a less ambitious goal not have some effect?'[311] Indeed a less ambitious goal could have had certain effects, if only there had been the necessary political will to determine it. From the outset, the ENP documents have been rather ambiguous as to what is on offer for the neighbouring states in place of EU membership.

The urgency of establishing new relations with the neighbours, as well as determining the offer for all 16 of them, without disappointing the willing neighbours, compelled the Commission to turn 'to the well-known delaying strategy of constructive ambiguity'.[312] Indeed, ambiguity has been following the ENP incentives since the initiation of the policy. Initially, grand promises were voiced in the form of 'more than partnership and less than membership' and 'sharing everything, but institutions'.[313] The Wider Europe Communication referred to 'a stake in the EU's internal market and further integration and liberalisation to promote the four freedoms'.[314] Although the ENP Strategy Paper preserved the language of 'stake in the internal market',[315] the incentives of cooperation were narrowed in scope due to the intervention of the Council.

The Council then replaced the extension of the internal market with the possibility of 'participating progressively in the internal market and its regulatory structures', where the prospect of movement of persons was exchanged with enhanced cooperation on matters related to legal migration as noted before.[316] Thus, the lack of connection between the objectives for reform and the level of integration on offer turned the policy into a 'modernisation' framework.[317] The ambiguity surrounding the ENP incentives in the early years diminished the leverage of the EU in the neighbourhood and contributed to limited political support in the governing circles of the neighbouring states.[318]

Later it gradually transpired that a 'deeper economic integration' and an 'improved market access' are the watered-down incentives on offer.[319] Cremona considers that such integration would go significantly beyond a model free trade area (FTA) not necessarily with all four freedoms, but most importantly it will allow for flexible integration in different areas.[320] The DCFTA was the preferred form of the deeper economic integration,[321] which was confirmed in practice

---

[311] Prodi, note 30 above.

[312] Comelli et al, note 19 above, 213.

[313] Prodi, note 30 above.

[314] Wider Europe Communication, 4.

[315] ENP Strategy Paper, 8, 14.

[316] General Affairs and External Relations Council, Conclusions on Wider Europe – New Neighbourhood, 16 June 2003, endorsed at Thessaloniki European Council, 19– 20 June 2003. See also Chapter 2, note 87.

[317] Cremona, note 164 above, 9.

[318] D Helly, 'EU's Influence in its Eastern Neighbourhood: The Case of Crisis Management in the Southern Caucasus' (2007) 7 *European Political Economy Review* 102, 108.

[319] Communication on Strengthening the ENP, 3–4; General Affairs and External Relations Council, Presidency Progress Report, Strengthening the European Neighbourhood Policy, 18–19 June 2007, 3.

[320] Cremona, note 164 above, 12.

[321] Commission Non-paper, 'ENP – A Path towards Further Economic Integration', 3; Council Conclusions on European Neighbourhood Policy, 18 February 2008, 1.

when the negotiations on launching a DCFTA were commenced with Ukraine in 2008. In this way the integration itself has taken the role of an element of the ENP methodology.[322] Offering deeper economic integration as the core of the relationship went further than the previous relations with the ENP partners, while simultaneously neutralising short-term promises of becoming a part of the internal market. An ordinary FTA, characterised by removal of quotas and tariffs, would not have gone far in satisfying the ambitions of the neighbours. Besides, the association agreements with the South Mediterranean states already made provisions for FTAs. A 'comprehensive' FTA refers to liberalisation of trade in both goods and services, while a 'deep' FTA entails regulatory approximation and reduction of non-tariff barriers.[323]

Although defining the incentive as a DCFTA finally denoted the level of commitment that was to be reciprocated by the EU, it is a much smaller 'carrot' than 'sharing everything, but institutions', and one that cannot be considered as an overarching incentive.

In Georgia, following the Rose Revolution in 2003, within its marked pro-Western course the government set an unrealistic short-term objective of joining both NATO and the EU.[324] Offering anything less than membership was a clear disincentive, while the promise of the DCFTA materialised too late to sustain the political momentum. Moreover, the advantages of the DCFTA for Georgia at that stage were not straightforward, given the 'strongly liberal' economic course adopted by the national government.[325]

Despite its interests in the economic cooperation with the EU, Azerbaijan does not demonstrate much eagerness to integrate into the EU: the integration into 'the European and Euro-Atlantic political, security, economic and other institutions' constitutes a more general strategic goal of the country.[326] The ruling regime controlling the large revenues from the country's rich natural resources has no sense of urgency to integrate into the internal market.[327] The promise of the DCFTA is, therefore, hardly an incentive for the governing regime to transform itself. The opening of DCFTA negotiations is currently not an option for

---

[322] Cremona, note 240 above, 237–38.

[323] S Gstohl, 'What is at Stake in the Internal Market? Towards a Neighbourhood Economic Community' in Lannon (ed), note 191 above, 85–108, 98.

[324] Following the fraudulent 2003 parliamentary election in Georgia, public protests led to a change of power with pro-Western Mikhail Saakachvili becoming president in January 2004; G Kandelaki, 'Georgia's Rose Revolution: A Participant's Perspective', Special Report, United States Institute of Peace, Washington, July 2006, 4–5; National Security Concept of Georgia, Ministry of Foreign Affairs of Georgia, Tbilisi, 8 July 2005.

[325] N Popescu, 'ENP and EaP: Relevant for the South Caucasus?' in *South Caucasus: 20 Years of Independence* (Friedrich Ebert Stiftung, 2011) 316–34, 331.

[326] National Security Concept of the Republic of Azerbaijan, Ministry of Foreign Affairs, 23 May 2007.

[327] 'Azerbaijan: Vulnerable Stability', ICG, Europe Report No 207, 3 September 2010, 2–5; F Guliyev, 'Oil Wealth, Patrimonialism, and the Failure of Democracy in Azerbaijan', *Caucasus Analytical Digest* 02/09, Bremen, 4–5.

Azerbaijan which is not a member of the World Trade Organization (WTO) – a precondition for commencing any such negotiations.[328]

The cooperation with the EU is a 'priority' for Armenian foreign policy, seeking to strengthen its economic ties to compensate for its political and economic isolation in the region.[329] Although this would suggest that a DCFTA is a weighty incentive, Armenia nevertheless has strong military and economic dependence on Russia,[330] where its precarious position forces the pursuit of a 'complementarity policy'.[331] It could be suggested that the promise of EU membership with sufficient guarantees of Armenia's security would have incentivised the latter to make independent choices, especially in the view of the growing pressure exerted by Russia to join a competing project of the Eurasian Economic Community.[332]

The weaknesses of the ENP conditionality are not restricted to those mentioned. The language of conditionality has switched to emphasise partnership and differentiation.[333]

3.4.3.4 *Joint Ownership and Differentiation*

The rationale behind the ENP rooted in the security concerns of the EU could not rest solely on the conditionality mechanism, embodying hierarchical structure and asymmetry in the relationship, which is essentially a 'one way process'.[334] The 'profoundly asymmetrical power relationship' where the outsiders' dependence on the EU was unequal to the EU's dependence on the outsiders has been crucial for the transformation of the CEE countries.[335] However, the interests of the EU in its neighbourhood could not have been secured without the cooperation of the neighbours, and therefore the policy methodology is complemented by 'more compromising' measures.[336]

---

[328] Commission Communication, Eastern Partnership COM (2008) 823 final, 3 December 2008 (hereinafter Eastern Partnership Communication) 4.

[329] National Security Strategy of Armenia, Ministry of Foreign Affairs, 26 January 2007.

[330] Two Russian military bases are located in the country, and a Treaty on Friendship and Cooperation was signed in 1997. Russia has major stakes in various sectors of the Armenian economy, including banking and telecommunications. Armenia is one of the founding members of the Collective Security Treaty Organisation whereby Russia guarantees its security.

[331] S Vasilyan, 'The External Legitimacy of the EU in the South Caucasus' (2011) 16 *European Foreign Affairs Review* 341, 346; A Iskandaryan, 'Armenia–Russia Relations: Geography Matters' in A Hug (ed), *Spotlight on Armenia* (UK, Foreign Policy Centre, 2011) 54.

[332] The current members include Russia, Belarus and Kazakhstan; www.eurasec.com; 'Will Armenia Join EurAsEC? Russian President Medvedev is Pressing for the Three Observer Members of EurAsEc to Join as Full Members', *Commonspace EU*, 20 March 2012. See also the postscript to this book.

[333] N Tocci, 'Does the ENP Respond to the EU's Post-Enlargement Challenges?' (2005) 40 *International Spectator* 21, 27.

[334] S Blockmans, 'EU Enlargement as a Peacebuilding Tool' in Blockmans, Wouters, and Ruys (eds), note 241 above, 77–103, 100; E Korosteleva, *The European Union and its Eastern Neighbours: Towards a More Ambitious Partnership?* (London, Routledge, 2012) 33.

[335] Vachudova, note 35 above, 63.

[336] Tulmets, note 19 above, 35.

The principle of joint ownership in the ENP Strategy Paper entailed that the EU would not impose priorities on its partners, while the Action Plans would take into account a clear recognition of mutual interests.[337] The very fact of the possibility of determining the conditions with the participation of both parties has been considered to formally exclude the conditionality.[338] The function of joint ownership seems to be the engagement of the neighbours to secure their cooperation by guaranteeing 'national ownership and commitment'.[339] It has therefore been identified as one of the strengths of the policy, where the Action Plans are the result of negotiation and political consensus between the parties.[340] In this sense, the joint ownership element should supplement the conditionality principle.

However, there are apparent contradictions between these principles. On the one hand, joint ownership does not sit well with the unequal conditions implied by conditionality.[341] The conditionality principle assumes that there are certain requirements set up from the very beginning, where the party establishing the requirements is strictly monitoring the fulfilment of the obligations by the other party eager to achieve what is on offer. From this perspective, the principle of joint ownership is therefore compromised by conditionality: joint ownership is only possible within the limits of the requirements imposed through unequal conditionality.

In the ENP the principle of joint ownership has not been entirely followed during the process of policy formulation, as the parameters of cooperation are defined by the EU which *directs* its policy towards the neighbours. The objectives and means of the policy were set in the same fashion for all partners.[342]

On the other hand, the intentions behind the principles of conditionality and joint ownership are different.[343] Intended to reflect also the interests of the neighbouring countries, the principle of joint ownership suggests a certain degree of flexibility.[344] This seems to go against the presumed strictness of conditionality, which also has to be reconciled with the principle of differentiation whose rationale is closer to that of joint ownership than conditionality.

The principle of differentiation is another element of the ENP's methodology which intends to adapt the pre-accession strategy to new tasks and is reflected in the drafting of the Action Plans.[345] Although the differentiation has been applied during the last two rounds of enlargement, it acquired official status within the

---

[337] ENP Strategy Paper, 8.

[338] Leino and Petrov, note 303 above, 660.

[339] Wider Europe Communication, 15–16.

[340] Communication on Strengthening the ENP, 3.

[341] Cremona and Hillion, note 17 above, 40.

[342] Wider Europe Communication, 16; H Haukkala, 'A Hole in the Wall? Dimensionalism and the EU's New Neighbourhood Policy' The Finnish Institute of International Affairs, UPI Working Papers N.41, 2003, 18–19.

[343] Kelley, note 10 above, 36.

[344] Koutrakos, note 99 above, 377.

[345] ENP Strategy Paper, 8, 14.

ENP.[346] Moreover, for the ENP the application of this principle will entail different consequences. If the enlargement differentiation entails that the EU membership is a matter of time which might be different for different candidates, in the case of the ENP, the differentiation leads to different levels of integration with the EU.

On its own it appeared to be a promising basis for cooperation since, depending on the motivation and commitment of the partner state, the latter can achieve a higher level of integration in the absence of a single goal established for all the countries involved in the policy.[347] Its significance was already apparent during the process of developing the ENP, when it became possible to classify the neighbours depending on their ambitions.[348] At the same time, it is exactly this aspect of differentiation which is more likely to generate new dividing lines.[349] In combination with conditionality, differentiation can result in the level of integration differing from country to country, as noted above.[350]

Among the advantages of the principle of differentiation some saw the possibility of making the conditionality 'less arbitrary by negotiating a set of realistic objectives' with each state making progress more transparent and predictable.[351] Nevertheless, that does not suggest that differentiation will support conditionality, as it might well result in abandoning conditionality entirely or significantly. The effectiveness of conditionality in countries where there is no power asymmetry, either due to the EU's own interests or the neighbouring country's unwillingness to integrate into the internal market, can therefore be predicted to be limited. In this context differentiation potentially suggests different treatment of countries in comparable circumstances.

In terms of its function, the differentiation is close to the principle of joint ownership in according the ENP with the flexibility required for securing EU interests via responding to the neighbour's interests. In practice, these principles go against consistency understood in terms of similar treatment of third countries, discussed in Chapter 2.[352] Most importantly, it is not clear whether differentiation operates above the threshold set in EU values, including democracy. A minimum threshold of compliance should be required before applying 'differentiated' treatment. It is these principles which, depending on the EU's interests in a particular country, can undermine the Union's normative power, in particular by trumping democracy promotion. Therefore, while the conditionality principle

---

[346] K Inglis, 'Accession Treaties: Differentiation Versus Conditionality?' in Ott and Vos (eds), note 240 above, 139–56, 141; Ridder et al, note 295 above, 246.

[347] H Haukkala and A Moshes, 'Beyond "Big Bang": The Challenges of the EU's Neighbourhood Policy in the East', Helsinki, Finnish Institute of International Affairs, 2004, 52.

[348] These countries have been classified as willing, passive, reluctant and excluded partners in M Emerson, G Noutcheva, N Popescu, 'European Neighbourhood Policy Two Years On: Time Indeed for an "ENP Plus"' CEPS, Policy Brief No 126, 21 March 2007.

[349] Cremona and Hillion, note 17 above, 40–41.

[350] Van Elsuwege, note 206 above, 66.

[351] Balfour and Rotta, note 31 above, 13.

[352] KE Smith, *European Union Foreign Policy in a Changing World* (Cambridge, Polity Press, 2003) 65.

assumes values embedded in law, the joint ownership and differentiation entail a margin for securing interests deriving from political considerations embodying the 'norm versus interest' problem.

As the revisions of the ENP progressed, the principles of joint ownership and differentiation acquired a central status.[353] The differentiation is particularly emphasised in the ENP revisions following the Arab Spring revolutions in the so-called 'more for more approach', where it appears almost in an incentive-like role: conditionality in a form of promises will apply as long as the specific neighbour desires it.[354] Thus, the advancement in cooperation between the parties does not always depend on the adherence to the Action Plans, but often on internal or external political developments.[355] The consequences of the Arab Spring revolutions support this statement, as the internal political developments compelled the EU to reconsider its previous attitudes and promises. Most significantly, by emphasising differentiation as a central element of its methodology, it raises the risk, appreciated by the Parliament, of abandoning a minimum threshold of adhering to EU values.[356]

Thus, the absence of a membership perspective, the initial lack of precision as to the new incentives, together with the apparent contradictions implanted in its methodology deprived the ENP of a sound basis for the success of political reform within the latter. The EaP initiative failed to resolve these apparent contradictions.[357]

3.5 EASTERN PARTNERSHIP: ANOTHER EUROPEAN ECONOMIC AREA?

The application of a similar set of instruments and mechanisms within the ENP to the Eastern and Southern neighbours was not justified due to the past history of relations and distinct frameworks of cooperation between the parties. The geographic split that followed marks the return to the original rationale of the ENP, that is to offer preferential relations to its Eastern neighbours.[358] The EaP has therefore become the 'Eastern dimension' of the ENP and includes Ukraine, Moldova, Belarus, Georgia, Armenia and Azerbaijan.[359]

The initiative was met with reluctance by its addressees. While Ukraine disagreed with being treated similarly to other neighbours, the Moldovan leadership viewed it as a political move against Russia, and the South Caucasian republics

---

[353] Commission Communication, Taking Stock of the European Neighbourhood Policy COM (2010) 207, 12 May 2010, 4.

[354] 2011 Joint Communication, 2, 8–9, 20–21; Joint Communication, 'Delivering on a New European Neighbourhood Policy', JOIN (2012) 14 final, 15 May 2012, 2–4.

[355] Van Elsuwege, note 206 above, 66–67.

[356] Parliament Resolution on EU External Policies in Favour of Democratisation (2011/2032(INI)) 7 July 2011, para 26.

[357] N Ghazaryan, 'The Evolution of the ENP and the Consistent Evolvement of its Inconsistencies' (2012) 7 *Russian and European Affairs Review* 1, 10–12.

[358] Lannon and Van Elsuwege, note 41 above, 286.

[359] Brussels European Council Conclusions, 19–20 June 2008, 19.

preferred finding their way with the EU on an individual basis.[360] In this sense, the EaP is essentially a unilateral policy initiated without prior consultations with the neighbours,[361] as it did not represent the aspirations of some of the neighbours at the time.

Moreover, varying degree of eagerness or progress were apparent in relation to each of the countries in 2008. If the EaP was to signify a closer relationship, then it represented an opportunity to incorporate *ex-ante* conditionality within the ENP prior to offering the new initiative to those partners who had achieved a certain level of adherence to political reform. Not only was this a missed opportunity, but also the relationship between the EaP and the ENP is unclear in respect of its contribution to the latter, or perhaps its effect on the latter.

3.5.1 Eastern Dimension

In its proposal for the EaP the Commission envisaged that the new initiative would 'make a step change in relations with these partners' in comparison with the ENP.[362] Whether this 'step change' had a political or legal underpinning is not easy to discern.

In terms of the ENP rationale of providing an alternative to enlargement, the grouping of the Eastern partners in a separate multilateral framework could be suggested to amount to recognising the 'Europeanness' of Ukraine, Moldova, Belarus and the states of the South Caucasus as opposed to the Southern Mediterranean states. However, the official documents on the EaP are careful to avoid stressing the 'Europeanness' of the Eastern partners.[363] Instead, the EaP Communication mentions only that the initiative is 'without prejudice to individual countries' aspirations for their future relationship with the EU',[364] raising the dormant issue of accession prospects. It is not the definition of 'Europeanness' that is important here, which in any case is a contested concept, but rather the branding of a country as 'European' constituting the central condition for accession under Article 49 TEU.[365]

There is no consensus among the EU foreign policy actors as to the 'Europeanness' of all Eastern neighbours. Although previously the Commission included Georgia,

---

[360] S Tumanov, A Gasparishvili and E Romanova, 'Russia–EU Relations, or How the Russians Really View the EU' in E Korosteleva (ed), *Eastern Partnership: A New Opportunity for the Neighbours* (London, Routledge, 2012) 132.

[361] O Stegny, 'Ukraine and the Eastern Partnership: "Lost in Translation?"' in E Korosteleva (ed), *The Eastern Partnership Initiative: A New Opportunity for the Neighbours?* (London, Routledge, 2012) 52–74, 59.

[362] Eastern Partnership Communication, 2.

[363] 'Brussels to Recognise "European Aspirations" of Post-Soviet States', *EU Observer*, 24 November 2008.

[364] Eastern Partnership Communication, 2.

[365] Hillion, note 277 above, 403; D Kochenov, *EU Enlargement and the Failure of Conditionality: Pre-Accession Conditionality in the Field of Democracy and the Rule of Law* (Austin, Wolters Kluwer Law and Business, 2008) 29–30.

Armenia and Azerbaijan within 'European states', currently the EEAS makes a distinction between 'other European states' – Ukraine, Belarus, Moldova and Russia – and the South Caucasus,[366] therefore supporting the view doubting the 'Europeanness' of the South Caucasian republics.[367] The Parliament, on the other hand, is unequivocal on the European prospects of all EaP partners.[368] The EaP documents fail to clarify whether the initiative marks a departure from the ENP in this respect.

The perceived 'step change' in relations between the EU and EaP participants should be judged with reference to the incentives of cooperation. While it was perceived that the EaP would entail an almost 'complete integration' into the internal market,[369] including liberalisation of protectionists areas such as agriculture,[370] it ultimately incentivised trade liberalisation by affirming the prospect of a DCFTA, better mobility and energy cooperation.[371]

In relation to mobility issues, the EaP Communication referred to the possibility of a visa-free travel regime, and 'targeted' opening up of EU labour markets for the citizens of neighbours.[372] However, instead of facilitating a visa-free travel regime immediately, the EaP has incorporated the mobility partnerships as its central element.[373] The flexibility of mobility partnerships complements the visa facilitation and readmission agreements which are the hard law instruments related to mobility. The latter is an example of softening the reality of exclusion in the absence of the promise of free movement, and is a first step towards visa liberalisation. The first visa facilitation agreements were concluded in 2007 with Ukraine and Moldova – the most promising neighbours in the East by then.[374] In the case of Georgia the reliance on this instrument came as a reaction to security threats aimed at increasing the Union's presence in the region following the August 2008 war. The Extraordinary European Council in September 2008 decided 'to step up relations with Georgia, including visa facilitation measures'.[375] The visa facilitation agreement was finally concluded with Georgia in 2011, followed by Armenia in 2012.[376] In essence, the EaP in the area of mobility does not mark a departure from the ENP, since the discourse is similarly framed in terms

---

[366] See the website of the EEAS, www.eeas.europa.eu/regions/index_en.htm.

[367] Koutrakos, note 99 above, 364; Blockmans and Prechal, note 308 above, 5.

[368] European Parliament Resolution on the Review of the European Neighbourhood Policy (2011/2157(INI)) 14 December 2011, para 37; European Parliament Resolution on the review of the European Neighbourhood Policy – Eastern Dimension P7_TA(2011)0153, 7 April 2011, para 10.

[369] C Hillion and A Mayhew, 'The Eastern Partnership – Something New or Window-dressing', SEI Working Paper No 109, 2009, 6.

[370] Eastern Partnership Communication, 10; R Balfour and A Missiroli, 'Dealing with Troubled Neighbourhoods', Commentary, European Policy Centre, 12 February 2009.

[371] Eastern Partnership Communication, 3, 10.

[372] Ibid, 6.

[373] Ibid, 6–7.

[374] [2007] OJ L334/169; [2007] OJ L332.

[375] Presidency Conclusions, Extraordinary European Council Conclusions, 1 September 2008, 3.

[376] [2011] OJ L52/34; 'EU–Armenia Agreement on Facilitating the Issuing of Visas' 17866/12 Press Release 538, 17 December 2012. Council Decision 2013/2/EU [2013] OJ L3/1.

of visa facilitation, rather than free movement of persons. Besides, the prospect of similar cooperation is also offered to certain Southern neighbours, suggesting no specific treatment of the Eastern neighbours.[377]

The third area where the cooperation is intensified is energy security, which similarly does not depart from the original exclusionary rationale, but rather makes it more obvious. The subsequent Joint Declaration of the EaP Summit followed the Commission in prioritising trade, mobility and energy cooperation.[378]

As to the promise of the DCFTAs, their effect in terms of incentives for cooperation should be assessed within the bilateral framework of cooperation.

3.5.2 Seeking Novelty in Bilateral Cooperation?

Here the EaP merely confirmed that the new agreements would take the form of association agreements. In isolation this cannot be considered as a step change in relations between the parties, as the negotiation process with Ukraine commenced in 2007 had already confirmed the type of the agreement. The significance of this promise is possibly linked to the indication that the new agreements would be without prejudice to the neighbours' 'aspirations for their future relationship with the EU'.[379] This might suggest that similar to Europe Agreements with the CEE states, the association agreements with Eastern partners can pave the way for future membership given the necessary political context. However, the EaP itself has not created such political context, especially when no consensus is apparent on the 'Europeanness' of all partners involved and given the disengagement of certain Member States.[380] The EaP, therefore, does not clarify the political purpose of the association agreements to be concluded. It rather focuses on the possible content of the agreements, which is linked primarily to economic integration.

According to the EaP Communication, cooperation through the association agreements has been envisaged to lead to the creation of a network of FTAs that can eventually evolve into a neighbourhood economic community 'taking inspiration from the European Economic Area where appropriate'.[381] Although not an entirely original proposal,[382] the official reference to the European Economic Area (EEA) model within the EaP was rather significant due to the mere possibility of such development. Initially created as an alternative to membership of the EC in 1994, the EEA included European Free Trade Association countries who were not

---

[377] 'Communication on a Dialogue for Migration, Mobility and Security with the Southern Mediterranean Countries' COM (2011) 292/3, 24 May 2011; Joint Communication, 'Delivering on A New European Neighbourhood Policy' JOIN (2012) 14 final, 15 May 2012, 13; 'Migration and Mobility Partnership signed between the EU and Morocco', Press Release, IP/13/513, 7 June 2013.

[378] Joint Declaration of the Prague Eastern Partnership Summit, 7–8.

[379] Eastern Partnership Communication, 2.

[380] See note 405 below.

[381] Eastern Partnership Communication, 10.

[382] Communication on Strengthening the ENP, 5.

members of the EC.[383] The main purpose of the EEA agreement was to create a 'dynamic and homogeneous [EEA], based on common rules and equal conditions of competition'.[384] The homogeneity of the economic area is based on embracing law substantially replicating EU law interpreted in conformity with the rulings of the Court of Justice.[385]

However, establishing a single neighbourhood area based on the model of the EEA again raises the issue of membership. This could be a possible significant difference between the ENP and the EaP. The EEA does not exclude the membership of European Free Trade Area (EFTA) countries of the EU, although at the same time it is an alternative type of integration from accession.[386] Sweden, Finland and Austria were members of the EEA prior to their accession to the EU. Iceland has opted for accession, and is currently among the candidate countries.[387] Non-membership of the EU by Norway and Liechtenstein is not by virtue of exclusion by the EU, but due to the choice of the citizens of the countries concerned. Since the EaP does not solve the issue of the bar on membership, the possible reliance on the EEA example creates further confusion as to the ENP rationale. Besides, building anew an economic community *à la* EEA raises the question of extending the EEA itself to the willing neighbouring states.

However, participating in the EEA as an alternative is not without problems either. The latter has been noted to bring a 'difficulty of managing deep integration in the absence of shared law-making institutions'.[388] For countries such as Ukraine or Moldova, seeking full economic and political union with the EU, the EEA or an EEA-like integration falls short of reciprocation of their aspirations, and might be viewed as a 'second-class membership'.[389]

Ultimately, the subsequent documents, including the Joint Declaration of the EaP Summit remained silent on such a prospect, instead referring to the possibility of establishing 'a network of deep and comprehensive free trade areas'.[390] The 2011 Joint Communication revising the ENP mentioned in passing the possibility of *economic community*, making a reference to the 2006 Communication on Strengthening the ENP.[391] The peculiarity of this reference lies in the fact that it makes a general statement on the possibility of establishing an economic

---

[383] Agreement on the European Economic Area [1994] OJ L1; M Cremona, 'The "Dynamic and Homogeneous" EEA: Byzantine Structures and Various Geometry' (1994) 19 *European Law Review* 508, 508.

[384] Fourth Recital, Preamble to EEA Agreement, Art 1 [1994] OJ L1/1.

[385] Art 6, EEA Agreement.

[386] The Preamble to the EEA Agreement states that it 'shall not prejudge in any way the possibility of any EFTA State to accede to the European Communities'.

[387] Brussels European Council Conclusions, 17 June 2010, 9.

[388] Cremona, 'Enlargement', note 270 above, 410.

[389] A Lazowski, 'Box of Chocolates Integration: The European Economic Area and the Swiss Model Revisited' in Blockmans and Prechal (eds), note 308 above, 87–109, 110.

[390] Joint Declaration of the Prague Eastern Partnership Summit, Prague, 7 May 2009, 7.

[391] Joint Communication, A New Response to a Changing Neighbourhood: A Review of the European Neighbourhood Policy COM (2011) 303, 25 May 2011, 8–9 (hereinafter Joint Communication on A New Response).

community involving *all* ENP partners, therefore discrediting the step change that the EaP was meant to signify for the Eastern neighbours.[392]

The prospect of establishing a neighbourhood economic community is nonetheless dubious given the retention of the principles of differentiation and joint ownership within the EaP.[393] The latter, combined with selective application of conditionality, dictates variations in the level of economic cooperation among the partner states, whereas establishing a common economic area will require a common denominator in terms of economic regulation. Such common denominator will require convergence with EU economic *acquis*, and accession to the WTO, which is not a prospect actively sought in either Azerbaijan or Belarus.[394] Hence, the methods the EaP inherited from the ENP could prove to be counterproductive for solving the task of bringing all the partners to the same level of cooperation with the EU within the bilateral framework of cooperation.

The Communication on the EaP noted that progress in the evolution of the relationship will depend on commitment to the rule of law, good governance, respect for human rights and minorities, and the principles of the market economy and sustainable development, therefore retaining the principle of conditionality.[395] It has been suggested that the EaP strengthens the conditionality element by bringing more focus to the role of democracy among other things by establishing the platform on democracy, good governance and stability.[396] On the one hand, this proposition is supported by the Communication on EaP, according to which the starting of negotiations on association agreements would depend on progress made in the area of political reform,[397] therefore embodying an *ex-ante* political conditionality. However, in practice this has been disregarded at the stage of starting the negotiations: the latter were commenced with all willing partners despite their democratic record.[398] Therefore it is rather an *ex-post* conditionality that can be expected, if at all, within the EaP.

As noted earlier the negotiations on the association agreement with Ukraine have been concluded, but it has not yet been signed.[399] The negotiations on association agreements were opened with Georgia, Armenia, Azerbaijan and Moldova in 2010. Two years on negotiations were launched on establishing a DCFTA with Georgia,

---

[392] DCFTA negotiations are under way with Morocco, Tunisia and Jordan: 'EU Started Preparations for DCFTA Negotiations with Morocco, Tunisia and Jordan', Press Release, IP/13/245, 20 March 2013.

[393] ENP Strategy Paper, 8, 14; Eastern Partnership Communication, 3, 8.

[394] Azerbaijan applied for WTO membership in 1997, but has since made little progress in satisfying the entry requirements. Belarus applied for WTO membership in 1993, however the negotiations were halted in 2005. In recent years more active engagement with the issue is noticeable on behalf of Belarus, linked to the Russian accession to the WTO in 2012. T Mkrtchyan, T Huseynov, K Gogolashvili, 'The European Union and the South Caucasus: Three Perspectives on the Future of the European Project from the Caucasus', Europe in Dialogue 2009/01, 81.

[395] Eastern Partnership Communication, 4.

[396] S Stewart, 'EU Democracy Promotion in the Eastern Neighbourhood: One Template, Multiple Approaches' (2011) 16 *European Foreign Affairs Review* 607, 609.

[397] Eastern Partnership Communication, 2, 3, 4.

[398] See Chapter 6, section 6.4.

[399] See note 225 above.

Armenia and Moldova. Azerbaijan is currently negotiating an investment and non-preferential trade agreement.

Within this context Blockmans and Van Vooren view the prospect of neighbourhood economic community as potentially tied to legally binding sectoral multilateralism following the neofunctionalist rationale of 'spillover'.[400]

3.5.3 Multilateral Framework of Cooperation

The EaP, in addition to bilateral relations, introduced a multilateral framework of cooperation for Eastern neighbours. The original Polish-Swedish proposal on EaP considered the multilateral framework to be the 'added value' of the new project. For the Polish policymakers the EaP was to transform the Eastern neighbourhood based on the Visegrad accession experience.[401] In this context the novelty of the EaP was not the incentives or instruments on offer, but rather the intention to enhance the relations between the Eastern partners themselves.[402] The EaP was nonetheless aimed not only at introducing qualitative changes to the ENP: the initiative was to a certain extent directed at counterbalancing the Russian presence, since its launching was linked also to the August 2008 war in Georgia.[403]

On a structural level the EaP introduced new fora for multilateral high-level meetings, which supports the suggestion that the EaP takes the political association between the EU and its partners further than 'classical association'.[404] The structural platform consists of meetings of the heads of the states or governments of Eastern partners held every two years and annual spring meetings of Ministers of Foreign Affairs, which nevertheless are not perceived important enough to attend by all heads of EU Member States.[405]

On a substantive level four thematic platforms have been established for a multilateral cooperation in a form of exchange of practice operating through meetings held twice a year at the level of senior officials. The platforms established are on democracy, good governance and stability; economic integration and convergence with EU policies; energy security; and contacts between people. Substantively the thematic platform on democracy and good governance follows the Action Plan requirements mainly referring to the obligations the neighbouring states undertake in the Council of Europe or the Organization for Security and Co-operation in Europe (OSCE).[406] Its added value should therefore be sought in

---

[400] S Blockmans and B Van Vooren, 'Revitalizing the European "Neighbourhood Economic Community": The Case for Legally Binding Sectoral Multilateralism' (2012) 17 *European Foreign Affairs Review* 577, 580.

[401] AK Cianciara, '"Eastern Partnership" – Opening a New Chapter of Polish Eastern Policy and the European Neighbourhood Policy?' No 4, June 2008, The Institute of Public Affairs, Warsaw, 3, 6.

[402] Van Vooren, note 235 above, 156.

[403] Popescu, note 325 above, 327.

[404] Hillion and Mayhew, note 369 above, 8–9.

[405] 'Split over Direction Overshadows Eastern Partnership Summit', *EU Observer*, 22 September 2011; 'Big Names to Stay Away from Prague Summit', *EU Observer*, 4 May 2009.

[406] See Chapter 5, section 5.2.2.

its multilateral framework. However, the EaP's multilateralism, given its soft nature, does not itself guarantee cooperation between neighbours, where some, including Armenia and Azerbaijan have openly hostile relations with each other.

The real added value of the EaP for the purposes of EU democratic values can be argued to be linked to the enhanced role of national parliaments and civil society. Parliamentary exchange is made possible through the Euronest parliamentary cooperation framework, which according to the ENP Commissioner represents more than another EaP structure: it is a tool to 'advance democratisation' via shared experience between parliamentarians.[407] The Euronest developed a practice of adopting resolutions, which, although non-binding in nature, develop a common political denominator and establish a ground for cooperation.[408] The establishment of the civil society forum in 2009, meeting on an annual basis, is another important development within the EaP. This can be suggested to be aimed at compensating the sidelined role of the civil society within the ENP.[409] The forum has established its own working groups, including on democracy, good governance and stability. Although it does not as such affect the ENP implementation processes at national level, the civil society cooperation nevertheless contributes to the formation of public opinion and raising awareness on the issues of European integration in relevant countries.

In addition to the above-mentioned aspects of the multilateral framework, the EaP provides for common positions on various issues between the EU and the Eastern partners, as well as implementation of 'flagship initiatives'.[410] The latter include sector-specific initiatives, such as the Small and Medium Enterprise facility, the Integrated Border Management Programme, regional electricity markets and others. Although the multiplication of projects and tasks leads to sectoral cooperation and enhancement of links between the parties, it arguably bears the risks of detracting from comprehensive integration that a fully fledged bilateral association would allow. On the other hand, due to the preservation of the ENP methodology, it has been considered that there is a possibility of 'subordination' of the multilateral partnership to bilateral cooperation.[411]

Ultimately the success of the EaP depends on political momentum, which is not present due to the variable degree of interest on behalf of Member States, as well as the funding available.[412] Although it initially appeared that the Commission

---

[407] Š Füle, European Commissioner for Enlargement and European Neighbourhood, Speech at the Euronest Parliamentary Assembly, EuroNest Parliamentary Assembly Baku, Speech/12/256, 3 April 2012.

[408] During the last session in April 2012 five resolutions were adopted on a range of issues. They included challenges to democracy in EaP countries, trade agreements, energy security threats, strengthening of civil society, and the situation with former Ukrainian Prime Minister Yulia Timoshenko. Available at www.euronest.europarl.europa.eu/euronest/.

[409] See Chapters 5 and 6; Š Füle, Speech/12/256, EuroNest Parliamentary Assembly 3 April 2012; Š Füle, 'Strengthening the Role of Civil Society in Democratic Governance', Speech/12/654, European Commission, 27 September 2012.

[410] Hillion and Mayhew, note 369, above 11–12.

[411] Lannon and Van Elsuwege, note 41 above, 315.

[412] Ibid, 321.

was more eager to fund the EaP in comparison with the UfM,[413] following the Arab Spring revolutions significantly larger funds have been directed at the Southern neighbours during 2011–13.[414] Taking into account the complicated negotiations over the EU budget for 2014–20, one can hardly expect more funds to be directed at the Eastern neighbours for the next budgetary term.

3.6 CONCLUSION

A sole finding that emerges from the discussion on institutional, instrumental and methodological aspects of the ENP is that the political nature of the ENP has left its imprint on the legal features of the policy.

Although the ENP's institutional pattern was largely reminiscent of the enlargement experience, with a distinctive role for the Commission, the Member States nevertheless played their part in impacting the policy via the Council and mostly the Presidency, in particular by 'rationalising' the policy. In terms of EU democratic values the role of the Parliament should be noted due to its eagerness to uphold the normative image of the EU.

The Lisbon Treaty introduced new institutional arrangements to increase the coherence of EU external action, which nevertheless create new complexities. Due to the introduction of the permanent Presidency and the office of the High Representative in a 'double-hatted' capacity, as well as the existence of a separate DG on the ENP, there are currently more offices representing the EU in its neighbourhood than previously. In practice the multiplicity of actors means a slower response on behalf of the EU, as well as the lack of a definite stance on particular issues. Moreover, multiple actors with multiple agendas create scope for rivalry where the effect of the new institutional arrangements ultimately depends on personalities.[415] Thus, it can hardly be argued that there is a more unified vision of the EU identity in its neighbourhood than prior to the Lisbon Treaty.

In substantive terms the ENP has been drafted ambitiously to achieve all-encompassing security. The cooperation on offer cut across the different rationales pursued in the EU foreign policy, but also the three pillars of the EU's constitutional order prior to the Lisbon Treaty. It therefore raised complex issues of legal competence. As a cross-pillar policy, the competence to conduct the ENP was to be found in express and implied provisions, and shared and exclusive external competence. To avoid complications in legal terms, the policy was largely framed in terms of soft law instruments, advantageous due to securing flexibility

---

[413] A budget of €600 million of redeployed and newly allocated funds was made available for the first period; Eastern Partnership Communication, 13; Van Vooren, note 235 above, 157.

[414] 540 million euro was directed at the Southern neighbourhood, with only 130 million euro allocated to the EaP states; 'European Neighbourhood Policy in 2012: Continuing Engagement for a Stronger Cooperation with Neighbours Despite Turbulent Political and Economic Cooperation', Press Release, IP/13/245, March 2013.

[415] Dougan, note 102 above, 691–92.

in shaping and adapting the policy to the needs of the EU without creating new legal obligations for either itself or the Member States.

The promise of a new bilateral agreement first materialised in relations with Ukraine (although not finally concluded yet) and confirmed the presumption that it would take the form of an association agreement. This raises the issue of the added value of Article 8 TEU which, although it 'constitutionalises' the ENP, is nevertheless not legally necessary for concluding new agreements in the neighbourhood as other Treaty provisions can be used instead. Instead the presence of Article 8 TEU in the Treaty is aimed at the 'legalisation' of the political rationale of the ENP by offering an alternative to accession.

With this rationale in mind, the ENP was to be based on the very policy it attempted to replace by adopting the accession instruments, as well as by relying on the main driving force behind the accession policies, that is the conditionality principle. The latter was modified to the concept of 'shared values', and created a credibility problem as the 'carrot' at stake was not clearly defined. Currently, 'deeper economic integration', a vague notion of its own, is the reward on offer for undertaking economic and political reforms. Besides, the conditionality element is to be reconciled with joint ownership and differentiation. The latter can be argued to have transformed the ENP into what the Council called 'a policy of encouragement and support'.[416] The flexibility offered by the principle of joint ownership and differentiation is vital for achieving policy objectives, which are secured more efficiently by cooperative means. The ENP therefore carries an intrinsic tension 'between engaging partners in a cooperative relationship and the transformative content' of the policy.[417]

The EaP, by inheriting the ambiguities of the ENP, does not clarify the purpose of cooperation with the Eastern partners. On the positive side, its multilateral framework creates an avenue for socialisation between the countries concerned and the facilities for parliamentary and civil society participation aimed at engaging the hitherto sidelined actors.[418]

Facing the changes and challenges in the neighbourhood following the Arab Spring revolutions, the ENP underwent a revision in 2011. A more enhanced outlook has been envisaged for a closer partnership to build democracy, pursue economic development and manage migration.[419] Besides the 'more for more approach', the revised ENP also refers to 'a new approach' in democracy promotion to signal a reinforced commitment to political reforms.[420] Although it can be suggested that the reinforced commitment to democracy is reflective of the commitment in Article 8 TEU, the surprising aspect of it is the phrasing of this commitment in language of 'the new approach' as its substance does not change

---

[416] Council Conclusions, Strengthening the European Neighbourhood Policy, General Affairs and External Relations Council, 18–19 June 2007.
[417] Balfour and Rotta, note 31 above, 19.
[418] See Chapter 5, section 5.3.
[419] Joint Communication on A New Response, 1.
[420] Ibid, 2–3.

in practice.[421] It can be suggested that the latter is about the external rehabilitation of the EU's normative image. The 'new approach' aims to reiterate – for the attention of the neighbours and for the sake of its credibility – that the Union would adhere to its values, despite its past willingness to cooperate with authoritarian regimes. It therefore comes across as an acknowledgement of the Union's failure to adhere to its rhetoric of democracy promotion previously in the Southern neighbourhood. As noted by the Parliament, the EU risks undermining its credibility further if the new differentiated approach has no common minimum threshold in democracy promotion.

Before passing judgement on whether this minimum threshold is upheld in the ENP implementation in the countries concerned, it is necessary to identify what exactly 'democracy' or 'democratic values' stand to denote in the EU.

---

[421] Council Conclusions on the European Neighbourhood Policy, Foreign Affairs, 20 June 2011.

4

Democratic Values of the EU

4.1 INTRODUCTION

T
HAT 'EUROPE NEEDS to project its model of society into the wider world', a model which is based on 'the principles of democracy, freedom and solidarity', was the normative vision for EU external relations adopted prior to the ENP.[1] The Lisbon Treaty legalises this vision in its common provisions on upholding EU values in external relations generally, and in the neighbourhood specifically through Article 8 TEU. When an actor claims to project externally its *own* model based on the principle of democracy, it is legitimate to expect certain normative underpinning to such model.

In 2001 the Commission noted that the EU's substantial political and moral weight to promote democracy derives from the fact that its Member States are democracies,[2] and hence it can promote democracy by 'virtue of what it is'.[3] However, the EU is more than a mere union of its democratic Member States. Such a minimalist view does not reflect the status of democracy as an independent principle or value in the EU legal order. Moreover, to sideline the long-existing debate on the democratic discourse in the EU would significantly limit the standing of the Union to promote democracy as a value of its own. Besides, it is exactly because of the internal democratic evolution of the EU that democracy promotion has acquired such prominence on its external agenda. The intertwined nature of the Union's external stance on democracy and its own democratic development comes across in the 1991 European Council Declaration on Human Rights.[4]

The EU is a remarkable example of democratic experimentation with its incrementally evolving democratic model. The pledge for a 'more democratic' Union in the Laeken Declaration has eventually led to a separate Title in the revised TEU on Provisions on Democratic Principles.[5] While internally this development is

---

[1] R Prodi, '2000–2005: Shaping the New Europe', Speech to EP, Strasbourg 15 February 2000, Speech/00/41.

[2] Commission Communication, 'The European Union's Role in Promoting Human Rights and Democratisation in Third Countries' COM (2001) 252 final, 8 May 2001.

[3] R Balfour, 'Principles of Democracy and Human Rights. A Review of the European Union's Strategies Towards its Neighbours' in S Lucarelli and I Manners (eds), *Values and Principles in European Union Foreign Policy* (London, Routledge, 2006) 114–29, 114.

[4] Luxembourg European Council Conclusions, Declaration on Human Rights, 28–29 June 1991.

[5] Laeken Declaration on the Future of the European Union, Laeken European Council, 14–15 December 2001, s II, para I.

considered to be 'a dramatic step towards political union',[6] externally it justifies the Union's stance on democracy promotion. However, a question arises as to a genuine commitment to democracy in view of the so-called 'democratic deficit' of the EU.[7] Within the enlargement policy there was a place for irony in that 'a democratically deficient body' was indicating how to establish democratic systems.[8] Is such an irony appropriate in the neighbourhood? To answer this question the identification of the features that best describe the democratic model of the EU is required. Since one cannot expect the EU to promote its own model to nation states, it is rather the features or the values comprising the model that can be promoted in external relations.

Within this narrative the chapter is structured as follows. An overview of the democratic discourse in the EU, including on the issue of 'democratic deficit', is considered first. The discussion further identifies those features of governance that the EU can claim as its own democratic values. Part four of the chapter focuses on the transposition of the EU democratic values in the 2004 and 2007 rounds of enlargement, which serves as a precedent for the ENP. The chapter will be summarised with conclusions on the democratic values of the EU as part of its normative identity.

4.2 THE NORMATIVE BASIS FOR DEMOCRACY PROMOTION: FROM ROME TO LISBON

Defining the Union's legal order as an international organisation, a federation, a *sui generis* multi-level governance system, or in any other way creates a different premise for the democratic discourse of the EU. The discussion that follows does not aim to contribute to this discourse on qualifying the EU legal and political order as it is outside the scope of this research, although at times references are made to certain approaches. Instead it intends to trace those features of its governance that are viewed as democratic in modern societies.

4.2.1 The Founding Treaties and Democracy

As an international organisation at the time of its foundation, the EC was not intended to be democratic.[9] Democracy did not feature in the Rome Treaty in any

---

[6] R Schütze, *European Constitutional Law* (Cambridge, CUP, 2012) 43.

[7] Foreign diplomats note the democratic deficit of the EU as a discrediting factor for its stance on democracy promotion: C Carta, 'Close Enough? The EU's Global Role Described by Non-European Diplomats in Brussels' in S Lucarelli and L Fiaramonti (eds), *External Perceptions of the European Union as a Global Actor* (London, Routledge, 2011) 207–17, 213–14.

[8] H Grabbe, 'How Does the EU Measure when the CEECs are Ready to Join?' in C Jenkins (ed), *The Unification of Europe? An Analysis of EU Enlargement* (London, Centre for Reform, 2000) 37–46, 45.

[9] F Mancini, *Democracy and Constitutionalism in the European Union: Collected Essays* (Oxford, Hart Publishing, 2000) 31–32.

capacity, although concerns over popular consent and democracy were raised early on over the non-representative Commission.[10] These concerns were set aside by the belief of Jean Monnet that the problem of popular consent should be postponed until the efficiency of European governance resulted in improvements in the economic welfare of society ultimately securing public support.[11]

Thus, the delivery of economic benefits would ensure 'output' democracy as defined by Scharpf.[12] He considers democracy as a two-dimensional concept related to inputs and outputs of governance aimed at collective self-determination. 'Input' democracy requires citizens to be the source of political choices for which governments should be held accountable.[13] 'Output' democracy implies 'effective fate control',[14] where the government is able to offer the most efficient solutions to its citizens' concerns.

Delivering economic benefits, nevertheless, did not neutralise the issue of popular consent, which became more prominent due to the transformation of the EC and the establishment of the EU with competences in new fields being transferred to a supranational level. From a mere economic entity it has evolved into a political union assuming new internal and external obligations. Most significantly, the EU was no longer solely a Union of its Member States, but also a Union of its citizens, prompting reconsideration of the nature of its legal order.[15] The rejection of the Maastricht Treaty by the voters eventually sent a signal of detachment of the political system from its popular base.[16]

Democracy and related issues therefore acquired significant attention from EC institutions in the early 1990s. Although various preceding developments had led to the democratisation of the EC, democracy previously was not per se considered as an EC value. The Community did not have its own values and was merely incorporating the values of its Member States, including 'pluralist democracy'.[17] The Preamble to the Maastricht Treaty merely confirmed that the Member States were attached to the principles of liberty, democracy, respect for human rights and fundamental freedoms and the rule of law, and ensured the Union's respect for the national identities of its Member States, whose governance is based on the principle of democracy in Article F.[18]

---

[10] W Wallace and J Smith, 'Democracy or Technocracy? European Integration and the Problem of Popular Consent' (1995) 18 *West European Politics* 137, 143–44.

[11] Ibid, 143–44.

[12] F Scharpf, 'Economic Integration, Democracy and the Welfare State' (1997) 4 *Journal of European Public Policy* 18, 19.

[13] Ibid.

[14] Ibid.

[15] Art G of the EU Treaty established the citizenship of the Union [1992] OJ C191/1.

[16] The Danish voters rejected the EU Treaty with a 52% No vote in 1992. In France the Treaty was ratified with only a 51.05% Yes vote.

[17] C Hoskyns and M Newman (eds), *Democratising the European Union. Issues for the Twenty-first Century* (Manchester, Manchester University Press, 2000) 185; J Pinder, 'The European Community and Democracy in Central and Eastern Europe' in G Pridham, E Herring and G Sanford (eds), *Building Democracy? The International Dimension of Democratisation in Eastern Europe* (London, Leicester University Press, 1994) 110–32, 120.

[18] Fifth recital, Preamble to the EU Treaty.

It was not until 1997 that the Amsterdam Treaty recognised democracy as a founding principle of the Union, according it with a European status.[19] Furthermore, the EU assumed an obligation of exercising oversight of the Member States' actions in respecting the principle of democracy.[20] The Treaty thus acknowledged the role democracy has to play at the EU level by adding 'another layer' to the protection of the democratic models of the Member States.[21]

The Lisbon Treaty is the latest stage of constitutionalising the democratic evolution of the EU. Apart from acknowledging democracy as a value to be upheld internally and externally, the Treaty for the first time provides an insight into the elements of the Union's democratic governance. The relevant provisions followed decades of incremental changes and institutional developments feeding the debates on the nature of democracy in a political entity such as the EU.

4.2.2 Democratic Theories and the EU 'Democratic Deficit'

Democracy has been one of the most debated concepts in political theory since the time of Aristotle. Scholars can hardly agree on its content and elements, rendering it a highly contested notion. In international relations, the lack of common understanding as to the meaning of democracy particularly complicates intervention in third countries.[22]

Therefore, the initial problem to encounter while studying democracy is that 'there is no democratic theory – there are only democratic theories'.[23] Different models of democracy have been developed, including direct and indirect or representative democracy, majoritarian, pluralistic, consensus, liberal democracy, parliamentary democracy, participatory and deliberative democracy etc. While some of these models will be discussed further below in relation to democratic values of the EU, it should be noted that political equality, popular sovereignty and rule by majority are key concepts shared by the leading democratic theories.[24] A widely accepted conceptualisation of democracy is Dahl's definition of institutions of large-scale democracy or polyarchy with its focus on electoral aspects of democracy, freedom of expression etc.[25] Weale defines democracy in contrast to non-democratic forms of government with reference to its minimal conditions: it is vital that public decisions are made based on public opinion 'formally expressed by citizens of the community, the vast bulk of whom have equal political rights'.[26]

---

[19] Former Art 6 EU.

[20] Former Art 7 EU.

[21] B Laffan, 'Democracy and the European Union' in L Cram, D Dinan and N Nugent (eds), *Developments in the European Union* (Basingstoke, Palgrave, 1999) 330–49, 341.

[22] KE Smith, *European Union Foreign Policy in a Changing World* (Cambridge, Polity Press, 2003) 123.

[23] R Dahl, *A Preface to Democratic Theory* (Chicago, University of Chicago Press, 1956) 1.

[24] Ibid, 34.

[25] R Dahl, *On Democracy* (New Haven, Yale University Press, 2000) 85–86, 90; R Dahl, *Democracy and Its Critics* (New Haven, Yale University Press, 1989) 221.

[26] A Weale, *Democracy* (Basingstoke, Palgrave, 2007) 18.

Various approaches have been adopted for conceptualising the democracy of the EU, comparing it to the republican model of separation of powers,[27] viewing it as consensual democracy,[28] a pluralist democracy,[29] or 'a Schumpeterian competitive elite' democracy.[30] It should be noted that the democratic discourse also stems from two presumptions of democracy, that is as a system of governance and a means to ensure legitimacy. As a system of governance, democracy is said to constitute two pillars: popular and constitutional, representing respectively the expression of popular will and choice and constitutional mechanisms of checks and balances.[31] Lord refers to a specific political meaning of democracy where the 'irreducible core' of the concept would seem to be the 'responsive rule' based on the principles of popular control and equality.[32]

Others highlight the importance of democracy as a necessary prerequisite for the acceptance of EU governance by the public with reference to its legitimacy. For instance, Weiler describes it as 'a condition for the long-term stability and acceptability of European governance'.[33] Others also link the issue of legitimacy to the effectiveness of the organisation in exercising public authority.[34] Taking the two strands into account, EU democracy can be described as a multi-level system of governance, which represents the will of the peoples of Europe to be governed also at the European level in a way that would lead to the acceptance of such governance. This definition manifests the intertwined nature of democracy and legitimacy of EU governance, which in turn can be linked to outsiders' expectations. The promotion of democracy by the EU in its neighbourhood can be legitimate if European governance is accepted as democratic by its own people. Nevertheless, the simplicity of this definition does not do justice to the EU constitutional order, in particular since it excludes the Member States from the picture.

Remarkably, the EU democratic discourse predominantly developed to criticise the practices of the EU, where a picture of EU governance emerged often with

---

[27] A Moravcsik, 'In Defence of the "Democratic Deficit": Reassessing Legitimacy in the European Union' (2002) 40 *Journal of Common Market Studies* 603, 610.

[28] I Manners, 'The Constitutive Nature of Values, Images and Principles in the EU' in Lucarelli and Manners (eds), note 3 above, 19–41, 34.

[29] J Coultrap, 'From Parliamentarism to Pluralism. Models of Democracy and the European Union's "Democratic Deficit"' (1999) 11 *Journal of Theoretical Politics* 107, 124.

[30] JHH Weiler, U Haltern and F Mayer, 'European Democracy and its Critique' (1995) 18 *West European Politics* 4, 32; P Craig, 'Democracy and Rule-making Within the EC: An Empirical and Normative Assessment' (1997) 3 *European Law Journal* 105, 126–27.

[31] Y Meny, 'De la Democratie en Europe: Old Concepts and New Challenges' (2002) 41 *Journal of Common Market Studies* 1, 4.

[32] C Lord, *Democracy in the European Union* (Sheffield, Sheffield Academic Press, 1998) 12.

[33] From political theory he draws on such notions as autonomy, dignity and self-determination of the individual and in similar societal notions of freedom, justice and equality. From social sciences he links the democratic imperative to the social legitimacy of European governance; JHH Weiler, 'Amsterdam and the Quest for Constitutional Democracy' in D O'Keeffe and PM Twomey (eds), *Legal Issues of the Amsterdam Treaty* (Oxford, Hart Publishing, 1999) 1–21, 5.

[34] K Lenaerts and E de Smijter, 'The Question of Democratic Representation' in J Winter, D Curtin, AE Kellermann and B de Witte (eds), *Reforming the Treaty on European Union: The Legal Debate* (London, Kluwer Law International, 1996) 173–197, 175.

deficient or unsuitable features. This trend is exemplified in the literature on the so-called 'democratic deficit' of the EU.

There is no clear definition of 'democratic deficit' and it is a 'powerful catchword' which allows its meaning to be manipulated by anyone who, for whatever reason, is not satisfied with the operation of the EU institutions.[35] Although various characteristics have been attached to this concept,[36] the 'classical democratic deficit theory' is reflected in the 'dispossession' of national representative institutions, which is only partially rectified at the European level.[37] The 1988 Toussaint Report of the Parliament highlighted two central elements, namely the transfer of sovereign powers from the Member States to the Community level, and the exercise of such powers by institutions other than the EP.[38] Ideally the central place within the then EC institutions should have been awarded to the Parliament based on the theory of parliamentary democracy, with the focus on the notions of popular sovereignty and party government.[39]

Prior to the Lisbon Treaty, the main criticism was directed at the fact that the EP did not occupy a central place within the institutions of the Union even after the introduction of the co-decision procedure, since the ultimate decision-making power in many policy areas still rested with the non-elected Council, and the legislative initiative belonged to the appointed Commission. Although the Parliament has been directly elected since 1979, the elections were considered to be 'second-order' with a low turnout and no strong party politics.[40] The European elections were noted to have been dominated by national politics,[41] thereby detaching the citizens from decision making at the supranational level.

Another feature of classical 'democratic deficit' theory was the inability of the electorate to hold the Council accountable. Only national governments could be held accountable at domestic level. This was viewed as problematic due to the diverse and complex nature of decision making at Union level, as well as the qualified majority voting in the Council which complicated the process of holding national governments responsible for positions they had not taken.[42] Thus, despite the constitutional developments transforming the EP, the EU constitutional

---

[35] Meny, note 31 above, 8.

[36] See for example Weiler et al, note 30 above, 7–9; S Andersen and KA Eliassen (eds), *The European Union: How Democratic Is It?* (London, Sage, 1996) 3; VA Schmidt, *Democracy in Europe: The EU and National Polities* (Oxford Scholarship Online, January 2007) 21, 28, 29, 39; P Craig, 'The Nature of the Community: Integration, Democracy and Legitimacy' in P Craig and G de Burca (eds), *The Evolution of EU Law* (Oxford, OUP, 1999) 1–54, 23–24.

[37] C Lord, 'Assessing Democracy in a Contested Polity' (2001) 39 *Journal of Common Market Studies* 641, 642.

[38] EP, Committee on Institutional Affairs, 1 February, 1988 PE 111.236/fin (Toussaint Report) 10–11.

[39] R Katz, 'Models of Democracy: Elite Attitudes and the Democratic Deficit in the European Union' (2001) 2 *European Union Politics* 53, 55.

[40] Laffan, note 21 above, 337; Schmidt, note 36 above, 21.

[41] B Crum, 'Legislative–Executive Relations in the EU' (2003) 41 *Journal of Common Market Studies* 375, 380; Weiler et al, note 30 above, 8.

[42] Wallace and Smith, note 10 above, 147; Weiler et al, note 30 above, 7; Crum, note 41 above, 379–80.

arrangements were viewed as non-satisfactory from the perspective of parliamentary or Westminster democracy.[43]

While the vast critique of the 'democratic deficit' mainly focuses on the deficiencies of the 'input' democracy, some commentators, including Moravcsik and Majone, have argued in defence of the 'democratic deficit' based on 'output' democracy.[44] Moravcsik considers the EU to be well positioned to deal with issues of social welfare and redistribution as an intergovernmental bargaining forum.[45] In an arrangement of separation of powers with vertical division among the EU institutions and horizontal division at the local, national and transnational level, he finds an effectively functioning system of checks and balances, indirect democratic control exercised through national governments, and sufficient representation of the popular will due to the increasing powers of the EP.[46] Describing the EU as a 'regulatory state', Majone considers its main task to be undertaking 'Pareto-efficient' policies, which render traditional democratic discourse 'unintelligible' at the EU level.[47] Along this rationale, the introduction of majoritarian practices at supranational level even creates complications undermining the 'output' legitimacy, and thereby the capacity of the EU as a problem solver.[48]

In response, Follesdal and Hix, while accepting that there is increased democratic contestation both in the Parliament and the Council, contend that the link between the latter and the societal preferences cannot be justified by 'large distributive consequences, rendering a purely unique Pareto-improvement argument insufficient'.[49] They dismiss the qualifications of the supranational governing practices as democratic based on 'output' democracy only. The latter cannot be viewed separately from 'input' elements, one of which is the formation of citizens' preferences. Moreover, outputs themselves have to be legitimised.[50]

Whichever side of the argument one finds oneself on, the process of a continuous democratisation of the EC/EU over the past decades cannot be denied. The

---

[43] The Westminster system is a form of parliamentary democracy, see further Weale, note 26 above, 43.

[44] Schmidt, note 36 above, 36, 47–48.

[45] Moravcsik, note 27 above, 618.

[46] Ibid, 605, 610.

[47] The concept of Pareto efficiency refers to a situation where arrangements to make one person better off cannot be made without making someone else worse off; G Majone, *Europe as the Would-be World Power: The EU at Fifty* (Cambridge, CUP, 2009) 33. See also G Majone, 'The Rise of the Regulatory State in Europe' (1994) 17 *West European Politics* 78; G Majone, *Regulating Europe* (London, Routledge, 1996); G Majone, 'The Credibility Crisis of Community Regulation' (2000) 38 *Journal of Common Market Studies* 273.

[48] S Weatherill, 'Competence and Legitimacy' in C Barnard and O Odudu (eds), *The Outer Limits of European Union Law* (Oxford, Hart Publishing, 2009) 17–34, 25–26.

[49] A Follesdal and S Hix, 'Why There is a Democratic Deficit in the EU: A Response to Majone and Moravcsik' (2006) 44 *Journal of Common Market Studies* 533, 551–57. On the necessity of 'input' see also R Bellamy, 'Democracy without Democracy? Can the EU's Democratic "Outputs" be Separated from the Democratic "Inputs" Provided by Competitive Parties and Majority Rule' (2010) 17 *Journal of European Public Policy* 2.

[50] EO Eriksen and JE Fossum, 'A Done Deal? The EU's Legitimacy Conundrum Revisited' in EO Eriksen, C Joerges and F Rodl (eds), *Law, Democracy and Solidarity in a Post-National Union: The Unsettled Political Order of Europe* (London, Routledge, 2008) 230–52, 234.

central issue in this respect is 'a false problem'[51] of the application of the theories of democracy developed for states to the EU.[52] An alternative is seen in potential comparisons of the EU with intergovernmental institutions aimed at solving global issues in an interdependent world.[53] In comparison with traditional international organisations (viewed as a legitimate comparison),[54] there would be no need to defend the democracy of the EU as in cases of international organisations, national democracies have no link with the decisions made outside their constitutional system.[55] Nevertheless, the EU cannot be reduced to a traditional international organisation due to its pattern of transfer of powers from the national level, its political union and increasing diffusion of supranational governance into the democratic, political and economic life of its members. Thus, due to lack of an alternative, and because the statist model of democracy allows for a 'fallback' position, the statist concept of democracy can be used to trace the democratic evolution of the EU.[56] However, any 'fallback' position should be taken with caution. First of all, one should bear in mind the gap existing between 'ideal' democracy and the practices of states in reality.[57] Second, normative concepts developed at the national level can hardly be transferred to the supranational level without substantial modifications in their operation, or their conceptualisation in a new light.[58]

The mere comparison of the Rome Treaty, silent on any expression of democracy, and the provisions of the Lisbon Treaty, stipulating the principles of representative and participatory democracy in the Union, accompanied by decades of changing practices, makes it necessary to acknowledge the development of the EU into *a* democracy. The provisions of the revised TEU for the first time provide normative indications as to the EU's democratic values. It is at this most recent phase of constitutional development that democracy promotion by the EU can be considered most justified.

4.3 IDENTIFICATION OF DEMOCRATIC VALUES

The EU evolved by incorporating certain values into its constitutional order. Instead of focusing on the development of separate institutions in the EU, the discussion that follows places these developments in a context of certain values.

---

[51] Schütze, note 6 above, 74.

[52] A Heriter, 'Elements for Democratic Legitimation in Europe: an Alternative Perspective' (1999) 6 *Journal of European Public Policy* 269, 280; M Jachtenfuchs, 'Democracy and Governance in the EU' (1997) 1 *European Integration Online Papers* 40; Meny, note 31 above, 10; JC Piris, 'Where Will the Lisbon Treaty Lead Us' in A Arnull, C Barnard et al (eds), *A Constitutional Order of States? Essays in EU Law in Honour of Alan Dashwood* (Oxford, Hart Publishing, 2011) 59–74, 71.

[53] Heriter, note 52 above, 280.

[54] Craig, note 36 above, 27.

[55] MP Maduro, 'Europe and the Constitution: What if This is as Good as It Gets?' in JHH Weiler and M Wind (eds), *European Constitutionalism Beyond the State* (Cambridge, CUP, 2003) 74–102, 84.

[56] Meny, note 31 above, 10.

[57] Dahl, *On Democracy*, note 25 above, 31.

[58] Weale, note 26 above, 239.

4.3.1 Representation as a Democratic Value

While majority rule is behind every notion of democracy, it is the mechanism of representation that is used in modern democracies to ensure popular governance. In large-scale systems instead of direct democracy representation is secured via elections to choose citizens' representatives.

4.3.1.1 Supranational Representation

The original Assembly established in the Rome Treaty was a rather different institution from the Parliament of today. Comprised of members of national parliaments, the legislative role of the Assembly was confined to consultation and it had limited powers of oversight of other institutions.[59]

The 'Communitarian' outlook of the Parliament combined with its proactive attitude gradually necessitated a change in its position. At the 1974 Paris Summit, it urged the Council to facilitate direct elections to the Parliament, and subsequently found support in the Tindemans Report linking the issue of direct elections to popular interest.[60] The first direct elections to the EP took place in 1979.

In its turn the Court was instrumental in enhancing the role of the Parliament in the decision making of the EU, exemplified in the stance taken in *Roquette Frères*, *Le Verts*, *Chernobyl* and other cases.[61] The importance of representation was acknowledged in relation to the consultation procedure in *Roquette Frères*, which was said to reflect at Community level 'the fundamental democratic principle that the peoples should take part in the exercise of power through the intermediary of a representative assembly'.[62] The Court therefore went beyond the original Treaties to transpose a 'fundamental democratic principle' to Community level,[63] by placing representation at its centre.

Subsequent Treaty amendments gave the Parliament more power to supplement its representative function. The SEA introduced the cooperation procedure, enhancing the Parliament's role in EU decision making.[64] The co-decision procedure which followed in the Maastricht Treaty was by far the most far-reaching method of Parliament's involvement, allowing the latter to feature as a joint legislator with the

---

[59] Art 138, Treaty Establishing the European Economic Community, 11957E/TXT.

[60] Meeting of the Heads of Government, 9–10 December 1974, Paris, EC Bulletin No 12, 1974, para 5; Report by Mr Leo Tindemans to the European Council, 'European Union', EC Bulletin Supplement 1/76, 28.

[61] In *Le Verts* the Court added the Parliament to the list of the institutions against whose actions annulment proceedings can be brought; Case 294/83 *Parti Ecologiste 'Le Verts' v Parliament* [1986] ECR 1339, para 23. In *Chernobyl* the EP was allowed to bring annulment proceedings against other institutions to defend its prerogatives; Case C-70/88 *Chernobyl* [1990] ECR I-2041, para 3; Case 138/79 *SA Roquette Frères v Council of the European Communities* [1980] ECR-03333, para 37; Case T-135/96 *UEAPME* [1997] ECR I-01061.

[62] Case 138/79 *SA Roquette Frères v Council of the European Communities* [1980] ECR-03333, para 33.

[63] Mancini, note 9 above, 35.

[64] Art 6 SEA.

Council.[65] The co-decision procedure also contributed to a change of perceptions of the EP held by other institutions. The Commission, for instance, acknowledged the Parliament's role in enhancing the 'two-fold legitimacy' of the EU.[66] The co-decision procedure has been further extended to more policy areas by the Amsterdam and Nice Treaties, ultimately turning the Parliament into a power to be reckoned with, to which the Council increasingly diverts its attention.[67]

The Lisbon Treaty goes further than any other Treaty in increasing the powers of the EP, the real 'winner' of the Treaty amendments.[68] Co-decision has become the 'ordinary' legislative procedure and has been extended to almost 40 areas.[69] The flexibility provision in Article 352 TFEU currently requires the consent of the Parliament instead of consultation. As noted previously, Article 218 TFEU guarantees increased participation for the EP in the process of concluding international agreements, while Article 48 TEU entitles it to initiate Treaty revisions. Besides, the revised Treaty provisions also no longer distinguish between 'compulsory' and 'non-compulsory' expenditure, thus extending the Parliament's position.[70]

The enhancement of the EP's role even before the Lisbon Treaty meant that the EU could be viewed as a 'classic two chamber legislature'.[71] The Lisbon Treaty for the first time acknowledges this evolved feature of the EU legal order with reference to the principle of representative democracy. Article 10 TEU establishes the principle of EU dual representation: Union citizens are directly represented at supranational level via the Parliament, while the Member States are represented in the European Council by their heads of state or government and in the Council by their governments. Such 'double capacity representation' has been linked to the integration processes: the role of each of the institutions primarily reflects the level of integration of the EU.[72]

The Lisbon Treaty makes further attempts to address the detachment of ordinary citizens from EU governance: the very language of the provisions on citizenship emphasises the obvious connection with the democracy at the supranational level.[73] The right of every citizen to participate in the democratic life of the Union is linked to the necessity to take decisions as openly and as closely as possible to the citizen as provided in Article 10 TEU. The article therefore recognises the

---

[65] Former Art 251 EC.

[66] Scope of the Co-decision Procedure, SEC (96) 1225/4, July 1996, Pt IIA, para 1.

[67] M Shackleton, 'The European Parliament' in J Peterson and M Shackleton (eds), *The Institutions of the European Union*, 3rd edn (Oxford, OUP, 2012) 124–47, 139.

[68] P Craig, *The Lisbon Treaty: Law, Politics, and Treaty Reform* (Oxford, OUP, 2010) 36–39; M Dougan, 'The Treaty of Lisbon 2007: Winning Minds, Not Hearts' (2008) 45 *Common Market Law Review* 617, 692.

[69] Almost 30 new legal bases changed their respective procedures to co-decision, and 14 new legal bases were added with the same procedure; JC Piris, *The Lisbon Treaty: A Legal and Political Analysis* (Cambridge, CUP, 2010) 118.

[70] Arts 14(1) and 16(1) TEU; Piris, ibid, 119–20.

[71] S Hix, *The Political System of the European Union* (Basingstoke, Palgrave, 1999) 56.

[72] Lenaerts and Smijter, note 34 above, 176.

[73] J Shaw, 'The Constitutional Mosaic Across the Boundaries of the European Union: Citizenship Regimes in the New States of South East Europe' in N Walker, J Shaw and S Tierney (eds), *Europe's Constitutional Mosaic* (Oxford, Hart Publishing, 2011) 137–70, 146.

importance of citizens' participation in such aspects of EU decision making as subsidiarity.[74] Article 10 TEU also addresses the political parties with a view to raising European awareness and facilitating the expression of citizens' will.

While the role of the EP does not have to be defended within the representation narrative, the role of the Council as a non-elected institution demands justification.

From a representative perspective, before transforming into a Union of its peoples or citizens, the EU as an entity has been and continues to be a Union of its Member States. The Council therefore has a direct mandate from the Member States, thus revealing the second element of the EU's 'twofold legitimacy'. It is also argued that this aspect goes beyond the representation of the Member States. The Council has an indirect democratic mandate, as it consists of members of national executives elected at national level. The participation of the governments is therefore an indirect representation of the citizens in their capacity as the Member States' citizens. Thus, ultimately it is not the Member States, but their peoples which comprise 'the other constitution building subject'.[75] In this context, both aspects of dual representation can be traced back to popular will.

From a functional perspective, the role of the Council can be also defended due to its position to resolve issues requiring solution at supranational level. Reliable commitment in terms of decision implementation can be ensured only by those who themselves participated in achieving the agreements and are in a position to guarantee the credibility of such commitments.[76] Moreover, in the view of the budget of the EU being resourced from the Member States, the role of national governments is crucial, as they are held accountable at national level.[77]

Despite the development of the representative feature of the Union's democracy, the absence of the basic condition of representative democracy, that at election time the citizens 'can throw the scoundrels out', has been noticed as a drawback.[78] However, such validation would involve radical changes in the EU, which were not envisaged in the process of Treaty revisions.[79] Not only, would it exclude the Member States as those creating the main assurances and fulfilling the commitments, but it would also strip the Union of the second aspect of its 'dual representation' stemming from indirect citizen representation through the Member States. This is evident in the language of Article 1 TEU where the reference to the 'high contracting parties' makes is clear that it is a Union of its states, as well as of its citizens.

This two-fold representation should therefore be viewed as a modification of the principle of representative democracy once transposed to the supranational level, which nevertheless should not question the role of representation as a value.

---

[74] Craig, note 30 above, 122–23.
[75] J Habermas, *The Crisis of the European Union: A Response* (Cambridge, Polity, 2012) 35.
[76] Weale, note 26 above, 240–41.
[77] Lenaerts and Smijter, note 34 above, 182–83.
[78] Weiler, note 33 above, 6.
[79] P Craig and G de Búrca, *EU Law: Text, Cases and Materials*, 5th edn (Oxford, OUP, 2011) 154–55.

Even more so, it is said to confirm the 'federal nature' of the EU.[80] In practice, it would justify the EU's stance on conduct of free and fair elections in the neighbourhood. Besides, one would expect the EU to attach significance to the role of parliaments in neighbouring countries, as a central element of representative democracy.

Although the discussion above demonstrates the normative development of the element of representative democracy, in reality there are still grounds to question the Parliament's ability to resolve the issues of democratic accountability and legitimacy.[81] The links with the EU citizens are still weak, exemplified by low turnout at elections, as well as the voting over domestic issues articulated at national level.[82] Moreover, the citizens cannot link the formation of the executive to the outcomes of the parliamentary elections in the EU as at the national level.[83] They therefore seek political legitimisation at national level.

According to Mancini the 'democratic deficit' should be tackled 'in the very fabric of the Union'.[84] The developments regarding the role of the Parliament can therefore be seen as an example of this. Others consider that further democratic legitimisation should be directed to the national level.[85] The Treaty reform upholds representative democracy by not only emphasising the importance of representation at supranational level, but also by enhancing the role of the national parliaments. The parliamentary form of democracy has been noted to have informed these constitutional developments.[86]

4.3.1.2 National Parliaments

As noted earlier, originally the Commission justified the EU's standing on democracy promotion by reference to the democratic governance in its Member States. The 28 Member States each have their own democratic models, some with centuries of democratic tradition, others still struggling with the institutionalisation of democratic practices. Although various democratic practices in certain old and new Member States can be criticised, the centrality of parliament in the political

---

[80] Schütze, note 6 above, 44; JE Fossum, 'The Future of the European Order' in P Birkinshaw and M Varney (eds), *The European Union Legal Order After Lisbon* (The Hague, Kluwer Law International, 2010) 33–56, 45.

[81] S Hix, T Raunio, R Scully, 'Fifty Years On: Research on the European Parliament' (2003) 41 *Journal of Common Market Studies* 191, 192.

[82] R Corbett, F Jacobs and M Shackleton, 'The European Parliament at Fifty: A View from the Inside' (2003) 41 *Journal of Common Market Studies* 353, 359; F Amtenbrink, 'Towards a More Democratic Union? Comments on the Treaty Establishing a Constitution for Europe' in K Inglis and A Ott (eds), *The Constitution for Europe and an Enlarging Union: Unity in Diversity?* (Groningen, Europa Law Publishing, 2005) 31–55, 50; Laffan, note 21 above, 337; S Hix, AG Noury and G Roland, *Democratic Politics in the European Parliament* (Cambridge, CUP, 2007) 28.

[83] R Corbett, 'The Evolving Roles of the EP and of National Parliaments' in A Biondi and P Eeckhout (eds), *European Union Law After Lisbon* (Oxford, OUP, 2012) 248–61, 256.

[84] Mancini, note 9 above, 65–66.

[85] Piris, note 69 above, 126.

[86] EO Eriksen, *The Unfinished Democratisation of Europe* (Oxford, OUP, 2009) 217.

life of the Members is not a matter of debate. However, it is national parliaments that are viewed as the 'biggest losers' in the process of Europeanisation.[87]

First of all, national parliaments lost power when competence was transferred to supranational level in the most important spheres of national politics, lacking efficient instruments to call the Council to accountability through national governments.[88] As noted earlier, governments cannot be held accountable domestically for positions they did not take at supranational level. Not many parliaments of the Member States can control or veto the position of their government in the Council.[89] The lack of information and competence in national parliaments was noted to contribute to their restricted participation, and in particular their inability to safeguard the principle of subsidiarity.[90]

Contrary to these arguments, it is considered that the cause of such transformation is not the *EU* democratic deficit, but the democratic deficit *in Europe*. The tendency to prioritise effectiveness over parliamentary control is common also in national political systems in Western Europe, as a result of 'post-parliamentary or organic democracy'.[91] The dominance of strong executives over the past decades with relative autonomy in policymaking,[92] bureaucratisation and depoliticisation have been noted to contribute to the diminishing role of the representative element of democracy at national level.[93] However, the lack of criticism of national democracies can be justified because the main requirement of democratic theory is formally satisfied: parliaments are able to control national decision making.

From this perspective, the 'democratic deficiencies' of the EU are not the cause of the 'democratic deficit' in its Member States, but rather a consequence of it. The Member States are said to give up their autonomy to ensure effective problem solving at other levels of governance, whether subnational or transnational.[94] But because the national parliaments continue to symbolise the link between the citizens and the political system, their undermined role threatens the legitimacy of national democracies.

---

[87] Schmidt, note 36 above, 54, 223.

[88] Lenaerts and Smijter, note 34 above, 185.

[89] W Sadurski, 'EU Enlargement and Democracy in New Member States' in W Sadurski, A Czarnota and M Krygie (eds), *Spreading Democracy and the Rule of Law: The Impact of EU Enlargement on the Rule of Law, Democracy and Constitutionalism in Post-communist Legal Orders* (Dordrecht, Springer, 2006) 27–49, 35.

[90] A Sajo, 'Becoming "Europeans": The Impact of EU "Constitutionalism" on Post-Communist Pre-Modernity' in Sadurski, Czarnota and Krygie (eds), ibid, 175–92, 183.

[91] S Andersen and T Burns, 'The EU and the Erosion of Parliamentary Democracy: A Study of Post-parliamentary Governance' in S Andersen and KA Eliassen (eds), *The European Union: How Democratic Is It?* (London, Sage, 1996) 227–51, 229–30; Mancini, note 9 above, 68.

[92] J O'Brennan and T Raunio, 'Deparliamentarisation and European Integration' in J O'Brennan and T Raunio, *National Parliaments within the Enlarged European Union: From 'Victims' of Integration to Competitive Actors* (London, Routledge, 2007) 1–26, 7–8.

[93] R Dehousse, 'Beyond Representative Democracy: Constitutionalism in A Polycentric Polity' in Weiler and Wind (eds), note 55 above 135–56, 137; M MacCarthaigh, 'Accountability through National Parliaments, Practice and Problems' in O'Brennan and Raunio (eds), note 92 above, 29–45, 39–41.

[94] W Wessels, 'The Modern West European State and the European Union: Democratic Erosion or a New Kind of Polity' in S Andersen and KA Eliassen (eds), note 91 above, 57–69, 62.

The importance of the national parliaments was first acknowledged in the Amsterdam Treaty's Protocol on the role of national parliaments with provisions on supply of information by the Commission and the Conference of Parliamentary Committees for Union Affairs of Parliaments (COSAC). The Lisbon Treaty is the most important development in this trend, introducing a separate provision on the role of national parliaments in the text of the Treaty, elaborated further in additional protocols.[95]

Article 12 TEU accentuates the role of participation by national parliaments in EU decision making in a number of aspects. First, the Treaty and the protocol aim at creating a permanent information chain between the supranational and national levels. For the purpose of exercising efficient control over national governments, the Council must send the agendas for, and the outcome of, its meetings directly to national parliaments.[96] It has been noted that the Protocol on the national parliaments is about the national parliaments 'being better informed'.[97] In practice it can signify more than better information supply: their position in day-to-day legislation is strengthened vis-à-vis the executive, on whom they previously depended for information. A more inclusive approach is established inter alia in relation to Treaty revisions and accession applications. Moreover, obliging the Council to meet in public when considering and voting on a draft legislative act, the Lisbon Treaty further reinforces the positioning of the national parliaments and electorates vis-à-vis their governments.[98]

Another related issue is the safeguarding of the principle of subsidiarity, facilitated by sending the annual legislative programme of the Commission and draft legislative acts to national parliaments, which can forward their reasoned opinions to the EU institutions.[99] The combination of the provisions on the national parliaments facilitates engagement of national parliaments in EU affairs, and collaboration with national governments on their position in the Council.[100] In practice it also depends on the national parliaments' willingness to make full use of the provided mechanism.

Such engagement seems more realistic also due to the inter-parliamentary cooperation both between national parliaments and with the EP. This, perhaps, should be considered as a means of counterbalancing the dominance of the executive branch at European level, but most importantly at national level as regards European issues.[101]

---

[95] Protocol on the Role of National Parliaments in the European Union; Protocol on the Application of the Principles of Subsidiarity and Proportionality.

[96] Art 5, Protocol on the Role of National Parliaments.

[97] T Raunio, 'National Legislatures in the EU Constitutional Treaty' in O'Brennan and Raunio (eds), note 92 above, 79–92, 83.

[98] Art 16 TEU; Amtenbrink, note 82 above, 40.

[99] Art 4, Protocol on Subsidiarity; Arts 1, 2, 3, Protocol on the role of national parliaments.

[100] Corbett, note 83 above, 258.

[101] Art 12 TEU provides for participation of national parliaments in the evaluation of mechanisms for the implementation of policies in the area of freedom, security and justice.

Nevertheless, there are still limitations on the role of national parliaments. Some criticise the Treaties for not extending the new procedures beyond the application of the principle of subsidiarity.[102] Besides, the Treaty revisions missed an opportunity to clarify the role of national parliaments by not setting minimum conditions for their involvement.[103] It is therefore left to the national parliaments to determine the extent of their engagement. The danger is that national parliaments might still consider the oversight of the national government to be their priority.[104] Moreover, they are restricted in their options of following such established procedures, as comitology or trilogues.[105]

Despite these shortcomings, the inclusion of provisions on national parliaments among democratic principles of the EU supports the existence of representation as a democratic value of the EU. They demonstrate an attempt to preserve the democratic values of the Member States with their respective democracies, where the parliament is the main source of legitimacy. In its most recent statement on democracy promotion abroad, the Council places the representative aspects of democracy at the basis of the EU's vision of promotion of democracy.[106] One can therefore expect to see the promotion of representative democracy in the EU neighbourhood.

While representation satisfies one of the basic conditions in traditional democracies, in order to prevent the tyranny of the minority there should be restrictions on the exercise of power as developed in the liberal democratic approach. Here the EU has been noted to suffer from 'democratic overload'.[107]

4.3.2 Liberal Constitutionalism

Liberal democracy, or liberal constitutionalism is characterised by accountability of the executive branch of power to the parliament, a clear division of power between legislative, executive and judicial branches and the 'counter-majoritarian devices' of checks and balances.[108] A key feature of liberal democracies is the protection of citizens' rights and freedoms.

---

[102] Sadurski criticises the arrangements noted above for not being extended beyond the principle of subsidiarity: W Sadurski, *Constitutionalism and the Enlargement of Europe* (Oxford, OUP, 2012) 173.

[103] C Bengston, 'Interparliamentary Cooperation in Europe' in O'Brennan and Raunio, note 92 above, 46–65, 57.

[104] A Cygan, 'Collective' Subsidiarity Monitoring by National Parliaments after Lisbon: The Operation of the Early Warning Mechanism' in M Trybus and L Rubini (eds), *The Treaty of Lisbon and the Future of European Law and Policy* (Cheltenham, Edward Elgar Publishing Limited, 2012) 55–73, 71–72.

[105] D Curtin, 'The Council of Ministers: The Missing Link?' in L Verhey, P Kiiver, and S Loeffen (eds), *Political Accountability and European Integration* (Groningen, Europa Law Publishing, 2009) 125–35, 131, 133.

[106] EU Agenda for Action on Democracy Support in EU External Relations, Democracy Support in the EU's External Relations, Council Conclusions, External Relations, 17 November 2009, s 2.

[107] Meny, note 31 above, 4, 9.

[108] Weale, note 26 above, 331–32.

4.3.2.1 Institutional Balance

Although the EU is not characterised by a clear separation of powers, it is the idea of 'institutional balance' of the Union as established in Article 13 TEU that serves as a reference point for drawing parallels with the republican understanding of democracy based on separation of powers.[109] According to this notion, different institutions represent divergent interests within society, and the public good is served through a balanced cooperation between them.[110] Consequently, each EU institution fulfils its own democracy- and legitimacy-related role.[111] The institutions not only perform the functions allocated to them, but also balance the other branches of power. The balancing exercise aims to guarantee the safeguarding of the principle of conferred powers in accordance with Article 13 TEU. For instance, the Court performs the function of an independent judicial authority, but it is also called upon to decide on matters of competence delimitation for other institutions.

It is Parliament–Council and Parliament–Commission relations that have occupied the central place within the debate on institutional balance. These relations have a rather dynamic nature,[112] as the constitutional amendments and institutional practices significantly altered the original arrangements. As noted earlier, the evolution of legislative processes and the introduction of the co-decision procedure have turned the Parliament into the centre of the Council's attention to the detriment of the Commission.[113] Thus, the Parliament's ability to veto legislation in the co-decision procedure has proved to have become a powerful instrument in balancing the Council's power.[114] Nevertheless, the role of the EP is still limited in certain areas, of which the CFSP is an example.

As to Parliament–Commission relations, the EU does not strictly satisfy the conditions of accountability of the executive to parliament. The peripheral role of the EP changed with the post-Maastricht vote of confidence, and the post-Amsterdam power to veto the choices of the Member States for the President and the members of the Commission.[115] On a few occasions the Parliament demonstrated a willingness to 'throw the scoundrels out', with the examples of the Santer Commission or the withdrawal of the proposed Italian Commissioner Rocco Buttiglione due to an expected negative vote.[116] Over time the accountability of the Commission increased via such practices, as the scrutiny of the Commission's

---

[109] P Van Elsuwege and A Vermeersch, 'Institutional Reform in the European Union: A Difficult Balancing Act' in Inglis and Ott (eds), note 82 above, 57–84, 80; Craig, note 30 above, 113; Corbett et al, note 82 above, 368.

[110] Craig, *Democracy and Rule-making*, note 30 above, 115–16.

[111] J Shaw, *Law of the European Union* (Basingstoke, Palgrave, 2000) 238–39.

[112] Van Elsuwege and Vermeersch, note 109 above, 81.

[113] J Peterson, 'The College of Commissioners' in Peterson and Shackleton (eds), note 67 above, 71–93, 88.

[114] Amtenbrink, note 82 above, 73, 37.

[115] Currently Art 17(7) and (8) TEU.

[116] 'EP Comes of Age', *EU Observer*, 27 October 2004; EO Eriksen and JE Fossum, 'Democracy through Strong Publics in the European Union' (2002) 40 *Journal of Common Market Studies* 401, 412.

activities through the appearance of individual Commissioners in the Parliament's specialised committees.[117] Besides, the budgetary powers of the Parliament contribute to the control exercised over the Commission.[118]

The dynamics in Parliament–Commission relations have once again been altered by the Lisbon Treaty. The Parliament is currently entitled to elect the President of the Commission, instead of giving mere approval of his candidacy.[119] Most importantly the European Council should propose the candidacy taking into account the elections to the Parliament, which can be compared to the national context of appointing a prime minister representing the parliamentary majority.[120] Although this might undermine the Commission's independence, a principle enshrined in Article 17 TEU,[121] it might contribute to creating the image the citizens are most accustomed to, that is the link between elections and formation of the executive.

Although the Lisbon Treaty continued the trend in extending the Parliament's control over the Commission, it nevertheless created new causes for concern. Instead of concentrating all issues of accountability in one institution, namely the Commission, the constitutional reform resulted in multiplication of executives, further fuelling the accountability debate.[122] General scrutiny rights are provided over the office of the permanent President, who has to present a report to the EP after the meetings of the European Council.[123] The position of the High Representative has been discussed previously.[124]

4.3.2.2 What Type of Demos?

As noted above, the protection of individuals' rights is an inalienable feature of any liberal democratic polity. Established as a community of states, the EU institutions were not created in order to safeguard or promote rights in general. Besides, to which basis should such rights have been attached?

In this regard the EU's democratic model has been viewed to be incomplete due to a lack of 'demos' or 'Volk' constituting the basis of a democratic regime.[125] Although the most common reference to demos is in its ethno-cultural understanding, even the traditional models of democracy have been noted to fail in providing a

---

[117] Peterson, note 113 above, 88.

[118] Arts 318–319 TFEU; Corbett et al, note 82 above, 366.

[119] Arts 14(1), 17(7) TEU.

[120] Hix et al, note 82 above, 17; Corbett, note 83 above, 250–51; Craig, note 68 above, 34.

[121] Dougan, note 68 above, 693–94.

[122] M Shackleton, 'The European Commission and Parliamentary Oversight' in L Verhey, P Kiiver, and Sr Loeffen (eds), *Political Accountability and European Integration* (Groningen, Europa Law Publishing, 2009) 79–83, 82; P Craig, 'Executive Accountability and the Contestability of the Executive Domain' in Verhey, Kiiver, and Loeffen (eds), ibid, 153–71, 171.

[123] Art 15(6) TEU.

[124] See Chapter 3, section 3.2.2.3.

[125] JHH Weiler, 'In Defence of the Status Quo: Europe's Constitutional Sonderweg' in Weiler and Wind (eds), note 55 above, 7–23, 8–9; Weiler et al, note 30 above, 12–15.

clear theory of 'demos'.[126] Defining 'demos' traditionally has become even more difficult in multicultural and multi-ethnic societies. Weiler noted an alternative to statist 'demos' existing 'on the basis of shared values, shared understanding of rights and societal duties and shared rational, intellectual culture which transcend ethno-national differences' without replacing the national ethno-cultural dimension.[127] According to Habermas what unites 'a nation of citizens' is not a common ethno-cultural background, but rather 'an intersubjectively shared context of possible understanding' which is part of the democratic processes itself.[128] Others propose a 'demos' consisting of 'multiple and shifting demoi' characterised as groups of those who are affected by EU decisions.[129] A diverse demos united in its shared understanding of its political and social context can therefore coexist with traditional understanding of national demos without replacing it. Thus, instead of the notion of 'Volk' it has been suggested that the concept of 'citizenship' should be used for the supranational discourse.[130] The concept of EU citizenship within the wider Treaty framework can be argued to provide a framework for exploring alternative visions of demos described above.

The peculiarity of the EU lies in the fact that the 'rights' and 'freedoms' discourse preceded the introduction of the concept of citizenship in the Maastricht Treaty. While the Rome Treaty merely provided economic freedoms for mobile citizens of its Member States, the Court of Justice was instrumental in the development of this feature of the EU model. Based on the national constitutional traditions and international instruments, the Court carved out the EC's own niche for protecting fundamental rights and freedoms as a general principle of law.[131] Thus, rights were affirmed prior to identifying the subjects of those rights in the EU context. Citizenship of the EU constitutionalised the bearers of those rights transforming them from Member State citizens to Union citizens. Introduced in the Maastricht Treaty, EU citizenship enhanced democratic decision making by concretising the link between the people and the European system.[132] Although citizenship rights were limited to traditional mobility rights and

---

[126] F Requejo, 'Liberal Democracy's Timber is Still Too Straight: The Case of Political Models for Coexistence in Composite States' in N Walker, J Shaw and S Tierney (eds), note 73 above, 231–52, 238–39.

[127] Weiler et al, note 30 above, 19, 23.

[128] J Habermas, 'Remarks on Dieter Grimm's "Does Europe Need a Constitution?"' (1995) 1 *European Law Journal* 303, 305.

[129] JW Müller, 'The Promise of "Demoi-Cracy": Democracy, Diversity, and Domination in the European Public Order' in J Neyer and A Wiener (eds), *Political Theory of the European Union* (Oxford, OUP, 2011) 187–203, 200.

[130] A Von Bogdandy, 'The European Lesson for International Democracy: The Significance of Articles 9 and 12 EU Treaty for International Organisations', Jean Monnet Working Paper 01/11, NYU School of Law, 2011, 10; A Von Bogdandy, 'Founding Principles' in A Von Bogdandy and J Bast (eds), *Principles of European Constitutional Law*, 2nd edn (Oxford, Hart Publishing, 2010) 11–54, 49.

[131] Case 11/70 *Internationale Handelsgesellschaft* [1970] ECR 1125, para 4; Case 4/73 *Nold v Commission* [1974] ECR 491, para 13.

[132] Hoskyns and Newman, note 17 above, 196.

certain political rights, they proved to be 'dynamic',[133] and due to judicial activism have become a 'fundamental status' of the Union citizens.[134]

EU citizenship provides an alternative to statist 'demos' by uniting the citizens of the Member States via the list of shared values in Article 2 TEU. Besides, the principle of equality, implanted in the concept of citizenship in the Treaties and actively upheld by the Court,[135] is said to complement the mutual recognition of diversity.[136] Moreover, the very location of Article 9 TEU on citizenship within Title II on provisions on democratic principles demonstrates the link between democracy in the EU and the citizenship as its popular basis as noted earlier.

Even the sceptics acknowledged the potential of the concept of EU citizenship if political rights were accompanied by certain social underpinning to make citizens' political rights a reality.[137] The declaration of the Charter of Fundamental Rights in 2000 further contributed to the protection of citizens' rights. The Charter has acquired a binding legal force in the Lisbon Treaty and therefore constitutes a part of the current regime on human rights protection. Not less important is the provision in Article 6 TEU obliging the EU to accede to the European Convention of Human Rights, which would provide an additional catalogue of rights and would allow further scrutiny. In continuation of the trend of a more reinforced protection of human rights, a Fundamental Rights Agency was established to specialise in issues of fundamental rights, and provide assistance to the EU institutions as regards policies affecting the latter.[138] Its capacity regrettably does not extend to such important areas as the CFSP and cooperation in criminal matters – a criticism that can be added to others directed at the protection of human rights in the EU.[139]

Besides, the concept of EU citizenship and the expanded catalogue of rights did not lead to popular citizen participation. The latter has become an additional ground for criticising EU decision making, viewed as 'a cartel of elites' controlling the political agenda.[140] Such criticism, however, should be placed in the context of the shortcomings of modern representative democracies in Western Europe

---

[133] D O'Keeffe, 'Union Citizenship' in D O'Keeffe and PM Twomey (eds), *Legal Issues of Maastricht Treaty* (New Jersey, John Wiley and Sons, 1994) 87–107, 102.

[134] Case C-413/99 *Baumbast and R v Secretary of State for the Home Department* [2002] ECR I-7091, para 82.

[135] Case C-85/96 *Maria Martinez Sala v Freistaat Bayern* [1998] ECR I-2691, paras 62–63; Case C-184/99 *Rudy Grzelczyk v CPAS* [2001] ECR I-6193, para 36; Case C 456/02 *Trojani v CPAS* [2004] ECR I-7573, paras 39–40.

[136] S Kadelbach, 'Union Citizenship' in Von Bogdandy and Bast (eds), note 130 above, 443–78, 476.

[137] R Kuper, 'Democratisation: a Constitutionalising Process' in Hoskyns and Newman (eds), note 17 above, 156–73, 168–72.

[138] Art 1, Council Regulation No 168/2007, [2007] OJ L53/1.

[139] E Spaventa, 'Fundamental What? The Difficult Relationship between Foreign Policy and Fundamental Rights' in M Cremona and B de Witte, *European Union Foreign Relations Law: Constitutional Fundamentals* (Oxford, Hart Publishing, 2008) 233–55, 234. For criticism of human rights protection in the EU see for instance J Coppel and A O'Neill, 'The European Court of Justice: Taking Rights Seriously?' (1992) *Common Market Law Review* 669; A Williams, *EU Human Rights Policies: A Study in Irony* (Oxford, OUP, 2004).

[140] Dehousse, note 93 above, 149, 156.

generally where non-democratic political bargaining coexists with traditional democratic processes.[141] In this context the need for legitimisation through a more process-orientated approach becomes more pressing.

4.3.3 Participation and Deliberation as a Democratic Value

In polities operating on a large scale the effective participation of citizens in the political process, that is the reflection of the opinion of those affected by decision making, is more challenging.[142] Large-scale political organisations are capable of providing effectiveness in decision making in comparison with the national level, but they also create a dilemma between effectiveness and participation linked to the 'input' and 'output' democracy. In the EU context its legitimacy was inter alia criticised due to targeting only groups of people with minimal access to decision making.[143]

The issue of citizens' participation has been reflected in democratic theory. Within the normative understanding of participatory democracy, with its focus on the central role of citizens' participation in the democratic process, different approaches have been elaborated. These include 'discursive' democracy as developed by Habermas, the 'strong' democracy of Barber, and the 'directly-deliberative' model developed by Cohen and Sobel.[144] Fuchs notices two common features of these approaches, namely the direct nature of citizens' participation in governance and the central place of deliberation in political will formation.[145] According to Habermas, deliberative politics exists within two spheres: democratically institutionalised will formation and informal opinion formation, where communication takes place among those who are potentially affected, which ultimately results in a solution to relevant problems in the political public sphere.[146] Discourse among those who will be affected by decision making is a necessary element in the chain of this process.[147] It should be noted that the quest for participation through deliberation does not require replacement of traditional repre-

---

[141] Dahl, *On Democracy*, note 25 above, 113.

[142] Ibid, 110, 125–231; Laffan, note 21 above, 339.

[143] Petitioning through the EP was the only available method of direct involvement for citizens, and only after the institution of Ombudsman was introduced by the EU Treaty did citizens acquire another possibility for bringing complaints at the EU level; Schmidt, note 36 above, 28.

[144] D Fuchs, 'Participatory, Liberal and Electronic Democracy' in T Zittel and D Fuchs (eds), *Participatory Democracy and Political Participation: Can Participatory Engineering Bring Citizens Back in?* (London, Routledge, 2007) 29–54, 39.

[145] Ibid.

[146] J Habermas, *Contributions to a Discourse Theory of Law and Democracy* (Cambridge, Polity Press, 1996) 308, 365.

[147] BR Barber, *Strong Democracy: Participatory Politics for a New Age* (Berkeley, University of California Press, 1984) 136; J Dryzek, 'Legitimacy and Economy in Deliberative Democracy' (2001) 29 *Political Theory* 651, 651; Cohen, as cited in Weale, note 26 above, 78; A Verhoeven, *The European Union in Search of a Democratic and Constitutional Theory* (London, Kluwer Law International, 2002) 39.

sentative institutions, rather it 'supplements the processes'.[148] Thus 'functional representation' should not replace 'political representation'.[149]

Another shared feature of various conceptions of participatory democracy is adaptation of the models to the circumstances of modern societies.[150] The EU is not an exception in this sense, with major debates over participatory aspects of its decision making developing throughout the last two decades. Since the early 1990s, public participation has attracted attention mainly in connection with the issues of openness and transparency.[151] The White Paper on Governance declared participation as one of the principles of good governance in the EU in 2001.[152] The Charter of Fundamental Rights and the conventional manner of its drafting was considered to be directed at citizens in order to acknowledge the EU's 'commitments in a public process' with a view to enhancing its dual legitimacy.[153] The significance of the drafting of the Charter lies in the composition of the drafting Convention and its participative and deliberative nature which served as a relatively 'open forum for constitutional debate'.[154] The Convention was also unprecedented due to the availability of information on the procedure and content of the drafting process, as well as the limited involvement of civil society through hearings.[155]

A similar method was adopted subsequently for the Convention on the Future of Europe responsible for drafting the Treaty establishing a Constitution for Europe.[156] The Convention has been considered to be an improvement and a success in terms of deliberation and consensus making and openness of its proceedings.[157] At the same time, the Convention and the subsequent IGC only

---

[148] Weale, note 26 above, 81.

[149] A Verhoeven, 'Democratic Life in the European Union, According to its Constitution' in DM Curtin and RA Wessel (eds), *Good Governance and the European Union: Reflections on Concepts, Institutions and Substance* (Antwerp, Intersentia, 2005) 153–71, 170.

[150] Fuchs, note 144 above, 39.

[151] D Chryssochoou, 'Democracy and the European Polity' in M Cini (ed), *European Union Politics*, 2nd edn (Oxford, OUP, 2007) 359–73, 363; Scope of the Co-Decision Procedure, Commission Report under Article 189b (8), SEC (96) 1225/4, July 1996, paras 23, 39; Inter-Institutional Declaration on Democracy, Transparency and Subsidiarity, adopted by the Commission, Council and the EP at the Brussels European Council, October 1993.

[152] European Commission, White Paper on European Governance COM (2001) 428 final, 25 July 2001, 10.

[153] [2000] OJ C3634; G de Búrca, 'The Drafting of the European Union Charter of Human Rights' (2001) 26 *European Law Review* 126, 130.

[154] The Convention had European and national level representatives of the Member States, EP, national parliaments and one representative of the Commission; de Búrca, ibid, 138; MP Maduro, 'The Double Constitutional Life of the Charter of Fundamental Rights of the European Union' in T Hervey and J Kenner (eds), *Economic and Social Rights under the EU Charter of Fundamental Rights – A Legal Perspective* (Oxford, Hart Publishing, 2003) 269–99, 271.

[155] Eriksen and Fossum, note 116 above, 417–18.

[156] The Convention was composed of representatives of the Member States and candidate state governments, members of national parliaments and the EP, two representatives of the Commission, and representatives of other Community institutions with observer status.

[157] J Schonlau, 'The Convention Method' in D Castiglione, J Schonlau et al, *Constitutional Politics in the European Union: The Convention Moment and its Aftermath* (Basingstoke, Palgrave, 2007) 90–111, 90, 96, 98, 110.

demonstrated that participation is a nascent phenomenon. Certain criticism has been directed towards the President's excessive power, 'hearing' and 'consultation' instead of 'dialogue' with the civil society,[158] as well as the exclusion of EU and national parliamentarians from the IGC following the Convention.[159] Another major lacuna was noted to be the general public's inability to reflect its concerns through the Convention method.[160]

It should be noted that the Convention method was not adopted for the Lisbon Treaty revisions, which nevertheless did not depart from the Constitutional Treaty in substance.   Besides, under Article 48 TEU the ordinary revision procedure is based on a Convention method unless the European Council decides otherwise due to the extent of the proposed amendments.

To mainstream citizens' participation in the political process, the Lisbon Treaty specifies the participatory aspects of EU decision making in Article 11 TEU, which is said to be the 'culmination' of previously existing institutional practices.[161] The participation of citizens is elevated to the status of a democratic principle. The safeguarding of citizens' participation is imposed on the institutions, which, it can be argued, institutionalises informal opinion formation. Although Article 11 TEU is rather general and much is left for elaboration, its language is mandatory, and is therefore not to be dismissed.[162]

In addition to the institutionalisation of will formation, Article 11(4) TEU allows for citizens' right to invite the Commission to submit a legislative proposal if the support of one million citizens is secured. This can be compared with Habermas's 'outside initiative model', where the initiative stems from the outside of the political system.[163] In this model the pressure created by public opinion compels official consideration of the matter causing concern. With a view to enhancing the accessibility of the Union to its citizens based on Article 11(4) TEU the Council and the Parliament adopted the Regulation on citizens' initiative.[164]

Thus, previous practices and the Lisbon Treaty provisions testify to the emergence of participation as a democratic principle of the EU. The drafters of the initial Constitutional Treaty accepted deliberative politics as central to the understanding of participatory democracy in the EU context. Adopting participatory models in its constitutional practice and obliging the institutions to ensure citizens' participation can entail that the EU will require its neighbours to share the same democratic value.

It can therefore be concluded that the EU has its own evolutionary and dynamic non-ideal democratic model. Democracy as a value is shared between the EU and its Members States: the EU has attempted to enhance its democratic credentials,

---

[158]   Ibid, 95; E Lombardo, 'The Participation of the Civil Society' in ibid, 153–69, 154, 155.
[159]   Bengston, note 103 above, 54.
[160]   R Bellamy, note 49 above, 10.
[161]   J Mendes, *Participation in EU Rule-making: A Rights Based Approach* (Oxford, OUP, 2011) 140, 451.
[162]   Craig, note 68 above, 67.
[163]   Habermas, note 146 above, 379–84.
[164]   Recital 2 in the Preamble; Regulation (EU) No 211/2011 of the European Parliament and of the Council of 16 February 2011 on the citizens' initiative [2011] OJ L65/1.

but also to preserve the democratic models of its Member States. Although the specific characteristics of the EU as a multi-level polity often require different application of state-based democratic concepts, the democratic values of representation, liberal constitutional values and participation are values shared between the EU and its Member States. It is these values that the EU claims to promote in its neighbourhood. As the enlargement is viewed to have succeeded in the democratic transformation of the candidate countries, and since the ENP attempts to replicate this practice, it is apt to consider how the EU democratic values have been reflected in this process of transformation.

4.4 THE PRECEDENT OF ENLARGEMENT

Due to preparations by a large number of countries for the 2004 accession round their democratic transformation had become a matter of 'retaining the EU's essential identity'.[165] While previously the EU had not set out the prerequisites of democracy promotion, its 'basic tenets' were laid down during the last two rounds of enlargement.[166]

4.4.1 Creating Democracies in Accession States

As a general rule democratic practices are the result of predominantly cumulative transformation under domestic pressure occurring over a period of time. External influences play a secondary role in this process. The accession process of the CEE states is considered to be an exception to this general rule,[167] where the membership incentive was perceived to be the main driving force behind the democratic changes.

On a note of caution, the attribution, largely, of the perceived success of political transformation in the CEE states to the accession process is problematic, since it dismisses the larger political context. First, the timing of the accession process was crucial: the offer of the EU model had coincided with the efforts of the CEE political leadership to replace or establish new institutions.[168] Second, their accession took place in parallel with the integration into other organisations advocating the principles of liberal democracy, including the Council of

[165] R Youngs, 'Normative Dynamics and Strategic Interests in the EU's External Identity' (2004) 42 *Journal of Common Market Studies* 415, 416.

[166] R Balfour, *Human Rights and Democracy in EU Foreign Policy: The Cases of Ukraine and Egypt* (London, Routledge, 2012) 7.

[167] C Hillion, 'The Copenhagen Criteria and their Progeny' in C Hillion (ed), *EU Enlargement: A Legal Approach* (Oxford, Hart Publishing, 2004) 1–22, 4; G Pridham, 'The International Dimension of Democratisation: Theory, Practice, and Inter-regional Comparisons' in G Pridham, Herring and Sanford (eds), *Building Democracy? The International Dimension of Democratisation in Eastern Europe* (London, Leicester University Press, 1994) 7–31, 9.

[168] H Grabbe, 'How Does Europeanisation Affect CEE Governance? Conditionality, Diffusion and Diversity' (2001) 8 *Journal of European Public Policy* 1013, 1014.

Europe, the OSCE and NATO.[169] It is therefore difficult to delimit specifically the influence of EU conditionality on the democratic transformation of the countries concerned.

Although the Rome Treaty itself did not refer to democratic conditionality in Article 237, the latter slowly emerged outside the Treaties. For the first time, in approving the Birkelbach Report, the Parliament referred to the necessity of observing democratic practices in the candidate states.[170] The European Council of 1978 specified that representative democracy is an 'essential element' of membership in the EC.[171] 'Pluralist democracy' was specified by the Commission as an element essential for pre-accession.[172] This conditionality in its early underdeveloped form was first tested in the accession of Greece, Spain and Portugal, who satisfied formal conditions of liberal democracies when joining the EU.[173] As discussed previously, the accession of the CEE states stood out due to the institutional recognition of the political conditionality and the subsequent linking of the membership perspective to democracy in Article 49 EU by making a reference to Article 6 EU in the Amsterdam Treaty.

However, references to democracy as a condition for membership did not simultaneously provide the prerequisites or the specificities of democracy the candidate countries were expected to build, rendering the implementation of democratic conditionality 'disaggregated' without full awareness of its meaning.[174]

The change arrived in 1997 when the Commission initiated an evaluation of the candidates' progress in annual reports, with political conditionality said to acquire a 'real bite'.[175] The necessity to assess the progress was the main rationale for specifying the content of democracy within political conditionality.[176] Thus, in 1997 the Council specified the following prerequisites:

- representative government, accountable executive;
- government and public authorities to act in a manner consistent with the constitution and the law;

---

[169] F Schimmelfennig and U Sedelmeier, 'Conclusions: The Impact of the EU on the Accession Counties' in F Schimmelfennig and U Sedelmeier (eds), *The Europeanisation of Central and Eastern Europe* (London, Cornell University Press, 2005) 210–28, 212; Sadurski, note 102 above, 154; P Magnette and K Nicolaidis, 'The European Union's Democratic Agenda' in M Telo (ed), *The EU and Global Governance* (London, Routledge, 2009) 43–63, 49.

[170] Report on the Political and Institutional Aspects of Accession to or Association with the Community, 19 December 1961.

[171] Copenhagen European Council, 7–8 April 1978, Declaration on Democracy, EC Bulletin, No 3 (1978) 6.

[172] Commission Opinion on the application for accession to the European Communities by the Hellenic Republic [1979] OJ L291/3; Commission Opinion on the applications for accession to the European Communities by the Kingdom of Spain and the Portuguese Republic [1985] OJ L302/3.

[173] G Pridham, 'The European Union's Democratic Conditionality and Domestic Politics in Slovakia: the Meciar and Dzurinda Governments Compared' (2002) 54 *Europe-Asia Studies* 203, 205–06.

[174] G Pridham, 'EU Enlargement and Consolidating Democracy in Post-Communist States – Formality and Reality' (2002) 40 *Journal of Common Market Studies* 953, 958.

[175] Sadurski, note 89 above, 77, 29.

[176] D Kochenov, *EU Enlargement and the Failure of Conditionality: Pre-Accession Conditionality in the Fields of Democracy and the Rule of Law* (Austin, Wolters Kluwer Law and Business, 2008) 86.

• separation of powers;
• free and fair elections at reasonably intervals by secret ballot.[177]

Although rather general, these prerequisites served as an indication for reforms, and were supplemented by other documents, where reference was made to 'the consolidation of pluralist democratic procedures and practice', including support for 'acquisition and application of knowledge and technique of parliamentary practice and organisation'.[178] In addition, the strengthening of NGO capacity was considered to contribute to development of a pluralist society.[179]

In this connection, Kaldor and Vejvoda differentiated between formal and substantive conditions for democracy. The formal conditions imply inclusive citizenship, the rule of law, separation of powers, elected power-holders, free and fair elections, freedom of expression, associational autonomy, and civilian control over the security forces; and substantive democracy assumes political equality, power distribution and a political culture of democratic participation.[180]

The most detailed reference to democracy as an element of the Copenhagen political criteria was provided in the Commission's 'Agenda 2000',[181] which was aimed primarily at evaluating whether accession negotiations should be opened.[182] The Commission referred to formal criteria of democracy under the heading of 'Democracy and Rule of Law', mixing these concepts together. The constitutions of applicant countries were to guarantee democratic freedoms, including political pluralism, freedom of expression and freedom of religion, establishment of democratic institutions and independent judicial and constitutional authorities. The conduct of free and fair elections should allow the alternation of different political parties in power, and a greater role for opposition parties.[183]

Based on these prerequisites the Commission then evaluated the political practice of democracy in the applicant countries, including the distribution of power in reality, the political culture of participation, the level of protection of constitutional freedoms in practice and others.[184] The Union was therefore thought to have transgressed the criteria of formal democracy and embraced those of substantive democracy.[185] However, the 'process' aspect of transformation was noted to be more problematic in terms of foreign influence in comparison with the

---

[177] Council Conclusions of 29 April 1997 on the application of conditionality with a view to developing a coherent EU strategy for its relations with the countries in the region, s 1.4.67.

[178] Guidelines, The European Union's Phare and Tacis Democracy Programme, as cited in GR Olsen, 'Promotion of Democracy as a Foreign Policy Instrument of "Europe": Limits to International Idealism' (2000) 7 *Democratisation* 142, 148.

[179] Olsen, ibid, 149.

[180] M Kaldor, 'Eastern Enlargement and Democracy' in Hoskyns and Newman (eds), note 17 above, 139–55, 140–41; M Kaldor and I Vejvoda (eds), *Democratisation in Central and Eastern Europe* (London, Continuum, 2002) 4–5.

[181] European Commission, 'Agenda 2000: For a Stronger and Wider Union' EU Bulletin Supplement 5/97 (hereinafter 'Agenda 2000').

[182] KE Smith, 'The Evolution and Application of EU Membership Conditionality' in M Cremona (ed), *The Enlargement of the European Union* (Oxford, OUP, 2003) 105–39, 115.

[183] Agenda 2000, 40.

[184] Ibid, 40–41.

[185] Pridham, note 173 above, 203, 222.

'procedure'.[186] The question then comes down to whether the formal criteria have been complied with satisfactorily.

The conditions specified by the EU institutions, although indicative, were not particularly detailed or specific. On the one hand, this helped the Commission to avoid the challenge of imposing a particular model on candidate countries, and therefore allowed for national variations.[187] On the other hand, the lack of precision and clarity of the criteria and compliance benchmarks eventually resulted in a lower threshold for fulfilling the criteria, difficulty in assessment of progress, and 'poor analysis quality provided by the Commission, including random choice of issues, unreliable conclusions, numerous contradictions and a curious approach to democracy'.[188] Moreover, the evaluation was reduced to the overview of the functioning of the executive, parliament, judiciary, and anti-corruption measures.[189] Such important elements of democratic transformation as functioning of political parties and the civil society have been considered to be 'the forgotten elements of transformation'.[190] For other elements of political conditionality, such as minority rights, the political conditionality was noted to be of limited impact.[191] The enlargement conditionality was therefore suffering from 'sequencing controversy': prioritising certain features of democracy over others.[192] The conditionality fell short of offering sufficiently 'specific and detailed institutional solutions and devices' necessary for political transformation.[193] In this light the Commission's evaluation of the progress was said to be based not on concrete achievements, but rather on 'whether the country is moving in the right direction, and if so, how fast'.[194] The Commission's reports were viewed 'as contextual assessments' arrived at on the basis of understanding reached between governments and the Commission, influenced by the opinions of both EU and local experts.[195] There was, therefore, scope for political bargaining resulting in uncertainty.[196]

Furthermore, the application of democratic criteria was overshadowed by a greater focus on compliance with the *acquis*, its economic part in particular.[197]

---

[186]   M Light, 'Exporting Democracy' in KE Smith and M Light (eds), *Ethics and Foreign Policy* (Cambridge, CUP, 2001) 75–92, 90.

[187]   Kochenov, note 176 above, 94.

[188]   Ibid, 300–01.

[189]   Ibid, 88; Sadurski, note 89 above, 29.

[190]   Pridham notices that political parties did not feature in EU programmes for democracy assistance in general: Pridham, note 173 above, 959; G Pridham, 'Change and Continuity in the European Union's Political Conditionality: Aims, Approach and Priorities' (2007) 17 *Democratisation* 446, 450; Kochenov, note 176 above, 162.

[191]   Sadurski, note 102 above, 187–88.

[192]   Magnette and Nicolaidis, note 169 above, 53.

[193]   Sadurski, note 102 above, 152.

[194]   K Henderson, 'Reforming the Post-Communist States: Meeting the Political Conditions for Membership' in C Jenkins (ed), *The Unification of Europe? An Analysis of EU Enlargement* (London, Centre for Reform, 2000) 27–35, 30.

[195]   Smilov as cited in Kochenov, note 176 above, 311.

[196]   C Hillion, 'Enlargement of the European Union: A Legal Analysis' in A Arnull and D Wincott (eds), *Accountability and Legitimacy in the European Union* (Oxford, OUP, 2002) 401–18, 418; Kochenov, note 176 above, 312.

[197]   Olsen, note 178 above, 149; Kochenov, note 176 above, 301.

This can be seen as justifiable if the political conditionality is primarily to serve the purpose of establishing a new reform-orientated leadership able to undertake necessary economic reforms.[198] Warning about repeating the same mistakes in the neighbourhood, Kochenov distinguished between 'acquis conditionality' and 'non-acquis conditionality', where few expectations can be attached to the latter,[199] ie to the promotion of values by the EU.

In this respect, it is important to distinguish between the phases of conditionality preceding and following the opening of accession negotiations. Democratic conditionality was prominent more in the first phase, while the emphasis on democratic conditionality was much weaker in the second phase due to the absence of a direct link with accession, as the membership negotiations had been already started.[200] Besides, there was an obvious gap identified between the Commission's assessment of democratic reform and the progress of the countries in their pre-accession processes.[201]

Thus, the positive effect of the pre-accession process mainly affected the formal prerequisites of democracy prior to the opening of the accession negotiations, while substantive prerequisites of democracy were not significantly influenced.[202] In addition, political conditionality failed to deliver the desired results in certain country-specific issues, such as minority rights in the Balkan states. Democratic conditionality seemed to be less efficient than the *acquis* conditionality, which in its turn undermined the democratic processes in the CEE countries.[203]

4.4.2 Spreading the 'Democratic Deficit' to Candidate States

The debate on the 'democratic deficit' was not confined to the EU institutions and the parliaments of the Member States, but also spread to the candidate countries, where it was noted to have potentially widened the gap between ruling elites and the masses in CEE countries struggling to overcome their Communist heritage.[204]

It was the structural aspects of the accession process that deserved criticism, where national governments played the most important role in the transformation process. The needs of European transformation demanded a compact team ensuring efficient and coordinated management creating a powerful 'core executive'.[205]

[198] Henderson, note 194 above, 29.

[199] D Kochenov, 'The ENP Conditionality: Pre-Accession Mistakes Repeated' in L Delcour and E Tulmets (eds), *Pioneer Europe? Testing EU Foreign Policy in The Neighbourhood* (Baden-Baden, Nomos, 2008) 105–20, 108–10.

[200] Smith, note 182 above, 114; E Ridder, A Schrijvers, and H Vos, 'Civilian Power Europe and Eastern Enlargement: The More the Merrier' in J Orbie (ed), *Europe's Global Role: External Policies of the EU* (Aldershot, Ashgate, 2008) 240–57, 250–51.

[201] Kochenov, note 176 above, 309–11.

[202] Kaldor, note 180 above, 141.

[203] F Schimmelfennig and U Sedelmeier, 'Governance by Conditionality: EU Rule Transfer to the Candidate Countries of Central and Eastern Europe' (2004) 11 *Journal of European Public Policy* 661, 675–76.

[204] Pridham, note 174 above, 954.

[205] Grabbe, note 168 above, 1018.

The Europe Agreements concluded with the CEE established Association Councils composed of EU representatives and representatives of national governments, which were the main institutions responsible for the supervision of the agreement.[206] They were endowed with a competence to adopt legally binding decisions which would take precedence over national law, therefore avoiding the national legislator.[207] Thus, national parliaments had a limited role and awareness in the adoption of legislation in contradiction to the requirement of 'stable democratic institutions and the development of capable law-makers' required by the Copenhagen political criteria.[208] In addition, the accession negotiations took place in a secretive atmosphere, where national parliaments could hardly have challenged the role of the executive.[209]

The legislative–executive relations were not the only relations distorted during the accession process. Certain weakening of checks and balances was noted also as regards the guarding role of constitutional courts, which could not revise the executive regulations implementing the EU legislation.[210] Therefore, integration in the prominent areas of the relationship was favoured over democratic processes, which was part of the conditionality itself.

The problem was aggravated by the EU favouring the political consensus in former applicant countries, which ultimately resulted in discouraging serious debate about accession.[211] Even when the national parliaments made an effort to play a more prominent role in their oversight of *acquis*-related legislative reforms, it was met by a negative attitude from the Commission.[212] Thus, the integration process concerned only the top governing circles in candidate countries, where the parliaments had limited opportunities for serious engagement and the general public had little knowledge of and participation in the process of integration.[213] As in their Communist past, citizens of these countries should have considered accession politics as external and distant, with the process losing its democratic credentials.[214]

---

[206] See for instance, Arts 109 and 110 of the Europe Agreement establishing an association between the European Communities and their Member States, of the one part, and the Republic of Estonia, of the other part [1998] OJ L68/3, Title X.

[207] Art 111, ibid.

[208] Grabbe, note 168 above, 1017.

[209] Sadurski, note 89 above, 34.

[210] A Sajo, 'Accession's Impact on Constitutionalism in the New Member States' in G Bermann and K Pistor (eds), *Law and Governance in an Enlarged European Union* (Oxford, Hart Publishing, 2004) 415–35, 432.

[211] Pridham, note 173 above, 207.

[212] Sadurski, note 102 above, 169.

[213] Sajo, note 210 above, 415; A Albi, *European Union Enlargement and the Constitutions of Central and Eastern Europe* (Cambridge, CUP, 2005) 62–65; A Lazowski, 'The Polish Parliament and EU Affairs: An Effective Actor or an Accidental Hero?' in O'Brennan and Raunio, note 92 above, 203–19, 214; S Blockmans, 'EU Enlargement as a Peacebuilding Tool' in S Blockmans, J Wouters, and T Ruys (eds), *The European Union and Peace Building: Policy and Legal Aspects* (The Hague, TMC Asser Press, 2010) 77–103, 94; G Eniko, 'The Role of the Hungarian National Assembly in EU Policy-making After Accession to the Union: A Mute Witness or a True Controller?' in J O'Brennan and T Raunio, note 92 above, 220–240, 223–224; P Stoykova, 'Parliamentary Involvement in the EU Accession Process' in O'Brennan and Raunio, note 92 above, 255–71, 269.

[214] Kaldor and Vejvoda, note 180 above, 164.

Therefore, the enlargement process, while arguably having a positive influence on the formal prerequisites for democracy, may also have had an adverse effect on the substantive aspects of democracy in these particular countries. It is this example that is being followed in the neighbourhood.

4.5 CONCLUSION

The retrospective overview of the constitutional development of the EU and its institutions demonstrates the evolving and dynamic nature of its democratic model. The latter, although in a number of aspects coming close to practices at national level, nevertheless cannot be explained purely by state-developed notions without qualifications. The Treaty revisions and institutional practices have steadily moved over the time towards adapting those features of democratic models in the EU's Member States which were operative at the European level. Most of the development has taken place to legitimise the European project and to consolidate public support.

The Lisbon Treaty is the most far-reaching constitutional development in the democratic evolution of the EU. For the first time the Treaty spells out the democratic values of the EU inter alia by introducing new features into its decision-making processes. The culmination of the legal and political developments of several decades in the provisions of the Lisbon Treaty are a testimony to the evolving nature of the EU democratic model, where the Lisbon Treaty is not yet the last word. The Eurozone crisis and its consequences once again raised the issue of the legitimacy of governance at EU level, which might require further means of legitimising the Union governance and connecting it with its popular base.

At the present time, the Union's democratic model has embraced the value of representation characterised by dichotomy. The importance attributed to the role of national parliaments upholds the intrinsic value of representation, and attempts to prevent the spillover effect of the classic understanding of 'democratic deficit'. The increased role of the Parliament appears to enhance the institutional balance in the EU. Obligations are imposed on the EU institutions to increase citizens' participation by giving them 'a say' in the governance process. Although the Lisbon Treaty far from transformed the EU into an ideal democracy, it nevertheless contributed to the development of the latter's democratic credentials and established a normative ground for democracy promotion. Democracy as a concept is 'valued' by the EU and its Member States since it was necessary to legitimise the project itself, which was incorporated in its constitutional obligations, and therefore has become part of its normative image. At the same time, it is clear that no particular model is being offered to the outside world, an approach confirmed also during the accession process of the Balkan states.[215] Thus, instead

---

[215] Commission, 'Proposal for a Council Regulation on assistance for Albania, Bosnia and Herzegovina, Croatia, the Federal Republic of Yugoslavia and the former Yugoslav Republic of Macedonia' COM (2000) 281 final.

of searching for a model, it is the democratic values of the EU that should be traced in its external relations.

However, the Union's commitment to democracy when promoted to the accession countries has raised question marks as to the corners cut. Many gaps have been identified in the application of political conditionality, where the EU did not make the best use of the available legal framework. The countries that joined the EU in 2004 and 2007 accession rounds have been considered to satisfy formally the criteria of modern democracies, but in practice the political conditionality failed in many respects, including its substantive aspects, as well as inconsistent and selective progress evaluation. Besides, satisfying the formal criteria of democracy did not prove to be sufficient in practice, as the process could be reversed in a short period of time. The recent Hungarian political reforms and practices provide such an example.[216] Thus, the assumption that the enlargement was a success story of EU-led democratic transformation is tenuous and serves as an inauspicious precedent for the ENP.

This conclusion casts another shadow over the potential of the ENP to positively influence democratic development of the Southern Caucasian countries. Democratic conditionality should be expected to be further compromised due to the political nature of the ENP and the reinforced principle of differentiation.

---

[216] 'MEPs Voice "Serious concern" on Hungary's Democracy', *EU Observer*, 16 February 2013.

5

EU Democratic Values and the ENP

Implementation in the South Caucasus I: Action Plans

5.1 INTRODUCTION

THE SUPPORT FOR democratic reform in the South Caucasian states is a challenge the EU has faced since their inclusion in the ENP. In contrast to the enlargement of the CEE countries, where imposition by the EU of the accession criteria had coincided with the post-independence identity search,[1] with the majority of ENP states the EU faced already-established models of governance. In the South Caucasus only Georgia, emerging after the Rose Revolution, signalled its quest for an improved political system, whereas for Armenia and Azerbaijan the political reforms were to be incentivised by the ENP.

To trace the role of the democratic values identified in the previous chapter, it is essential, therefore, to identify those instruments and mechanisms that are central to the purpose of practical engagement with the states concerned. These include the instrumental framework for setting the conditions reflecting the EU values, the consequences of their fulfilment or lack of it, and the main mechanism of sustaining motivation deployed by the EU. The Action Plans, the monitoring of their implementation, and the assistance programmes put in place to support the political transformation correspond to mentioned elements.[2] The overview of each element separately and in a chain of causation demonstrates the extent of the Union's loyalty to its obligation to promote democracy in its external relations. The focus of this chapter is on the Action Plans as the main instrumental basis for the ENP implementation in the three countries, as no Association Agenda has been set at the time of writing.

---

[1] H Grabbe, 'How Does Europeanisation Affect CEE Governance? Conditionality, Diffusion and Diversity' (2001) 8 *Journal of European Public Policy* 1013, 1014.

[2] Baracani identifies these components as the constituents of the 'ENP method': E Baracani, 'European Union Democratic Anchoring' in E Baracani (ed), *Democratisation and Hybrid Regimes: International Anchoring and Domestic Dynamics in European Post-Soviet States* (Florence, European Press Academic Publishing, 2011) 111–34, 118.

Van Vooren considers the Action Plans to be 'the central point of reference' for the application of the ENP conditionality.[3] A number of factors can be identified for the Action Plans' 'centrality.' Although the PCAs are incorporated within the Action Plans, the latter are the main instruments setting out the conditions for cooperation between the parties. Besides, progress in the relationship depends on the fulfilment of the criteria of the Action Plan,[4] which, according to a Commission official, attaches practical significance to them as opposed to the PCAs.[5] Therefore, analysis of the Action Plans is essential in identifying the role of EU democratic values with reference to the credibility of conditions established for compliance.

The first part of the chapter addresses the main advantages and disadvantages of the Action Plans in the context of democracy promotion. Next, the Action Plans for Armenia, Azerbaijan and Georgia are analysed in a comparative perspective to reveal the extent of consistent promotion of EU democratic values. The next part considers the process of Action Plan implementation in all three states to identify the effect of these processes on their political life. A brief summary of findings is finally presented on the role of the Action Plans in the process of democracy promotion in our case studies.

5.2 ACTION PLANS AND EU DEMOCRATIC VALUES: A REALISTIC PLAN FOR REFORM?

In order to analyse the role of EU democratic values within the Action Plans it is first of all necessary to consider the extent and manner of translation of the obligation to promote democracy into these documents.

5.2.1 The Democratic Rhetoric and the Action Plans: General Observations

In setting the framework of cooperation the Action Plans with the South Caucasian states reflect the blurred nature of the incentives of the policy, as discussed in Chapter 3. The main promise is contained in the opportunity for an 'increasingly close relationship, going beyond co-operation, to involve a significant measure of economic integration and a deepening of political cooperation' which assumes 'a stake in the EU's Internal Market' and a possibility 'to participate progressively in key aspects of EU policies and programmes'.[6] The vagueness and lack of clarity hardly suggests that the documents were to entail radical political and economic reforms.

---

[3] B Van Vooren, 'The Hybrid Legal Nature of the European Neighbourhood Policy' in F Maiani, R Petrov, E Mouliarova (eds), *European Integration without EU Membership: Models, Experiences, Perspectives*, EUI Working Papers, MWP 2009/10, 17–27, 17.

[4] Eg Armenia Action Plan, s 1; the Action Plans are available at www.ec.europa.eu/world/enp/documents_en.htm.

[5] Interview with anonymous Commission official, DG RELEX, European Commission (Brussels, 28 January 2009).

[6] Sections 1 and 2 common to all three Action Plans.

Only the Georgian Action Plan goes as far as offering a 'gradual extension of four freedoms'.[7] This can be interpreted as the Commission's response to Georgia's post-revolutionary European aspirations, which would boost the country's eagerness to undertake reforms within the ENP. On the other hand, for Georgia, which made clear its intentions to join the EU, it came rather more as a disincentive than an incentive, as mentioned previously. Furthermore, by the time the Action Plan was signed, the ENP documents revealed that the 'four freedoms' were not on offer as such. While not sufficient to incentivise a fully pro-European course in Armenia, the blurred incentives suited Azerbaijan rather well: subscribing to such vague promises, especially in a soft law framework, allows for intensification of energy links, while not committing to anything specific.

The next issue is related to the construction of the conditionality in the Action Plans. The progress in the development of the relationship between the parties is said to depend on the degree of the countries' 'commitment to common values, as well as [their] capacity to implement jointly agreed priorities'.[8] General arguments on the usage of the language of 'shared values' were considered in previous chapters. Here it is necessary to address a few concerns connected to the incorporation of this language into the Action Plans. Using the language of 'common values' in the framework ENP documents conceptualising the policy is one issue: ultimately we have noted that there had been sufficient indication that the values are those of the EU, which is also supported by the wording of Article 8 TEU. However, using the same language in the main document setting the conditions for cooperation is another matter. Preserving the vagueness embedded in this notion, the EU values themselves are not clearly spelled out as a threshold to comply with. Leino and Petrov suggest that this language is used to hide political choices behind the relations between the parties.[9] It is even more poignant when taking into account that the Action Plans are the reference documents for the Commission in undertaking the monitoring of progress. In these circumstances much flexibility and room for manoeuvre is created as the concept can be interpreted as widely or as narrowly as needed in terms of political expedience. The only factor capable of rectifying the language of 'shared values' is the translation of the 'values' directly into the priority areas of the Action Plans in a way that is specific, clear and measurable.

It has been noted that the Action Plans in general follow the broad Copenhagen criteria alluding to all areas of cooperation implied.[10] The political criterion, in particular, has been elevated to a priority area in all three Action Plans, which was

---

[7] EU–Georgia Action Plan, s 2.

[8] Introduction to the Action Plans.

[9] P Leino and R Petrov, 'Between "Common Values" and Competing Universals: The Promotion of the EU's Common Values through the European Neighbourhood Policy' (2009) 15 *European Law Journal* 654, 670.

[10] EU–Azerbaijan Action Plan, s 3, priority areas 2, 3, 4, 6, 7; EU/Georgia AP, s 3, priority areas 1, 2, 3; EU/Armenia AP, s 3, priority areas 1, 2, 3, 4, 5; G Sasse, 'The European Neighbourhood Policy Conditionality Revisited for the EU's Eastern Neighbours (2008) 60 *Europe–Asia Studies* 295, 302.

considered to be their distinguishing feature.[11] The prioritisation of political reform on the face of it appears to be an upgrade in line with the normative rhetoric of the policy. Although it is perceived in the Commission that the EU's insistence on democratic reform underlines its distinctness from other international actors,[12] the mere fact of prioritisation *alongside* other measures is not sufficient to secure such distinctness. The latter by itself does not entail a qualitatively different approach taking into account the non-binding legal nature of the document and the presence of numerous other priority areas. It therefore creates a problem of *prioritisation sequencing*. The Action Plans fail to clarify whether the conditions for political reform are intended to serve as *preconditions* for cooperation in other prioritised areas. The lack of sequencing of the priority areas is indicative of the EU's normative stance and its foreign policy objectives: political reforms are promoted alongside cooperation in other areas important for the EU.

While their prototype instrument, the Accession Partnership, made the accession criteria appear like 'primary law' by emphasising intermediate objectives to be achieved,[13] the Action Plans do not leave any doubts as to their political nature. The Action Plans provide an example of the criticism of soft law in the internal context related to lack of clarity and precision of the latter.[14] Thus, the conditionality element of the ENP is undermined by the way the conditions for progress are spelled out or, more precisely, are not spelled out, whereas the success of the conditionality depends on the precision and clarity with which the conditions, benchmarks and time frames are defined.[15] Various commentators have remarked on the lack of clear vision of the overall picture of the reforms and lack of operational basis in the Action Plans.[16] Their function can be summarised as being 'persua-

---

[11]   KE Smith, 'The Outsiders: The European Neighbourhood Policy' (2005) 81 *International Affairs* 757, 765.

[12]   Anonymous Commission official, note 5 above.

[13]   C Hillion, 'Enlargement of the European Union: A Legal Analysis' in A Arnull and D Wincott (eds), *Accountability and Legitimacy in the European Union* (Oxford, OUP, 2002) 401–18, 417; D Kochenov, *EU Enlargement and the Failure of Conditionality: Pre-Accession Conditionality in the Fields of Democracy and the Rule of Law* (Austin, Wolters Kluwer Law and Business, 2008) 74.

[14]   DM Trubek, P Cottrell, and M Nance ' "Soft Law", "Hard Law", and European Integration' in G de Búrca and J Scott (eds), *Law and New Governance in the EU and the US* (Oxford, Hart Publishing, 2006) 65–94, 66.

[15]   F Schimmelfennig and U Sedelmeier, 'Governance by Conditionality: EU Rule Transfer to the Candidate Countries of Central and Eastern Europe' (2004) 11 *Journal of European Public Policy* 661, 664; A Magen, 'The Shadow of Enlargement: Can the European Neighbourhood Policy Achieve Compliance?' Center on Democracy, Development and the Rule of Law, Stanford Institute for International Studies, Working Papers, No 68, August 2006, 411; D Lynch, 'The European Neighbourhood Policy', Institute for Security Studies, June 2004, 6.

[16]   D Kochenov, 'The ENP Conditionality: Pre-Accession Mistakes Repeated' in L Delcour and E Tulmets (eds), *Pioneer Europe? Testing EU Foreign Policy in The Neighbourhood* (Baden-Baden, Nomos, 2008) 105–20, 116; Magen, note 15 above, 415; Smith, note 11 above, 757, 765; N Tocci, 'Can the EU Promote Democracy and Human Rights Through the ENP? The Case for Refocusing on the Rule of Law' in M Cremona and G Meloni (eds), *The European Neighbourhood Policy: A New Framework for Modernisation?*, EUI Working Papers, LAW 2007/21, 23–35, 31; M Emerson, 'Is There to be a Real European Neighbourhood Policy?' in R Youngs (ed), *Global Europe: New Terms of Engagement*, Foreign Policy Centre, UK, 2005, 15–22, 20; P Seeberg, 'The European Neighbourhood Policy, Post-normativity and Pragmatism' (2010) 15 *European Foreign Affairs Review* 663, 676.

sive' documents setting out the expectations on behalf of the EU.[17] The Commission officers and the representatives of the authorities in Georgia and Armenia both perceive the documents to be a 'wish list' for reforms or the *preferred general* direction for development.[18] In Azerbaijan the document has been viewed by the government to be a mere expression of the cooperative nature of the relations between the parties.[19]

The Action Plans particularly fall short of establishing a framework of preconditions for political reform that would have matched the original rhetoric. According to the Commission the priorities were to be 'ambitious and realistic, and formulated in a manner as precise and specific as possible so as to allow concrete follow-up and monitoring of the commitments taken by both sides',[20] leading to the view the Action Plans were meant to be more than declaratory in nature.[21]

The Country Reports, on which the Action Plans were based, appeared 'fairly direct and concrete', including criticism of the deficiencies of the democratic practices.[22] The evaluation of democratic issues within the 'Democracy and the rule of law' section has been fairly consistent in all three Country Reports as regards the details and the issues of concern. The criticism of the Commission has mainly revolved around the separation of powers, elections, reform of the judiciary, reform of the executive, including the functioning of local authorities, and civil service reform.[23] Issues related to political participation and freedom of expression have found their way into the section on 'Human rights and fundamental freedoms'.[24] This demonstrates the flexible approach demonstrated towards the definition of democracy in the external policy of the EU, which has since become a trend. For instance, in the definition of democracy in Agenda 2000, freedom of expression and freedom of religion are considered to be elements of the democracy element of the political criteria.[25] A similar 'interlinked' approach to human rights and democracy is apparent in the Commission's Report on Furthering Human Rights and Democracy Across the Globe.[26] In practice

---

[17] M Cremona, 'The European Neighbourhood Policy: More than a Partnership?' in M Cremona (ed), *Developments in EU External Relations Law* (Oxford, OUP, 2008) 244–99, 277.

[18] Anonymous Commission official, note 5 above; Interview with Anonymous Official, State Ministry for European Integration of the Republic of Georgia (Tbilisi, 7 April 2009).

[19] A Gahramanova, 'Internal and External Factors in the Democratisation of Azerbaijan' (2009) 16 *Democratisation* 777, 794.

[20] Commission Communication, 'On the Commission Proposals for Action Plans under the European Neighbourhood Policy' COM (2004) 795 final, 3.

[21] P Koutrakos, *EU International Relations Law* (Oxford, Hart Publishing, 2006) 379.

[22] G Bosse, 'Values in the EU's Neighbourhood Policy: Political Rhetoric or Reflection of a Coherent Policy?' (2007) 7 *European Political Economy Review* 38, 49.

[23] Country Report Georgia, European Neighbourhood Policy, Commission Staff Working Paper, SEC (2005) 288/3, s 2.1; Country Report Armenia, European Neighbourhood Policy, Commission Staff Working Paper, SEC (2005) 285/3, s 2.1; Country Report Azerbaijan, European Neighbourhood Policy, Commission Staff Working Paper, SEC (2005) 286/3, s 2.1.

[24] Section 2.2 of the Country Reports.

[25] See Chapter 4, section 4.4.1.

[26] European Commission, Furthering Human Rights and Democracy Across the Globe, 2007. Available at www.eeas.europa.eu/human_rights/docs/brochure07_en.pdf.

this corresponds to the liberal understanding of democracy, which, as discussed previously, envisages a prominent role for protection of rights and the following analysis will be inclusive of human rights issues.

However, the vision of the Country Reports was gradually lost, resulting in much weaker language.[27] Tocci found an explanation for this in the shifting of priorities towards cooperation directed at tackling common security threats, including secure energy supply.[28] Bosse specifically includes the South Caucasian Action Plans in a separate group, arguing that the rationalist interests in energy security, crisis management and the fight against international crime and corruption have taken precedence over 'secondary' democracy promotion.[29] Besides, the principles of joint ownership and differentiation played their part in the drafting and negotiation of the specific priorities. In comparison with their prototype instruments, the Accession Partnerships, which were noted to be written predominantly by the officials in the Commission, the Action Plans' priorities are the outcome of negotiations between the Commission and the neighbouring countries, despite the agenda being unilaterally imposed by the EU.[30] In this context the Action Plans with Georgia, Armenia and Azerbaijan are noticeably less detailed than their counterparts with Ukraine and Moldova.

5.2.2 The South Caucasian Action Plans and their Democratic Agenda

The main challenge one encounters when analysing the issue of promotion of democratic values within the Action Plans is the choice of a relevant method. In search of a test to analyse the principle of coherence within the ENP, Van Vooren uses the test of linguistic vigour by which the policy initiatives are expressed in the Action Plans on a scale of one to ten.[31] The discussion that follows, although implying a certain degree of attention paid to the language of the documents, is not based on a particular scale, but instead focuses on the measurability of the priorities established. The measurability of actions provides the ground for linking the Action Plans with political monitoring and financial assistance. It therefore depends on the concreteness, the precision and the time frame of the measures established.

---

[27] E Johansson-Nogues, 'The (Non-)Normative Power EU and the European Neighbourhood Policy: An Exceptional Policy for an Exceptional Actor?' (2007) 7 *European Political Economy Review* 181, 188–89; Bosse, note 22 above, 50–52.

[28] Tocci, note 16 above, 31.

[29] Bosse, note 22 above, 57.

[30] E Tulmets, 'Adapting the Experience of Enlargement to the Neighbourhood Policy: the ENP as a Substitute to Enlargement?' in P Kratochvil (ed), *The European Union and Its Neighbourhood: Policies, Problems and Priorities* (Prague, Institute of International Relations, 2006) 29–57, 44; Tocci, note 16 above, 25.

[31] B Van Vooren, *External Relations Law of the EU and the European Neighbourhood Policy: A Paradigm for Coherence* (London, Routledge, 2011) 235.

5.2.2.1 EU–Armenia Action Plan

While political reforms are envisaged within the first two priority areas, the major focus of the Armenia Action Plan is on economic liberalisation, legislative reform in line with the economic *acquis*, and energy strategy.[32] The actions on political reform widely reflect the substance of the Copenhagen political criteria, including democracy, the rule of law, protection of human rights, and rights of minorities. Both priority areas contain relatively long lists of actions, the negotiation of which did not give rise to any opposition by the Armenian side.[33] It is assumed that the principle of joint ownership did not affect the negotiation process, since the country does not have any effective leverage over the EU.

The specific actions in priority area 1 are devoted to strengthening of democratic structures and the rule of law, thus combining these two concepts into one. Similar to the Country Report, the Action Plan requires actions on proper implementation of constitutional reform, ensuring better separation of powers. However, in the area of separation of powers, the main focus is on the independence and functioning of the judiciary and reform of the executive.[34] In terms of the representative element of democracy, full compliance of the electoral framework with OSCE commitments and recommendations of the Venice Commission of the Council of Europe is required by amending the Electoral Code and improving electoral administration. The priority area 2 on human rights, which also includes issues on the independence of the media, is to be implemented in its entirety in accordance with the international obligations of the country, including under the PCA, in the Council of Europe, the OSCE and the UN. Thus, although it has been noted that the Action Plans exercise a function of interpreting the PCAs,[35] the opposite also seems to be true, where the PCA serves as an interpretative basis for the Action Plan priorities.

Ultimately, the priorities for political reform are structured around the issues of separation of powers, the executive and judiciary, and the guarantee of basic rights. In terms of the EU values, two major omissions should be noted. The operation of parliament and political parties is a largely neglected area together with the role of the civil society and issues of public participation, noted in the Country Report. This is disappointing since in the case of Armenia joint ownership did not play any part in downgrading the political conditions, suggesting lack of insistence on behalf of the Commission.

---

[32] Actions for encouraging further economic development, improvement of investment climate and strengthening of private sector-led growth, further convergence of economic legislation and administrative practices, and development of energy strategy are the main priority areas; EU–Armenia Action Plan, s 3, priority areas 3, 4, 5, 6.

[33] Anonymous Commission official, note 5 above.

[34] Five out of 10 priorities are dedicated to the reform of the judiciary with reference to its independence, laws for the procuracy, and the status of the Council of Justice. The reform of the executive includes the functioning of local self-government and the civil service.

[35] Van Vooren, note 31 above, 182.

In terms of measurability, with the exception of the priority of developing the Ombudsman institution and the electoral framework with reference to an international standard,[36] the rest of the priorities can be summarised as a general call to develop and adopt laws. The actions not only lack precision in substance, but also, for the majority of conditions, no concrete deadlines are envisaged for their implementation. Only four actions had a deadline of 2006, which is at odds with the Plan's endorsement in late 2006. The Armenian Action Plan therefore fails to provide a measurable list of actions that can be monitored on an annual basis. If no specific benchmarks are highlighted for any intermediate period, it is not clear what can constitute progress in fulfilling a particular priority action.

Besides, the inadequate approach to prioritisation is not confined to the manner of spelling out the priorities. In addition to the priority areas, section 4 on general objectives and actions complements the prioritised actions with a further list of actions. The composition of the document is rather odd: it is drafted from specific to general, where the specific actions are presented first and mostly without precision and detail. The section on general actions contains a longer list of measures than the priority areas on political reform, and includes certain issues vital for Armenian political life that are disregarded or paid little attention in the priority areas.[37] They include the functioning of political parties and the strengthening of political pluralism, as well as the role of the civil society, although mentioned without much elaboration. That the document is drafted in such a manner is said to be explained by its political, non-binding character,[38] which therefore does not have to satisfy the principle of legal certainty. Besides, since the Action Plan is only a 'wish list', the division between priorities and general action is seen as 'a matter of presentation'.[39] One can therefore assume that there is no distinction between the prioritised actions and those identified in section 4, raising a question mark over the basis for exercising monitoring.

5.2.2.2 EU–Georgia Action Plan

From the outset of the ENP cooperation, Georgia was viewed as one of the most suitable countries for the implementation of the ENP with the potential to make progress in the short term.[40] The political ambition of the post-Revolution government appeared to have coincided with the ENP rhetoric on democracy

---

[36] In relation to the development of the Human Rights Ombudsman's institution, "Paris Principles" based on UN General Assembly Resolution 48/134 of December 1993 have been emphasised. The development of the electoral framework must take place in line with OSCE/ODIHR and CoE Venice Commission recommendations.

[37] More detail is provided for the reform of local self-government and the reform of the civil service. It requires the strengthening capacities of local communities and civil service institutions in line with European standards and the implementation of the European Charter of Local Self Government.

[38] Anonymous Commission official, note 5 above.

[39] Ibid.

[40] Ibid.

promotion: it was perceived to suit the alleged shift from 'leader-based' reforms to more 'programme or ideology'-orientated reforms.[41]

Therefore, it is in the case of Georgia that one would have expected a clearly expressed commitment to democratic reform in the document setting the main conditions for cooperation between the parties. The Georgian Action Plan does not live up to this expectation though. It merges democracy, rule of law and human rights-related issues within one priority area combining actions to be implemented in compliance with Georgia's international obligations under the PCA and in the Council of Europe, the OSCE and the UN.[42] Similar to Armenia, a major emphasis has been placed on the reform of the judiciary by continuing the criminal justice reform commenced under the EUJUST Themis Rule of Law Mission with reference to previously prepared reform strategy.[43] Although rather general in substance, the reference to the previously established reform strategy makes the priority action measurable in terms of its content. Nonetheless, none of the sub-actions has any intermediary deadlines.

The only relatively detailed action concerns the conduct of elections in accordance with international standards, through the implementation of OSCE Office for Democratic Institutions and Human Rights and Council of Europe recommendations.[44] Although the emphasis on free and fair elections demonstrates the importance attached to the representative element of Georgia's unstable post-revolutionary democracy, the absence of the role of parliament and political parties, or generally better separation of powers and checks and balances is a retreat from the values the EU has been keen to develop itself and safeguard in its Member States. Despite prioritising certain other issues, including civil service reform,[45] the priorities on political reform have largely omitted the issue of human rights and fundamental freedoms. The prohibition of torture is the only issue that features on the agenda with reference to relevant international standards but free from deadlines.

It can be suggested that the limited attention paid to democratic reform is explained by the consideration at the time that Georgia already had committed itself to democratic reform. However, it has been acknowledged in the Commission that democracy building requires a long-term commitment.[46] Besides, the

---

[41] R Balfour, 'Promoting Human Rights and Democracy in the EU's Neighbourhood: Tools, Strategies and Dilemmas' in R Balfour and A Missiroli, 'Reassessing the European Neighbourhood Policy', EPC Issue Paper No 54, June 2007, 20; Anonymous official, Georgia, note 18 above.

[42] EU–Georgia Action Plan, s 3, priority area 3.1.

[43] These measures include improvement of training of judges, prosecutors, and officials in the judiciary, Ministry of Justice administration, police and prisons, in particular with regard to human rights issues and judicial internal cooperation; improved access to justice, notably through the establishment of an effective legal aid system; penitentiary and probation service; and system of execution of court decisions.

[44] In particular, the need for a reliable voter registry and a transparent electoral commission has been noted.

[45] These also include the adoption of a new criminal procedural code and the finalisation and implementation of a strategy and programme for local government reform with deadlines in only two cases.

[46] Anonymous Commission official, note 5 above.

post-Revolutionary non-democratic practices of the new government, which were much criticised by international observers and were described as 'little more than "repackaging" ' of previous political practices, could not have escaped the attention of the Commission.[47]

Similar to the Armenian Action Plan, section 4 on democracy and the rule of law, human rights and fundamental freedoms provides for general actions complementing the priorities. The actions aimed at democratisation in this section can be summarised around the reform of the judiciary and the civil service and the strengthening of parliament and political pluralism by enhancing the role and functioning of political parties. However, including these important actions within a general list sent a signal of their relatively low importance on the agenda of cooperation between the parties. It should be noted that the issues of citizens' participation, including through development of civil society, have been disregarded in the Georgian Action Plan.

5.2.2.3 EU–Azerbaijan Action Plan

Some consider that democracy occupies the same prominent role in the Azerbaijani Action Plan as in the Action Plan with Georgia.[48] This view can be suggested to refer to the elevation of the status of the political reform to priority areas, since the content of the reform falls short of 'prominence'. As mentioned before, at the early stages of ENP involvement democracy was already a 'low-key' concern in relations between the parties dominated by energy cooperation.[49] Following the coloured revolutions in Georgia and Ukraine, the Azerbaijani regime became even more suspicious of foreign efforts to promote the democratic agenda.[50] However it was not only the Azerbaijani authorities, but also the EU officials, that shied away from strong wording.[51]

Taking into account Azerbaijan's democratic record, its Action Plan is most telling on the muted role that political reform plays on the agenda of the cooperation: only four very generally formulated actions found their way into the priority

---

[47]   J Whitley, 'Georgia's Democratic Veneer: Scraping the Surface' in Baracani (ed), note 2 above, 352–80, 376; M Muskhelishvili and G Jorjoliani, 'Georgia's Ongoing Struggle for a Better Future Continued: Democracy Promotion through Civil Society Development' (2009) 16 *Democratisation* 682, 693–94. See further, 'Honouring of obligations and commitments by Georgia' Resolution 1603 (2008), Parliamentary Assembly of Council of Europe, 15, 47–49; Human Rights Watch, 2006; Honouring of obligations and commitments by Georgia' Report, Doc 10383, 21 December 2004, Parliamentary Assembly of the Council of Europe, para 4, 6; 'Georgia: Sliding Towards Authoritarianism?' ICG, Europe Report No 189, 19 December 2007, 18.

[48]   EJ Stewart, 'Mind the Normative Gap? The EU in the South Caucasus' in R Whitman (ed), *Normative Power Europe: Empirical and Theoretical Perspectives* (Basingstoke, Palgrave, 2011) 65–82, 71.

[49]   M Emerson, G Noutcheva, N Popescu, 'European Neighbourhood Policy Two Years On: Time Indeed for an "ENP Plus"', Centre for European Policy Studies, Policy Briefs, No 126, 21 March 2007; E Nuriyev, 'EU Policy in the South Caucasus: A View from Azerbaijan', Centre for European Policy Studies, Working Document No 272/July 2007, 22; L Alieva, 'EU and South Caucasus', Discussion Paper, Bertesmann Group for Policy Research, Centre for Applied Policy Research, December 2006, 18.

[50]   Gahramanova, note 19 above, 786.

[51]   Ibid, 792.

area 2 on strengthening democracy. The principle of joint ownership appears to have played its part in downgrading political reform in comparison with Armenia and Georgia. To secure the cooperation of the opposite party in accepting the document, certain compromises had to be made with respect to actions the party was reluctant to undertake or deadlines.[52] Another factor affecting the composition of the Action Plan is the subjectivity inherent in the nature of the negotiation process, where the Commission officers can reflect their views in the negotiating position.[53] The fact that priority area 1 is dedicated to the contribution to the peaceful resolution of the Nagorno-Karabakh conflict also demonstrates the stronger leverage Azerbaijan had in relations with the EU, where Georgia failed to secure a stronger emphasis on its conflicts in the Action Plan at the same stage of relations.[54]

The actions within priority area 2 revolve around the issue of elections, including the continuous reform of the electoral process and the conduct of elections in line with general reference to the Council of Europe and OSCE standards without any precision or deadlines. A common reference to institutional reforms to ensure proper checks and balances between executive and legislative powers in conformity with the commitments to the Council of Europe is also among the priority actions. The last actions within priority area 2 are legislative and administrative reforms aimed at strengthening of local self-government. As a result, the Azerbaijani Action Plan is an example of preserving the normative rhetoric, but reducing it to a 'box ticking' exercise.

It should be noted that unlike the Action Plans with Armenia and Georgia, the action related to the reform of the judiciary is included in priority area 3 on the protection of human rights and fundamental freedoms and the rule of law in compliance with the country's international obligations. This priority area also contains an action on the development of civil society. The broad requirement to promote the growth of civil society and its organised forms is complemented by a more specific requirement to alleviate the complicated procedures required for NGO registration, which, although relatively precise, had no deadlines. Only the priority action related to the ratification and implementation of the Optional Protocol to the UN Convention against Torture had a deadline of 2006. It should also be noted that anti-corruption measures are included in a separate area related to the improvement of the business climate. On the one hand this suggests a certain acknowledgement on behalf of the EU of the culture of patronage networks in Azerbaijan, which scores the lowest among the South Caucasian states in the ranking on corruption.[55] On the other hand including these measures in a priority area related to the business climate suggests its depoliticisation.

---

[52] Anonymous Commission official, note 5 above.

[53] Ibid.

[54] N Popescu, 'Europe's Unrecognised Neighbours: The EU in Abkhazia and South Ossetia', Centre for European Policy Studies, Working Document No 260/March 2007, 8–9.

[55] See also Chapter 1, note 66. 'An Assessment of the Development of Political Parties in the Republic of Azerbaijan', USAID, 2003, 4; Azerbaijan Country Report, European Neighbourhood Policy, Commission Staff Working Paper COM(2005) 72 final, SEC (2005) 286/3, 2 March 2005, s 2.1;

Akin to the previous Action Plans, section 4 on general objectives and actions provides for further measures complementing the priorities, although it is a much shorter list in this case. References formulated similarly to priority actions are made to reform of the electoral process and local governance. Reform of the judicial system and civil service reform are envisaged, merely indicating the ultimate objectives.

5.2.2.4 Democratic Values Betrayed?

An overview of the Action Plans' content relevant to democratic reform suggests a preservation of the political rhetoric of the ENP on paper. However, it falls short of being translated into an operational and measurable plan of actions set for the five-year period for which the document was adopted.[56] Moreover, the Action Plans also failed in accentuating the values that have inspired the EU's own progress in democratising the European political project.

Although the principle of differentiation was applied with similar issues receiving varied attention, it nevertheless was not exploited to its full potential to highlight country-specific issues, such as the dominance of the executive in Azerbaijan, the post-Revolutionary practices in Georgia or the weaknesses of the Armenian political system. Such important issues for all three countries as the activity of parliament, separation of powers, and efficient functioning of checks and balances systems are muted even if they make an appearance. The absence of citizens' participation issues and the development of civil society is another manifestation of the EU's retreat from its democratic values. It is predominantly the formal prerequisites of democracy as entailed by the obligations of the countries in various international organisations that are the ones requiring attention. The focus on the conduct of elections and the reform of the judiciary is a common feature in all three Action Plans. The insistence on elections is a general approach deployed by the EU in its foreign policy,[57] which nevertheless is ignored in practice, resulting in 'electoralist fallacy'.[58]

Beyond the Action Plans, the ENP in its most recently revised version claims to support 'deep' democracy.[59] This understanding of democracy follows the trend of merging the concepts of democracy, human rights and rule of law. Although as noted above, it is not problematic as such, it allows commitments regarding core

'Azerbaijan: Vulnerable Stability', Europe Report No 207, 3 September 2010, 11–12; 'Azerbaijan's 2005 Elections: Lost Opportunity', ICG, Europe Briefing No 40, 21 November 2005, 1; 'Azerbaijan: Turning Over a New Leaf?' ICG, Europe Report No 156, 13 May 2004, 9–10.

[56] The three Action Plans were extended further following the expiry of the five-year period.

[57] S Füle, European Commissioner for Enlargement and European Neighbourhood, EuroNest Parliamentary Assembly, Speech/12/256, 3 April 2012, Baku; Foreign Affairs Council, Luxembourg, 15 October 2012, 18.

[58] M Light, 'Exporting Democracy' in KE Smith and M Light (eds), *Ethics and Foreign Policy* (Cambridge, CUP, 2001) 75–92, 89.

[59] Joint Communication, A New Response to a Changing Neighbourhood COM (2011) 303, 25 May 2011, 3.

democratic values to be avoided, with the focus instead on mainly formal criteria, which are the following:

- free and fair elections;
- freedom of association, expression and assembly and a free press and media;
- the rule of law administered by an independent judiciary and right to a fair trial;
- fighting against corruption;
- security and law enforcement sector reform (including the police) and the establishment of democratic control over armed and security forces.[60]

Thus, the representative element of democracy is reduced to free and fair elections, while separation of powers and political participation are the abandoned elements within so-called 'deep democracy'.

The overview of the Action Plan also suggests that the EU refrains from offering *its* democratic values to the countries of the South Caucasus. Within a general trend in the area of democratisation references are made to the international obligations of the partner countries as indicated above.[61] This approach was originally incorporated in recognition guidelines of the EC and its Member States for the CIS countries,[62] and was subsequently translated into the PCAs.[63] It has also been implanted in the ESS and EU Agenda for Action on Democracy Support in External Relations.[64] 'Multilateralism' is prescribed in Article 21(2) TEU, where the EU should seek cooperation with organisations functioning on the same principles as those of the Union. It therefore highlights the 'interaction between EU legal order and international norms',[65] whereby the Union accepts that its influence is not exercised in a legal void.[66] It also justifies the reliance by the Commission on the reports of relevant international organisations during the assessment of progress.

Another explanation for 'multilateralism' can be found in the soft law nature of the Action Plans. In order to achieve at least a certain level of compliance, reference is made to the obligations of the neighbouring countries in other organisations of which they potentially risk losing membership, such as the Council of

---

[60] Ibid.

[61] On this general trend see M Cremona, 'Values in the EU Constitution: the External Dimension' Center on Democracy, Development and the Rule of Law', Stanford Institute for International Studies, Working Papers, No 26, 2 November 2004, 11.

[62] F Hoffmeister, 'The Contribution of EU Practice to International Law' in M Cremona (ed), note 17 above, 37–127, 73.

[63] For instance Art 68 PCA with Armenia. Equivalent provisions are present in the PCAs with Georgia and Azerbaijan; see Title VII of the PCAs with Armenia, Georgia and Azerbaijan.

[64] H Sjursen, 'The EU as a "Normative" Power: How Can This Be?' (2006) 13 *Journal of European Public Policy* 235–51, 245; Council Conclusions, Democracy Support in the EU's External Relations, EU Agenda for Action on Democracy Support in EU External Relations, 17 November 2009, 6.

[65] M Cremona, 'Values in EU Foreign Policy' in M Evans and T Tridimas (eds), *Beyond Established Legal Orders: Policy Interconnections between the EU and the Rest of the World* (Oxford, Hart Publishing, 2011) 275–315, 275.

[66] P Magnette and K Nicolaidis, 'The European Union's Democratic Agenda' in M Telo (ed), *The EU and Global Governance* (London, Routledge, 2009) 43–63, 51.

Europe.[67] This also explains the reliance on the PCAs as a source of international obligations of the three countries, agreements which, despite their economic core, are nevertheless binding legal documents with an 'essential element'.

From this perspective, the multilateral approach can then be viewed as recognition of the EU's limited capacity in promoting democracy within the ENP. It also suggests that the EU shies away from taking a lead role in democracy promotion. This is complicating in terms of the perception of the Union's stance on democratic reform. A recent EU Neighbourhood Barometer poll suggests that the citizens of the EaP countries attach the highest importance to EU involvement in the areas of peace and security and poverty reduction, whereas the issues of human rights and democracy are ranked third and fifth in the list of priorities.[68]

As a result, the EU does not add much to the requirements the neighbouring states already have to satisfy, therefore rendering its role in the process of democratisation supplementary or ancillary to other international organisations. Early on, concerns were expressed by the representatives of civil society that the benchmarks of the Action Plans were not as strict as the commitments the South Caucasian countries had made to the Council of Europe.[69] In terms of reception by the authorities in Georgia, there was a presumption that the major discussions with EU representatives mainly revolved around economic and social issues, while issues on democratic development and protection of human rights were usually framed with reference to Georgia's obligations in the Council of Europe and OSCE, as well as the evaluation by those organisations and international non-governmental organisations.[70] In addition it is thought that the Council of Europe is better positioned and has weightier leverage in the country's democratisation process than the EU, since Georgia potentially risks losing its membership.[71] The issue of 'multilateralism' is also linked to measuring the success of the EU in promoting democracy as noted in the previous chapter, where any perceived success cannot be attributed merely to EU policies.

Besides the substantive reflection of the EU democratic values, the retreat from the democratic agenda is also noticeable as regards the rigour and precision of the documents. As noted by a Commission official, the lack of specificity should not necessarily be evaluated negatively, as restricting actions to certain measures and deadlines would 'bind the hands' of the parties.[72] From this perspective the imprecision inherent in the Action Plans allows the partner country to choose the

---

[67] For instance following the failures and post-election violence in Armenia after February 2008 presidential elections Armenia risked suspension of its voting rights due to Resolution 1609 of the Parliamentary Assembly of the Council of Europe (17 April 2008) unless certain measures were taken.

[68] 'EU Cooperation Positively Perceived by its Neighbours', Press Release, IP/13/246, 20 March 2013.

[69] 'Conflict Resolution in the South Caucasus: The EU's Role', IGC, Europe Report No 173, 20 March 2006, 13.

[70] Interview with David Darchiashvili, Chairman of the Committee on EU Integration, Parliament of the Republic of Georgia (Tbilisi, 7 April 2009).

[71] Interview with Ivane Chkhikvadze, Eurasia Partnership Foundation (Tbilisi, 6 April, 2009); the Eurasia Partnership Foundation is a public organisation with a mandate to increase civic participation inter alia in the area of EU integration.

[72] Anonymous Commission official, note 5 above.

measures of implementation flexibly and to decide its own timetable. It is perceived in the Commission that the implementation of the actions established will potentially transform the relevant countries into EU membership candidates,[73] that is to say that even the measures provided are sufficient to induce democratic compliance. However, if the lack of an intense approach in the Azerbaijani case can be justified by the joint ownership of the process, the Georgian case is also instructive in this sense. Even in the case of a country with the most expressed European aspirations, the Action Plan provisions on democratic reform do not seem to be of any assistance, failing to establish a clear and detailed set of actions that would address contemporary issues of political governance. That the Action Plans fall short of requiring clear commitments based on measurable criteria was acknowledged by the main critic in this area, that is the Parliament. It has called for the main policy documents to 'tighten up' the wording of the requirements on democratisation.[74]

Such an outlook contributes to the presumption that it is the commencement of the reform process that matters to demonstrate that the country is moving in the right direction,[75] as was the case with the accession policy. However, such an approach undermines the conditionality by creating scope for avoiding implementation of any chosen undesirable action for an indefinite term. It also questions the basis on which the Commission is supposed to evaluate the progress of the ENP partners.

The lack of prioritisation of political reform over other areas of cooperation suggests two possible scenarios if viewed from the perspective of the partner states. Under the first scenario, the country is reluctant to undertake democratic reforms, however the progress in other priority areas secures general compliance and thus creates scope for avoiding compliance in political reforms. Under the second scenario, there are other pressing matters, such as economic development or poverty reduction requiring concerted national efforts, which can distract even a willing country in its attempts to reform the country.

The second scenario can be suggested to describe the reality of Georgia, where pressing domestic or external factors have required urgent attention by the government, therefore diverting political efforts. The external environment of Russian embargoes and military pressures following the Rose Revolution has had a distracting effect on Georgia's political reforms, requiring the government to concentrate on short-term priorities.[76] This is a clear example of the geopolitics of the region impeding the success of the ENP. In Armenia the civil society representatives have also noted the government's discretion as to the choice of reforms affecting their implementation in practice.[77]

---

[73] Ibid.
[74] Parliament Resolution on EU External Policies in Favour of Democratisation (2011/2032(INI)) 7 July 2011, 12.
[75] Interview with Darchiashvili, note 70 above.
[76] Popescu, note 54 above, 20.
[77] Interview with Artak Kirakosyan, NGO Civil Society Institute (Yerevan, 21 April 2009). The NGO aims to assist and promote the establishment of a free and democratic society in Armenia.

The problem with prioritisation sequencing has been acknowledged in the EU. The Court of Auditors in its assessment of the effectiveness of the ENPI funding directed at the South Caucasus states criticised the Action Plans as having too many priorities.[78] The Commission defended the Action Plan format as being comprehensive, flexible and inclusive of all areas of cooperation.[79] However, in practice it makes it impossible to answer the question whether the EU should advance relations with a party which, despite the worsening political situation, makes progress in other areas of cooperation, such as energy or economic development.[80] The difficulty in answering this question lies in the lack of prioritisation among the general objectives of EU external action as discussed in Chapter 2. Ultimately it is the process of monitoring and its consequences that reveal the balancing exercise between cooperation in various areas, which is considered in Chapter 6.

5.3 ACTION PLAN IMPLEMENTATION: DEMOCRATIC CREDENTIALS

In addition to the democratic agenda of the Action Plans, the discussion of their implementation process is indicative in terms of upholding EU democratic values. The openness of national elites to the Union's influence is demonstrated inter alia through the institutional and legislative framework created for the purpose of integration. This first of all assumes assigning the task of policy programming and monitoring to certain institutions of the state. Two prominent approaches to the institutional arrangements were developed within the enlargement experience, including the assigning of relevant responsibilities to a certain ministry or the establishment of a separate institution responsible for the integrative processes.[81] All three South Caucasian Republics have distinct approaches to these matters which indirectly reflect the level of each country's political commitment.

5.3.1 Action Plan Implementation in Georgia

Georgia's 'willing' status[82] is exemplified by the existence of a separate institution entrusted with the task of EU integration. The State Ministry for European and Euro-Atlantic Integration is a permanent institution established in 2004 to deal with the issues of EU integration.[83] The vice prime minister holds the position of

[78] European Court of Auditors Report, 'Is the New European Neighbourhood and Partnership Instrument Successfully Launched and Achieving Results in the Southern Caucasus (Armenia, Azerbaijan and Georgia)?' Special Report No 13, 49.

[79] Ibid.

[80] J Kelley, 'New Wine in Old Wineskins: Policy Learning and Adaptation in the New European Neighbourhood Policy' (2006) 44 *Journal of Common Market Studies* 29, 51.

[81] Grabbe, note 1 above, 1018.

[82] Tocci, note 16 above, 27.

[83] Later on the task of the Ministry was widened to include also Euro–Atlantic integration; anonymous official, Georgia, note 18 above.

minister for European integration, ensuring a high-level political representation. A state committee on integration with the EU was also established, chaired by the prime minister and essentially replicating the composition of the cabinet of ministers, with the Ministry for European Integration as its secretariat. The main task of the committee is to coordinate the activity of the government in the area of European integration.[84] Apart from these vertical institutions there is also a horizontal network involving officials responsible for the issues of EU integration in each ministry in an expert capacity, as well as a relevant vice-minister or vice head of other state institutions.[85]

A Committee on European Integration was established in 2004 within the Georgian Parliament with its main task assisting in the process of harmonisation of Georgian legislation to the *acquis*. The latter introduced an amendment to Georgian legislation obliging all initiators of legislation to ensure *non-contradiction* to EU rules.[86] Two possible scenarios for parliament's involvement have been identified by the former chairman of the committee, including initiation of the legislation and monitoring of the process.[87] Taking into account the number of legislative acts to be adopted and the fact that the executive is better positioned for identifying the areas where priority action is required, involvement in the ENP implementation process by scrutinising the government's activity is considered to be a task most suited to parliament.[88] This position suggests that parliament's participation in ENP implementation is limited to the process of monitoring the government's activity in general without exercising much initiative. This pattern corresponds to the criticism referred to in the previous chapter in the context of enlargement practices.

The government's European aspiration was translated into its programme for 2008–12, which included an ambitious objective of achieving integration in the four freedoms of the internal market. Within this framework annual programmes have been prepared by the Ministry for European Integration in cooperation with other ministries in a form of matrix indicating the specific measures to be taken by responsible institutions, their deadlines and the financial assistance allocated.[89] The government's leading role in the Action Plan implementation is also strengthened because of the role it plays in allocating the financial assistance issued by the EU.[90]

Georgia's civil society expressed its eagerness to play an active role in programming and monitoring of the ENP implementation. During the elaboration of the Action Plan almost 70 organisations forwarded their recommendations to the

---

[84] Ibid.
[85] Ibid.
[86] Interview with Darchiashvili, note 70 above.
[87] Ibid.
[88] Ibid.
[89] Anonymous official, Georgia, note 18 above. Decree No 498 Government of the Republic of Georgia. The first implementation programme was adopted for 2007 only.
[90] See Chapter 6, section 6.3.2.

Georgian government in 2005.[91] Government officials claimed many of these recommendations served as a basis for its activity,[92] suggesting initial willingness to involve the civil society.

The same association of NGOs established a monitoring group in 2006 by organising public debates on the issues of EU integration, as well as maintaining the dialogue with the representatives of the Commission and the European Parliament.[93] Nevertheless, the civil society institutions encountered certain barriers to their participation. The absence of any formal or official arena for establishing contacts between the civil society and the government, as well as the EU representatives, was noted to be an obstacle for its efficient involvement.[94] The actual engagement is left to informal contacts and personal relationships.[95] Examples of informal practices are the participation of the civil society representatives in the meetings of the Parliament's committee on European integration, which in turn forwards the recommendations made by the civil society representatives to the government.[96]

Although according to a public survey conducted in 2006, the vast majority of the population supported Georgia's integration into the EU,[97] the public lacks knowledge as to the EU itself and the process of EU integration, including its 'costs and benefits'.[98] According to the representatives of the government and the Parliament measures are undertaken to provide objective information on the European integration processes, EU values and institutions.[99] Nevertheless, these measures are considered to be insufficient, especially due to the passive attitude of the media in enlightening the public on issues related to European integration.[100] The limited awareness of the population is mostly restricted to the capital.[101]

Thus, the ENP-related reforms are undertaken with the leadership of the executive, isolated efforts of the civil society and a mostly unaware public.

5.3.2 Action Plan Implementation in Armenia

Though Armenia has been classified as a 'hesitant' partner,[102] major institutional developments have taken place in the country manifesting its determination to implement the ENP Action Plan.

[91] Interview with Chkhikvadze, note 71 above; Civil Society Report, 'Civil Society on priorities of the ENP AP for Georgia 2007–2009'.
[92] Civil Society Report, note 91 above.
[93] Ibid.
[94] Interview with Chkhikvadze, note 71 above; Civil Society and Monitoring Implementation of ENP AP, Civil Society Survey Results, Open Society Georgia Foundation and Eurasia Partnership Foundation, Tbilisi 2008.
[95] Civil Society Survey Results, note 94 above.
[96] Interview with Chkhikvadze, note 71 above.
[97] Interview with Darchiashvili, note 70 above.
[98] Interview with Chkhikvadze, note 71 above.
[99] Anonymous official, Georgia, note 18 above; interview with Darchiashvili, note 70 above.
[100] Interview with Chkhikvadze, note 71 above.
[101] Ibid.
[102] Tocci, note 16 above, 27.

A national council for cooperation with the EU was established in 2006, chaired by the prime minister and assigned with the task of introducing a mechanism for coordinating activities and contacts between all interested parties, including the civil society, on the issues of EU integration.[103] The members of the council include the ministers, the vice-speaker of the Parliament and the representatives of civil society, whose meetings should take place at least once a year.[104] Together with the national council, a committee for coordinating the cooperation with the EU was created a similar composition (with the exception of the representatives of the civil society) and with a task of elaborating a strategy for EU integration.[105] It is worth mentioning that both institutions were established for the implementation of the National Programme for PCA implementation for 2006–09, thus expressing a fragmented approach by the government, without yet acknowledging the ENP Action Plan.

The main institution entrusted with the task of the coordination of policy preparation and implementation is the Ministry of Economy coordinating a working group established by a presidential decree.[106] Entrusting the task of ENP implementation to the Ministry of Economy demonstrates the importance of economic cooperation for Armenia. Within the latter the ENP is perceived to offer an outstanding opportunity for Armenia's economic development, where economic and democratic reforms are required for a functioning market economy.[107]

In September 2008, a council on cooperation with European institutions under the president of the national security council was established, involving all vice-ministers and aimed at exercising an oversight of the Action Plan implementation.[108] On the one hand, it can be suggested that the establishment of a number of high-level institutions demonstrates the importance of the integrative processes for the Armenian authorities. However, it simultaneously causes confusion as to their tasks and roles in the integration processes.

The Ministry of Economy coordinates the process of the Action Plan implementation in practice. After the adoption of the document, the Ministry, in cooperation with other ministries, drafted a programme for the measures to be implemented in 2007.[109] The programme was much criticised by the civil society for allowing only six months for its implementation and lack of 'deliverables resulting from implementation or any benchmarks towards which the implementation

---

[103] Decree No 1282-N, 7 September 2006, Government of the Republic of Armenia.

[104] Ibid.

[105] Ibid.

[106] Interview with Varos Simonyan, Head of Department of EU and International Economic Affairs, Ministry of Economy of the Republic of Armenia (Yerevan, 20 April 2009).

[107] Ibid.

[108] Ibid; Armenia Progress Report 2008, Commission Staff Working Document Accompanying the Communication from the Commission to the European Parliament and the Council SEC (2009) 511/2, 23 April 2009, 3.

[109] Decree No 927, 22 August 2008, Government of the Republic of Armenia.

shall be measured'.[110] Subsequently, a different approach has been adopted by the government in order to avoid a lengthy preparatory drafting process involving different ministries on an annual basis.[111] Following the Georgian example the programmes for Action Plan implementation were established to set actions for more than one year. The 2009–11 programme for Action Plan implementation comprised almost 200 legislative measures, while the 2012–13 programme aimed inter alia at the facilitation of the opening of the DCFTA negotiations.[112]

Similarly to Georgia, a committee on European integration was established in the Parliament in 2008, responsible for links with the Union and the Council of Europe. In the initial few years of its operation the committee underwent a process of identifying its own role, and therefore could not claim a strong presence for the Parliament in the process of the ENP implementation. The committee was the only institution in Armenia directly entrusted with the task of EU legislation approximation.[113] However, the lack of knowledge on issues of EU *acquis* and limited human resources of the Committee hindered the performance of this task.[114] Ultimately, in 2012 the Committee was stripped of such competence and therefore was given no opportunity to play a decisive role in the process of ENP Action Plan implementation.

Public awareness of the ENP and its implementation in Armenia is rather low as likewise noted by the civil society representatives and state officials.[115] Similarly to Georgia, awareness decreases from the capital to the regions, which are less informed on matters of cooperation between Armenia and the EU.[116] The failures of the media have been noted, where even the events organised within the ENP framework are presented without highlighting their connection with the policy.[117] As to the civil society, it expressed willingness to participate in the programming and subsequent implementation of the Action Plan by organising public events, discussions, and seeking foreign grants for undertaking monitoring activities.[118]

However, its role in the actual integration processes has been limited in practice. Government officials are reluctant to attend events organised by the civil society, and there are no guarantees that the results of the public monitoring will be taken into account.[119] For instance, the process of the preparation of the

---

[110] Partnership for Open Society, Armenia, Analyses of the RA Government Decision on ENP AP Implementation Tools for 2007, July 2007; Interview with Karen Bekaryan, Head of NGO European Integration (Yerevan, 20 April 2009).

[111] Interview with Simonyan, note 106 above.

[112] Presidential Decree No NK-52-A, 16 April 2012; Decree No NK-68-A President o the Republic of Armenia 6 May 2009.

[113] The Law on National Assembly rules of procedure provided that 'the Parliament's Standing Committee on European Integration is responsible for links with the European Union and the Council of Europe, *harmonisation of laws* of the Republic of Armenia with European legislation'; LA-308, 21 March 2002.

[114] Ibid.

[115] Interview with Simonyan, note 106 above; Interview with Bekaryan, note 110 above; Interview with Kirakosyan, note 77 above.

[116] Interview with Bekaryan, note 110 above.

[117] Ibid.

[118] Ibid; interview with Kirakosyan, note 77 above.

[119] Interview with Kirakosyan, note 77 above.

government's 2007 programme on Action Plan implementation was described as 'closed and not accountable to the civil society and to the Armenian public'.[120] The contacts between the government and the representatives of the public sector are based on the reputation or the status of the organisation.[121] Thus, it would seem that as in Georgia the absence of an official framework within the ENP ensuring contacts between the government, the public and EU representatives contributed to the exclusion of the civil society from the implementation process. In Armenia the institutional framework has existed from 2006, at least on paper. The national council for cooperation with the EU mentioned above was designed to involve the representatives of civil society, although none of the representatives of the civil society interviewed was aware of its existence. The representative of the government, acknowledging the importance of the civil society, noted that a reform of the council has been initiated to ensure the effective presence of the civil society in the process.[122] A government official noted that steps had been taken to address the exclusionary practices in relation to the Parliament and the civil society, for instance by publishing the 2009–11 Action Plan implementation programme on the government's website.[123]

Hence, it can be concluded that Armenia's approach generally follows a similar pattern to Georgia, although falls short of creating a separate state institution entrusted with the process of European integration. The major role in the ENP implementation rests with the government with limited involvement from the Parliament and the general public.

5.3.3 Action Plan Implementation in Azerbaijan

The classification of Azerbaijan as a 'passive' or 'hesitant' ENP partner places it in a category of states where limited efforts are undertaken to implement the Action Plan.[124] The limited efforts are said to be explained by the 'vague' attitude of the Azerbaijani government on the issue of European integration.[125] As noted previously, integrating into European organisations is part of the general foreign policy, while cooperation with the EU has been dominated by energy cooperation issues. The country as such seeks no comprehensive integration framework. Even the provision acknowledging the country's 'European aspiration' in the Action

---

[120] 'Analyses of the RA Government Decision on ENP AP Implementation Tools for 2007', Partnership for Open Society Armenia.

[121] For instance, the European Integration NGO cooperates with the Parliament's Committee on EU integration, and the EU Department of Ministry of Foreign Affairs; Bekaryan, note 110 above.

[122] Interview with Simonyan, note 106 above; during 2009 some measures were undertaken by the government to involve representatives of the civil society in the process of the Action Plan implementation. With the assistance of the EU Social and Economic Committee a workshop was organised in Yerevan with the participation of representatives of the Armenian civil society.

[123] Ibid.

[124] Emerson et al, note 49 above, 24; Tocci, note 16 above, 27.

[125] J Boonstra, 'Azerbaijan' in R Youngs (ed), *Is the European Union Supporting Democracy in its Neighbourhood?* (Fride, 2008) 136.

Plan, common also for Georgia and Armenia, was not included in the initial draft, and was incorporated only under pressure from the Azerbaijan National Committee for European Integration (ANCEI), involving representatives from different segments of public life.[126]

The EU is seen by the Azerbaijani government and its population as an important economic partner.[127] Most importantly there is wide mistrust over the sincerity of the EU's attempt to promote democracy and human rights.[128] The tolerance of the international community, including the EU, of the false elections in Azerbaijan have also affected the perception of the local population.[129] It is said the government is mostly interested in EU assistance and certain economic projects,[130] with the implementation of the ENP depending on 'cost-benefit' calculations.[131] Since the assistance promised by the EU is rather minuscule when compared to Azerbaijan's budget,[132] no significant efforts can be expected from the Azerbaijani government in implementing the ENP Action Plan.

Following the inclusion of Azerbaijan within the ENP a state commission on European integration was established in 2005 comprised of the members of government. A number of ministries are therefore in charge of different aspects of cooperation with the EU, dealing with the issues of representation, aid allocation or assistance projects. The commission is assisted by a number of working groups dealing with various issues.[133] However, the nature of the commission is one of a coordinating institution and as such does not entail a comprehensive legislative approach to Action Plan implementation similar to Georgia or Armenia. The leading ministry chairing a task group on economic issues is the Ministry of Economic Development.[134]

In contrast with Georgia and Armenia, Azerbaijan did not embark on the implementation of the Action Plan after its adoption. Following the introduction of the EaP an 'Action Plan on the approximation of the legislation of Azerbaijan to EU legislation over 2010–2012' based on Article 43 PCA was adopted in 2010, becoming the first national measure on EU integration-related issues. The plan is not aimed at Action Plan implementation as such, and is rather limited to

---

[126] 'European Neighbourhood Policy and Azerbaijan', Annual Report of the Azerbaijan National Committee for European Integration, 18 July 2007, 10; available at www.osi.az/download/eurointegration/ANCEI_report_eng.pdf.

[127] Boonstra, note 125 above, 131; Popescu makes similar general observation as regards the South Caucasus: N Popescu, 'ENP and EaP: Relevant for the South Caucasus?' in *South Caucasus: 20 Years of Independence* (Friedrich Ebert Stiftung, 2011) 316–34, 331.

[128] A Mammadli, 'EU–Azerbaijan Relations: Enhancing Human Rights and Democracy within Eastern Partnership Initiatives', Caucasus Analytical Digest No 35-36 February 2012, 17.

[129] A Yunusof, 'Twenty Years of Independence in Azerbaijan' in '*South Caucasus*', note 127 above, 60–75, 70.

[130] Mammadli, note 128 above.

[131] 'Institutional Convergence of CIS towards European Benchmarks,' Report No 82/2008, Centre for Social and Economic Research, Warsaw, 2008.

[132] See Chapter 6, section 6.3.2; Boonstra, note 125 above, 135.

[133] Mammadli, note 128 above, 16.

[134] The minister of economic development currently chairs the commission; Orders of the President of the Republic of Azerbaijan December No 2597, 13 December 2012 and No 2786, 7 March 2013.

acquis approximation under the responsibility of the Ministry of Economic Development.[135] The majority of the measures are related to the integration of Azerbaijan into the world economy and other regulatory issues provided in Article 43 PCA. The above-mentioned programme can be contrasted to the practice of Georgia and Armenia where comparable programmes have been in place since 2007 following the adoption of their respective Action Plans. Besides, the Armenian and Georgian programmes are not restricted to '*acquis* conditionality' and provide for measures aimed at compliance with the political conditionality of the ENP.

Among the parliamentary committees none is specifically responsible for EU integration. Only recently a special unit on European integration has been established within the committee on international relations in charge of the cooperation with international organisations.[136] The Azerbaijani Parliament could not claim a significant presence on the issue of EU integration or political transformation due to domestic power imbalance: the national Parliament is largely dependent on the executive.[137] In particular, the Azerbaijani law on standard normative acts adopted in June 2010 requires parliament to 'coordinate' its legislative programme with that of the executive, that is the presidential administration, implying a lack of initiative.[138]

At the early stages of ENP cooperation the civil society expressed its fears that deepening of energy cooperation, by the signing of a Memorandum on EU–Azerbaijan energy cooperation in 2006 without imposing any preconditions on the country, would weaken the strength of the ENP.[139] In contrast to the official policy, the Azerbaijani civil society considers integration with the EU to be a priority for the country's future development.[140] The representatives of various segments of civil society established the ANCEI in February 2006 and claimed a prominent role in preparing proposals for the Action Plan and demonstrating willingness to undertake monitoring activities.[141] However, the latter was largely deprived of an opportunity to comment on the elaboration of the Action Plan due

---

[135] See the website of the Ministry of Economic Development, at www.economy.gov.az/index.php/en/international/europe-union.

[136] F Chiragov, 'Visa Facilitation Baseline Study', Center for Economic and Social Development, Policy Association for an Open Society, supported by the Local Government and Public Service Reform Initiative of Open Society Foundations, 2011, available at: http://visa-free-europe.eu/wp-content/uploads/2011/06/Azerbaijan-countryraportPASOS.pdf.

[137] 'The honouring of obligations and commitments by Azerbaijan', Report, PACE, Committee on the Honouring of Obligations and Commitments by Member States of the Council of Europe, Doc. 13084, 20 December 2012, 19.

[138] 'Azerbaijan: Vulnerable Stability', International Crisis Group, Europe Report No. 207, 3 September 2010, 6.

[139] Alieva, note 49 above, 16.

[140] 'Azerbaijan National Committee for European Integration and Increase of Civil Society Participation in European Neighbourhood Policy', External Evaluation of the Project, 2; Boonstra, note 125 above, 136.

[141] Alieva, note 49 above, 10–11; 'European Neighbourhood Policy and Azerbaijan', Annual Report of the Azerbaijan National Committee for European Integration, 8–10.

to the government's refusal to publicise the draft document.[142] Despite the civil society's efforts to engage in a dialogue with the authorities, it has been suggested that the past contacts were far from being classified as a real dialogue and rather performed a 'box ticking' function.[143] The current negotiation process between Azerbaijan and the EU inter alia on the future association agreement is said to be non-transparent, limiting the capacity of the civil society to influence the process.[144]

5.4 CONCLUSION

The Action Plans initially appear to take political reform to a new level within the agenda of cooperation due to the inclusion of respective issues within priority areas. Nevertheless, the picture is not as promising as it appears.

The major issues which are commonly addressed in the priority actions in the three Action Plans mainly revolve around the reform of the judiciary, reform of the executive and the conduct of elections. The majority of the priority actions are unmeasurable due to lack of substance, precision, detail and deadlines, turning the actions into a rhetorical call for reform. Besides, the Commission demonstrated a rather fragmented approach to the democratic values of the EU by practically omitting such vital issues as the role of parliament, political parties and the development of civil society from the priority areas, the latter being included only in the case of Azerbaijan. The EU's retreat from its normative stance is apparent in Azerbaijani and, surprisingly, Georgian Action Plans. While the principle of joint ownership explains the weak language on political reform in Azerbaijan's case, few priorities have been included on the agenda of democratic reform in Georgia, which focuses primarily on the judiciary and elections. In this light, the Armenian Action Plan appears to be the most true to the democratic rhetoric of the EU.

The status of political reform on the Action Plan agenda is also undermined due to the multiplicity of priority actions: political reform is only *one of* the areas of prioritised actions. The weaknesses of the Action Plans might explain the reliance on the countries' commitments in other international organisations, where they have binding obligations to implement democratic reforms. Such 'multilateralism' might be perceived as an effort to ensure the continuity of political reform. However, simultaneously the EU risks strengthening its image of an economic actor which does not aim at promoting democratic reforms.

Besides the very process of the Action Plan implementation distorts the democratic processes in Georgia and Armenia, where significant institutional and legislative measures were established to implement the Action Plans. The process is led by

---

[142] Ibid, 10.
[143] 'Azerbaijan National Committee for European Integration and Increase of Civil Society Participation in European Neighbourhood Policy', External Evaluation of the Project, 11.
[144] Mammadli, note 128 above, 16.

the executive with a marginal role for the national parliaments or the civil society. Fewer efforts are undertaken in Azerbaijan to implement the Action Plan where the pro-European civil society lacks power to influence the political agenda. Thus, the EaP civil society forum is met by much enthusiasm by the representatives of the civil society in the countries concerned.[145] Although, as discussed previously, the forum creates a necessary platform for socialisation enhancing the capacity of the civil society, it nevertheless does not guarantee any role in the ENP implementation processes domestically.

Democratisation – as part of the ENP – is not considered to be a priority for any of the countries. For both Armenia and Georgia democratic reforms are viewed as a precondition for necessary economic reform which is considered to be the core of the cooperation with the EU. Democratic reform in Georgia has also been perceived to pave the way for the country's integration into Western organisations, including NATO. In practice it suggests that democratic reforms feature on the agenda of Action Plan implementation as actions related to economic reforms. Thus, the formal prerequisites of democracy can be expected to be developed to ensure the continuation of cooperation and its possible advancement. However, even the formal criteria might not need to be satisfied as the case of Azerbaijan demonstrates. The importance of the democratic reforms is undermined due to the lack of perception of the ENP as a policy requiring political and economic transformation. It comes as a result not only of the national government's reluctance to undertake political reforms, but also the EU's permissive attitude to democratic conditionality, where the stability of present energy agreements is a top priority.

It is therefore left to the elements of monitoring and financial assistance to instil some dynamism into the political conditionality of the ENP.

---

[145] Interview with Kirakosyan, note 77 above; Mammadli, note 128 above.

6

EU Democratic Values and the ENP

Implementation in the South Caucasus II: Monitoring and Assistance

6.1 INTRODUCTION

IT IS SAID that the EU possesses sufficient tools to exercise the ENP conditionality even without the membership incentive.[1] It is suggested that such tools can include the monitoring of policy implementation in combination with the assistance mechanisms deployed by the EU.

In the enlargement experience the control of the progress of political and economic reforms has been viewed to be the best means of guaranteeing the ultimate success of candidate countries.[2] Likewise within the ENP the absence of monitoring would render the Action Plans devoid of any practical significance and would diminish the EU's role in policy implementation in our case studies. The monitoring of the Action Plan implementation demonstrates the determination on behalf of the EU to send a regular message to the partner countries on their potential to come closer to the EU.[3]

It is undertaken through the mechanism of joint evaluation and progress reports issued unilaterally by the Commission.[4] The PCA joint institutions advance and monitor the implementation of the Action Plans, while the Commission produces reports on implementation in cooperation with the High Representative.[5] The lack of clarity and detail in the Action Plan priorities sets a

---

[1] R Balfour and A Rotta, 'Beyond Enlargement: The European Neighbourhood Policy and its Tools' (2005) 40 *International Spectator* 7, 10.

[2] D Kochenov, *EU Enlargement and the Failure of Conditionality: Pre-Accession Conditionality in the Fields of Democracy and the Rule of Law* (Austin, Wolters Kluwer Law and Business, 2008) 51; P Dunay, 'Strategy with Fast Moving Targets: East-Central Europe' in R Dannreuther (ed), *European Union Foreign and Security Policy: Towards a Neighbourhood Strategy* (London, Routledge, 2004) 27–47, 32.

[3] Wider Europe – Neighbourhood: A New Framework for Relations with our Eastern and Southern Neighbours, Communication from the Commission to the Council and the European Parliament COM (2003) 104 final, 11 April 2003, 18.

[4] Commission Communication, Proposals for Action Plans under the European Neighbourhood Policy COM (2004) 795 final, 9 December 2004, 4.

[5] See s 5 of EU–Georgia, EU–Armenia, EU–Azerbaijan Action Plans.

tenuous ground for monitoring the implementation of these documents, and challenges the Commission with a task of measuring progress.

The assistance provided to the partner countries is the last element of the conditionality mechanism. Its overview helps to identify the extent of upholding the EU's democratic rhetoric at various stages of policy implementation. It is this element that, combined with the incentives of the policy, can deliver significant effects in practice, as neighbouring countries such as Armenia and Georgia depend on foreign assistance for internal transformation. It is therefore necessary to identify to what extent the ENPI legal framework prioritises assistance for democratic reform in general, and in the countries concerned in particular.

The chapter is structured as follows. First, the process of monitoring and its role in securing consistency between various elements of policy implementation is considered. The progress reports issued by the Commission will be discussed in order to reveal its efficiency in the conditionality mechanism. The next part of the chapter addresses the ENPI legal framework as the main instrument for providing assistance to the South Caucasian states. The role of other assistance measures affecting democracy promotion is also discussed within this part. The last substantive part reflects on the chain of conditionality of the ENP and its effects in policy implementation in the South Caucasus. The chapter is summarised with observations on the consistency of securing the EU's normative image within the operative elements of the ENP conditionality.

6.2 MONITORING POLITICAL REFORM IN THE SOUTH CAUCASUS

The monitoring element within the ENP methodology can be considered to be the epicentre of conditionality as it should link the advancement of cooperation between the parties to the progress achieved. Taking into account both the positive and negative elements of ENP conditionality, it is suggested that the purpose of monitoring is either to reward those states which demonstrate sufficient progress in meeting the targets set or to ensure adverse consequences for those states which fail to deliver on political reforms. A related issue is the nexus between the results of monitoring and the assistance provided.

The two types of monitoring identified in the introduction do not necessarily suggest such linking. Each type of monitoring is addressed in turn.

6.2.1 Political Dialogue: What Monitoring?

The element of political dialogue in EU external relations was noted to provide a platform for promoting the objectives of EU external action, and for assessing respect for democratic governance, democratic principles and human rights in its external agenda generally.[6] This dialogue is said to have a 'preventive' aspect to it and is aimed at securing compliance.[7]

Within the ENP the political dialogue takes place either at high official level or within the institutional framework of the PCAs. Hence, the Presidency, the Troika visits, or meetings with the ENP Commissioner or the High Representative should be considered as high-level monitoring, which guarantee that the issues of democracy promotion and human rights protection are constantly present on the dialogue agenda.[8] In addition to official visits, declarations and *démarches* can also be added to the monitoring element, which is suggested to have certain practical effects in the states concerned.[9] Although declarations are meant to express the position the Union takes regarding a particular situation,[10] often the final statement is a result of a compromise involving various actors with diverging positions as noted in Chapter 3.[11] A related problem is the slow operation of the heavy bureaucratic machinery of the EU, where the element of swift response is at times missing.[12] Thus, often the statements and declarations fail to indicate the position taken by the EU or to do so in a timely manner.

Since 2009 monitoring via dialogue has also been taking place with Georgia and Armenia through the EU Human Rights Dialogues, aimed at mainstreaming political reform within EU external action. It takes place at various levels and concerns the issues of human rights protection, democracy and rule of law.[13] The level of representation varies: in 2012 the EU was represented by the Director of the Human Rights and Democracy Department of the EEAS.[14]

A lower level of political dialogue is recorded at the level of institutions established within the PCAs, highlighting the joint ownership element of the ENP methodology.[15] The practice demonstrates that the 'jointness' of the monitoring is more of an engagement than monitoring, and therefore cannot have a 'preventive' function. The highest level of PCA engagement is recorded at the Cooperation Council meetings, which take place annually at a ministerial level. On a declaratory level the Cooperation Councils consistently highlight the essential elements

---

[6] Council Conclusions, External Relations Council, Democracy Support in the EU's External Relations, 17 November 2009, 4; European Union Guidelines on Human Rights Dialogues, Council, December 2001, 5.

[7] Council Conclusions, note 6 above.

[8] Interview with anonymous Commission official, DG RELEX, European Commission (Brussels, 28 April 2009).

[9] A Gahramanova, 'Internal and External Factors in the Democratisation of Azerbaijan' (2009) 16 *Democratisation* 777, 795; Interview with Karen Bekaryan, Head of NGO European Integration (Yerevan, 20 April 2009).

[10] R Wessel, *The European Union's Foreign and Security Policy: A Legal Institutional Perspective* (The Hague, Kluwer Law International, 1999) 186.

[11] See Chapter 3, section 3.2.2.2; U Khaliq, *Ethical Dimensions of the Foreign Policy of the European Union: A Legal Appraisal* (Cambridge, CUP, 2008) 91.

[12] Interview with Bekaryan, note 9 above.

[13] EU Guidelines on Human Rights Dialogues with Third Countries, 5. Available at www.consilium.europa.eu/uedocs/cmsUpload/16526.en08.pdf.

[14] EU–Georgia Human Rights Dialogue (Tbilisi, 26 June 2012).

[15] Commission Communication, ENP Strategy Paper COM (2004) 373 final, 12 May 2004, 10.

of political dialogue, namely the rule of law, democratic principles, protection of human rights and fundamental freedoms, political pluralism, freedom of expression and freedom of the media. This guarantees the *representation* of the EU as a normative actor. However, a closer look at the minutes of the Cooperation Council meetings indicates that, in practice, no assessment of progress is undertaken as such. There is a perception in the Commission that the task of the Councils is limited to summarising the developments taking place throughout the year, including the activities of other joint bodies under the PCA, where the meetings do not last more than half an hour and are akin to a 'hand-shaking exercise'.[16] Besides, unlike their counterparts established under Europe Agreements with the CEE states, the PCA Cooperation Councils do not have a power of adopting decisions binding on the parties, which diminishes their importance.

The lower-level joint institutions cannot claim a major role in the task of monitoring via political dialogue: democracy promotion issues require high-level interaction according to a Commission official.[17] The significance of these institutions rather lies in technical cooperation on a lower level. The chronology of establishing the subcommittees is suggestive of the importance of a particular area of cooperation not only for the EU, but also for the partner states, since the establishment of new subcommittees depends on the agreement of the partner states. The subcommittee related to democracy is the justice, liberty and security subcommittee first established in Georgia in 2007. The first subcommittee established in Armenia was on trade, economic and related legal issues, and in Azerbaijan the first two subcommittees were established on energy, environment and transport, and on trade and economic issues in 2008.

In 2008 the Parliament called on the Commission to negotiate the establishment of human rights subcommittees with all three states.[18] However, in Georgia the mentioned subcommittee remained in place without new developments, and equivalent subcommittees were established for Armenia and Azerbaijan in 2010. In the case of Azerbaijan the relevant subcommittee's title also includes 'human rights and democratisation', to a certain extent satisfying the Parliament's vision, or perhaps suggesting that the issues of human rights and democratic development are more pressing in Azerbaijan. It can be suggested that the subcommittees, meeting at civil servant level, have a minimal role in steering political reforms on a grand scale, and rather can be viewed as a platform for socialisation. Besides, the mentioned subcommittees have a rather narrow profile in terms of the scope of issues they tend to address.

The Parliamentary Cooperation Committees established under the respective PCAs in 2004 secure the interaction between the EP and the representatives of the national parliaments. The minutes of the committee meetings demonstrate a keen attitude towards exercising an oversight over democracy and human rights-related

---

[16] Anonymous Commission official, note 8 above.
[17] Ibid.
[18] European Parliament Resolution of 17 January 2008 on a More Effective EU Policy for the South Caucasus: from Promises to Actions (2007/2076(INI)) para 21.

issues.[19] Although the outcome of the Committee meetings does not have an immediate influence on the advancement of relations, the meetings nevertheless perform
an informative function which might be of assistance to the Parliament when it
gives its consent to concluding new agreements.[20] Likewise, the involvement of the
national parliamentarians in such cooperation facilitates a more active role in relation to EU integration issues at domestic level.

Therefore, it can be concluded that the role of the PCA joint institutions in the
monitoring of progress is rather insignificant, as their function is confined to
nothing more than declarations on an annual basis. The factual evaluation of the
progress achieved is left to the Commission (currently jointly with the EEAS),
whose judgement carries more political weight.

6.2.2 Commission Monitoring: 'Under Western Eyes'?

The monitoring element of the accession conditionality secured the transfer of
the Commission's traditional role of the 'guardian of the Treaty' to progress evaluation of the candidate states.[21] Determined to preserve its central role within the
ENP, the Commission adopted a similar mechanism of annual monitoring based
on progress reports. Despite the perceived importance of monitoring in securing
the success of the accession states, the very process of monitoring did not escape
the criticism, raised in Chapter 4, that the evaluation process was marred by various drawbacks and had a political element to it.[22] Combined with the political
nature of the ENP, such precedent therefore suggests a higher degree of politicisa-
tion within the evaluation process.

The Action Plans are the main point of reference for evaluating progress. In
view of the mostly unmeasurable nature of the conditions in the Action Plans, the
question turns into the adequacy of the monitoring exercised by the Commission
related to the level of compliance sought in adhering to democratic values. The
discussion below is based on three premises. First, it aims at revealing the consistency between the Commission's choice of issues to evaluate and the prioritised
actions in the Action Plans, and therefore answers the question as to what is being
evaluated. On the one hand, the priorities are so widely defined that the
Commission's hands are not tied in its choice of issues to monitor. On the other
hand, for this very reason, rigour and continuity in the assessment become very
important, which is the second dimension of the discussion and answers the question on how progress is measured. Lastly, and most importantly, the consequences
of the Commission's evaluation should be placed in the context of the ENP conditionality to answer the question for what political end the monitoring is being

---

[19]   Available at www.europarl.europa.eu/delegations/en/dsca/publications.html.
[20]   Art 218(6) TFEU.
[21]   C Hillion, 'The Copenhagen Criteria and their Progeny' in C Hillion (ed), *EU Enlargement: A Legal
Approach* (Oxford, Hart Publishing, 2004) 1–22, 13.
[22]   See Chapter 4, section 4.4.1.

undertaken. The next sections of this part address the first two questions, while the last question is discussed in the final substantive part of this chapter.

6.2.2.1 Assessing the Priorities: Consistency, Continuity and Rigour

A cursory examination of the reports evaluating progress for the 2007–12 period reveals a peculiar continuity pattern and at times a lack of it.[23]

In the Georgian reports, in terms of its choice of issues the Commission consistently addressed the actions contained in the priority area on democratic reform of the Action Plan in 2008–11 progress reports.[24] However, omitted from the 2012 and 2013 reports were issues of separation of powers, public service reforms and local governance reform, as well as the implementation of recommendations of the European Committee for the Prevention of Torture and Inhuman or Degrading Treatment or Punishment, thus undermining the continuity of evaluation. Besides, the evaluation of progress on political reform has not been restricted to the prioritised actions only. Issues such as minority rights, media pluralism and others, which are included in section 4 on general actions of the Action Plan, have also been evaluated by the Commission.[25] Other issues of which there was no mention in the Action Plan were also evaluated,[26] indicating a lack of distinction between prioritised actions and those included in the general actions list, as well as those not mentioned in the Action Plan. This confirms the assumption made in the previous chapter as to the non-significance of prioritising the actions. It can be argued that non-prioritised issues became part of the assessment due to certain developments in particular areas presenting the progress achieved in a positive light, rather than because compliance was sought in that area.

In terms of the rigour of evaluation, the latter depends on the issue considered. For instance, in assessing the action on 'ensuring proper separation of powers' prioritised in the Action Plan, the Commission duly notes certain reforms achieved or planned for the future, and at times indicates the outstanding issues. However, the evaluation comes across as one of a passive observer, often reserving judgement, where the reforms achieved are presented as the central feature, while the outstanding issues are mentioned in passing without much elaboration. It is suggested that in comparative perspective a few specific issues are most rigorously assessed in terms of the level of scrutiny and the indications as to further compliance. These areas include electoral reform and practice, the independence and efficiency of the judiciary and the justice system, and prevention of torture.

---

[23] The progress reports are available at www.ec.europa.eu/world/enp/documents_en.htm.

[24] Progress Report Georgia 2008, Commission Staff Working Document SEC (2008)393, 3 April 2008; Progress Report Georgia 2009, Commission Staff Working Document SEC (2009) 513/2, 23 April 2009; Progress Report Georgia 2010, Commission Staff Working Document SEC (2010) 518, 12 May 2010; Progress Report Georgia 2011, Commission Staff Working Document SEC (2011) 649, 25 May 2011; Progress in 2011 and Recommendations for Action Georgia, Joint Staff Working Document SWD (2012) 114 final, 15 May 2012; Progress in 2012 and Recommendations for Action Georgia Joint Staff Working Document SWD (2013) 90 final, 20 March 2013.

[25] See Georgia Progress Reports for 2008, 3–5; 2009, 5–6; 2010, 4–6; 2011, 3–5.

[26] These include women's rights, children's issues, freedom of association, labour rights.

Similar observations can be made regarding Armenian progress reports. In terms of the selection of issues considered, the progress reports are mostly consistent in addressing the prioritised measures.[27] However, other prioritised issues such as the reform of prosecution and property rights have been omitted from the evaluation from the start.[28] The issue of property rights makes a brief appearance in the 2010 report, while reform of prosecution returns to the evaluation radar in 2010 and 2011, although without much rigour or continuity in the following years. Certain issues disappear from the assessment spectrum, including separation of powers and local self-governance after 2011.[29]

In terms of the evaluation rigour the Commission focuses more on the electoral reform, independence of media and freedom of assembly, prevention of torture, as well as anti-corruption strategies. It should be noted that often when demonstrating rigour in its assessment by indicating the outstanding issues the Commission relies on the evaluation results by other international organisations.[30] Similarly to Georgia, the Commission continuously engages in the assessment of actions not prioritised or not mentioned in the Action Plan, including freedom of expression, gender equality, labour rights, prohibition of discrimination and freedom of religion. It should be noted that unlike the Georgian progress reports, which make no recourse to the role of the civil society, the Armenian progress reports assess the position of the civil society from 2009. Thus, it can be confirmed that the Commission is not restricted in its choice of issues subject to evaluation.

The Azerbaijani progress reports, although mostly consistent in addressing the Action Plan priorities, have their peculiarities.[31] One of the central elements of the prioritised actions, that is securing proper checks and balances between parliament and the executive, has appeared on the Commission's radar only once in six years.[32] Cautious in its language, the Commission falls back on the assessment by the Council of Europe, and makes no return to this issue in subsequent years. Thus, it can be suggested that in this area, which would have directly challenged

---

[27] Progress Report Armenia 2008, Commission Staff Working Document SEC (2008)392, 3 April 2008; Progress Report Armenia 2009, Commission Staff Working Document SEC (2009) 511/2, 23 April 2009; Progress Report Armenia 2010, Commission Staff Working Document SEC (2010) 516, 12 May 2010; Progress Report Armenia 2011, Commission Staff Working Document SEC (2011) 639, 25 May 2011; Progress in 2011 and Recommendations for Action Armenia, Joint Staff Working Document, SWD (2012) 110 final, 15 May 2012; Progress in 2012 and Recommendations for Action Armenia SWD (2013) 79 final, 20 March 2013.

[28] They also include the accession to the European Code of Social Charter.

[29] The improvement of the legal aid system and the establishment and functioning of the administrative courts also disappear from the reports after 2008.

[30] Eg the assessment of local self-governance reform relies on the Council of Europe conclusions; Armenia 2008 Progress Report, 3.

[31] Progress Report Azerbaijan 2008, Commission Staff Working Document SEC (2008) 39, 3 April 2008; Progress Report Azerbaijan 2009, Commission Staff Working Document SEC (2009) 512/2, 23 April 2009; Progress Report Azerbaijan 2010, Commission Staff Working Document SEC (2010) 519, 12 May 2010; Progress Report Azerbaijan 2011, Commission Staff Working Document SEC (2011) 640, 25 May 2011; Progress in 2011 and Recommendations for Action Azerbaijan, Joint Staff Working Document SWD (2012) 111 final, 15 May 2012; Progress in 2012 and Recommendations for Action Azerbaijan, Joint Staff Working Document SWD (2013) 88 final, 20 March 2013.

[32] Azerbaijan 2010 Progress Report, 3.

the executive's autocratic rule, the Commission is tiptoeing around the matter, focusing instead on other issues not prioritised in the Action Plan. For those matters the Commission is often open about stating the lack of progress or in some cases clear worsening of the situation on the ground. Certain prioritised measures, such as the proper implementation of the law on freedom of information or the establishment of an independent broadcasting media do not directly feature within the report, while the Commission continually addresses issues of freedom of expression and media not mentioned in the Action Plan. As in the Georgian and Armenian reports, other matters included in the general actions feature continually within the evaluation.[33] Consistent attention is paid to fighting corruption, which is a separate priority of its own, as noted in the previous chapter but which the Commission includes in its evaluation on democratic progress.

In terms of the rigour of assessment, the Azerbaijani progress reports stand out due to the frequency of recording the lack of progress, or even worsening, of the political situation in various areas. This suggests that despite the low-key priority of democratic reform in the relations between the parties, the Commission has to evaluate the state's progress, at least formally.

To summarise, in the case of Georgia the Commission consistently concentrates on representative democracy and elements of liberal governance in a general manner. At times the detail of the evaluation demonstrates that the Commission is ready to engage in assessment, especially via positive evaluation, where the country's leadership is undertaking reforms and seeks appreciation.[34] The Georgian progress reports are, however, silent on the participative element of democracy, in particular the role of the civil society, which is a feature present in almost all Armenian progress reports. The representative element of democracy and the functioning of the judiciary and certain political freedoms are continual elements in the Armenian progress reports, while the issue of separation of powers has been ignored since 2010. The latter, particularly relevant for Azerbaijan with its dominant executive, has been practically omitted from the evaluation exercise, which instead focuses on the representative elements of democracy, the fight against corruption and other issues.

Thus, the following observations should be made regarding the adequacy of the Commission's evaluation. First of all, the approach taken in the evaluation results in the discrediting of the Action Plan priorities as such. Second, the Commission addresses progress as regards prioritised action with varying detail and rigour, not only depending on the country concerned, but also depending on the year. In addition, the evaluation is not indicative as to further actions and as such does not provide guidance for the future. Third, the forgetfulness of the Commission

---

[33] These include the functioning of the institution of Ombudsman, freedom of assembly, national minorities, gender equality.

[34] This urgency on behalf of the Georgian government to reassure the EU of its commitment to democratic values after the August 2008 war has been reciprocated by the EU. It made this commitment part of the new package of political conditionality linked to increased EU post-conflict assistance agreed in January 2009.

should be noted where continuity of assessment is undermined by omitting or abandoning certain priorities.

Since the involvement of the EEAS within the process of drafting the progress reports, certain developments can be recorded. The 2012 and 2013 progress reports make a reference in their headings to 'deep and sustainable' democracy in line with the Joint Communication on the revised ENP.[35] While it did not entail any changes in the evaluation technique in comparison with previous years, a new element has been introduced to the progress reports by inviting attention to certain actions prior to undertaking sector-related reform evaluation. Perhaps by incorporating a list of outstanding issues, the Commission and the EEAS avoid seeking the agreement of the partner states that would be required in the revision of the Action Plans. Although the majority of the outstanding issues concern democracy- and human rights-related issues, they are mostly formulated in the style of the Action Plans and likewise cannot be viewed as 'benchmarks'. Only some of them have specificity in requiring certain actions to be taken.[36] Taking into account the tendency to evaluate progress on issues not even mentioned in the Action Plans or mentioned within general non-prioritised actions, this means that a revision of the Action Plan is long overdue.

6.2.2.2 The Judgement Process

So, how does the Commission arrive at its conclusions? It has been suggested that the annual picture of progress is obtained in a continuous process of contacts between the EU delegation and the national governments, interaction with the national parliaments and NGOs, and communication between the EU embassies, aimed at elaboration of a comprehensive vision on political reform.[37] Having an EU delegation in relevant countries is a major source of contact and point of reference for analysis for the Commission. The reports are also based on the data prepared in close cooperation with the Council of Europe, the OSCE, relevant UN bodies, and other international organisations.[38] The Communication stresses the contribution of the membership of the partners to the OSCE and the Council of Europe 'to a particular reform agenda aiming at close approximation to the fundamental standards prevailing in the EU'.[39]

However, ultimately the composition of the progress report is a subjective exercise by a Commission official, who can influence the language of the document in terms of his or her particular vision of the progress.[40] Thus, the evaluation process

---

[35] Joint Communication, A New Response to a Changing Neighbourhood: A Review of the European Neighbourhood Policy COM (2011) 303, 25 May 2011 (hereinafter 2011 Joint Communication).

[36] For instance, the requirement to adopt the draft law on defamation, which provides for the abolition of criminal liability for defamation and insult in the 2012 Azerbaijan Progress Report, 3.

[37] Anonymous Commission official, note 8 above.

[38] This approach was confirmed in the Commission Communication on Implementation of the ENP in 2007, COM (2008) 164, 3 April 2008, 3.

[39] Ibid.

[40] Anonymous Commission official, note 8 above.

is inevitably a flexible exercise where a wide margin is preserved for political considerations and subjectivity. It can be argued that the Commission refrains from making harsh judgements even when noticing lack of progress. For instance, the evaluation of progress by the Commission following the post-election violence in Armenia in 2008 was much criticised by the Armenian civil society due to the perceived muted tone of the report at a time when freedom of association was being violated and dozens of political prisoners were being held in detention.[41]

The assessment is undertaken on an individual basis without any regional comparative perspective. Only after the report is prepared does a horizontal unit on Neighbourhood Policy coordination in Directorate D compare the progress reports in order to ensure 'that the evaluation of Azerbaijan makes sense in comparison with Tunisia'.[42] Most importantly, in the absence of a clear vision of democratic values being promoted, it is logical to assume certain discretion on behalf of the Commission in evaluating the progress in the Action Plan implementation with subjectivity creeping in.

The impact of political monitoring by the international community has been noted in relation to Armenia as regards the financial assistance issued to it: the position of those financially supporting the country is one of the reasons the latter does not succumb to authoritarianism.[43] This observation highlights the effect of linking the results of political monitoring to the assistance provided.

6.3 FINANCIAL ASSISTANCE AND THE DEMOCRATIC VALUES OF THE EU

The presence of democratisation issues within the external assistance provided by the EU is a testimony to the 'mainstreaming' of democracy promotion within the EU decision-making processes.[44] Technical assistance is identified as a significant element of promotion of EU values.[45] An example of EU technical assistance for democracy is the first ESDP mission to Georgia, EUJUST Themis, in support of the rule of law and established at the request of the Georgian authorities.[46] Another example is a Twinning project launched in 2008 in Armenia to support the reform of the Ombudsman office.[47]

---

[41] T Mkrtchyan, T Huseynov and K Gogolashvili, 'The European Union and the South Caucasus: Three Perspectives on the Future of the European Project from the Caucasus', Europe in Dialogue 2009/01, Bertelsmann Stiftung, 2009, 23.

[42] Anonymous Commission official, note 8 above.

[43] B Navasardian, 'Politics and Governance in Armenia: The Prospects for Democracy' (Friedrich Ebert Stiftung, 2011) 92–107, 99.

[44] The European Union: Furthering Human Rights and Democracy Across the Globe, European Commission 2007, 13.

[45] M Cremona, 'Values in EU Foreign Policy, in M Evans and T Tridimas (eds), *Beyond Established Legal Orders: Policy Interconnections between the EU and the Rest of the World* (Oxford, Hart Publishing, 2011) 275– 315, 293.

[46] Council Joint Action 2004/523/CFSP of 28 June 2004; E Baracani, 'European Union Democratic Anchoring' in E Baracani (ed), *Democratisation and Hybrid Regimes: International Anchoring and Domestic Dynamics in European Post-Soviet States* (Florence, European Press Academic Publishing, 2011) 111–34, 129.

[47] Armenia 2009 Progress Report, 17.

Democracy assistance can also take the form of financial assistance.[48] Budgetary support is therefore an element of the Union's leverage in its relations with its neighbours.[49] The financial and technical assistance provided to the ENP states reflects the above-mentioned democracy 'mainstreaming' in its legal framework. Democratic assistance has been incorporated within the ENPI legal framework, the main financial instrument providing assistance to the ENP states. It has been noted that democracy assistance is characterised by dual purpose, where political reforms are either supported for their own sake or as part of general stabilisation assistance.[50] The ENPI can be suggested to follow the second pattern.

It should be noted that the establishment of the Action Plans with Georgia, Armenia and Azerbaijan in late 2006 coincided with the establishment of the ENPI, which made the latter the main assistance instrument for Action Plan implementation until the time of writing.[51]

6.3.1 The Role of Democratic Values within the ENPI

The Regulation establishing the ENPI was adopted on the basis of former Articles 179 and 181a EC, both providing for developing and consolidating democracy promotion as a general objective. The ENPI accordingly upholds the ENP rhetoric on democracy promotion by incorporating a commitment to promote EU values to neighbouring countries via dialogue and cooperation,[52] reiterating the EU's normative image. It also specifies that supporting democratisation by enhancing the role of civil society and promoting media pluralism, as well as through electoral observation assistance, is one of the areas for channelling assistance.[53]

Although the Regulation is set to assist the implementation of the PCAs or future agreements, the Action Plans are used as a point of reference for establishing the priorities for assistance.[54] It is therefore legitimate to expect that the prioritisation of democracy-related issues in the Action Plans would be reflected in the assistance allocation.

A better use of funds has been identified as one of the strengths of the ENPI where the allocation of funds is 'explicitly policy-driven' and marks a major development for the countries previously covered by 'Technical Aid to the Commonwealth

---

[48] Burnell as cited in Baracani, note 46 above, 129.

[49] For instance in the case of Ukraine Solonenko suggests that the increase of budgetary support will enhance the leverage of the EU: I Solonenko, 'European Neighbourhood Policy Implementation in Ukraine: Local Context Matters' in E Lannon (ed), *The European Neighbourhood Policy's Challenges* (Brussels, College of Europe Studies, PIE Peter Lang, 2012) 345–79, 356–57.

[50] T Carothers, 'Democracy Assistance: The Question of Strategy' (1997) 4 *Democratisation* 109, 110.

[51] Regulation No 1638/2006 of the European Parliament and of the Council laying down general provisions establishing a European Neighbourhood and Partnership Instrument (ENPI Regulation) [2006] OJ L310/1.

[52] Art 1, ENPI Regulation.

[53] Art 2(2), ENPI Regulation.

[54] Arts 2(1) and 3(1), ENPI Regulation.

of Independent States' (TACIS), moving 'from technical assistance to fully-fledged cooperation'.[55] A number of distinctions between these two instruments could be highlighted.

According to the Regulation, assistance under the ENPI is established in partnership between the Commission and the beneficiary, involving national, regional and local authorities, economic and social partners, civil society representatives etc.[56] In comparison with TACIS, which engaged with the respective governments only, the ENPI Regulation marked a major shift on paper towards a more inclusive approach. Moreover, Article 14 of the Regulation establishes the list of participants eligible for funding, which, besides state actors, also includes decentralised bodies and non-state actors, thus incorporating the bottom-up approach in contrast to the top-down approach of TACIS assistance. The Regulation prioritises the civil society both in terms of its participation in the allocation of EU assistance and its development being one of the target areas.[57] The ENPI National Indicative Programmes for three states also emphasised the bottom-up approach to governance.[58]

A common feature of TACIS and ENPI is the negative conditionality element. The preconditions for triggering the negative conditionality mechanism are included in Article 28, which includes the failure on behalf of the partner states to observe the principles of liberty, democracy, respect for human rights and fundamental freedoms and the rule of law. Although spelling out the grounds for suspension of assistance might imply the significance of these issues on the cooperation agenda, it nevertheless does not indicate what counts as a 'failure' or which level of 'failure' is required for triggering negative conditionality.

It is the positive conditionality that was considered to be the 'real development' in the use of conditionality to neighbouring countries, where the future development of relations would depend on the achievements of mutually agreed goals.[59] It can be suggested that in this context the negative conditionality merely fulfils a complementary or a deterring function. On the other hand, since the positive conditionality is not affirmed in any binding legal instrument, the negative conditionality incorporated in the ENPI Regulation perhaps aims to support the positive conditionality by highlighting its political element.

A major issue related to the ENPI is its 'budget problem'.[60] The financial envelope amounting to approximately €11 billion for the 2007–13 period, intended for all neighbours including Russia, has been inadequate for financing reforms in

---

[55] Commission Communication, Strengthening the European Neighbourhood Policy COM (2006) 726 final, 4 December 2006, 3; Council Regulation 99/2000 concerning the provision of assistance to the partner states in Eastern Europe and Central Asia [2000] OJ L12.

[56] Art 4(2), ENPI Regulation.

[57] Arts 2 and 4, ENPI Regulation.

[58] Armenia ENPI National Indicative Programme 2007–2010, 7–8; Georgia ENPI National Indicative Programme 6; Azerbaijan ENPI National Indicative Programme 2007–2010, 6, 9.

[59] M Cremona, 'The European Neighbourhood Policy: More than a Partnership?' in M Cremona, (ed), *Developments in EU External Relations Law* (Oxford, OUP, 2008) 244–99, 284.

[60] R Seidelmann, The EU's Neighbourhood Policies' in M Telo (ed), *The European Union and Global Governance* (London, Routledge, 2009) 261–82, 277.

all desired sectors similar to the pre-accession strategy.[61] Budgetary constraints are particularly expressive when viewed in the context of country-specific annual allocations, discussed below.

The role of the ENPI assistance in exercising the positive conditionality is also not straightforward, despite proclaiming democracy-related issues to be one of the lines for assistance. Although it is part of the ENP conditionality, the assistance element is also affected by joint ownership incorporated in Article 4 of the ENPI Regulation.

The implementation of the Regulation depends on soft law instruments, such as the ENPI country strategy papers 2007–13 and the national indicative programmes for 2007–10 and 2011–13.[62] The country strategy papers provide a general overview of the objectives of the cooperation, the political and economic situation and a review of past and future EU assistance.[63] Among the previous programmes and instruments operating in the South Caucasus, only the European Initiative for Democracy and Human Rights had been directly concerned with democracy promotion,[64] however its sole focus on small-scale projects involving NGOs implied a major gap in this area of funding. TACIS, the main assistance instrument for PCA implementation has been considered to have had limited effect on reform generally due to being 'cash-starved'.[65] Also, the lack of continuity and absence of links to progress in democratisation were factors that had undermined the effectiveness of previous instruments as identified by the Commission.[66]

The ENPI national indicative programmes establish certain priority areas for providing assistance including support for democratic development with sub-priorities for each of the countries.[67] Based on these programmes annual action

[61] E Tulmets, 'Adapting the Experience of Enlargement to the Neighbourhood Policy: the ENP as a Substitute to Enlargement?' in P Kratochvil (ed), *The European Union and Its Neighbourhood: Policies, Problems and Priorities* (Prague, Institute of International Relations, 2006) 29–57, 46.

[62] Art 3, ENPI Regulation.

[63] ENPI, Armenia Country Strategy Paper, 2007–2013; ENPI, Georgia Country Strategy Paper, 2007–2013; ENPI, Azerbaijan Country Strategy Paper 2007–2013. Available at www.ec.europa.eu/world/enp/documents_en.htm.

[64] Council Regulations EC 975/1999 laying down the requirements for the implementation of development cooperation operations which contribute to the general objective of developing and consolidating democracy and the rule of law and to that of respecting human rights and fundamental freedoms [1999] OJ L120/1, 8 May 1999, and EC No 976/1999 laying down the requirements for the implementation of Community operations, other than those of development cooperation, which, within the framework of Community cooperation policy, contribute to the general objective of developing and consolidating democracy and the rule of law and to that of respecting human rights and fundamental freedoms in third countries [1999] OJ L120/8, 8 May 1999.

[65] V Stritecky, 'The South Caucasus: A Challenge for the ENP' in Kratochvil (ed), note 61 above, 59–76, 63–64.

[66] Armenia Country Strategy Evaluation, Final Report, January 2006; EuropeAid Co-operation Office, Directorate General for Development and External Relations, 2, available at www.ec.europa.eu/europeaid/how/evaluation/evaluation_reports/reports/2006/804_vol1_en.pdf; Evaluation of EC Tacis Country Strategy: Azerbaijan 1996–1999, March 2000, 4, available at www.ec.europa.eu/europeaid/how/evaluation/evaluation_reports/reports/tacis/951538_en.pdf.

[67] Section 4 in Armenia ENPI National Indicative Programme 2007–2010; Georgia ENPI National Indicative Programme 2007–2010; Azerbaijan National Indicative Programme 2007–2010.

programmes are adopted subject to a number of measures with 'inbuilt flexibility', implying that there are no fixed programmes.[68] According to a Commission official, instead of fixing particular projects, a dialogue with the national government is maintained to decide the specific objectives for providing support, representing a 'more forward-looking, more structural approach'.[69] Various forms of assistance, including budgetary (sectoral budget or general budget) and non-budgetary support are envisaged.[70] It also supports new cooperation tools such as TAIEX and Twinning in the areas of regulatory reform and administrative capacity building, also borrowed from the accession instruments.[71]

Following the adoption of the ENPI Regulation, it was noted that the commitment to shared values would be tested once the actual measures were financed.[72] A general review of the annual action programmes reveals a limited role for financial assistance within the democratic conditionality of the ENP.

6.3.2 In Search of Democratic Values in Measures Financed

In light of the reinforced commitment towards democracy promotion in the ENPI Regulation and the Commission's realisation of past mistakes as mentioned earlier, two issues must be addressed when considering the ENPI soft law instruments. These include the prioritisation of democratic reform when allocating the funds in practice, and the nexus between progress in implementing political reforms and the assistance allocated.

The actual allocation of the assistance takes place on the basis of priorities identified in the national indicative programme. The 2007–10 national indicative programmes set three main priority areas, one of which is the 'strengthening of democratic structures and good governance'. In Armenia out of €98.4 million for 2007–10, 30 per cent of the general assistance was allocated to this priority area, the others including regulatory reform/administrative capacity building and support for poverty reduction.[73] In the 2011–13 national indicative programme 30–35 per cent of the general sum of €157.3 million was similarly allocated to democratic structures and good governance.[74]

In the case of Georgia, support for democratic development, rule of law and governance received 26 per cent of €120.4 million for the period of 2007–10.[75] Other priorities included economic development, poverty reduction and peaceful

---

[68] Georgia ENPI National Indicative Programme 2007–2010, 15.

[69] Anonymous Commission official, note 8 above.

[70] Georgia ENPI National Indicative Programme 2007–2010, 16; Armenia ENPI National Indicative Programme 2007–2010, 14.

[71] Tulmets, note 61 above, 30; Cremona, note 59 above, 265.

[72] G Bosse, 'Values in the EU's Neighbourhood Policy: Political Rhetoric or Reflection of a Coherent Policy?' (2007) 7 *European Political Economy Review* 38, 57.

[73] Armenia ENPI National Indicative Programme 2007–10, 4.

[74] Armenia ENPI National Indicative Programme 2011–13, 7.

[75] Georgia ENPI National Indicative Programme 2007–10, 4.

settlement of conflicts. In the 2011–13 programme support for democratic development, rule of law and good governance received 25–35 per cent of the sum of €180.[76]

Support for Azerbaijan's democratic development and good governance received 32.6 per cent out of €92 million to include also priorities of socio-economic reform, the fight against poverty, and support for reforms in the transport, energy and environmental sectors.[77] In the 2011–13 national indicative programme 25–30 per cent of €122.5 million was allocated to democratic structures and good governance.[78]

Although allocating almost a third of the budget to democracy-related issues appears promising, certain observations should be made. First of all, the change of language in the national indicative programme towards 'democratic structures' and 'good governance' can be noted to be a downgrade from the EU values, pertaining merely to formal criteria of democracy. Despite the presence of priorities and sub-priorities established in the national indicative programmes, they are formulated generally and vaguely and are not translated into the annual action programmes. Second, as noted above, the allocation takes place through a dialogue with the national government, which should consent to prioritise certain projects. For the period 2008–12 democracy-related issues feature only in a handful of cases. It was only in 2008 that the respective annual programmes prioritised the reform of the judiciary in Armenia and Azerbaijan, and criminal justice system reform in Georgia.[79] In the case of Armenia it has been noted that the judiciary and the rule of law are the main areas of EU continuous engagement.[80] However, the allocation of the assistance does not confirm such continuity in respect of the assistance provided. After 2008, the Armenian annual action programmes returned to prioritising action on independence and the efficiency of the judiciary only in 2012, without any other democracy-related issue being prioritised for five years. No democracy-related issues have been prioritised in Azerbaijan following the 2008 action programme. In Georgia after 2008 only the rule of law and human rights protection by supporting criminal justice reform was prioritised once again in 2011. It can therefore be concluded that the annual assistance provision has largely abandoned prioritisation of concrete areas or steps related to the Action Plan democratic priorities. Democratic reform has

---

[76] Georgia ENPI National Indicative Programme 2011–13, 10.

[77] Azerbaijan ENPI National Indicative Programme 2007–10, 5.

[78] Azerbaijan ENPI National Indicative Programme 2011–13, 7.

[79] Commission Decision C (2008) 3494 of 15 July 2008 on the ENPI Annual Action Programme 2008 in favour of Armenia to be financed under Art 19 08 01 03 of the general budget of the European Communities; Commission Decision C (2008) 8238 16 December 2008 on the ENPI Annual Action Programme 2008 in favour of Azerbaijan Armenia to be financed under Art 19 08 01 03 of the general budget of the European Communities; Commission Decision C (2008) 3516 of 15 July 2008 on the ENPI Annual Action Programme 2008 in favour of Georgia to be financed under Art 19 08 01 03 of the general budget of the European Communities.

[80] V Shkolnikov, 'European Assistance to Human Rights, Democracy and Rule of Law in Armenia: Incremental Results, no Breakthroughs' in A Hug, *Spotlight on Armenia* (UK, Foreign Policy Centre, 2011) 51–53, 51.

been abandoned in favour of support for economic and other reforms required for the establishment of new agreements.

First of all, this demonstrates that assistance allocation does not rely on the Action Plans in practice, as other issues prioritised in the democracy-related area would have featured within six years of annual allocation. Besides, the annual allocation programmes do not reflect the findings of the Commission's evaluation, which therefore has no bearing on the allocation of assistance. The progress reports provide the most up-to-date indication as to the elements of democratic conditionality, but their potential seems to have been abandoned in terms of directing assistance where it is needed.

Besides, the budgetary constraints also play their part in prioritising democratisation. For instance, poverty reduction or post-conflict rehabilitation in Georgia might legitimately be perceived as a more pressing problem than media independence.[81] Within a limited budget, democracy-related issues might concede their role to other pressing domestic concerns demanding a pragmatic approach. However, there is another side to this coin, which is the perpetuation of the ruling regime. While the EU allocates funds for tackling poverty reduction or addressing pressing social issues in Azerbaijan, these funds are a grain of sand in comparison with the country's annual national revenues, directed inter alia at its military budget. For instance, the Azerbaijani government made the largest increase in military expenditure worldwide in 2011 amounting to billions of euros,[82] when the EU allocation for that year was directed inter alia to rural development. There are therefore no surprises in the finding that the effectiveness of financial conditionality has been low in respect to Azerbaijan.[83]

In the absence of fixed programmes on democracy, the assistance is allocated as a result of dialogue between parties, which according to the ENPI Regulation should be an inclusive process as noted earlier. However, this does not appear to be the case in either of the countries. In Georgia the government makes decisions on the expenditure of the financial assistance issued by the EU as there are no concrete programmes established to that extent.[84] The funds are spent without the participation of the civil society on the presumption that the EU ultimately exercises monitoring.[85] Besides, the funds admitted to the budget are not available to the civil society, which is one of the addressees of the assistance according to the ENPI Regulation. According to a Georgian government official, the assistance allocated to state institutions can be further redirected through certain established

---

[81] See, for instance, Georgia 2009 and 2012 annual action programmes.

[82] 'New EU support for governance and economic development in Azerbaijan', European Commission, Press Release, available at www.ec.europa.eu/europeaid/documents/aap/2011/pr_aap_2011_aze.pdf; 'Recent Trends in Military Expenditure', Stockholm International Peace Research Institute, available at www.sipri.org/research/armaments/milex/resultoutput/trends.

[83] Mkrtchyan, Huseynov and Gogolashvili, note 41 above.

[84] Interview with anonymous Commission official, note 8 above.

[85] Interview with anonymous official, State Ministry for European Integration of the Republic of Georgia (Tbilisi, 7 April 2009); Interview with Ivane Chkhikvadze, Eurasia Partnership Foundation (Tbilisi, 6 April 2009).

procedures to non-state organisations for implementation of relevant projects.[86] In simple terms, the civil society does not benefit directly from the ENPI assistance. The switching of assistance in Georgia from the civil society to the government following the Rose Revolution suggested that the assistance was being issued not to support the democratic process as such but rather to achieve a particular political outcome – establishment of a pro-Western political course.[87]

The assistance allocation process in Armenia follows the same pattern, where the government is said to be better positioned to decide which areas should be financed as priorities.[88] Since budgetary assistance merges with the national budget, it is impossible to trace whether measures on democratic reform, if any, are related to the assistance allocated through the ENPI. Besides, the civil society representatives have been estranged from the process of allocation of assistance, and no programmes can be noted to be financed through the ENPI to support the civil society. No surprises are recorded in the case of Azerbaijan, where the government enjoys similar flexibility in spending the financial assistance without any participation or oversight by other stakeholders, including the civil society.

Thus, it should be noted that while the ENPI Regulation appeared to put a greater emphasis on shared values and democratisation, the way the assistance is allocated in practice and the issues to which the assistance is allocated is almost a missing link in the ENP conditionality. That the assistance element does not deliver in terms of supporting the element of conditionality has been most extensively criticised by the Court of Auditors in its report on the provision of aid to the South Caucasian states. Such weaknesses as lack of connection between the Action Plans, country strategy papers and national indicative programmes, insufficient prioritisation, lack of dialogue and direct support to the civil society under the ENPI have been identified.[89] As a result the provision of assistance has essentially created a gap in the element of conditionality, where it has allowed the advancement of sectoral cooperation without checks on the democratic progress, also questioned by the Court of Auditors.[90]

Similar observations can be made regarding the financial assistance issued for the EaP. Although the ENPI East regional strategy paper and indicative programme for the period 2010–13 prioritise inter alia democracy, good governance and stability, the annual action programmes since 2010 make no reference to any specific projects or issues related to democratisation.[91] Instead they prioritise

---

[86] Interview with anonymous official, State Ministry for European Integration of Georgia, note 85 above.

[87] R Youngs, *The EU's Role in the World Politics: A Retreat from Liberal Intergovernmentalism* (London, Routledge, 2011) 62; S Stewart, 'The Interplay of Domestic Contexts and External Democracy Promotion: Lessons from Eastern Europe and the South Caucasus' (2009) 16 *Democratisation* 804, 810.

[88] Interview with Varos Simonyan, Head of Department of EU and International Economic Affairs, Ministry of Economy of the Republic of Armenia (Yerevan, 20 April 2009).

[89] 'Is the New ENPI Successfully Launched and Achieving Results in the Southern Caucasus (Armenia, Azerbaijan and Georgia)?' Court of Auditors, Special Report, No 13, 2010, 15–17, 22, 35.

[90] Ibid 35–36.

[91] Commission Decision of 26 July 2010 on the Regional East Action Programme 2010 Part I in favour of ENP countries and Russia to be financed under Art 19 08 01 03 of the general budget of the

intra-neighbourhood cooperation on border management, transport, climate and other issues.

Perhaps in view of the criticism above the 2011 Joint Communication revising the ENP has acknowledged the need for better 'linking of policy objectives and assistance programming' and a 'more flexible and more focused delivery of financial assistance' for its next multi-annual financial framework.[92] The planned measure for the 2014–20 financial period is said to provide 'greater differentiation, more flexibility, stricter conditionality and incentives for best performers'.[93] The growing pressure to link flexibility of financing to democratic scrutiny exerted by the Parliament and the Court of Auditors creates a challenge for the Commission and the EEAS.[94] The Commission appears gradually to be incorporating the new approach in its practice. For instance in 2012 Commissioner Stefan Füle linked the prospect of allocating additional funds to Armenia to the outcome of the next progress report.[95]

6.3.3 Other Support Mechanisms

Besides the ENPI, there are a number of other instruments and facilities through which the EU provides assistance to its neighbours in support of democratisation and human rights protection. The country progress reports 2008–11 in their overview of the financial cooperation made references to the assistance provided through horizontal thematic programmes, such as the European Instrument for Democracy and Human Rights (EIDHR) and the Non-State Actors and Authorities in Development.

The EIDHR, which replaced its predecessor in 2006, intended to introduce more flexibility to support for democracy and human rights worldwide.[96] Adopted through the same legal basis as the ENPI Regulation, the EIDHR's distinguishing feature is that the assistance does not depend on securing the agreement of governments of third states. As noted above, the ENPI as such fails to engage

---

European Union; Commission Implementing Decision 13 July 2011 on the ENPI East Regional Action Programme 2011 Part I in favour of ENP countries and Russia to be financed under Art 19 08 01 03 of the general budget of the European Union, C (2011) 4965; Commission Implementing Decision of 28 November 2011 on the ENPI East Regional Action Programme 2011 Part II in favour of ENP countries and Russia to be financed under Art 19 08 01 03 of the general budget of the European Union C (2011) 8563; Commission Implementing Decision of 31 July 2012 on the ENPI East Regional Action Programme 2012 Part I in favour of ENP countries and Russia to be financed from the general budget of the European Union C(2012) 5517 final; Commission Implementing Decision of 21 September 2012 on the ENPI East Regional Action Programme 2012 Part II in favour of ENP countries and Russia to be financed from the general budget of the European Union.

[92] 2011 Joint Communication, 18.

[93] Available at www.enpi-info.eu/main.php?id_type=2&id=402.

[94] European Parliament Resolution on the Review of the European Neighbourhood Policy (2011/2157(INI)) 14 December 2011.

[95] 'EU–Armenia: Joint work on Partnership for Reform', MEMO/12/169, 7 March 2012.

[96] Regulation No 1889/2006 concerning the financing instrument for the promotion of democracy and human rights worldwide [2006] OJ L386/1.

non-state actors. Only in the case of suspension of general assistance in using negative conditionality does Article 28 of the ENPI Regulation provide for support for non-state actors. Thus, it can be said that this niche is left open for other instruments, such as the EIDHR. According to Balfour, it was due to pressure from the Parliament that the EIDHR was not merged with regional or thematic assistance programmes.[97] On the other hand it can be suggested that as long as there are other instruments issuing support to the civil society, there is no pressing need to increase the profile of the civil society within the ENPI.

Besides, there are a number of issues that can be identified in connection with the operation of the EIDHR. The total budget of the EIDHR for the period 2007–13 is over €1 billion for a worldwide instrument, where the South Caucasus is included within a general group of ENPI and Middle Eastern addressee states.[98] The instrument focuses on small-scale projects and is described as 'a drop in the ocean' as opposed to the enormous tasks on the agenda of democratisation of relevant states.[99] The EIDHR Strategy Paper 2011–2013, which claims to place 'more emphasis on the situations where human rights are the most at risk', has omitted Azerbaijan, which had the worst record in terms of human rights in the South Caucasus, from its 2011 annual allocation programme.[100]

Besides, problems have been identified with the long chain of command in the Commission,[101] where the instrument is perceived to suffer from excessive bureaucracy. Although the assistance supports the vibrancy of the civil society, many projects concentrate on social issues indirectly relevant for democracy and human rights,[102] which nevertheless in their limited outreach fall short of changing public perceptions or mobilising society in favour of political transformation.

The EIDHR is not the only instrument supporting civil society. The Non-State Actors and Authorities in Development adopted under the Development Cooperation Instrument also provides assistance to representatives of the civil society in the areas of poverty reduction and sustainable development, and therefore has less significance for democratisation issues.[103]

---

[97] R Balfour, 'Promoting Human Rights and Democracy in the EU's Neighbourhood: Tools, Strategies and Dilemmas' in R Balfour and A Missiroli, *Reassessing the European Neighbourhood Policy*, EPC Issue Paper No 54, June 2007, 20.

[98] EIDHR Strategy Paper 2007–2010 (DG RELEX/B/1 JVK 70618), Indicative EIDHR Financial Allocations 2007–2010, Annex 1.

[99] Balfour, note 97 above, 20.

[100] EIDHR 2011–2013 Multiannual Indicative Planning, Global Calls for Proposals + CBSS. Available at www.ec.europa.eu/europeaid.

[101] F Bicchi, 'Dilemmas of Implementation: EU Democracy Assistance in the Mediterranean' (2010) 17 *Democratisation* 976, 991–92.

[102] See for instance 10 new projects financed in Armenia since 2010, available at http://eeas.europa.eu/delegations/armenia/press_corner/all_news/news/2010/20101125_01_en.htm. In early 2012, 16 projects were announced to be financed in Azerbaijan under a 2010 call for proposal, EU Delegation Azerbaijan, Press Release, 'European Union to support 16 new NGO projects', Baku, 07 February 2012.

[103] Established under Art 14 of Regulation EC No 1905/2006 of the European Parliament and of the Council of 18 December 2006 establishing a financing instrument for development cooperation [2006] OJ L378/41.

Another avenue for financing non-state actors is the Civil Society Facility launched in 2010 with a limited budget of over €26 million targeting the entire neighbourhood for the period 2011–13.[104] It is aimed at promoting the engagement of the civil society in policy dialogue, but also at increasing the interaction between the civil society members and the national authorities.[105] The facility is essentially aimed at compensating for the failure of the ENPI to involve the civil society. However, similarly to non-state actors, it is directed at a wide range of social affairs that are not necessarily linked to democratic transformation.[106]

To complicate things further, a European Endowment for Democracy was established in 2012 to support political parties, non-registered NGOs and political activists in third countries. A reaction to the Arab Spring revolutions, the new facility was established within the revised ENP to support 'deep democracy' by engaging with those opposing the ruling regimes. The first allocation of €6 million was made available at the end of 2012.[107] The instrument is devised to bypass any procedural issues and allow direct engagement with political activists. Established principally under pressure from the EEAS,[108] the new measure has raised a number of concerns, emphasised by the Parliament, including the criteria for selection, relationship with other instruments, and, importantly, the accountability for using the funds and possibility of monitoring.[109]

On the one hand, it can be suggested that these measures do not undermine the ENP conditionality, as they bypass the national governments and engage only with the civil society. However, having a number of instruments promoted by different actors not only appears to be a reflex reaction, but most significantly carries the risk of fragmentation and lack of synergy. The Commission itself acknowledges the need for enhancing complementarity between various funding programmes.[110] In addition, it is doubtful to what extent the assistance issued under these instruments is informed by the ENP and how it complements the measures undertaken within the ENPI. Moreover, other facilities are used in addition to those identified, raising concerns as to their position within the ENP conditionality mechanism.

---

[104] 2011 Joint Communication, 4; 'EU Response to the Arab Spring: the Civil Society Facility', MEMO/11/638, 27 September 2011.

[105] See www.enpi-info.eu/mainmed.php?id=393&id_type=10.

[106] S Richter and J Leininger, 'Flexible and Unbureaucratic Democracy: Promotion by the EU? The European Endowment for Democracy between Wishful Thinking and Reality', Comments 2012/C 26, August 2012, German Institute for International and Security Affairs, 6.

[107] 'The European Endowment for Democracy – Support for the Unsupported', Press Release IP/12/1199, 12 November 2012.

[108] Richter and Leininger, note 106 above, 3.

[109] European Parliament Recommendation of 29 March 2012 to the Council on the modalities for the possible establishment of a European Endowment for Democracy (2011/2245(INI)); See also L Skoba, 'European Endowment for Democracy: Hopes and Expectations', Library Briefing, European Parliament, 30 April 2013.

[110] See, for instance, 'Evaluation of the EIDHR Programme in Georgia 2005–2007', 44, available at www.ec.europa.eu/europeaid/what/human-rights/documents/georgia_eidhr_evaluation_2007-2009_2010_en.pdf.

One such measure is the Stability Instrument established in 2007 under development and cooperation policy aimed at reacting to political crises. It was deployed in Armenia in 2009 to provide immediate support to the post-election stabilisation efforts in the form of an Advisory Group for a total budget of €2 million.[111] The assistance was renewed in 2011 under the ENPI with a further €4.2 million in 2009 and focuses mainly on support of already existing structures for parliamentary participation, prevention of torture and combating anti-discrimination.[112] Although these issues are well worth paying attention to, the problem lies somewhere else, namely the role of this assistance in the conditionality chain of the ENP. The Advisory Group was established following the post-election violence in Armenia resulting in human deaths and injuries as a result of police intervention.[113] In view of the Action Plan's focus on adequate elections, this could have been considered to be a breach of the ENPI conditionality, especially when the Presidency made its concerns officially known.[114] It can therefore be suggested that the breach of conditionality resulted in issuing more assistance through a different measure at the request of the national government. Financing the Advisory Group under the ENPI the second time around therefore meant incorporating this conditionality-bypass into the framework of the ENPI. Most importantly, it demonstrated that negative conditionality is not desirable.

The Stability Instrument was also used in Georgia to support the electoral process in 2008 with a view to addressing the shortcomings of the elections noted by the international observers. The support under this facility continued in subsequent years and inter alia focused on the issue of political parties.[115]

Apart from the envisaged ENPI budget for 2007–12, after the Georgian–Russian war, the Commission issued post-conflict assistance amounting to €500 million for the period 2008–10.[116] Within this assistance, €181.9 million was provided for 2008 and distributed into several areas, including 'ongoing assistance' under various programmes, among which were democracy, human rights and support for non-state actors without specifications as to particular issues the assistance was to be directed at. It demonstrated the EU's responsiveness to political declarations, in which the Georgian president announced a new wave of democratic reforms following the 2008 war.[117] However, the coinciding of the assistance with the political declarations delivered certain tangible results when some of the proclaimed reforms were initiated and partially implemented by the end of the year, including the strengthening of parliamentary opposition and involvement in the

[111] Armenia 2010 Progress Report, 19.

[112] Ibid, 18–19; Quarterly Report, 1 October–31 December 2012, European Advisory Group.

[113] Republic of Armenia, Presidential Election, OSCE/ODIHR Election Observation Mission Report, 19 February 2008.

[114] The EU Presidency expressed its concerns about the aftermath of the elections, calling on the Armenian authorities to release detained citizens and to refrain from further arrests of leaders of opposition; 'EU Presidency Statement on the Situation in Armenia', 12 March 2008.

[115] Georgia 2010 Progress Report, 22.

[116] EU Assistance Fact Sheet, Website of EC Delegation to Georgia, available at www.europa.eu/rapid/press-release_MEMO-08-645_en.htm?locale=en.

[117] Interview with anonymous Commission official, note 8 above.

constitutional reform process.[118] This can be viewed as an example of the application of the principle of differentiation, responsive to domestic dynamics.[119]

Another mechanism, the Governance Facility, is said to embody 'positive financial conditionality'.[120] Through this facility the Commission aims to reward those neighbours that demonstrated progress in Action Plan implementation, and in particular in 'core' governance issues: democratic practice, respect for human rights and fundamental freedoms and the rule of law.[121] The Governance Facility has not been used for any of the South Caucasian states. However, the positive aspect of financial conditionality has been noted to depend not so much on the progress achieved but rather on the importance of the relevant state for the EU or its Member States.[122] The latter is determined inter alia by physical proximity facilitated by the principle of differentiation, which is reflected also within the ENP, where some addressees continuously receive more than others, despite political conditionality.[123]

While the Commission acknowledges the necessity of simplifying the next financial instrument to replace the ENPI, it is said nevertheless to reflect the 'more for more approach' also in the allocation of assistance.[124] 'More for more' will not only mean increased differentiation, but will depend on what counts as the second 'more', since current practice suggests it is not the progress achieved in political reform.

The Eastern Partnership Integration and Cooperation Programme established in 2012 and providing for a budget of €130 million for the 2012–13 period took a similar stance of linking assistance to the progress achieved in the areas of political reform based on the principle of 'more for more' of the revised ENP.[125] As a result the 2012 fund of €65 million was allocated to Moldova, Georgia and Armenia as the countries making the most progress in the area.[126] Thus, the financial assistance has taken over a role of an incentive, which can become a significant motivator for countries dependent on external assistance. Furthermore, it demonstrates that it is mostly the 'move in the right direction' that matters rather than a specific level of compliance.

---

[118] 2008 Georgia Progress Report, 4.

[119] P Van Elsuwege, 'Variable Geometry in the European Neighbourhood Policy: The Principle of Differentiation and its Consequences' in E Lannon (ed), *The European Neighbourhood Policy's Challenges* (PIE Peter Lang, College of Europe Studies, 2012) 59–84, 66–67.

[120] Ibid, 78.

[121] Principles for the Implementation of a Governance Facility under ENPI, 3, available at www.ec.europa.eu/world/enp/pdf/governance_facility_en.pdf.

[122] N Popescu, 'More for More in the Neighbourhood' (22 March 2011), www.blogs.euobserver.com.

[123] Ibid.

[124] 2011 Joint Communication, 20; Council Conclusions on the European Neighbourhood Policy, Foreign Affairs, 20 June 2011.

[125] Commission Implementing Decision on the Eastern Partnership Integration and Cooperation programme 2012–2013 in favour of the Eastern Neighbourhood to be financed under Article 19 08 01 03 of the general budget of the European Union, C(2012) 4170 final, 26 June 2012.

[126] Available at www.ec.europa.eu/europeaid/where/neighbourhood/regional-cooperation/enpi-east/eapic_en.htm.

6.4 CONDITIONALITY: *QUO VADIS?*

That the positive conditionality of the ENP was not to be taken seriously became apparent early on in the South Caucasus when the EU signed a Memorandum of Understanding with Azerbaijan in the same year as the respective Action Plan. It demonstrated at the start that despite the fact that the country had the worst democratic record in the region, the EU was willing to cooperate, a step which was perceived as an example of trumping EU norms.[127]

Although political reform found its way into priorities of the Action Plans, it nevertheless did not become a precondition for development in any other area. The documents have not been established to assist with a democratisation agenda. They have merely indicated the direction favoured by the EU and testified to the cooperative nature of the relations. Although the progress evaluation by the Commission highlighted – often in a muted tone – the failures in undertaking relevant actions in meeting the Action Plan priorities, it did not lead to any steps aimed at changing the pattern of cooperation. While the progress evaluation demonstrated the unsuitability of the Action Plans in guiding political reform in partner states, the Plans' main advantage of flexibility and adaptability had not been relied upon. Although having been in force for more than six years, the documents have not been revised or amended to reflect either the criticism addressed to them or to update the list of actions the parties are required to undertake. Hence, it can be argued that they did not intend to create a demanding plan on political reform in the first place. At the same time the revision of the Action Plans was not required as they adequately performed the function of ensuring the engagement of the neighbours. The rumoured replacement of the Action Plans with Association Agendas for Georgia and Armenia, although a welcome development, is nevertheless linked to the prospect of concluding new agreements, and as such does not aim at stimulating political reform.

Second, the evaluation of political progress also had minimal impact on the provision of assistance. The assistance allocated to the countries concerned was not adapted to address the problematic issues identified by the Commission.

Third and most importantly, the progress in the relations between the parties did not depend on either positive or negative outcomes of the Commission's evaluation. Within the bilateral track of cooperation a few developments took place, including the opening of negotiations on association agreements, the establishment of mobility partnerships, the conclusion of visa facilitation agreements and the launch of DCFTA negotiations with Georgia and Armenia. The opening of negotiations with Ukraine earlier than with other partners implied that this development was part of the positive conditionality due to Ukraine's advanced status, yet the same cannot be said about all countries. The establishment of mobility

---

[127]   EJ Stewart, 'Mind the Normative Gap? The EU in the South Caucasus' in R Whitman (ed), *Normative Power Europe: Empirical and Theoretical Perspectives* (Basingstoke, Palgrave, 2011) 65–82, 72.

partnerships, visa facilitation agreements and DCFTA talks in Georgia and Armenia might be seen to indicate the application of positive conditionality, with Azerbaijan being left out due to its democratic record. However the launch of negotiations on establishing a mobility partnership and visa facilitation agreement with Azerbaijan, despite its worsening democratic record, does not support such a presumption.[128] Moreover, the negotiations on association agreements were launched in 2010 simultaneously with all three states. This concurrence confirmed that it was not the conditions of engagement or cooperation that mattered but rather the cooperation itself. There are therefore no identifiable distinctions in the EU's approach towards a state which is clearly unwilling to undertake democratic reforms.

The application of the instruments mentioned above in combination is part of the engagement process, and not a specific reward for achieving progress in the area of political reforms. That it is not the progress that matters but the political statement is supported by an example of the Council instructing the Commission to speed up the negotiation of the visa facilitation with Georgia following the August 2008 war. Although the agreement was not concluded immediately, it nevertheless demonstrated that the advancement in relations does not depend on political conditionality.

The engagement rationale also suggests that the initiation of DCFTA negotiations with Georgia and Armenia came as a reward for undertaking reforms in other areas, particularly in areas of economic reform and regulatory convergence. The non-negotiation of a DCFTA with Azerbaijan is not due its negative political record, but because the latter is not undertaking relevant economic reforms and does not actively pursue WTO accession. The signing of the Declaration on the Southern Gas Corridor with Azerbaijan in 2011 demonstrated the Union's determination to continue its cooperation with a state characterised by authoritarian features. Furthermore, it reaffirmed the importance of the partners to each other with respect to bilateral energy cooperation. The quest for security and stability implanted in the ENP requires a gradual closer engagement, which the named instruments aim to secure without, however, requiring a particular level of adherence to democratic reform. The instrumental progression is still accompanied by an apparent appeal for democratic reform, upholding the normative image of the EU. Nevertheless, this appeal factor is not included *to influence* the relations between the parties. That political conditionality was stripped of its positivity was confirmed by the Council in 2012. Despite noting that progress in strengthening democracy was required in all three states, it continued to uphold the negotiations on the association agreements and the DCFTA with Georgia and Armenia as well as 'good energy cooperation' with Azerbaijan.[129]

---

[128] 'European Neighbourhood Policy in 2012: Continuing Engagement for a Stronger Cooperation with Neighbours Despite Turbulent Political and Economic Conditions', Press Release IP/13/245, 20 March 2012; 'The Negotiations on Visa Facilitation between Azerbaijan and the EU Started', Press Release, EU Delegation in Azerbaijan, 5 March 2012.

[129] Council Conclusions on the South Caucasus, Foreign Affairs, 27 February 2012.

Besides, the proposed Strategic Modernisation Partnership with Azerbaijan might lead to a complete abandonment of the ENP conditionality. In practice this would suggest a special attitude to Azerbaijan, acknowledging its unique role for the EU in the Eastern neighbourhood and discarding the agenda of political or economic transformation.[130] It remains to be seen whether the Azerbaijani initiative can materialise in the future.

In addition to the context of positive conditionality, the relations between the parties provided for certain opportunities for applying *ex-ante* conditionality. The failure to prioritise democratic reform in the Action Plans could have been compensated outside the framework of their implementation, akin to the pre-accession approach, where the opening of accession negotiations depended on the fulfilment of political criteria.[131] As discussed previously, the launch of the EaP could have become a factor equivalent to the opening of the accession negotiations. If the new initiative was to denote a step change in the relations between the parties then certain preconditions could have been established. This was not the case, and even Belarus was invited to participate.[132]

In connection to the DCFTA negotiations, a form of *ex-ante* conditionality has been incorporated within the policy. It appeared in a set of short-term conditions presented to the partner state before the conclusion of a new agreement. For instance, the 'Füle matrix' was presented to Ukraine in 2010 in advance of the signing of an association agreement containing a DCFTA.[133] This approach has been incorporated in the 2011 ENP communication, which adds a new dimension to the conditionality through having a 'limited number of short and medium-term priorities' and 'incorporating more precise benchmarks and a clearer sequencing of actions'.[134] While the association agreements negotiations were launched with all three states without preconditions, the DCFTA negotiations with Georgia and Armenia in 2012 were linked only to trade-related preconditions, ie 'acquis conditionality'.[135] Whether the conclusion of the new agreements will ultimately depend on 'non-*acquis*', that is political conditionality, is not straightforward. The Ukrainian example potentially suggests that for once the ENP political conditionality might acquire a bite at the final stage of concluding the agreement.[136] But if so,

---

[130] See Chapter 3, note 255.

[131] KE Smith, 'The Evolution and Application of EU Membership Conditionality' in M Cremona (ed), The *Enlargement of the European Union* (Oxford, OUP, 2003) 105–39, 114.

[132] Stewart, note 87 above, 812.

[133] Solonenko, note 49 above, 356–57.

[134] 2011 Joint Communication, 18.

[135] In 2008 the Council noted that it would look forward to the Commission's recommendations, including feasibility studies in relation to the launch of DCFTA negotiations with Armenia and Georgia, but it did not make any references to democratic preconditions. After the Commission's fact-finding mission to Armenia in 2009 three key priorities were identified, including technical barriers to trade, sanitary and phytosanitary standards, as well as intellectual property rights. In Georgia preconditions for launching a DCFTA were similarly trade related; 'EU–Georgia Trade Talks Proving "Difficult", Minister Says', *EU Observer*, 15 February 2009; Council Conclusions on European Neighbourhood Policy, External Relations, 18 February 2008.

[136] 'EU Sets May Deadline for Ukraine's Reforms', *Euractiv*, 26 February 2013.

why start the negotiations in the first place with a state characterised by authoritarian features?

Finally, the element of negative conditionality at the disposal of the Commission can be dismissed in terms of its effects, as it appears to be a method of last resort, which is avoided at all costs. The negative conditionality has not been relied upon in any of the South Caucasian states, despite political turbulence related to post-electoral violence resulting in fatalities and repression, or simply the gradually worsening political situation in Azerbaijan regularly recorded in the Commission's progress reports. These examples clearly do not count as breach of the 'essential elements' clause in the PCAs, nor do they satisfy the 'failure to respect democracy' test in Article 28 of the ENPI Regulation allowing for suspension of aid.

Thus, the political conditionality of the ENP has not been used to influence the relations between the parties.

6.5 CONCLUSION

To conclude on the operative elements of the ENP methodology, it should be emphasised that the monitoring of the process and the assistance provided for the Action Plan implementation renders the democratic reform subsidiary, or in some cases irrelevant, within the ENP.

Expectations attached to the Commission's evaluation of the progress achieved in the partner states could not have been high at the outset due to the political nature of the Action Plans. Analysis of the progress reports of the three countries manifests the discrediting of the Action Plan priorities and the Commission's forgetfulness and lack of continuity and rigour in addressing the prioritised actions. The Commission chooses to bypass or ignore major shortfalls in the democratic lives of its partners, and therefore appears to evaluate, but not judge.

Most importantly, the progress reports serve little purpose in the chain of conditionality. The advancement or the stagnation in relations between the parties has not been made conditional upon the results of the progress evaluation. Nor have any of the Action Plans been revised in order to bring certain actions under the spotlight or require further reform. Instead, since the involvement of the EEAS in the progress evaluation, the reports have assumed the function of setting further conditions for compliance, albeit in the same unhelpful fashion as the Action Plans.

As regards the element of negative conditionality allowing for suspension of the PCA or provision of assistance through the ENPI, the latter has not been restored in relation to any of the South Caucasian states to date. Despite the fact that Azerbaijan made no or limited progress in political reform, the negative conditionality was practically disregarded. It is apparent that the progress on energy cooperation would be unlikely to be compromised by invoking negative conditionality. Another explanation for the reluctance to use negative conditionality can be offered in the case of a state demonstrating willingness and efforts to implement the policy, or elements of the policy. An instance of non-compliance triggering the negative conditionality mechanism would undermine the prospect of future cooperation. Even if a partner is not willing to implement the Action Plan as such, but its cooperation in one crucial area is evaluated as positive, then a protracted authoritarian record is not viewed as a failure to respect the principles of democracy and respect for human rights. Not only does this demonstrate one of the drawbacks of the application of negative conditionality, but it also illustrates the mostly political nature of this type of conditionality.

Another gap in the ENP conditionality is revealed in relation to the assistance allocation, despite the ENPI's greater emphasis on promotion of democracy. Although the national indicative programmes prioritise democratisation, the only democracy-related action to receive fixed assistance was justice-related reforms, making a rare appearance. Besides, the allocation of funds does not depend on the outcomes of the progress evaluation, unlinking these two elements of conditionality. Only in 2012 within the EaP Integration and Cooperation Programme was the allocation of additional funds seemingly linked to the performance of the neighbouring states. The effectiveness of assistance issued is also questioned due to the multiplicity of instruments deployed outside the ENPI framework. Although some of them engage the civil society and therefore compensate for the failure of the ENPI to deliver on its promise of a more inclusive approach, their support for the ENP agenda is not straightforward. Other facilities issuing additional assistance to the national governments confirm that the financial support does not have to be a part of the ENP conditionality mechanism. While this can be justified in terms of assistance issued to the civil society, the same cannot be said about facilities providing direct budgetary support to the state.

It can therefore be summarised that the elements of monitoring and assistance fail to strengthen the already weak political conditionality of the ENP.

7

Conclusion

TO CONCLUDE THE book we need to start from the beginning. Following Wolfers's formula, the role of democracy promotion within the ENP was predetermined by the policy rationale. A sweeping policy, it was to tackle the security issues in the neighbourhood and to meet halfway the expectations of Eastern neighbours with pro-European aspirations.

At the heart of the initiative were the interests of the EU around the issue of security and stability – no longer separable from the stability of the neighbours. These interests necessitated a political engagement and association of some sort. It is in this context that democracy promotion and the political transformation of the EU neighbours makes an entrance. The ENP was to promote democracy in the surrounding regions and the neighbours were to become democratic states, but only to the extent they wished to do so. The political transformation of partner states was not a policy end goal, it was rather to play an instrumental role in contributing to the achievement of the main objectives of security and stability. As part of the stability strategy, democracy promotion does not have a fixed role. On the one hand, according to the presumption that democratic states do not fight wars with each other, long-term security in the EU's vicinity requires democratisation of its neighbours. On the other hand, security and stabilisation in the short-term perspective at times require the cooperation of non-democratic regimes. The ENP therefore suffers from a conflict of goals and sub-goals, where the EU's narrow self-interest potentially undermines the achievement of its normative, identity-based objectives, of which democracy promotion is an example.

The role democracy promotion has acquired within the EU external framework is a reflection of democracy becoming a constituent element of the EU's internal identity. At no stage of the EC/EU normative existence would external democracy promotion have been more justified than currently due to the acceptance of democracy as a value and a principle in the EU legal order. The past decades have witnessed the continuous enhancement of EU democratic credentials: the democratic model of the EU is first of all characterised by its dynamic and evolving nature. The Lisbon Treaty is the most current indicator of the EU democratic values which one can legitimately expect the latter to aspire to promote in its neighbourhood. As such the EU does not impose any model of democracy on its neighbours, but the values of representation of citizens' will, liberal governance (broadly characterised by separation of powers and protection of citizens' rights) and political participation in decision making are those that have been steadily incorporated into its constitutional and political life, and that therefore can legitimately be expected to be advocated abroad. However, there are many obstacles to such endeavours within the ENP.

Since the early days of articulating the idea of a neighbourhood policy, democracy has been cited as one of the values the EU intends to spread in wider Europe. At the time of the ENP initiation, democracy promotion was considered to be a general objective common to the CFSP and certain Community external policies. The Lisbon Treaty has further implanted the objective of democracy promotion within the legal framework of EU external relations. The Union in its external relations 'shall uphold and promote' and 'safeguard' its values, which includes democracy under Article 2 TEU. It shall also be 'be guided by' the principle of democracy, and 'consolidate and support democracy' in its foreign relations. Democracy promotion is, therefore, an external identity objective and, due to its incorporation within the common list of foreign policy objectives in Article 21 TEU, has to be pursued in all areas of EU external action. Despite being an identity related objective, democracy promotion is not an absolute objective. The common list of external action objectives does not prioritise democracy promotion vis-à-vis other objectives. Article 21(2) TEU is drafted rather extensively to accommodate all areas of EU external relations in their pursuit of various interests of the EU. Thus, the legal framework of EU external relations accommodates both rationalist and normative accounts for EU external action. A balancing exercise is therefore required to ensure that efforts to achieve other policy objectives do not undermine democracy promotion as a general objective, where the principle of consistency plays a significant role.

The objectives of the policy implanted a conflict within the policy framed in terms of the interests of the EU, which at times transpired to be the interests of its Member States. The EU's interests varied across regions; for example, in the case study of South Caucasus its involvement related predominantly to energy cooperation and post-conflict rehabilitation. Depending on the EU's interests a different asymmetry of power emerged in relations with each of the states, Azerbaijan having become the most important partner in the region. Besides, all three states had different ambitions regarding their future with or within the EU, a factor also capable of influencing the political conditionality. While Georgia was keen on EU membership, Armenia was eager to integrate economically, shying away from making membership claims due to its military and economic dependence on Russia. Azerbaijan, on the other hand, was interested in energy cooperation where the EU's power of persuasion had been restricted. Such a combination of interests and incentives assumed objective external limitations on the ability of the EU to promote democracy. The analysis of various aspects of the ENP suggests the perpetuation of the above-mentioned conflict within the legal framework of the policy.

Despite the approach in the Treaties towards external democracy promotion as an identity objective, securing it within the ENP is problematic as the identity of the EU still remains divided. In particular, in view of the EU institutional arrangements in the external relations domain, one can hardly expect a shared vision of the EU in the neighbourhood. Despite the Commission's initial 'Communitarian' outlook for the neighbourhood, the Council proved powerful in steering the policy in a rationalist direction. The Member States had the capacity to provide leadership but could not agree on a common stance for the EU's action in the neighbourhood. The perceptions of the Member States as to their prerogative in foreign relations played their part in influencing the policy according to national interests, demonstrating a lack of unitary vision of the external role of the Union, and in particular on democracy promotion within a complex neighbourhood. Among the EU institutions the Parliament most frequently displayed a normative vision of the Union's role in its neighbourhood.

The institutional innovations introduced by the Lisbon Treaty did not aid tremendously in creating a common vision on the neighbourhood. The permanent Presidency of the European Council was to ensure the continuity of the policies, diminishing the importance of the rotating Council Presidency and leading to policy fluctuations. The 'double-hatted' position of the High Representative was to achieve a Commission–Council synergy creating a united front for EU action. However, a separate DG on the ENP still exists within the Commission, and there are currently more offices representing the EU in its neighbourhood than previously. In practice, the establishment of these offices led to the multiplication of actors, presenting a new challenge of slower response on behalf of the EU, and a continuous quest for coherence. Moreover, a common agenda for the neighbourhood did not suddenly materialise as a result of these innovations. The Presidency still plays an important role. The High Representative's linking role has not been exploited to its full potential. The post-Lisbon High Representative appears to have entered the scene with a lesser vision of the EU's role in the neighbourhood. The establishment of the EEAS is another factor to reconcile with, where coordination is required between the latter and the Commission to ensure the policy is heading in one direction.

Therefore, the EU legal order as such allowed for institutional and vertical divisions due to a multiplicity of actors and its divided legal nature over the CFSP action. The latter feature of the EU decision making has been preserved in the revised Treaties, where the CFSP is a distinct policy in terms of its intergovernmental nature. To secure the engagement of the neighbours in all areas akin to enlargement the ENP turned out to be a cross-pillar, and currently a cross-Treaty, policy cutting across the entire rationale of the EU foreign policy pertaining to all types of EU external competence. The policy therefore raised cumbersome issues of legal competence if any new hard law instrument was to be adopted. New international agreements would have been mixed in nature due to incorporation of a political dialogue in line with a previously established trend, therefore delaying the engagement of the neighbours. Besides, initially there was no clarity as to what exactly would be offered to the neighbours. Thus, a cure was found in the form of soft law instruments facilitating institutional interactions and allowing for a common ground for developing relations between the EU and each neighbour. The hard law instruments, including the previously established PCAs and the ENPI Regulation, added a negative conditionality element, which nevertheless was not destined to be influential.

It was the positive conditionality instead which was envisaged to determine the outcome of the cooperation. Together with the instruments of the pre-accession it was adapted to a different rationale of the ENP. The conditionality was to accord the ENP with the same transformationist logic that was deployed during the enlargement via the Copenhagen criteria. The latter appear to have been substantively incorporated within the ENP, requiring reforms along the same lines. However, the manner of incorporation is rather different. Instead of strict conditions, it is 'shared values' that the neighbours should adhere to – a much weaker and not entirely clear concept. Although it became evident that it was the EU values that were at stake, the language of 'shared values' is nevertheless too vague to become a credible basis for exercising conditionality. The positive conditionality has also been undermined due to the lack of clarity as to the incentives on offer, which failed to create a political momentum in the interested countries or reorientate others. The finally clarified incentive of a DCFTA is a 'disincentive' for some countries.

The ENP methodology was also complemented by other means, namely the principles of joint ownership and differentiation, which have a different rationale than conditionality. Conditionality manifests the coercive (in civilian understanding) approach aimed at transformation. On the contrary, principles of joint ownership and differentiation entail a cooperative approach.

Joint ownership allows the neighbours to have 'a say' in the cooperation, whereby the neighbours that have their own leverage over the EU can influence the course of relations. The differentiation on the other hand has a two-fold connection with conditionality. It allows each country to establish closer links with the EU at its own pace depending on its progress. At the same time, the EU can treat similar countries differently, since differentiation presumes a flexible approach, and therefore in practice can lead to an inconsistent approach, potentially questioning the normative threshold of EU actions. With the ENP revisions prompted by the Arab Spring revolutions, a 'more for more' approach embodying differentiation acquired a central role within the policy. Despite ensuring greater flexibility for the EU, it undermines the latter's stance on democracy unless a basic threshold of compliance is required. Thus, the rationale of the policy which translated into a goal conflict has also found its way into the ENP methodology, which most vividly displays the dilemma between norms and interests.

The neighbourhood-specific Article 8 TEU introduced by the Lisbon Treaty appears to have incorporated the contradictions present within the ENP. The provision in its language preserves the security rationale of the policy and points towards the collaborative nature of the relations between the EU and its neighbours. Although it establishes a legal obligation for the Union to cooperate with its neighbours, Article 8 appears to be of a political nature, where its ENP-like language and also textual location highlight the alternative role the neighbourhood policies play in relation to Article 49 TEU. Article 8 TEU also provides for the possibility of concluding new international agreements with the neighbours, which may contain reciprocal rights and obligations for the parties. While the language of the provision and current practice suggest that the new agreements would take the form of an association agreement, it raises the question of the necessity of the new provision in view of a separate legal basis in Article 217 TFEU enabling the conclusion of such agreements. Besides, a 'special relationship' can be implied even in agreements concluded under Article 212 TFEU.

Eventually, the choice of any of these legal bases depends on the message the EU intends to send to its neighbours, therefore confirming the political element of Article 8 TEU. For the purpose of democracy promotion, Article 8 TEU can be argued to denote a number of things. First, it suggests that an 'essential element' clause, together with political dialogue, will be incorporated into any new agreement concluded under this provision. By itself it would not herald any changes as it has been an established practice in relation to trade agreements. Second, it can be argued to have clarified the normative basis of the policy by making a reference to EU values. Nonetheless, Article 8 TEU does not indicate what level or extent of adherence is required to advance the relations between the EU and the neighbours. The start of association agreement negotiations with Azerbaijan suggests that adhering to values is not a precondition for the latter. Certain adherence to EU values might be expected at the stage before the conclusion of the agreements. During the accession of 2004 and 2007 the political conditionality was said to have been most influential at the stage prior to the opening of accession negotiations. Nevertheless, even in the case of enlargement, where democratic transformation of third states was closely related to the identity of the EU, its record of promoting democratic values was marred by deficiencies and inconsistencies. Such drawbacks can similarly be traced within the operative elements of the ENP, that is the Action Plans, the monitoring of their implementation and the assistance issued to the neighbours.

The Action Plans fall short of signifying a serious intention to promote democracy. The EU's retreat from its normative stance is apparent in the Azerbaijani and, surprisingly, Georgian Action Plans. The principle of joint ownership is most evident in the EU–Azerbaijan Action Plan, since the Nagorno-Karabakh conflict found its place in the first priority area as opposed to the EU–Georgia and EU–Armenia Action Plans. While joint ownership can explain the weak language on political reform in Azerbaijan's case, a few priorities have been included on the agenda of democratic reform in Georgia focusing primarily on the judiciary and elections. In this light, the Armenian Action Plan appears to be the most loyal to the democratic rhetoric of the EU. While certain key matters such as the role of parliaments, political parties and the development of civil society (the latter is included only in the case of Azerbaijan) are omitted from the Action Plans, the majority of the priority actions are unmeasurable due to their lack of substance, concreteness and deadlines. As a result the documents come across as a mere indication of the preferred direction of cooperation.

Besides, the prospect of political reform was also undermined by the issue of prioritisation sequencing, where democratic reform is only one of many other areas for cooperation. The Action Plans failed to establish whether the progress in democratic reform was a precondition for the advancement in relations between the parties. The political nature of these documents is also exemplified by the manner of their drafting, questioning the basis on which the monitoring of progress is exercised. The weaknesses of the Action Plans might explain the reliance on the countries' commitments in other international organisations, where they have binding obligations to implement democratic reforms. Although it does make practical sense, this approach supports the already established perceptions of the EU in the countries concerned. The latter is perceived mainly as an economic actor, where in some cases its genuine commitment to promoting democracy is doubted.

Besides, the very process of the Action Plan implementation distorts the democratic processes in Georgia and Armenia, where significant institutional and legislative measures were established to implement the Action Plans. The process is led by the executive with a marginal role for the national parliaments or the civil society. Fewer efforts are undertaken in Azerbaijan to implement the Action Plan where the pro-European civil society lacks power to influence the political agenda.

The main monitoring of the progress is undertaken by the Commission and currently the EEAS via annual reports. The results of the monitoring demonstrate that although the Commission evaluates the progress, it nevertheless attempts to refrain from judgement. The approach taken in fact demonstrates the unsuitability of the Action Plans as a ground for monitoring where their priorities do not play a significant role. The evaluation is not restricted to the prioritised actions only, as the Commission is free to evaluate progress in general actions, but also those not mentioned in the Action Plans at all. Besides, progress as regards prioritised actions is considered with varying detail, rigour and continuity, not only depending on the country, but also on the year concerned. Forgetfulness on the part of the Commission should be noted where the continuity of assessment is undermined by omitting or abandoning certain priorities. Following the establishment of the EEAS the progress reports appear as joint working documents introducing a slightly different approach. Although the method of evaluation has not changed as such, the progress reports for 2012 and 2013 include a list of actions demanding the attention of partner states, with the majority of these actions relating to democracy and human rights. This development should be viewed in light of the 'deep democracy' approach included in the revised ENP in the 2011 Joint Communication, which nevertheless focuses on formal criteria of democracy, contrary to what its title might suggest. Besides, the new conditions are mostly formulated in the same style as the Action Plans, rendering them unmeasurable.

The monitoring outcome does not appear to be linked to the financial assistance issued under the ENPI Regulation. The latter upheld the ENP democratic rhetoric, envisaging democracy promotion as one of the areas for assistance, and seemingly incorporated a more inclusive approach towards the civil society. However, issuing assistance as the third element in the chain of the EU's involvement with neighbouring countries can be controversial. The allocation of assistance for Georgia, Armenia and Azerbaijan provides for approximately one-third of the funds for political reform, including democratic development and human rights issues. Nonetheless, the only fixed line for assistance related to democratic development was judicial reform which was financed no more than twice in six years. The lack of prioritisation bears a risk of concentrating on other more pressing issues, especially when funds are restricted. The potential for financial assistance to become an important means of leverage is lost in the case of Azerbaijan due to its rich national revenues. Besides, the direct budgetary support issued to the countries leaves the national governments in charge of the assistance, thus excluding the civil society. Other aid mechanisms are used to finance civil society, raising the issue of their support for the ENP agenda. Moreover, other support facilities provide direct budgetary support, at times bypassing the ENP conditionality. Only in 2012 were the extra funds within the Eastern Partnership Integration and Cooperation Programme allocated to those neighbours that were perceived to have achieved the most success in their efforts.

The outcomes of the Commission's evaluation have not triggered any instances of application of negative conditionality, even in case of Azerbaijan with its steadily declining political record. Certain instances of democratic standards being breached have resulted in the EU issuing additional assistance to support the countries concerned. The negative conditionality is, therefore, a means of last resort, as it contradicts the rationale of continuous cooperation and engagement with the neighbours. Its application would undermine the pursuit of the EU's rationalist interests, such as energy cooperation with Azerbaijan, or it would alienate a country willing to undertake reforms and discourage it from further transformation. This could be the case in Georgia or Armenia if an instance of non-compliance were to lead to a breakdown of relations or suspension of aid.

Most importantly, it is not clear what the practical implications of the monitoring are. The progress reports did not lead to the revision of any of the three Action Plan priorities, even though such a possibility was envisaged. The results of the monitoring do not seem to be linked to progress in undertaking political reforms. On the one hand, Georgia and Armenia appear to be more advanced in their relations with the EU due to established mobility partnerships, visa facilitation agreements and the opening of the DCFTA negotiations, which can be linked to certain progress they have made in undertaking political reform. From this perspective, the developments in the Action Plan implementation, including political reform, demonstrate that the states are moving in the preferred 'right' direction. At the same time, the negotiation of a mobility partnership and visa facilitation agreement with Azerbaijan imply that the advancement of relations is not linked to political conditionality. In addition, the fact that a DCFTA has not been offered to Azerbaijan is due not to its failure to fulfil political reforms, but rather its unwillingness to undertake necessary reforms in accessing the WTO. The opening of negotiations on association agreements with all three states in 2010 similarly indicated the missing link between the progress achieved and the advancement in relations. If the example of the Ukrainian association agreement is followed in the South Caucasus, then a certain *ex-ante* conditionality can be expected at the stage before the conclusion of the agreement. *Ex-ante* conditions were attached to the opening of DCFTA negotiations with Georgia and Armenia, however they were related only to *acquis* and not political conditionality.

An opportunity in this sense was missed when no *ex-ante* conditionality was applied during the launch of the EaP. This initiative further demonstrated that it was the engagement that mattered, since Belarus was invited to participate. Although meant to signify a 'step change' in relations between the parties, the EaP did not significantly affect the relations between the parties as it reinstated the offers already on the plate within the ENP. Its potential of leading to an EEA-style economic community has not become the driving force behind the initiative. In addition, the retention of the principles of joint ownership and differentiation suggests differentiated integration with each of the states. Such a prospect is also not visible due to the lack of common vision as to the future of the EaP. The Union, and in particular its Member States, are still divided over the role of the EU in its neighbourhood. However, even if the level of political integration in the EU reaches a stage where it acts externally with a single voice and identity, it can still hardly be expected that the rationalist accounts for the Union's actions will be abandoned. The EU will continue to require secure energy supplies and cooperation with third states to tackle common security threats. Besides, the external limitations on promoting democracy, depending on the interests and ambitions of the neighbours, should also be acknowledged. A combination of these factors, linked to the mutual incentives of cooperation, reveals that in some cases, such as Azerbaijan, political conditionality is essentially abandoned. As to the other states, where the EU has leverage to stimulate political and economic reforms, the incentives for cooperation need clarification and magnification to sustain or create political momentum. In other words the EU needs to determine whether they belong to the club fully or partially. Democracy promotion will stand a chance in countries like Georgia and Armenia if a visible route-map to membership or a halfway house, such as an EEA-style arrangement, is promised. However, even such promises might not be sufficient in the Armenian case unless the EU replaces Russia as its security guarantor.

Ultimately, the ENP is not about democracy promotion. Although it has incorporated the normative identity of the EU, the ENP is ill suited for *ab extra* democratisation of neighbouring states.

Postscript

When choosing case studies from the Southern Caucasus one always bears the risks of swift political changes or developments . . . Following a meeting with the Russian President Putin in September 2013, the Armenian President declared that Armenia would join the Customs Union with Russia, Kazakhstan and Belarus. In view of the country's strong dependence on Russia in terms of military and economic security, Armenia had no choice but to succumb to Russian pressure to join the Eurasian Economic Community's Customs Union, as noted previously in the book. The EU institutions, taken by surprise, contained their reaction and refrained from passing judgment as to whether this development signified a major obstacle for the ENP efforts in Armenia. In its first response, the European Commission 'took note' of Armenia's 'apparent wish to join the Customs Union' and requested further information before making any 'conclusions on the way forward'.[1] Progress in concluding an association agreement and a DCFTA would certainly be affected by this declaration. First, the Russian 'offer that cannot be refused' undermines the very prospect of Armenia's economic integration with the EU via the DCFTA as both perspectives cannot be pursued simultaneously. It also deprives the EU of its most 'magnified' carrot to date – the DCFTA, which was a motivator for Armenia to undertake economic and political reforms – and therefore also of its main leverage. Second, the association agreement may still be concluded – at least so desires Armenia. It has expressed its intention to continue political cooperation with the EU and to conclude the association agreement without the DCFTA, but possibly with a trade component that is compatible with membership of the Customs Union in the Eurasian Economic Community.[2] In such a scenario it is unlikely the new agreement would establish a level of association that other neighbours in the East would be offered. Instead, the parties will have to adapt the ENP objectives to a more low-profile agreement. Although this will suggest an even lesser influence on behalf of the EU in terms of promoting its democratic values, it might nevertheless continue to play a certain role in this respect through financial assistance.

Finally and more generally, this development demonstrates an instance of the ENP's inability to provide a genuine alternative to membership.

---

[1] European Commission, 'Armenia: EU position on the latest developments', MEMO/13/766, Brussels, 4 September 2013.

[2] 'Armenia still hopes for Association Agreement with EU', *Armenia Now*, 5 September 2013.

Bibliography

Albi, A, *European Union Enlargement and the Constitutions of Central and Eastern Europe* (Cambridge, CUP, 2005)

Aliboni, R, 'The Geopolitical Implications of the European Neighbourhood Policy' (2005) 10 *European Foreign Affairs Review* 1

Alieva, L, 'EU and South Caucasus', Discussion Paper, Bertesmann Group for Policy Research, December 2006

Amtenbrink, F, 'Towards a More Democratic Union? Comments on Treaty Establishing a Constitution for Europe' in K Inglis and A Ott (eds), *The Constitution for Europe and an Enlarging Union: Unity in Diversity?* (Groningen, Europa Law Publishing, 2005) 31–55

ANCEI, 'European Neighbourhood Policy and Azerbaijan' Annual Report 18 July 2007

Andersen, S and Burns, T, 'The EU and the Erosion of Parliamentary Democracy: A Study of Post-parliamentary Governance' in S Andersen and KA Eliassen (eds), *The European Union: How Democratic Is It?* (London, Sage, 1996) 227–51

Andersen, A and Eliassen, KA (eds), *The European Union: How Democratic Is It?* (London, Sage, 1996)

Aspinal, M and Schneider, G (eds), *The Rules of Integration: Institutionalist Approaches to the Study of Europe* (Manchester, Manchester University Press, 2001)

Avery, G, 'The EU's External Action Service: New Actor on the Scene' European Policy Centre, 28 January 2011

Balfour, R, *Human Rights and Democracy in EU Foreign Policy: The Cases of Ukraine and Egypt* (London, Routledge, 2012)

——, 'Principles of Democracy and Human Rights. A Review of the European Union's Strategies Towards its Neighbours' in S Lucarelli and I Manners (eds), *Values and Principles in European Union Foreign Policy* (London, Routledge, 2006) 114–29

——, 'Promoting Human Rights and Democracy in the EU's Neighbourhood: Tools, Strategies and Dilemmas' in R Balfour and A Missiroli, 'Reassessing the European Neighbourhood Policy', EPC Issue Paper No 54, June 2007

—— and Missiroli, A, 'Dealing with Troubled Neighbourhoods', Commentary, European Policy Centre, 12 February 2009

—— and Missiroli, A, 'Reassessing the European Neighbourhood Policy', European Policy Issue Paper No 54, June 2007

—— and Rotta, A, 'Beyond Enlargement. The European Neighbourhood Policy and its Tools' (2005) 40 *International Spectator* 7

Baracani, E, 'European Union Democratic Anchoring' in E Baracani (ed), *Democratisation and Hybrid Regimes: International Anchoring and Domestic Dynamics in European Post-Soviet States* (Florence, European Press Academic Publishing, 2011) 111–34

——, 'From the EMP to the ENP: A New European Pressure for Democratisation?' (2005) 1 *Journal of Contemporary European Research* 54

Baracani, E, 'The EU and Democracy Promotion: A Strategy of Democratization in the Framework of Neighbourhood Policy?' in F Attina and R Rossi (eds), *European Neighbourhood Policy: Political, Economic and Social Issues*, The Jean Monnet Centre 'Euro-Med', Department of Political Studies, 2004, 37–57

Barber, BR, *Strong Democracy: Participatory Politics for a New Age* (Berkeley, University of California Press, 1984)

Bechev, D and Nicolaidis, K, 'From Policy to Polity: Can the EU's Special Relations with its "Neighbourhood" Be Decentred?' (2010) 48 *Journal of Common Market Studies* 475

Bellamy, R, 'Democracy without Democracy? Can the EU's Democratic "Outputs" be Separated from the Democratic "Inputs" Provided by Competitive Parties and Majority Rule?' (2010) 17 *Journal of European Public Policy* 2

Bendiek, A, 'European Realism in the EU's Common Foreign and Security Policy' in PJ Cardwell (ed), *EU External Relations Law and Policy in Post-Lisbon Era* (The Hague, TMC Asser Press, 2012) 35–57

Bengston, C, 'Interparliamentary Cooperation in Europe' in J O'Brennan and T Raunio (eds), *National Parliaments within the Enlarged European Union: From 'Victims' of Integration to Competitive Actors* (London, Routledge, 2007) 46–65

Berdiyev, B, 'The EU and Former Soviet Central Asia: An Analysis of the Partnership and Cooperation Agreements' (2003) 22 *Yearbook of European Law* 463

Bicchi, F, 'Dilemmas of Implementation: EU Democracy Assistance in the Mediterranean' (2010) 17 *Democratisation* 976

——, *European Foreign Policy Making Towards the Mediterranean* (Basingstoke, Palgrave Macmillan, 2007)

Biscop, S, 'The European Security Strategy and the Neighbourhood Policy: A New Starting Point for a Euro-Mediterranean Security Partnership?' in F Attina and R Rossi (eds), *European Neighbourhood Policy: Political, Economic and Social Issues*, The Jean Monnet Centre 'Euro-Med', Department of Political Studies, 2004, 25–36

Blockmans, S, 'EU Enlargement as a Peacebuilding Tool in S Blockmans, J Wouters and Ruys (eds), *The European Union and Peace Building: Policy and Legal Aspects* (The Hague, TMC Asser Press, 2010) 77–103

—— and Laatsit, M, 'The European External Action Service: Enhancing Coherence in EU External Action?' in PJ Cardwell (ed), *EU External Relations Law and Policy in the Post-Lisbon Era* (The Hague, TMC Asser Press, 2012) 135–59

—— and Prechal, S, The European Integration Process: A Continuum of "Deepening" and "Widening"' in S Blockmans and S Prechal (eds), *Reconciling the Deepening and Widening of the European Union* (The Hague, TMC Asser Press, 2007) 1–12

—— and Van Vooren, B, 'Revitalising the European "Neighbourhood Economic Community": The Case for Legally Binding Sectoral Multilateralism' (2012) 17 *European Foreign Affairs Review* 577

Boonstra, J, 'Azerbaijan' in R Youngs (ed), *Is the European Union Supporting Democracy in its Neighbourhood?* (Fride, 2008) 136.

Bosse, G, 'Values in the EU's Neighbourhood Policy: Political Rhetoric or Reflection of a Coherent Policy?' (2007) 7 *European Political Economy Review* 38

Broberg, MP, 'Don't Mess with the Missionary Man! On the Principle of Coherence, the Missionary Principle and the European Union's Development Policy' in PJ Cardwell (ed), *EU External Relations Law and Policy in the Post-Lisbon Era* (The Hague, TMC Asser Press, 2012) 181–96

Cardwell, PJ, *EU External Relations and Systems of Governance: The CFSP, Euro-Mediterranean Partnership and Migration* (London, Routledge, 2009)

——, 'Mapping Out Democracy Promotion in the EU's External Relations' (2011) 16 *European Foreign Affairs Review* 21

Carothers, T, 'Democracy Assistance: The Question of Strategy' (1997) 4 *Democratisation* 109

Carta, C, 'Close Enough? The EU's Global Role Described by Non-European Diplomats in Brussels' in S Lucarelli and L Fiaramonti (eds), *External Perceptions of the European Union as a Global Actor* (London, Routledge, 2009) 207–217

Chalmers, D, Davies, G and Monti, G, *European Union Law: Text and Materials*, 2nd edn (Cambridge, CUP, 2010)

Checkel, JT, 'Why Comply? Social Learning and European Identity Change' (2001) 55 *International Organisation* 553

—— and Moravcsik, A, 'A Constructivist Research Programme in EU Studies?' (2001) 2 *European Union Politics* 219

Christiansen, T, 'The European Union after the Lisbon Treaty: An Elusive "Institutional Balance"?' in A Biondi and P Eeckhout (eds), *European Union Law After Lisbon* (Oxford, OUP, 2012) 228–47

——, Jorgensen, KE and Weiner, A, 'The Social Construction of Europe' (1999) 6 *Journal of European Public Policy* 528

Chryssochoou, D, 'Democracy and the European Polity' in M Cini (ed), *European Union Politics*, 2nd edn (Oxford, OUP, 2007) 359–73

Cianciara, AK, ' "Eastern Partnership" – Opening a New Chapter of Polish Eastern Policy and the European Neighbourhood Policy?' No 4 June 2008, The Institute of Public Affairs, Warsaw

Comelli, M, 'The Challenges of the European Neighbourhood Policy' (2004) 3 *The International Spectator* 97

——, Greco, E and Tocci, N, 'From Boundary to Borderland: Transforming the Meaning of Borders through the European Neighbourhood Policy' (2007) 12 *European Foreign Affairs Review* 203

Corbett, R, 'The Evolving Roles of the European Parliament and of National Parliaments' in A Biondi and P Eeckhout (eds), *European Union Law After Lisbon* (Oxford, OUP, 2012) 248–61

——, Jacobs, F and Shackleton, M, 'The European Parliament at Fifty: A View from the Inside' (2003) 41 *Journal of Common Market Studies* 353

Coultrap, J, 'From Parliamentarism to Pluralism. Models of Democracy and the European Union's Democratic Deficit' (1999) 11 *Journal of Theoretical Politics* 107

Craig, P, 'Democracy and Rule-making Within the EC: An Empirical and Normative Assessment' (1997) 3 *European Law Journal* 105

——, 'Executive Accountability and the Contestability of the Executive Domain' in L Verhey, P Kiiver and S Loeffen (eds), *Political Accountability and European Integration* (Groningen, Europa Law Publishing, 2009) 153–71

——, *The Lisbon Treaty: Law, Politics and Treaty Reform* (Oxford, OUP, 2010)

——, 'The Nature of the Community: Integration, Democracy and Legitimacy' in P Craig and G de Búrca (eds), *Evolution of EU Law* (Oxford, OUP, 1999) 1–54

Cremona, M, 'Coherence in European Union Foreign Relations Law' in P Koutrakos (ed), *European Foreign Policy: Legal and Political Perspectives* (Cheltenham, Edward Elgar Publishing, 2011) 55–92

Cremona, M, 'Enlargement: A Successful Instrument of EU Foreign Policy?' in T Tridimas and P Nebbia (eds), *European Union Law for the Twenty-First Century* (Oxford, Hart Publishing, 2004) 317–414

——, 'EU Enlargement: Solidarity and Conditionality' (2005) 30 *European Law Review* 3

——, 'External Relations and External Competence of the European Union' in P Craig and G de Búrca (eds), *Evolution of EU Law*, 2nd edn (Oxford, OUP, 2011) 217–68

——, 'Human Rights and Democracy Clauses in the EC's Trade Agreements' in N Emiliou and D O'Keeffe (eds), *The European Union and World Trade Law: After the GATT Uruguay Round* (Chichester, Wiley, 1996) 62–77

——, 'The Draft Constitutional Treaty: External Relations and External Action (2003) 40 *Common Market Law Review* 1347

——, 'The "Dynamic and Homogeneous" EEA: Byzantine Structures and Various Geometry' (1994) 19 *European Law Review* 508

——, 'The European Neighbourhood Policy' in A Ott and E Vos (eds), *Fifty Years of European Integration: Foundations and Perspectives* (The Hague, TMC Asser Press, 2009) 221–45

——, 'The European Neighbourhood Policy as a Framework for Modernisation' in F Maiani, R Petrov and E Mouliarova (eds), *European Integration without EU Membership: Models, Experiences, Perspectives*, EUI Working Papers, MWP 2009/10, 5–15

——, 'The European Neighbourhood Policy: Legal and Institutional Issues' Center on Democracy, Development and the Rule of Law, Stanford Institute for International Studies, Working Paper No 25, 2 November 2004

——, 'The European Neighbourhood Policy: More than a Partnership?' in M Cremona (ed), *Developments in EU External Relations Law* (Oxford, OUP, 2008) 244–99

——, 'The Two (or Three) Treaty Solution: The New Treaty Structure of the EU' in A Biondi, P Eeckhout and S Ripley (eds), *EU Law After Lisbon* (Oxford, OUP, 2012) 40–61

——, 'The Union's External Action: Constitutional Perspectives' in G Amato, H Bribosia and B de Witte (eds), *Genesis and Destiny of the European Constitution* (Brussels, Bruylant, 2007) 1173–218

——, 'Values in EU Foreign Policy' in M Evans and T Tridimas (eds), *Beyond Established Legal Orders: Policy Interconnections between the EU and the Rest of the World* (Oxford, Hart Publishing, 2011) 275–315

——, 'Values in the EU Constitution: the External Dimension', Center on Democracy, Development and the Rule of Law, Stanford Institute for International Studies, Working Papers, No 26, 2 November 2004

—— and Hillion, C, 'L'Union Fait La Force? Potential and Limitations of the ENP as an Integrated EU Foreign and Security Policy' in N Copsey and A Mayhew (eds), *European Neighbourhood Policy: The Case of Europe*, Sussex European Institute, SEI Seminar Papers Series Number 1, 2006, 20–44

Crum, B, 'Legislative–Executive Relations in the EU' (2003) 41 *Journal of Common Market Studies* 375

Curtin, D, 'The Council of Ministers: The Missing Link?' in L Verhey, P Kiiver and S Loeffen (eds), *Political Accountability and European Integration* (Groningen, Europa Law Publishing, 2009) 125–35

Curtin, DM and Dekker, IF, 'The European Union From Maastricht to Lisbon: Institutional and Legal Unity of the Shadows' in P Craig and G de Búrca (eds), *Evolution of EU Law* (Oxford, OUP, 2011) 155–85

Cygan, A, ' "Collective" Subsidiarity Monitoring by National Parliaments after Lisbon: The Operation of the Early Warning Mechanism' in M Trybus and L Rubini (eds), *The Treaty of Lisbon and the Future of European Law and Policy* (Cheltenham, Edward Elgar Publishing Limited, 2012) 55–73

Dahl, R, *A Preface to Democratic Theory* (Chicago, University of Chicago Press, 1956)

——, *Democracy and Its Critics* (New Haven, Yale University Press, 1989)

——, *On Democracy* (New Haven, Yale University Press, 2000)

Dannreuther, R, 'Developing the Alternative to Enlargement: The European Neighbourhood Policy' (2006) 11 *European Foreign Affairs Review* 183

—— (ed), *European Union Foreign and Security Policy: Towards a Neighbourhood Strategy* (London, Routledge, 2004)

Dashwood, A, 'Implied External Competence of the European Community' in M Koskenniemi (ed), *International Law Aspects of the European Union* (Leiden, Martinus Nijhoff, 1998) 113–23

——, 'Mixity in the Era of the Treaty of Lisbon' in C Hillion and P Koutrakos, *Mixed Agreements Revisited: The EU and its Member States in the World* (Oxford, Hart Publishing, 2011) 351–66.

——, 'The Attribution of External Relations Competence' in A Dashwood and C Hillion (eds), *General Law of EC External Relations* (London, Sweet and Maxwell, 2000) 115–38

——, Dougan, M, et al, *Wyatt and Dashwood's European Union Law*, 6th edn (Oxford, Hart Publishing, 2011)

de Baere, G, *Principles of EU External Relations Law* (Oxford, OUP, 2008)

de Búrca, G, 'The Drafting of the European Union Charter of Human Rights' (2001) 26 *European Law Review* 126

Dehousse, R, 'Beyond Representative Democracy: Constitutionalism in A Polycentric Polity' in JHH Weiler and M Wind (eds), *European Constitutionalism Beyond the State* (Cambridge, CUP, 2003) 135–56

Delcour, L, 'Does the European Neighbourhood Policy Make a Difference? Policy Patterns and Reception in Ukraine and Russia' (2007) 7 *European Political Economy Review* 118

Del Sarto, R and Schumacher, T, 'From EMP to ENP: What's at Stake with the European Neighbourhood Policy towards the Southern Mediterranean?' (2005) 10 *European Foreign Affairs Review* 17

Denza, E, *The Intergovernmental Pillars of the European Union* (Oxford, OUP, 2002)

de Witte, B, 'Too Much Constitutional Law in the European Union's Foreign Relations' in M Cremona and B de Witte (eds), *EU Foreign Relations Law: Constitutional Fundamentals* (Oxford, Hart Publishing, 2008) 3–15

Diez, T, 'Constructing the Self and Changing Others: Reconsidering Normative Power Europe' (2005) 33 *Journal of International Studies* 613

Dougan, M, 'The Treaty of Lisbon 2007: Winning Minds, Not Hearts' (2008) 45 *Common Market Law Review* 617

Dragneva, R and Wolczuk, K, 'EU Law Export to the Eastern Neighbourhood' in PJ Cardwell (ed), *EU External Relations Law and Policy in the Post-Lisbon Era* (The Hague, TMC Asser Press, 2012) 217–40

Dryzek, J, 'Legitimacy and Economy in Deliberative Democracy' (2001) 29 *Political Theory* 651

Duchêne, F, 'The EC and the Uncertainties of Interdependence' in M Kohnstamm and W Hager (eds), *A Nation Writ Large? Foreign Policy Problems before the European Community* (London, Macmillan, 1973) 1–21

Duke, S, 'Consistency, Coherence and European Union External Action: The Path to Lisbon and Beyond' in P Koutrakos (ed), *European Foreign Policy: Legal and Political Perspectives* (Cheltenham, Edward Elgar Publishing, 2011) 15–54

——, 'The European External Action Service: Antidote against Incoherence?' (2012) 17 *European Foreign Affairs Review* 45

Dunay, D, 'Strategy with Fast Moving Targets: East-Central Europe' in R Dannreuther (ed), European Union Foreign and Security Policy: Towards a Neighbourhood Strategy (London, Routledge, 2004) 27–47

Edwards, G, 'The Pattern of the EU's Global Activity' in C Hill and M Smith (eds), *International Relations and the European Union*, 2nd edn (Oxford, OUP, 2011) 44–72

Eeckhout, P, *EU External Relations Law*, 2nd edn (Oxford, OUP, 2011)

——, *External Relations of the European Union: Legal and Constitutional Functions* (Oxford, OUP, 2011)

——, 'The EU's Common Foreign and Security Policy after Lisbon: From Pillar Talk to Constitutionalism in EU Law After Lisbon' in A Biondi, P Eeckhout and S Ripley (eds), *EU Law After Lisbon* (Oxford, OUP, 2012) 266–91

Emerson, M, 'Is There to be a Real European Neighbourhood Policy?' in R Youngs (ed), *Global Europe: New Terms of Engagement* (UK, Foreign Policy Centre, 2005) 15–22

——, 'The Wider Europe as the European Union's Friendly Monroe Doctrine' CEPS Policy Brief No 27, 2002

——, et al, 'European Neighbourhood Policy Two Years On: Time Indeed for an "ENP Plus"' CEPS Policy Brief No 126, 2007

——, et al, 'Just What is this "Absorption Capacity" of the European Union?' CESP Policy Brief No 113, 2006.

——, et al, 'The Reluctant Debutante: The European Union as Promoter of Democracy in its Neighbourhood', CEPS Working Document No 223, 2005

Eniko, G, 'The Role of the Hungarian National Assembly in EU Policy-making After Accession to the Union: A Mute Witness or a True Controller?' in J O'Brennan and T Raunio (eds), *National Parliaments within the Enlarged European Union: From 'Victims' of Integration to Competitive Actors* (London, Routledge, 2007) 220–40

Eriksen, EO, *The Unfinished Democratisation of Europe* (Oxford, OUP, 2009)

—— and Fossum, JE, 'A Done Deal? The EU's Legitimacy Conundrum Revisited' in EO Eriksen, C Joerges and F Rodl (eds), *Law, Democracy and Solidarity in a Post-National Union: The Unsettled Political Order of Europe* (London, Routledge, 2008) 230–52

——, 'Democracy through Strong Publics in the European Union' (2002) 40 *Journal of Common Market Studies* 401

Ferrero-Waldner, B, 'Europe's Neighbours – Towards Closer Integration,' Speech given at the Brussels Economic Forum, 22 April 2005

——, 'The European Neighbourhood Policy: The EU's Newest Foreign Policy Instrument' (2006) 11 *European Foreign Affairs Review* 139

Fiaramonti, L and Lucarelli, S, 'Self-Representation and External Perceptions – Can the EU Bridge the Gap?' in S Lucarelli and L Fiaramonti (eds), *External Perceptions of the European Union as a Global Actor* (London, Routledge, 2009) 218–22

Fierro, E, *The EU's Approach to Human Rights Conditionality in Practice* (The Hague, Martinus Nijhoff, 2003)

Follesdal, A and Hix, S, 'Why There is a Democratic Deficit in the EU: A Response to Majone and Moravcsik' (2006) 44 *Journal of Common Market Studies* 533

Fossum, JE, 'The Future of the European Order' in P Birkinshaw and M Varney (eds), *The European Union Legal Order After Lisbon* (The Hague, Kluwer Law International, 2010) 33–56

Fuchs, D, 'Participatory, Liberal and Electronic Democracy' in T Zittel and D Fuchs (eds), *Participatory Democracy and Political Participation: Can Participatory Engineering Bring Citizens Back in?* (London, Routledge, 2007) 29–54

Füle, S, European Commissioner for Enlargement and European Neighbourhood, EuroNest Parliamentary Assembly, Speech/12/256, Baku 3 April 2012

——, European Commissioner for Enlargement and European Neighbourhood, Strengthening the Role of Civil Society in Democratic Governance, Speech/12/654, 27 September 2012

Gahramanova, A, 'Internal and External Factors in the Democratisation of Azerbaijan' (2009) 16 *Democratisation* 777

Gebhard, C, 'Coherence' in C Hill and M Smith (eds), *International Relations and the European Union*, 2nd edn (Oxford, OUP, 2011) 101–27

Ghazaryan, N, 'Pre and Post-Lisbon Institutional Trends in the EU's Neighbourhood' in PJ Cardwell (ed), *EU External Relations Law and Policy in the Post-Lisbon Era* (The Hague, TMC Asser Press, 2012) 199–216

——, 'The ENP and the South Caucasus: Meeting Expectations?' in R Whitman and S Wolff (eds), *The European Neighbourhood Policy in Perspective* (Basingstoke, Palgrave, 2010) 223–46

——, 'The Evolution of the ENP and the Consistent Evolvement of it Inconsistencies' (2012) 7 *Russian and European Affairs Review* 1

Gould, T, 'The European Economic Area: A Model for the EU's Neighbourhood Policy?' (2004) 5 *Perspectives on European Politics and Society* 171

Grabbe, H, 'How Does Europeanisation Affect CEE Governance? Conditionality, Diffusion and Diversity' (2001) 8 *Journal of European Public Policy* 1013

——, 'How Does the EU Measure when the CEECs are Ready to Join?' in C Jenkins (ed), *The Unification of Europe? An Analysis of EU Enlargement* (London, Centre for Reform, 2000) 37–46

Gstohl, S, 'What is at Stake in the Internal Market? Towards a Neighbourhood Economic Community' in E Lannon (ed), *The European Neighbourhood Policy's Challenges* (Brussels, College of Europe Studies, PIE Peter Lang, 2012) 85–108

Habermas, J, *Contributions to a Discourse Theory of Law and Democracy* (Cambridge, Polity Press, 1996)

——, 'Remarks on Dieter Grimm's "Does Europe Need a Constitution?" ' (1995) 1 *European Law Journal* 303

——, *The Crisis of the European Union: A Response* (Cambridge, Polity, 2012)

Halbach, U, 'The European Union in the South Caucasus: Story of A Hesitant Approximation' in *South Caucasus: 20 Years of Independence* (Friedrich Ebert Stiftung, 2011) 300–15

Hanf, D, 'The European Neighbourhood Policy in the Light of the New "Neighbourhood Clause" (Article 8 TEU)' in E Lannon (ed), *The European Neighbourhood Policy's Challenges* (Brussels, College of Europe Studies, PIE Peter Lang, 2012) 109–23

Harasimowicz, A, 'European Neighbourhood Policy, 2004–2006: the Growing Need for Strategy' in M Cremona and G Meloni (eds), *The European Neighbourhood Policy: A New Framework for Modernisation?*, EUI Working Papers, LAW 2007/21, 81–94

Haukkala, H, 'A Hole in the Wall? Dimensionalism and EU's New Neighbourhood Policy' The Finnish Institute of International Affairs, UPI Working Papers No 41, 2003

Haukkala, H, and Moshes, A, 'Beyond "Big Bang": The Challenges of the EU's Neighbourhood Policy in the East', Helsinki, The Finnish Institute of International Affairs, Report 9/2004

Helly, D, 'EU's Influence in its Eastern Neighbourhood: The Case of Crisis Management in the Southern Caucasus' (2007) 7 *European Political Economy Review* 102

Henderson, K, 'Reforming the Post-Communist States: Meeting the Political Conditions for Membership' in C Jenkins (ed), *The Unification of Europe? An Analysis of EU Enlargement* (Centre for Reform, London, 2000) 27–35

Heriter, A, 'Elements for Democratic Legitimation in Europe: an Alternative Perspective' (1999) 6 *Journal of European Public Policy* 269

Herrmann, C, 'Much Ado About Pluto? The "Unity of the Legal Order of the European Union" Revisited' in M Cremona and B de Witte (eds), *EU Foreign Relations Law: Constitutional Fundamentals* (Oxford, Hart Publishing, 2008) 19–51

Hill, C, 'European Foreign Policy: Power Bloc, Civilian Model – or Flop?' in R Rummel (ed), *The Evolution of an International Actor: Western Europe's New Assertiveness* (Boulder, Westview, 1990) 31–55

——, 'The Capability–Expectations Gap, or Conceptualizing Europe's International Role' (1993) 31 *Journal of Common Market Studies* 305

Hill, C and Smith, M (eds), *International Relations and the European Union* (Oxford, OUP, 2005)

Hillion, C, 'A New Framework for the Relations between the Union and its East-European Neighbours' in M Cremona and G Meloni (eds), *The European Neighbourhood Policy: A New Framework for Modernisation?*, EUI Working Papers, LAW 2007/21, 147–54

——, 'Enlargement of the European Union: A Legal Analysis' in A Arnull and D Wincott (eds), *Accountability and Legitimacy in the European Union* (Oxford, OUP, 2002) 401–418

——, 'Enlarging the Constitutional Order of States' in A Arnull, C Barnard et al (eds), *A Constitutional Order of States? Essays in EU Law in Honour of Alan Dashwood* (Oxford, Hart Publishing, 2011) 485–99

——, 'Mapping-Out the New Contractual Relations between the European Union and its Neighbours: Learning from the EU–Ukraine "Enhanced Agreement"' (2007) 12 *European Foreign Affairs Review* 169

——, 'Mixity and Coherence in EU External Relations: The Significance of the "Duty of Cooperation"' in C Hillion and P Koutrakos (eds), *Mixed Agreements Revisited: The EU and its Member States in the World* (Oxford, Hart Publishing, 2010) 87–114

——, 'The Copenhagen Criteria and their Progeny' in C Hillion (ed), *EU Enlargement: A Legal Approach* (Oxford, Hart Publishing, 2004) 1–22

——, 'The EU's Neighbourhood Policy towards Eastern Europe' in A Dashwood and M Maresceau (eds), *Law and Practice of EU External Relations* (Cambridge, CUP, 2008) 309–333

——, 'Tous pour un, un pour tous! Coherence in the External Relations of the European Union' in M Cremona (ed), *Developments in EU External Relations Law* (Oxford, OUP, 2008) 10–36

——, 'Widen to Deepen? The Potential and Limits of Accession Treaties to Achieve EU Constitutional Reform' in S Blockmans and S Prechal (eds), *Reconciling the Deepening and Widening of the European Union* (The Hague, TMC Asser Press, 2007) 157–65

—— and Lefebvre, M, 'The European External Action Service: Towards a Common Diplomacy', European Issue No 184, Swedish Institute for European Policy Studies, 25 October 2010

——— and Mayhew, A, 'The Eastern Partnership – Something New or Window-dressing', SEI Working Paper No 109, 2009

Hix, S, *The Political System of the European Union* (Basingstoke, Palgrave, 1999)

———, Noury, AG and Roland, G, *Democratic Politics in the European Parliament* (Cambridge, CUP, 2007)

———, Raunio, T and Scully, R, 'Fifty Years On: Research on the European Parliament' (2003) 41 *Journal of Common Market Studies* 191

Hoffmeister, F, 'Curse or Blessing? Mixed Agreements in the Recent Practice of the European Union and its Member States' in C Hillion and P Koutrakos (eds), *Mixed Agreements Revisited: The EU and its Member States in the World* (Oxford, Hart Publishing, 2010) 249–68

———, 'The Contribution of European Union Practice to International Law' in M Cremona (ed), *Developments in EU External Relations Law* (Oxford, OUP, 2008) 37–127

Hoskyns, C and Newman, M (eds), *Democratising the European Union. Issues for the Twenty-first Century* (Manchester, Manchester University Press, 2000)

Howorth, J, 'European Defence and the Changing Politics of the European Union: Hanging Together or Hanging Separately' (2001) 39 *Journal of Common Market Studies* 765

Hyde-Price, A, 'The New Pattern of International Relations in Europe' in V Curzon Price, A Landau and R Whitman (eds), *The Enlargement of the European Union: Issues and Strategies* (London, Routledge, 1999) 111–17

ICG, 'Armenia: An Opportunity for Statesmanship', Europe Report No 217, 25 June 2012

———, 'Armenia: Picking up the Pieces', Europe Briefing No 48, 8 April 2008

———, 'Azerbaijan: Turning Over a New Leaf?', Europe Report No 156, 13 May 2004

———, 'Azerbaijan: Vulnerable Stability', Europe Report No 207, 3 September 2010

———, 'Azerbaijan's 2005 Elections: Lost Opportunity', Europe Briefing No 40, 21 November 2005

———, 'Conflict Resolution in the South Caucasus: The EU's Role', Europe Report No 173, 20 March 2006

———, 'Georgia: Securing a Stable Future', Europe Briefing No 58, 13 December 2010

———, 'Georgia: Sliding Towards Authoritarianism?', Europe Report No 189, 19 December 2007

Inglis, K, 'Accession Treaties: Differentiation Versus Conditionality?' in A Ott and E Vos (eds), Fifty Years of European Integration: Foundations and Perspectives (The Hague, TMC Asser Press, 2009) 139–156

———, 'EU Enlargement: Membership Conditions Applied to Future and Potential Member States' in S Blockmans and A Łazowski (eds), *The European Union and its Neighbours: a Legal Appraisal of the EU's Policies of Stabilisation, Partnership and Integration* (The Hague, TMC Asser Press, 2006) 61–92

Inotai, A, 'The CEECs: From the Association Agreements to Full Membership?' in J Redmond and G Rosenthal (eds), *The Expanding European Union: Past, Present, Future* (London, Linne Rienner Publishers, 1997) 157–76

A Iskandaryan, 'Armenia–Russia Relations: Geography Matters' in A Hug (ed), *Spotlight on Armenia* (UK, Foreign Policy Centre, 2011)

Jachtenfuchs, M, 'Democracy and Governance in the EU' (1997) 1 *European Integration Online Papers* 40

Johansson-Nogues, E, 'The EU and its Neighbourhood: an Overview' in K Weber, M Smith and M Baun (eds), *Governing Europe's Neighbourhood: Partners or Periphery* (Manchester, Manchester University Press, 2007) 21–35

Johansson-Nogues, E, 'The (Non-)Normative Power EU and the European Neighbourhood Policy: An Exceptional Policy for an Exceptional Actor?' (2007) 7 *European Political Economy* Review 181

Jorgensen, KE (ed), *Reflective Approaches to European Governance* (London, Macmillan, 1997)

Kaddous, C, 'Role and Position of the High Representative of the Union for Foreign Affairs and Security Policy under the Lisbon Treaty' in S Griller and J Ziller (eds), *The Lisbon Treaty: EU Constitutionalism without a Constitutional Treaty* (New York, Springer, 2008) 206–21

Kadelbach, S, 'Union Citizenship' in A Von Bogdandy and J Bast (eds), *Principles of European Constitutional Law*, 2nd edn (Oxford, Hart Publishing, 2010) 443–78

Kaldor, M, 'Eastern Enlargement and Democracy' in C Hoskyns and M Newman (eds), *Democratising the European Union. Issues for the Twenty-first Century* (Manchester, Manchester University Press, 2000) 139–55

—— and Vejvoda, I (eds), *Democratisation in Central and Eastern Europe* (London, Continuum, 2002)

Katz, R, 'Models of Democracy: Elite Attitudes and the Democratic Deficit in the European Union' (2001) 2 *European Union Politics* 53

Kok, W, *Enlarging the European Union: Achievements and Challenges*, Report to the European Commission, EUI, 19 March 2003

Korosteleva, E, *The European Union and its Eastern Neighbours: Towards a More Ambitious Partnership?* (London, Routledge, 2012)

Kelley, J, 'New Wine in Old Wineskins: Policy Learning and Adaptation in the New European Neighbourhood Policy' (2006) 44 *Journal of Common Market Studies* 29

Keukeleire, S and MacNaughtan, J, *The Foreign Policy of the European Union* (Basingstoke, Palgrave, 2008)

Khaliq, U, *Ethical Dimensions of the Foreign Policy of the European Union: A Legal Appraisal* (Cambridge, CUP, 2008)

——, 'The External Action of the European Union under the Treaty of Lisbon' in M Trybus and L Rubini (eds), *The Treaty of Lisbon and the Future of European Law and Policy* (Cheltenham, Edward Elgar Publishing, 2012) 239–61

Khasson, V, Vasilyan, S and Vos, H, ' "Everybody Needs Good Neighbours": The EU and its Neighbourhood' in J Orbie (ed), *Europe's Global Role: External Policies of the EU* (Aldershot, Ashgate, 2008) 217–37

Klabbers, J, *The Concept of Treaty in International Law* (The Hague, Kluwer Law International, 1996)

Kochenov, D, *EU Enlargement and the Failure of Conditionality: Pre-Accession Conditionality in the Fields of Democracy and the Rule of Law* (Austin, Wolters Kluwer Law and Business, 2008)

——, 'The ENP Conditionality: Pre-Accession Mistakes Repeated' in L Delcour and E Tulmets (eds), *Pioneer Europe? Testing EU Foreign Policy in the Neighbourhood* (Baden-Baden, Nomos, 2008) 105–20

Koskenniemi, M, 'International Law Aspects of the Common Foreign and Security Policy' in M Koskenniemi (ed), *International Law Aspects of the European Union* (Leiden, Martinus Nijhoff Publishers, 1998) 27–44

Koutrakos, P, *EU International Relations Law* (Oxford, Hart Publishing, 2006)

——, 'Legal Basis and Delimitation of Competence in EU External Relations' in M Cremona and B de Witte (eds), *EU Foreign Relations Law: Constitutional Fundamentals* (Oxford, Hart Publishing, 2008) 171–98

——, 'Primary Law and Policy in EU External Relations: Moving Away from the Big Picture' (2008) *European Law Review* 666

——, 'The Nexus Between the European Union's Common Security and Defence Policy and Development' in A Arnull, C Barnard et al (eds), *A Constitutional Order of States? Essays in EU Law in Honour of Alan Dashwood* (Oxford, Hart Publishing, 2011) 589–608

——, *Trade, Foreign Policy and Defence* (Oxford, Hart Publishing, 2001)

Kratochvil, P, 'The European Neighbourhood Policy: A Clash of Incompatible Interpretations' in P Kratochvil (ed), *The European Union and Its Neighbourhood: Policies, Problems and Priorities* (Prague, Institute of International Relations, 2006) 13–28

Kuper, R, 'Democratisation: a Constitutionalising Process' in C Hoskyns and M Newman (eds), *Democratising the European Union: Issues for the Twenty-first Century* (Manchester, Manchester University Press, 2000) 156–73

Labedzska, A, 'The Southern Caucasus' in S Blockmans and A Lazowski (eds), *The European Union and Its Neighbours: A Legal Appraisal of the EU's Policies of Stabilisation, Partnership and Integration* (The Hague, TMC Asser Press, 2006) 575–612

Laffan, B, 'Democracy and the European Union' in L Cram, D Dinan and N Nugent (eds), *Developments in the European Union* (Basingstoke, Palgrave, 1999) 330–49

Lang, KO, 'The Role of the German and the Czech Presidencies in the Definition of an Eastern Dimension for the ENP' in L Delcour and E Tulmets (eds), *Pioneer Europe: Testing EU Foreign Policy in the Neighbourhood* (Baden-Baden, Nomos, 2008) 77–101

Lannon, E and Van Elsuwege, P, 'The Eastern Partnership: Prospects of a New Regional Dimension within the ENP' in E Lannon (ed), *The European Neighbourhood Policy's Challenges* (Brussels, College of Europe Studies, PIE Peter Lang, 2012) 285–322

Lazowski, A, 'Box of Chocolates Integration: The European Economic Area and the Swiss Model Revisited' in S Blockmans and S Prechal (eds), *Reconciling the Deepening and Widening of the European Union* (The Hague, TMC Asser Press, 2007) 87–109

——, 'The Polish Parliament and EU Affairs: An Effective Actor or an Accidental Hero?' in J O'Brennan and T Raunio (eds), *National Parliaments within the Enlarged European Union: From 'Victims' of Integration to Competitive Actors* (London, Routledge, 2007) 203–19

——, 'With but Without You . . . The Europeanisation of Legal Orders of the Neighbouring Countries' in A Ott and E Vos (eds), *Fifty Years of European Integration: Foundations and Perspectives* (The Hague, TMC Asser Press, 2009) 247–70

Leino, P and Petrov, R, 'Between "Common Values" and Competing Universals – The Promotion of the EU's Common Values through the European Neighbourhood Policy' (2009) 15 *European Law Journal* 654

Lenaerts, K and de Smijter, E, 'The Question of Democratic Representation' in J Winter, D Curtin, AE Kellermann and B de Witte (eds), *Reforming the Treaty on European Union: The Legal Debate* (London, Kluwer Law International, 1996) 173–97

Light, M, 'Exporting Democracy' in KE Smith and M Light (eds), *Ethics and Foreign Policy* (Cambridge, CUP, 2001) 75–92

Lombardo, E, 'The Participation of the Civil Society' in D Castiglione, J Schonlau et al, *Constitutional Politics in the European Union: The Convention Moment and its Aftermath* (Basingstoke, Palgrave, 2007) 153–69

Longhurst, K and Nies, S, 'Recasting Relations with the Neighbours – Prospects for the Eastern Partnership', Institut Français des Relations Internationales, February 2009

Lord, C, 'Accountable and Legitimate? The EU's International Role' in C Hill and M Smith (eds), *International Relations and the European Union* (Oxford, OUP, 2005) 113–33

Lord, C, 'Assessing Democracy in a Contested Polity' (2001) 39 *Journal of Common Market Studies* 641

——, *Democracy in the European Union* (Sheffield, Sheffield Academic Press, 1998)

Lucarelli, S, 'Values, Identity and Ideational Shocks in the Transatlantic Rift' (2006) 9 *Journal of International Relations and Development* 304

Lynch, D, 'The European Neighbourhood Policy', Institute for Security Studies, June 2004

——, 'The Security Dimension of the European Neighbourhood Policy' (2005) 40 *The International Spectator* 33

——, 'Why Georgia Matters' Chaillot Paper No 86, February 2006, Institute for Security Studies

MacCarthaigh, M, 'Accountability through National Parliaments, Practice and Problems' in J O'Brennan and T Raunio (eds), *National Parliaments within the Enlarged European Union: From 'Victims' of Integration to Competitive Actors* (London, Routledge, 2007) 29–45

MacFarlane, N, 'The Caucasus and Central Asia: Towards a Non-Strategy' in R Dannreuther (ed), *European Foreign and Security Policy: Towards a Neighbourhood Strategy* (London, Routledge, 2004) 118–34

MacGoldrick, D, *International Relations Law of the European Union* (London, Longman, 1997)

MacLeod, I, Hendry, ID and Hyett, S, *The External Relations of the European Communities* (Oxford, Clarendon Press, 1996)

Maduro, MP, 'Europe and the Constitution: What if This is as Good as It Gets?' in JHH Weiler and M Wind (eds), *European Constitutionalism Beyond the State* (Cambridge, CUP, 2003) 74–102

——, 'The Double Constitutional Life of the Charter of Fundamental Rights of the European Union' in T Hervey and J Kenner (eds), *Economic and Social Rights under the EU Charter of Fundamental Rights – A Legal Perspective* (Oxford, Hart Publishing, 2003) 269–99

Magen, A, 'The Shadow of Enlargement: Can the European Neighbourhood Policy Achieve Compliance?' Center on Democracy, Development and the Rule of Law, Stanford Institute for International Studies, Working Paper No 68, August 2006

Magnette, P and Nicolaidis, K, 'The European Union's Democratic Agenda' in M Telo (ed), *The EU and Global Governance* (London, Routledge, 2009) 43–63

Maier, S and Schimmelfennig, F, 'Shared Values: Democracy and Human Rights' in K Weber, M Smith and M Baun (eds), *Governing Europe's Neighbourhood: Partners or Periphery* (Manchester, Manchester University Press, 2007) 39–57

Mammadli, A, 'EU–Azerbaijan Relations: Enhancing Human Rights and Democracy within Eastern Partnership Initiatives' Caucasus Analytical Digest No 35–36, February 2012

Mancini, F, *Democracy and Constitutionalism in the European Union: Collected Essays* (Oxford, Hart Publishing, 2000)

Manners, I, 'Normative Power Europe: A Contradiction in Terms' (2002) 40 *Journal of Common Market Studies* 235

——, 'The Constitutive Nature of Values, Images and Principles in the EU' in S Lucarelli and I Manners (eds), *Values and Principles in European Union Foreign Policy* (London, Routledge, 2006) 19–41

Marangoni, AC, 'One Hat Too Many for the High Representative – Vice President? The Coherence of EU's External Policies after Lisbon', EU Foreign Affairs Review, *Global Europe*, July 2012

March, GJ and Olsen, GR, *Rediscovering Institutions: The Organizational Basis of Politics* (New York, Free Press, 1989)

Marchetti, A, 'The European Neighbourhood Policy: Foreign Policy at the EU's Periphery' Discussion Paper C158, Centre for European Integration Studies, 2006

Maresceau, M, 'A Typology of Mixed Bilateral Agreements' in C Hillion and P Koutrakos (eds), *Mixed Agreements Revisited: The EU and its Member States in the World* (Oxford, Hart Publishing, 2010) 11–29

—— and Montaguti, E, 'The Relations between the European Union and Central and Eastern Europe: A Legal Appraisal' (1995) 32 *Common Market Law Review* 1327

Meloni, G, 'Is the Same Toolkit Used during Enlargement Still Applicable to the Countries of the New Neighbourhood? A Problem of Mismatching between Objectives and Instruments' in M Cremona and G Meloni (eds), *The European Neighbourhood Policy: A New Framework for Modernisation?* EUI Working Papers, LAW 2007/21, 97–111

——, 'Who's My Neighbour?' (2007) 7 *European Political Economy Review* 24

——, *Europe as the Would-be World Power: The EU at Fifty* (Cambridge, CUP, 2009)

——, *Regulating Europe* (London, Routledge, 1996)

——, 'The Credibility Crisis of Community Regulation' (2000) 38 *Journal of Common Market Studies* 273

——, 'The Rise of the Regulatory State in Europe' (1994) 17 *West European Politics* 78

Mendes, J, *Participation in EU Rule-making: A Rights Based Approach* (Oxford, OUP, 2011) 140

Meny, Y, 'De la Democratie en Europe: Old Concepts and New Challenges' (2002) 41 *Journal of Common Market Studies* 1

Merlingen, M and Ostrauskaite, R, 'EU Peacebuilding in Georgia: Limits and Achievements' in S Blockmans, J Wouters and T Ruys (eds), *The European Union and Peace Building: Policy and Legal Aspects* (The Hague, TMC Asser Press, 2010) 269–93

Missiroli, A, 'The EU and its Changing Neighbourhood' in R Dannreuther (ed), *European Union Foreign and Security Policy: Towards a Neighbourhood Strategy* (London, Routledge, 2004) 12–26

—— and Quille, G, 'European Security in Flux' in F Cameron (ed), *The Future of Europe: Integration and Enlargement* (London, Routledge, 2004) 114–34

Mkrtchyan, T, Huseynov, T and Gogolashvili, T, 'The European Union and the South Caucasus: Three Perspectives on the Future of the European Project from the Caucasus', Europe in Dialogue 2009/01, Bertelsmann Stiftung, 2009.

Moravcsik, A, 'In Defence of the "Democratic Deficit": Reassessing Legitimacy in the European Union' (2002) 40 *Journal of Common Market Studies* 603

——, 'Preferences and Power in the European Community: A Liberal Intergovernmentalist Approach' (1993) 31 *Journal of Common Market Studies* 473

Morillas, P, 'Institutionalisation or Intergovernmental Decision-Taking in Foreign Policy: The Implementation of the Lisbon Treaty' in PJ Cardwell (ed), *EU External Relations Law and Policy in the Post-Lisbon Era* (The Hague, TMC Asser Press, 2012) 119–34

Müller, JW, 'The Promise of 'Demoi-Cracy': Democracy, Diversity and Domination in the European Public Order' in J Neyer and A Wiener (eds), *Political Theory of the European Union* (Oxford, OUP, 2011) 187–203

Mungiu-Pippidi, A, 'Facing the "Desert of Tartars": The Eastern Border of Europe' in J Zielonka (ed), *Europe Unbound: Enlarging and Reshaping the Boundaries of the European Union* (London, Routledge, 2002) 51–77

Muskhelishvili, M and Jorjoliani, G, 'Georgia's Ongoing Struggle for a Better Future Continued: Democracy Promotion through Civil Society Development' (2009) 16 *Democratisation* 682

Natorski, M, 'National Concerns in the EU Neighbourhood: Spanish and Polish Policies on the Southern and Eastern Dimensions' in L Delcour and E Tulmets (eds), *Pioneer Europe: Testing EU Foreign Policy in the Neighbourhood* (Baden-Baden, Nomos, 2008) 57–75

Neuwahl, N, 'Foreign and Security Policy and the Implementation of the Requirement of "Consistency" under the Treaty on European Union' in D O'Keeffe and PM Twomey (eds), *Legal Issues of the Maastricht Treaty* (Chichester, Chancery Law Publishing, 1994) 227–46

Nuriyev, E, 'EU Policy in the South Caucasus: A View from Azerbaijan' CEPS, Working Document No 272/July 2007

Nuttal, S, 'Coherence and Consistency' in C Hill and M Smith, International Relations and the European Union (Oxford, OUP, 2005) 91–112

O'Brennan, J and Raunio, T, 'Deparliamentarization and European Integration' in J O'Brennan and T Raunio (eds), *National Parliaments within the Enlarged European Union: From 'Victims' of Integration to Competitive Actors* (London, Routledge, 2007) 1–26

O'Keeffe, D, 'Exclusive, Concurrent and Shared Competence' in A Dashwood and C Hillion (eds), *General Law of EC External Relations* (London, Sweet and Maxwell, 2000) 179–99

——, 'Union Citizenship' in D O'Keeffe and PM Twomey (eds), *Legal Issues of the Maastricht Treaty* (New Jersey, John Wiley and Sons, 1994) 87–107

Olsen, GR, 'Promotion of Democracy as a Foreign Policy Instrument of "Europe": Limits to International Idealism' (2000) 7 *Democratisation* 142

Ott, A and Wessel, R, 'The EU's External Relations Regime: Multilevel Complexity in an Expanding Union' in S Blockmans and A Lazowski (eds), *The European Union and its Neighbours: A Legal Appraisal of the EU's Policies of Stabilisation, Partnership and Integration* (The Hague, TMC Asser Press, 2006) 19–59

Pace, M, 'Paradoxes and Contradictions in EU Democracy Promotion in the Mediterranean: The Limits of EU Normative Power' (2009) 16 *Democratisation* 39–58

Pardo, S, 'Europe of Many Circles: European Neighbourhood Policy' (2004) 9 *Geopolitics* 731

Parliamentary Assembly of the Council of Europe, 'The Functioning of Democratic Institutions in Azerbaijan', Report of Monitoring Committee, Doc 11627, 6 June 2008

——, 'Honouring of obligations and commitments by Armenia', Report, Doc 10027, 27 January 2004

——, 'Honouring of obligations and commitments by Georgia', Report, Doc 10383, 21 December 2004

——, 'Honouring of obligations and commitments by Georgia', Resolution 1603 (2008), 24 January 2008

——, Resolution 1359 (2004) on Political Prisoners in Azerbaijan

Partnership for Open Society, 'Analyses of the Republic of Armenia Government Decision on ENP Action Plan Implementation Tools for 2007', July 2007

Passos, R, 'Mixed Agreements from the Perspective of the European Parliament' in C Hillion and P Koutrakos (eds), *Mixed Agreements Revisited: The EU and its Member States in the World* (Oxford, Hart Publishing, 2010) 269–94

Peers, S, 'EC Frameworks of International Relations: Co-operation, Partnership and Association' in A Dashwood and C Hillion (eds), *The General Law of EC External Relations* (London, Sweet and Maxwell, 2000) 160–76

——, 'From Cold War to Lukewarm Embrace: the European Union's Agreements with the CIS States' (1995) 44 *International and Comparative Law Quarterly* 829

Peterson, J, 'The College of Commissioners' in J Peterson and M Shackleton (eds), *The Institutions of the European Union* (Oxford, OUP, 2002) 71–93

Petrov, R, 'Association Agreement Versus Partnership and Co-operation Agreement. What is the Difference?' Eastern Partnership Community, 27 January 2011

——, 'The New EU Ukraine Enhanced Agreement versus the EU–Ukraine Partnership and Cooperation Agreement: Transitional Path or Final Destination?' in F Maiani, R Petrov and E Mouliarova (eds), *European Integration without EU Membership: Models, Experiences, Perspectives*, EUI Working Papers, MWP 2009/10, 39–45

Pinder, J, 'The European Community and Democracy in Central and Eastern Europe' in G Pridham, E Herring and G Sanford (eds), *Building Democracy? The International Dimension of Democratisation in Eastern Europe* (London, Leicester University Press, 1994) 110–32

Piris, JC, *The Lisbon Treaty: A Legal and Political Analysis* (Cambridge, CUP, 2010)

——, 'Where Will the Lisbon Treaty Lead Us?' in A Arnull, C Barnard et al (eds), *A Constitutional Order of States? Essays in EU Law in Honour of Alan Dashwood* (Oxford, Hart Publishing, 2011) 59–74

Popescu, N, 'ENP and EaP: Relevant for the South Caucasus?' in *South Caucasus: 20 Years of Independence* (Friedrich Ebert Stiftung, 2011) 316–34

Pridham, G, 'Change and Continuity in the European Union's Political Conditionality: Aims, Approach and Priorities' (2007) 17 *Democratisation* 446

——, 'EU Enlargement and Consolidating Democracy in Post-Communist States – Formality and Reality' (2002) 40 *Journal of Common Market Studies* 953

——, 'The European Union's Democratic Conditionality and Domestic Politics in Slovakia: the Meciar and Dzurinda Governments Compared' (2002) 54 *Europe-Asia Studies* 203

——, 'The International Dimension of Democratisation: Theory, Practice and Inter-regional Comparisons' in G Pridham, E Herring and G Sanford (eds), *Building Democracy? The International Dimension of Democratisation in Eastern Europe* (London, Leicester University Press, 1994) 7–31

Prodi, R, '2000–2005: Shaping the New Europe', Speech to the European Parliament, Speech/00/41, Strasbourg 15 February 2000,

——, 'A Wider Europe – A Proximity Policy as the Key to Stability', Speech to the Sixth ECSA-World Conference, Speech/02/619, 5–6 December 2002

Puetter, U, 'The Latest Attempt at Institutional Engineering: The Treaty of Lisbon and Deliberative Intergovernmentalism in EU Foreign and Security Policy Coordination' in PJ Cardwell (ed), *EU External Relations Law and Policy in the Post-Lisbon Era* (The Hague, TMC Asser Press, 2012) 17–34

Raik, K, 'Promoting Democracy through Civil Society: How to Step up the EU's Policy towards the Eastern Neighbourhood', CEPS, Working Document No 237/February 2006

Raube, K, 'Parliamentary Legitimacy in EU External Relations: How So?' Paper presented at UACES 42 Annual Conference, 'Old Borders, New Frontiers' 3–5 September 2012, Passau

Raunio, T, 'National Legislatures in the EU Constitutional Treaty' in J O'Brennan and T Raunio (eds), *National Parliaments within the Enlarged European Union: From 'Victims' of Integration to Competitive Actors* (London, Routledge, 2007) 79–92

Requejo, F, 'Liberal Democracy's Timber is Still Too Straight: The Case of Political Models for Coexistance in Composite States' in N Walker, J Shaw and S Tierney (eds), *Europe's Constitutional Mosaic* (Oxford, Hart Publishing, 2011) 231–52

Richter, S and Leininger, J, 'Flexible and Unbureaucratic Democracy: Promotion by the EU? The European Endowment for Democracy between Wishful Thinking and Reality' Comments 2012/C 26, August 2012, German Institute for International and Security Affairs

Ridder, R, Schrijvers, A and Vos, H, 'Civilian Power Europe and Eastern Enlargement: The More the Merrier' in J Orbie (ed), *Europe's Global Role: External Policies of the EU* (Aldershot, Ashgate, 2008) 240–257

Rosamond, B, 'New Theories of European Integration' in M Cini (ed), *European Union Politics*, 2nd edn (Oxford, OUP, 2007)

Rosas, A, 'Mixed Union-Mixed Agreements' in M Koskenniemi (ed), *International Law Aspects of the European Union* (Leiden, Martinus Nijhoff, 1998) 125–48

——, 'The European Union and Mixed Agreements' in A Dashwood and C Hillion (eds), *General Law of EC External Relations* (London, Sweet and Maxwell, 2000) 200–20

Rossi, LS, 'Does the Lisbon Treaty Provide a Clearer Separation of Competences between EU and Member States?' in A Biondi, P Eeckout and S Ripley (eds), *EU Law After Lisbon* (Oxford, OUP, 2012) 85–106

——, 'The European Neighbourhood Policy' in F Attina and R Rossi (eds), *European Neighbourhood Policy: Political, Economic and Social Issues*, The Jean Monnet Centre 'Euro-Med', Department of Political Studies, 2004, 8–14

Sadurski, W, *Constitutionalism and the Enlargement of Europe* (Oxford, OUP, 2012)

——, 'EU Enlargement and Democracy in New Member States' in W Sadurski, A Czarnota and M Krygie (eds), *Spreading Democracy and the Rule of Law: The Impact of EU Enlargement on the Rule of Law, Democracy and Constitutionalism in Post-communist Legal Orders* (Dordrecht, Springer, 2006) 27–49

Sajo, A, 'Accession's Impact on Constitutionalism in the New Member States' in G Bermann and K Pistor (eds), *Law and Governance in an Enlarged European Union* (Oxford, Hart Publishing, 2004) 415–35

——, 'Becoming "Europeans": The Impact of EU "Constitutionalism" on Post-Communist Pre-Modernity' in W Sadurski, A Czarnota and M Krygie (eds), *Spreading Democracy and the Rule of Law: The Impact of EU Enlargement on the Rule of Law, Democracy and Constitutionalism in Post-communist Legal Orders* (Dordrecht, Springer, 2006) 175–92

Sasse, G, 'The European Neighbourhood Policy Conditionality Revisited for the EU's Eastern Neighbours' (2008) 60 *Europe-Asia Studies* 295

Scharpf, F, 'Economic Integration, Democracy and the Welfare State' (1997) 4 *Journal of European Public Policy* 18

Schimmelfennig, F, 'European Neighbourhood Policy: Political Conditionality and its Impact on Democracy in Non-Candidate Neighbouring Countries', Paper prepared for the EUSA Ninth Biennial International Conference Austin, March 31–April 2 2005

—— and Sedelmeier, U, 'Conclusions: The Impact of the EU on the Accession Countries' in F Schimmelfennig and U Sedelmeier (eds), *The Europeanisation of Central and Eastern Europe* (London, Cornell University Press, 2005)

——, 'Governance by Conditionality: EU Rule Transfer to the Candidate Countries of Central and Eastern Europe' (2004) 11 *Journal of European Public Policy* 661

Schmidt, VA, *Democracy in Europe: The EU and National Polities* (Oxford Scholarship Online, January 2007)

Schonlau, J, 'The Convention Method' in D Castiglione, J Schonlau et al, *Constitutional Politics in the European Union: The Convention Moment and its Aftermath* (Basingstoke, Palgrave, 2007) 90–11

Schütze, R, *European Constitutional Law* (Cambridge, CUP, 2012)

——, 'Federalism and Foreign Affairs: Mixity as a (Inter)-national Phenomenon' in C Hillion and P Koutrakos (eds), *Mixed Agreements Revisited: The EU and its Member States in the World* (Oxford, Hart Publishing, 2010) 57–86

——, *From Dual to Cooperative Federalism: The Changing Structure of European Law* (Oxford, OUP, 2009)

Sedelmeier, U, *Constructing the Path to Eastern Enlargement* (Manchester, Manchester University Press, 2005)

Seeberg, P, 'The EU as a Realist Actor in Normative Clothes: EU Democracy Promotion in Lebanon and the European Neighbourhood Policy' (2009) 16 *Democratisation* 81

——, 'The European Neighbourhood Policy, Post-normativity and Pragmatism' (2010) 15 *European Foreign Affairs Review* 663

Seidelmann, R, The EU's Neighbourhood Policies' in M Telo (ed), *The EU and Global Governance* (London, Routledge, 2009) 261–82

Senden, L, *Soft Law in European Community Law* (Oxford, Hart Publishing, 2005)

Shackleton, M, 'The European Commission and Parliamentary Oversight' in L Verhey, P Kiiver and S Loeffen (eds), *Political Accountability and European Integration* (Groningen, Europa Law Publishing, 2009) 79–83

——, 'The European Parliament' in J Peterson and M Shackleton (eds), *The Institutions of the European Union*, 3rd edn (Oxford, OUP, 2012) 124–47

Shaw, J, *Law of the European Union* (Basingstoke, Palgrave, 2000)

——, 'The Constitutional Mosaic Across the Boundaries of the European Union: Citizenship Regimes in the New States of South East Europe' in N Walker, J Shaw and S Tierney (eds), *Europe's Constitutional Mosaic* (Oxford, Hart Publishing, 2011) 137–70

Shkolnikov, V, 'European Assistance to Human Rights, Democracy and Rule of Law in Armenia: Incremental Results, no Breakthroughs' in A Hug, *Spotlight on Armenia* (UK, Foreign Policy Centre, 2011) 51–53

Sjursen, H, 'The EU as a "Normative" Power: How Can This Be?' (2006) 13 *Journal of European Public Policy* 235

Sjursen, H, 'The EU's Common Foreign and Security Policy: The Quest for Democracy' (2011) 18 *Journal of European Public Policy* 1069

Smith, KE, 'Engagement and Conditionality: Incompatible or Mutually Reinforcing?' in R Youngs (ed), *Global Europe: New Terms of Engagement* (UK, The Foreign Policy Centre, 2005)

——, 'Enlargement, The Neighbourhood and European Order' in C Hill and M Smith (eds), *International Relations and the European Union*, 2nd edn (Oxford, OUP, 2011) 299–323

——, *European Union Foreign Policy in a Changing World* (Cambridge, Polity Press, 2003)

——, 'The End of Civilian Power EU: A Welcome Demise or Cause for Concern?' (2000) 35 *The International Spectator* 11

Smith, KE, 'The Evolution and Application of EU Membership Conditionality' in M Cremona, *The Enlargement of the European Union* (Oxford, OUP, 2003) 105–39

——, *The Making of EU Foreign Policy: The Case of Eastern Europe* (Basingstoke, Palgrave, 1999)

——, 'The Outsiders: The European Neighbourhood Policy' (2005) 81 *International Affairs* 757

——, 'The Use of Political Conditionality in the EU's Relations with Third Countries: How Effective?' (1998) 3 *European Foreign Affairs Review* 253

Smith, M, 'Enlargement and European Order' in C Hill and M Smith (eds), *International Relations and the European Union* (Oxford, OUP, 2005) 270–91

——, 'The Accidental Strategist? Military Power, Grand Strategy and the EU's Changing Global Role', 2008, European Institute, Edinburgh, Mitchell Working Paper Series 2008

—— and Webber, K, 'Political Dialogue and Security in the European Neighbourhood Policy: The Virtues and Limits of "New Partnership Perspective"' (2008) 13 *European Foreign Affairs Review* 73

——, 'South Caucasus: 20 Years of Independence' (Friedrich Ebert Stiftung, 2011)

Solonenko, I, 'European Neighbourhood Policy Implementation in Ukraine: Local Context Matters' in E Lannon (ed), *The European Neighbourhood Policy's Challenges* (Brussels, College of Europe Studies, PIE Peter Lang, 2012) 345–79

Spaventa, E, 'Fundamental What? The Difficult Relationship between Foreign Policy and Fundamental Rights' in M Cremona and B de Witte, *European Union Foreign Relations Law: Constitutional Fundamentals* (Oxford, Hart Publishing, 2008) 233–55

Stavridis, S, ' "Militarising" the EU: the Concept of Civilian Power Revisited' (2001) *The International Spectator* 43

Stegny, O, 'Ukraine and the Eastern Partnership: "Lost in Translation?"' in E Korosteleva (ed), *The Eastern Partnership Initiative: A New Opportunity for the Neighbours?* (London, Routledge, 2012) 52–74

Stewart, EJ, 'Mind the Normative Gap? The EU in the South Caucasus' in R Whitman (ed), *Normative Power Europe: Empirical and Theoretical Perspectives* (Basingstoke, Palgrave, 2011) 65–82

Stewart, S, 'EU Democracy Promotion in the Eastern Neighbourhood: One Template, Multiple Approaches' (2011) 16 *European Foreign Affairs Review* 607

——, 'The Interplay of Domestic Contexts and External Democracy Promotion: Lessons from Eastern Europe and the South Caucasus' (2009) 16 *Democratisation* 804

Stoss, S, 'The Review of the European Neighbourhood Policy: Increasing the Coherence and Coordination of EU External Action?' TEPSA Brief (2011)

Stoykova, P, 'Parliamentary Involvement in the EU Accession Process' in J O'Brennan and T Raunio (eds), *National Parliaments within the Enlarged European Union: From 'Victims' of Integration to Competitive Actors* (London, Routledge, 2007) 255–71

Stritecky, V, 'The South Caucasus: A Challenge for the ENP' in P Kratochvil (ed), *The European Union and Its Neighbourhood: Policies, Problems and Priorities* (Prague, Institute of International Relations, 2006) 59–76

Tassinari, R, 'Security and Integration in the EU Neighbourhood: the Case for Regionalism' Working Document No 226, CEPS, July 2005

Thym, D, 'Parliamentary Involvement in European International Relations' in M Cremona and B de Witte (eds), *EU Foreign Relations Law: Constitutional Fundamentals* (Oxford, Hart Publishing, 2008) 201–32

Timmermans, C, 'Opening Remarks – Evolution of Mixity since the Leiden 1982 Conference' in C Hillion and P Koutrakos (eds), *Mixed Agreements Revisited: The EU and its Member States in the World* (Oxford, Hart Publishing, 2010) 1–8

Tocci, N, 'Can the EU Promote Democracy and Human Rights Through the ENP? The Case for Refocusing on the Rule of Law' in M Cremona and G Meloni (eds), *The European Neighbourhood Policy: A New Framework for Modernisation?*, EUI Working Papers, LAW 2007/21, 23–35

——, 'Comparing the EU's Role in Neighbourhood Conflicts' in M Cremona (ed), *Developments in EU External Relations Law* (Oxford, OUP, 2008) 216–43

——, 'Does the ENP Respond to the EU's Post-Enlargement Challenges?' (2005) 40 *International Spectator* 21

——, 'The European Union as a Normative Foreign Policy Actor', Centre for European Policy Studies, Working Document No 281, 2008

Tonra, B, 'Constructing the Common Foreign and Security Policy: The Utility of a Cognitive Approach' (2003) 41 *Journal of Common Market Studies* 731

Tridimas, T and Eeckhout, P, 'The External Competence of the Community and the Case-Law of the Court of Justice: Principle versus Pragmatism' (1994) 14 *Yearbook of European Law* 143

Trubek, DM, Cottrell, P and Nance, M, ' "Soft Law", "Hard Law" and European Integration' in G de Búrca and J Scott (eds), *Law and New Governance in the EU and the US* (Oxford, Hart Publishing, 2006) 65–94

Tulmets, E, 'Adapting the Experience of Enlargement to the Neighbourhood Policy: the ENP as a Substitute to Enlargement?' in P Kratochvil (ed), *The European Union and Its Neighbourhood: Policies, Problems and Priorities* (Prague, Institute of International Relations, 2006) 29–57

Tumanov, S, Gasparishvili, A and Romanova, E, 'Russia–EU Relations, or How the Russians Really View the EU' in E Korosteleva (ed), *Eastern Partnership: A New Opportunity for the Neighbours* (London, Routledge, 2012)

Vachudova, MA, *Europe Undivided: Democracy, Leverage and Integration after Communism* (Oxford, OUP, 2005)

Vahl, M, 'EU–Russia Relations in EU Neighbourhood Policies' in K Malfliet, L Verpoest and E Vinokurov (eds), *The CIS, the EU and Russia* (Basingstoke, Palgrave, 2007) 121–41

Van Elsuwege, P, 'The Four Common Spaces: New Impetus to the EU–Russia Strategic Partnership?' in A Dashwood and M Maresceau (eds), *Law and Practice of EU External Relations: Salient Features of a Changing Landscape* (Cambridge, CUP, 2008) 334–59

——, 'Variable Geometry in the European Neighbourhood Policy: The Principle of Differentiation and its Consequences' in E Lannon (ed), *The European Neighbourhood Policy's Challenges* (Brussels, College of Europe Studies, PIE Peter Lang, 2012) 59–84

—— and Petrov, R, 'Article 8 TEU: Towards a New Generation of Agreements with the Neighbouring Countries of the European Union?' (2011) 36 *European Law Review* 688

—— and Vermeersch, A, 'Institutional Reform in the European Union: A Difficult Balancing Act' in K Inglis and A Ott (eds), *The Constitution for Europe and an Enlarging Union: Unity in Diversity?* (Groningen, Europa Law Publishing, 2005) 57–84

Van Hoof, L, 'Why the EU is Failing in its Neighbourhood: The Case of Armenia' (2012) 17 *European Foreign Affairs Review* 285

Vanhoonacker, S, 'Inter-Institutional Dynamics in Common Foreign and Security Policy Post-Lisbon: Who are the Winners?' Paper Presented at UACES 42 Annual Conference, 'Old Borders, New Frontiers', 3–5 September 2012, Passau.

Vanhoonacker, S, 'The Institutional Framework' in C Hill and M Smith (eds), *International Relations and the European Union* (Oxford, OUP, 2011) 67–90

Van Vooren, B, 'A Case-study of "Soft Law" in EU External Relations: the European Neighbourhood Policy' (2009) 34 *European Law Review* 696

——, 'A Legal-Institutional Perspective of the European External Action Service' (2011) 48 *Common Market Law Review* 475

——, *EU External Relations Law and the European Neighbourhood Policy: A Paradigm for Coherence* (London, Routledge, 2011)

——, 'The European Union as an International Actor and Progressive Experimentation in Its Neighbourhood' in P Koutrakos (ed), *European Foreign Policy: Legal and Political Perspectives* (Cheltenham, Edward Elgar Publishing, 2011) 147–71

——, 'The Hybrid Legal Nature of the European Neighbourhood Policy' in F Maiani, R Petrov and E Mouliarova (eds), *European Integration without EU Membership: Models, Experiences, Perspectives*, EUI Working Papers, MWP 2009/10, 17–27

Vasilyan, S, 'The "European" "Neighbourhood" "Policy"' in J Wunderlich and DJ Bailey (eds), *The European Union and Global Governance: A Handbook* (London, Routledge, 2010) 177–86

——, 'The External Legitimacy of the EU in the South Caucasus' (2011) 16 *European Foreign Affairs Review* 341

Verhoeven, A, 'Democratic Life in the European Union, According to its Constitution' in DM Curtin and RA Wessel (eds), *Good Governance and the European Union: Reflections on Concepts, Institutions and Substance* (Antwerp, Intersentia, 2005) 153–71

Verhoeven, A, *The European Union in Search of a Democratic and Constitutional Theory* (London, Kluwer Law International, 2002)

Von Bogdandy, A, 'Founding Principles' in A Von Bogdandy and J Bast (eds), *Principles of European Constitutional Law*, 2nd edn (Oxford, Hart Publishing, 2010) 11–54

——, 'The European Lesson for International Democracy: The Significance of Articles 9 and 12 EU Treaty for International Organisations', Jean Monnet Working Paper 01/11, NYU School of Law, 2011

Wallace, W, 'Looking after the Neighbourhood: Responsibilities for the EU-25', Policy Papers No 4, Notre Europe 2003

—— and Smith, J, 'Democracy or Technocracy? European Integration and the Problem of Popular Consent' (1995) 18 *West European Politics* 137

Weale, A, *Democracy* (Basingstoke, Palgrave, 2007)

Weatherill, S, 'Competence and Legitimacy' in C Barnard and O Odudu (eds), *The Outer Limits of European Union Law* (Oxford, Hart Publishing, 2009) 17–34

Weiler, JHH, 'Amsterdam and the Quest for Constitutional Democracy' in D O'Keeffe and PM Twomey (eds), *Legal Issues of the Amsterdam Treaty* (Oxford, Hart Publishing, 1999)

——, 'In Defence of the Status Quo: Europe's Constitutional Sonderweg' in JHH Weiler and M Wind (eds), *European Constitutionalism Beyond the State* (Cambridge, CUP, 2003) 7–23

——, Haltern, U and Mayer, F, 'European Democracy and its Critique' (1995) 18 *West European Politics* 4

Wendt, A, *Social Theory of International Politics* (Cambridge, CUP, 1999)

Wessel, R, 'Cross-pillar Mixity: Combining Competences in the Conclusion of EU International Agreements' in C Hillion and P Koutrakos (eds), *Mixed Agreements Revisited: The EU and its Member States in the World* (Oxford, Hart Publishing, 2011) 30–54

——, *The European Union's Foreign and Security Policy: A Legal Institutional Perspective* (The Hague, Kluwer Law International, 1999)

Wessels, W, 'The Modern West European State and the European Union: Democratic Erosion or a New Kind of Polity' in S Andersen and KA Eliassen (eds), *The European Union: How Democratic Is It?* (London, Sage, 1996) 57–69

——, 'The Multilevel Constitution of European Foreign Relations in Transnational Constitutionalism: International and European Perspectives' in N Tsagourias, *Transnational Constitutionalism: International and European Perspectives* (Cambridge, CUP, 2010) 160–206

Whitley, J, 'Georgia's Democratic Veneer: Scraping the Surface' in E Baracani (ed), *Democratisation and Hybrid Regimes: International Anchoring and Domestic Dynamics in European Post-Soviet States* (Florence, European Press Academic Publishing, 2011) 352–80

Whitman, R, *From Civilian Power to Superpower? The International Identity of the European Union* (Basingstoke, Palgrave, 1998)

Wolfers, A, *Discord and Collaboration: Essays on International Politics* (Baltimore, The Johns Hopkins University Press, 1968)

Wouters, J, Coppens, D and de Meester, B, 'The European Union's External Relations after the Lisbon Treaty' in S Griller and J Ziller (eds), *The Lisbon Treaty: EU Constitutionalism without a Constitutional Treaty* (New York, Springer, 2008) 143–203

Youngs, R, 'European Union Democracy Promotion Policies: Ten Years On' (2001) 6 *European Foreign Affairs Review* 355

——, 'Normative Dynamics and Strategic Interests in the EU's External Identity' (2004) 42 *Journal of Common Market Studies* 415

——, *The EU's Role in the World Politics: A Retreat from Liberal Intergovernmentalism* (London, Routledge, 2011)

Zaiotti, R, 'Of Friends and Fences: Europe's Neighbourhood Policy and the "Gated Community Syndrome" ' (2007) 29 *European Integration* 143

Index